FACILITATING DEVELOPMENT

Readings for Trainers, Consultants and Policy-Makers

edited by

ROLF P. LYNTON
UDAI PAREEK

Sage Publications
New Delhi/Newbury Park/London

Copyright © Rolf P. Lynton and Udai Pareek, 1992

First published in 1992 by

Sage Publications India Pvt Ltd
M-32 Market, Greater Kailash-I
New Delhi 110 048

Sage Publications Inc
2455 Teller Road
Newbury Park, California 91320

Sage Publications Ltd
6 Bonhill Street
London EC2A 4PU

Published by Tejeshwar Singh for Sage Publications India Pvt Ltd., phototypeset by Pagewell Photosetters, Pondicherry, and printed at Chaman Enterprises, Delhi.

Library of Congress Cataloging-in-Publication Data

Facilitating development: readings for trainers, consultants, and policy-makers / edited by
   Rolf P. Lynton, Udai Pareek.
      p.   cm.
   Includes index.
   1. Employees—Training of—Developing countries. 2. Economic development. I.
Lynton, Rolf P.   II. Pareek, Udai Narain, 1925-.
HF5549.5.T7F22   1992   658.3'124—dc20   92–17104

ISBN 81-7036-269-5 (India)
        0-8039-9417-6 (U.S.)

FACILITATING DEVELOPMENT

To our wives Ronnie and Rama
who have made the essential foursome
of these thirty years of close friendship
and collaboration.

'The intellectual echo of the earthy din'

'To put away one's own original thought
in order to take up a book
is a sin against the Holy Ghost.'
Schopenhauer

Concepts, those 'willow sands that in the right hands
will bend at the right place,
showing the biographer where to dig.
Mavis Gallant on Marquerite Yourcenar

CONTENTS

PART II: SPECIFIC ROLES, FUNCTIONS AND METHODS

Section 5: Planning: Strategy and Design

PREFACE

'. . . he stood with the Odyssey itself behind his back, and here he laid it on the table.

"Look, Msabu," he said, "this is a good book. It hangs together from the one end to the other. Even if you hold it up and shake it strongly, it does not come to pieces. The man who has written it is very clever. But what you write," he went on, both with scorn and with a sort of friendly compassion, "is some here and some there . . . ."

He stood for sometime in silence and then expressed his greater hopes of my book, and perhaps also repentance of his doubts, by picking up the scattered pages from the floor and laying them on the table.'[1]

WELL-ANCHORED COMPETENCE

The readings included in the original edition of *Training for Development*, seventeen of them placed at the end of chapters, allowed us to offer fuller and often particularly interesting treatments of some specific aspects of training while still keeping the main themes of our book clear and each chapter balanced. In this new volume, with close to a *hundred* readings in ten sections, each with an overview, we have been more ambitious.

One purpose, especially urgent in developing countries, is to make some important readings easily available. These countries, with the possible exceptions of India and the Philippines, have as yet little professional literature of their own and offer only very limited access to books and journals published abroad. So trainers and consultants are therefore only slowly developing habits of professional reading and writing.

But the new volume also gives us the opportunity to address some of the concerns we feel as we scan the training field in the late 1980s. About the escalating technologies of training, for instance, and the excessive attention paid to them. Training technologies have developed apace since the 1960s and trainers have many more options available with regard to strategies, methods and materials. To be fully competent in their craft it

[1] Isak Dinesen, *Out of Africa*, Vintage Book Edition, New York 1985, 50–51.

is important that trainers be familiar with these options and keep abreast with new ones that may prove useful in professional practice. They make up the tool kit, and competent trainers have good kits. But good kits do not of themselves guarantee good work, in training and consulting no more than in carpentry on in bridge building. What is important about technique, reflects Picasso, is 'that one has so much of it . . . that it completely ceases to exist'. It is a precondition, in short. In training and consulting, the connection between tool kit and quality performance may in fact be even more tenuous than in other crafts because these are interactional activities and the trainer consultants' understanding of clients and their needs springs from a deeper level of competence than the knowledge and use of tools. Preoccupations with techniques can crowd out attention to the personal dimensions involved in learning, and activities at the lighter level quickly become razzle-dazzle entertainment, fun perhaps but not necessarily useful, and possibly distracting and damaging. Trainers and consultants can be especially adept at using techniques to hide behind, or to continue unaware of blind spots in their engagement. They may keep to themselves the most sensitive—which may also be the most essential—information for making interventions succeed; about what clients need most to learn, for instance, what they are afraid of learning or of failing at, and what would help them most to overcome the difficulties they experience or anticipate. In short, the basis for deciding which tools the practitioner pulls out of the kit is soft and uncertain at best when he first meets the participants and a useful relationship between them is still to be built. Even that basis disintegrates if the trainer consultant, engaging himself only a little, faces participants who calibrate their engagement to his and in turn stay unengaged.

This illustration can be drawn from only one part of the trainer's world, the training session itself, the transaction with participants. Similarly enlarging—or stifling—are the contacts trainer consultants have with organizational clients, immediate colleagues, their professional fields and the larger world around them. Readings about the personal and the collegiate dimensions of training and consulting, therefore, come early in this volume and, in our attempt to offset prevailing tendencies to trivialize professional practice and the dispositions and competences it calls for, they overshadow readings about techniques.

A second concern we have and want to address in this volume is that too much training and consulting remains vague and its relation to concrete action unfocussed. This may be quite closely related to the concern mentioned above, that of the excessive attention to tools. We regard that preoccupation as quite possible serving the more basic wish to disperse any sense of the concrete, of the essential, frustrating, assertive, life-affirming stubbornness of actual persons and things, as they exist, which makes real life situations complex and translate into exacting demands on creative practitioners. Trainer consultants, no less than their trainees or clients, are susceptible to the comforting delusion that they can control meetings (sessions) and other people (participants). Broad generalizations, abstract content, lofty concepts are *personally* quite undemanding for all parties. In this book, therefore, we put our weight on the other foot and start the readings with real life concreteness, with readings about what professionals in fact need to learn and how they actually do learn to improve their practice. Other foci for readings in this volume include the place of training and consulting in manpower development and in broad change strategies, system building, and in ensuring sufficient personal development.

READING HABITS

What trainers read, of course, is only one stream among many that provoke learning but it ought at least to be a clear tributary: readings should open out new perspectives, deepen recognitions, raise questions, as well as confirm or add new tools. That these facets of developing and maintaining competence are all very important commands ready agreement among the trainers and consultants we know. But enquiry about what a practitioner has in fact read recently, or the suggestion that some reading might be useful, usually results in diffidence and quite restricted references, e.g., to one or two standard professional journals or, even narrower, to specific exercises or collections of them in annuals.

Quite different from this restricted response seem to be answers to the question of what readings they remember that really influenced them, made a difference, are ones they refer to again and again, have by their desk or in a cherished spot at home. Then eyes light up and voices rise and all manner of readings come into focus, which, while certainly not excluding strictly professional papers and books, range far more widely, to other professions, to history, fables, poetry, often drama: formulations, in whatever form, that perfectly captured an important thought.

To clarify for ourselves what we wanted to do with this volume and yet also not range too far, we asked ourselves what we read as a matter of routine and which recent readings stood out.

For one of us the 'recent list' is heavy on biography: Cole's on Erikson, Lewis Thomas and Oliver Sachs, the Maharani of Jaipur, Dorothy Sayers, Laurens Van der Post and several 'Profiles' in last year's *New Yorker*: the owner of a football club, two conductors of world famous orchestras and two musicians, a set of poker players (in other words, risk takers), a mental patient, a scientist, a geologist turned entrepreneur, a banker. Each describes and reflects on how an actual person (or a family or small group or community) actually put his life together as he moved along the grooves into which life had thrust him. Last year's pieces from journals, cut out and stacked for keeping, also include accounts of journeys to distant places, both recent and long past; and expeditions into the wilderness, for hunting or fishing, for instance, though these are not one's own hobbies. These, the best, tell of what people notice, do, think about and learn when some of the everyday constraints are absent. Also carefully preserved are many years of *New York Review of Books*. That the *Review* covers so wide a range of topics, using one book or often an accumulation of recent books as take-off for refreshing the vision of a whole field, is its attraction; also that it is so well written: a joy to read, and good for one's own writing. Essays and book reviews in the weekly *Guardian* ensure some continuing acquaintance with developments in Great Britain and the Continent.

More narrowly professional is literature about how people in different times and places set about doing the same things differently; Kakar's *Shamans, Mystics and Doctors* is an example. In the training/change area the organization development literature is most represented, especially descriptive and analytical studies of the interfaces between communities and service systems (David Korten, Eric Trist) and attempts to interrelate them more effectively; also studies of using small-scale experiences for large-scale programming (Pyle, Israel); attempts to embrace concerns with quality of life in job and organizational design (Weisbord) and the creation of institutional settings (Sarason). There is little reading on training itself, except that of quick specific reference to books and papers on the shelf, for an immediate purpose. *That* knowledge seems more readily to hand, apparently, than help with understanding contents and what and how people 'see'. Knowledge—or confirmation—seems to exhaust what to look for on those shelves. (The impersonal language in which most of this literature is written also inhibits free exploration.) Where normative and organizational support for training are effective, what to do in a program or a training session seems clear enough. The concerns that the bulk of readings seem to address have more to do, first, with keeping oneself fully alive, fresh, open and connected with the world around and, second, with maintaining a reflective stance and also making fresh observations. Conceptual reformulations that seem to be nurtured through these readings are welcome: new ways of seeing and doing.

For the other also the range of reading is wide, from books on art and culture to scientific reports and papers in journals; from philosophical treatises to new techniques of measuring behavior; from humanistic writings on personal and organizational change to behavioral technology. Last year's readings were dominated by books on culture (e.g. Geertz and Hofstede), and more specifically Indonesian culture (Geertz on Balinese culture, Peacock's anthropological insight into Indonesian culture, so also Drake's), on the history of modern Indonesia (Ricklefs) and dynamics of a specific society in Indonesia (Dobbin's book on Central Sumatra).

The journal readings have been more specifically on social issues. The *Journal of Social Issues* carries stimulating discussions, each number focussing on a specific current theme (e.g.,two recent numbers were devoted to social support). *The Harvard Educational Review* has an excellent book review section, often carrying integrated reviews of books on a single theme. *Organizational Dynamics, The Journal of Applied Behavioral Science*, and *The Administrative Science Quarterly* have been other sources of readings in the professional area. *Psychology Today* and *Society* give a large survey of current thinking. *Group and Organization Studies* and the *Review of Educational Research* have also inspired new ideas, the former through interviews with organizational thinkers, the latter through critical reviews of specific topics. *The Educational Researcher* occasionally carries articles by persons doing some exciting work on their current interests, and captures the process of thinking and enquiry.

All such readings have been sources of inspiration for examining existing frameworks, and exploring new areas in the field of current work. They have directly stimulated new empirical enquiry and further thinking. Culture and management, and organizational learning, are two directions in which recent exploratory work and writing have been carried out.

With these differing habits and preoccupations we have put aside any idea of ordering readings in this book according to the interests of the respective editors. Instead, we have chosen and grouped the readings around the trainer, consultant, policy maker, each in his or her practice and in the center of his or her world. Some readings about that world itself come first: how professional people in general learn. Then, immediately after, come readings about the professional as a person in a particular role and in his or her association with colleagues: the lone, unconnected practitioner soon runs a singular, unreliable practice.

The role calls for particular competences. We then in the succeeding sections see trainers, consultants, policy makers practising their crafts: as colleague; in action settings of different types; constructing a training or broad development system and taking account but also influencing larger organizational, cultural and political environments.

Right through all ten sections of readings we see these top rank practitioners—who also write—remain learners, essentially and habitually: they are credible—they model—through their own continued learning and growing. Two more points about this as it affects the content and structure of the book. Women practitioners who also write are still few; this remains true even though some practitioners have become prominent in training and, though to a small extent, also in consulting. Training and consulting are not peculiar in this deficiency[2] but it strikes us as particularly regretable in professional work where we often get stuck in logics and formal structures and the work could well use more creative, intuitive, holistic approaches. So we made special efforts to correct the imbalance and contacted twenty women colleagues we knew around the world. With *some* success: the majority of readings and references we received were on the same lines as the men's. We have included those with distinctly fresh perspectives.

The second point which we clarified in the course of preparing the final version: many pieces could be quite properly included in several sections. That this remains true even after our shortening them, often very substantially, to suit our purpose, reflects the importance we attach to positioning parts in their proper contexts. But it reflects more basically our experiences of learning and professional development: not one but several dimensions are in play at any time—outside and inside dimensions, strategic and immediately tactical, action and reflection; past, present, future; learning and the use of it in action. So, in the event, we moved a handful of readings from the last section on large system development into the section on planning strategies and designs, in order to illumine potential uses. But the reading on 'alone time' we left in the section on colleagueship, paired with others that confirm the essentially social, companionable confirmation of personal worth and worthwhile direction—the two poles for 'oscillation' (see 3.9). How professionals learn (Section 1) and seeing them at work (4) are quite integrative in any case. Given our understanding of learning and development processes we note the overlaps, redundancies, interconnections in all sections. At the very least, like the revolving radar screens at airports, they will ensure that data from all directions will surface for sure, for attention and incorporation, again and again.

Among the writers of pieces in this volume are many long-time friends and colleagues, yet others have drawn our attention to pieces that serve them well. We thank them all. The following have also read and commented on the volume as a whole, to guide what to include, exclude, extract or, in some cases, lengthen. All that involves much

[2] See Harriet Zuckerman, and Jonathan R. Cole, 'Marriage, Motherhood and Research Performance in Science,' *Scientific American*, February 1987 and correspondence in subsequent issues.

trouble and adds to busy lives. They are: Dr. Abad Ahmed, Professor of Management and Director of the South Campus of Delhi University; Ms. Kiran Bhatia, Program Officer, Ford Foundation in India; Dr. Somnath Chattopadhyah, Consultant; Ms. Sunita Dhar, Program Director; and Dr. Rajesh Tandon, Executive Director, Participatory Research in Asia (PRIA); Mr. Vijay Mahajan, Program Director, Professional Assistance for Development (PRADAN); and Mr. Deepankar Roy, Consultant.

Delhi & Jaipur   ROLF P. LYNTON
India   UDAI PAREEK
March 1990

PART I

Trainers and Consultants
in their Worlds

1. PROFESSIONAL LEARNING

Some focussing is necessary first, on content, context, direction and time.

Our concern is professional learning, learning for action; that is different from knowledge acquisition, basic skills development, scanning for career choice, more logical understanding or conceptual refining. Being so, it is for adults, not for beginners or college students; and for those adults who are for the most part in mid-career, that is when personalities, perceptions, life styles and routines are already embedded in a certain amount of experience and protective coverings. People at that stage of their lives have characteristic issues to occupy their most personal attention, characteristic difficulties to contend with, and also well developed learning styles. These may not be the most useful issues and styles but they dominate, at least to start with.

Scope and Situation

The first set of readings then is about this ballpark of professional learning: what settings and conditions favour it, what characterizes it, what are its sources and its sequels; in short, how to think about it. These initial readings, describing the ballpark and its surroundings, can then readily lead to the next set—about the kinds of persons who work there best, in *that* ballpark.

The first three readings are about 'change', 'transitions' and 'development', as adults engage with them without special 'training' or other deliberate interventions for accelerating and shaping them. Kurt Lewin, in his well-known conceptual formulation of changing into three phases—from 'unfreezing' through 'moving' to 'refreezing'—showed how lasting changes in action are achieved through involving groups of people in new, shared commitments, not through changing the preferences of a few individuals. So powerful are the social forces around an individual, not only of the immediate family or work group but also of wider cultural and professional groupings, that individuals tend not to move far out of line or, if they moved so during training, they soon retract, when back in familiar situations. Reducing the forces opposing change in a group's commitments is therefore often a more promising strategy than explaining and justifying new goals. The already familiar Forcefield Analysis stems from Lewin's work. Its direction is the opposite of all the additive approaches to training which prevail even now, forty years after the publication of Lewin's paper (so much for 'Readings'!).

From Lewin, then, the theorist from social experiments, to our first reading hereby, Erik Erikson, the artistic map-maker from clinical encounters. As a start to a small cluster of readings from his work, in various sections of this book, we reproduce his scheme of seven life stages (from 'Identity: Youth and Crisis') in which he details the series of tasks and dilemmas that confront the growing person in early adulthood. They include role choices, recognition of others and 'the will to be oneself'. Centrally at issue at that stage is 'identity versus identity confusion'; it is preceded by 'industry versus inferiority' and followed immediately by 'intimacy versus isolation'. After that follows 'generativity versus stagnation'. The next reading, by Levinson, supplements Erikson's by further detailing the characteristic sequence of stages in adulthood— at least for men and for those in industrialized North America.

The next reading by Sudhir Kakar then transfers us to India for a discussion of identity and adulthood in a developmental setting. 'This location of identity . . . that sense of *self-sameness* and *continuity* in time and space . . . (emerges) from the interplay of the psychological and the social, the developmental and the historical . . . (and) gives it its power and promise'. At present, writes Kakar, 'we are witnessing . . . an "identity vacuum" in Indian history . . . depression . . . loneliness . . . alienation . . . .' His observations may also fit other developing countries besides India and alert consultant trainers to the particular contexts in which adult learners are coping with the dominant themes of their lives. Under exacting conditions, the 'moving' towards change (Lewin's second phase), may well be better promoted by providing participants time 'to sort things out'—an Eriksonian 'moratorium'—than by training sessions designed to convey new information or to stimulate ideas about external things. In Harold Levinson's view, helping individuals at this stage of life to recapture and update their life's 'dream' is very important. All evidence points to the importance of reflective time. So training plans need to provide room for imaginative, personal, creative and recreative work by participants.

The Practitioner as Learner

The next three readings focus on how professionals in fact learn what experience shows about this. The model that emerges is quite different from the usual linear knowledge–to–application model in which 'the practitioner . . . comes into the chain of events only at the end of the process and it almost seems as if it would all work better without him. This one-directional chain', write Lombard and Turner, 'does not at all represent the actual development of knowledge and practice' which is circular and gives the practitioner a central role. The practitioner's intuitions, curiosities and feelings are therefore important as part of the 'total situation' to which he 'has to learn to respond ever more skillfully'. 'Experiential' education aims at providing this, deliberately and systematically. Contrary to much practice, we see active, even enthusiastic and joyful involvement of participants as only one component of it, and without proper focus on real life issues it can be misused to sidetrack those splendid emotions away from crucial learnings. The piece by Kolb and his colleagues discusses different learning styles of people as well as organizations. 'There are two goals in the experiential learning process . . . the specifics of a particular subject matter [and] to learn about one's own strengths and weaknesses as a learner', person or organization—i.e., learning how to learn from experience, also back home, on the job. Donald Schon's book, *The Reflective Practitioner*, enlarges on this scheme and documents it with professional 'dialogues' recorded in half a dozen professional offices. Practitioners 'converse' with the situations they are dealing with; that is, the practitioner tries out ideas against the fixed and not so fixed dimensions of the new situation, the situation 'back-talks', and this then 'guides his further moves'. In the course of this interchange, which may be protracted, till he is satisfied, the practitioner changes 'his stance towards the situation with which he converses'. Moreover, what he gains for his future practice is not mere general principles, the theoretician's goal, but a wider repertoire 'of exemplary themes from which, in the subsequent cases of his practice, he may compose new variations . . . . The artistry of a practitioner hinges on the range and variety of the repertoire that he brings to unfamiliar situations'. Perhaps this is the greater 'experience' for which clients chose one practitioner over another and the rationale for augmenting learning through practice with learning through cases and simulations.

Focus and Context

Techniques and concepts are tools, and the effective practitioner will choose which to use, when and for how long, according to his appreciation of the particular set of participants-in-their-situations (including himself in his own). Effective facilitation of learning for action, then, includes relevant contextual considerations.

This can be done in a variety of ways, as the next set of five readings illustrates. One is to focus outward and forward on the changed situations—technical, human, environmental, legal, structural—in which practitioners are to work competently in the future. Eric Trist and others at the Tavistock Institute, London, in mid-century pioneered conceptualization and practice in this direction with their work on 'socio-technical systems' and 'turbulent' environments. Readings on these specific areas are included in Sections IX and X. The reading included here is from A.K. Rice's work on conferences; he worked and also wrote similarly about reorganizing modern textile mills in India. *The Creation of Settings and the Future Societies* is the title Sarason gave to the book from which the next reading is taken. Whatever the source or rationale for the myriad new settings which modern and developing societies create for themselves, each brings together people, technologies and contexts in new constellations and provides fresh opportunities for learning. Focussing training on these changing and varied settings which societies keep on creating so busily may be more powerful and also more practical than creating yet more settings for the specific purpose of training.

Practitioners and their changing real life situations are two solid poles on which to exercise leverage for learning. Another focus is more basic: action to change the societal context in which practitioners and situations exist and interact. The extracts from Paulo Friere's work, highly distilled here because they are taken from a public lecture, can stand for the growing literature on achieving broad, even radical, social change through heightening the consciousness of whole groups of deprived and oppressed people—poor, women, low caste—about pervasive injustices and about possibilities of taking collective action. With resentments acknowledged, shared, analyzed and understood, community action can acquire the necessary driving force independent of and also unbeholden to established powers. Concrete action will then follow, attracting and developing whatever technical expertise it calls for. Friere uses this 'pedagogy of the oppressed' for a deliberate, steady strategy of direct action on society which also cuts through the dense mesh of dependencies that now keep people enslaved. Natasha Josefowitz' brief poem that follows, about a woman trying to move up in a men's world, highlights the double bind social pioneer's face. To be at all relevant for finding—or slashing—one's way through, a program of preparation must aim at personal, inner 'transformation' (not at adding knowledge or skills or even intellectual understanding). To be resolved are severe temptations to do to others what they do now to me, such as making *them* 'invisible', 'naming' *them*, subjecting *them* to 'reverse projections', 'split images' and 'ambivalences' in many situations and directions as pressures and doubts mount. The list is Rosemary Reuther's, a professor and writer in feminist and liberation theology.[1]

Kuhn, in his well known studies of 'scientific revolutions', noted that when a 'profession can no longer evade anomalies that subvert the existing tradition of scientific practice—then begin the extraordinary investigations that lead the profession at last to a new set of commitments, a new basis of science . . . tradition-shattering complements to the tradition-bound activity of normal science'.[2] Consultant trainers can help along this complex process by focussing attention on evident and predictable discrepancies. Friere would probably waive this aside as too slow and also too elitist: still shutting out the great mass of people in development.

The final two readings bridge the first with the next chapter. Carl Rogers' piece is another classic. If the ballpark of learning for action includes practitioner, sets of changing, particular situations and the general climate for change, all in complex interaction, then all participants in the transformation are learners. There can be no 'teachers'. 'For the vision of one man', reflects Gibran, 'lends not its wings to another man or woman'.

1.1 *Adult Crises and Growth: Identity, Intimacy, Generativity* [3]

ERIK H. ERIKSON

. . . a healthy personality actively masters his environment, shows a certain unity of personality, and is able to perceive the world and himself correctly—it is clear that all of these criteria are relative to the child's cognitive and social development. In fact, we may say that childhood is defined by their initial absence and by their gradual development in complex steps of increasing differentiation. How, then, does a vital personality grow or, as it were, accrue from the successive stages of the increasing capacity to adapt to life's necessities—with some vital enthusiasm to spare?

[1] 'Theologizing from the side of the "Other": Women, Blacks, Indians and Jews' in Leddy, Mary Jo and Mary Ann Hindsdale (ed.), *Faith that transforms, Essays in honor of Gregory Baum.*

[2] Kuhn, S. Thomas, *The Structure of Scientific Revolutions*, University of Chicago Press, Chicago, 1972.

[3] From Erik H. Erikson, *Identity, Youth and Crisis*, W.W. Norton & Company, Inc., New York, 1968, pp. 92–97, 138–41.

Whenever we try to understand growth, it is well to remember the epigenetic principle . . . somewhat generalized, this principle states that anything that grows has a ground plan, and that out of this ground plan the parts arise, each part having its time of special ascendancy, until all parts have arisen to form a functioning whole . . . . Inner laws of development, . . . create a succession of potentialities for significant interaction with those persons who tend and respond to (the growing person) and those institutions which are ready for him. While such interaction varies from culture to culture, it must remain within 'the proper rate and the proper sequence' which governs all epigenesis. Personality, therefore, can be said to develop according to steps predetermined in the human organism's readiness to be driven toward, to be aware of, and to interact with a widening radius of significant individuals and institutions.

It is for this reason that, in the presentation of stages in the development of the personality, we employ an epigenetic diagram . . . . The diagram [Figure 1] formalizes a progression through time of a differentiation of parts. This indicates (1) that each item of the vital personality to be discussed is systematically related to all others, and that they all depend on the proper development in the proper sequence of each item; and (2) that each item exists in some form before 'its' decisive and critical time normally arrives.

The Life Cycle: Epigenesis of Identity

If I say, for example, that a sense of basic trust is the first component of mental vitality to develop in life, a sense of autonomous will the second, and a sense of initiative the third, the diagram expresses a number of fundamental relations that exist among the three components, as well as a few fundamental facts for each.

Each comes to its ascendance, meets its crisis, and finds its lasting solution . . . toward the end of the stages mentioned. All of them exist in the beginning in some form . . . . Each state becomes a crisis (when) incipient growth and awareness in a new part function go together with a shift in instinctual energy and yet also cause a specific vulnerability in that part. One of the most difficult questions to decide, therefore, is whether or not a child at a given stage is weak or strong. Perhaps it would be best to say that he is always vulnerable in some respects and completely oblivious and insensitive in others, but that at the same time he is unbelievably persistent in the same respects in which he is vulnerable . . . .

Each successive step, then, is a potential crisis because of a radical change in perspective. Crisis is used here in a developmental sense to

Figure 1

	1	2	3	4	5	6	7	8
I	TRUST vs MISTRUST				Mutual Recognition vs Autistic Isolation			
II		AUTONOMY vs SHAME, DOUBT			Will to be Oneself vs Self-doubt			
III			INITIATIVE vs GUILT		Anticipation of Roles vs Role Inhibition			
IV				INDUSTRY vs INFERIORITY	Task Identification vs Sense of Futility			
V	Temporal Perspective vs Confusion Time	Self-Certainty vs Self-Consciousness	Role Experimentation vs Role Fixation	Apprenticeship vs Work Paralysis	IDENTITY vs IDENTITY CONFUSION	Sexual Polarization vs Bisexual Confusion	Leader and Followership vs Authority Confusion	Ideological Commitment vs Confusion of Values
VI						INTIMACY vs ISOLATION		
VII							GENERATIVITY vs STAGNATION	
VIII								INTEGRITY vs DESPAIR

connote not a threat of catastrophe, but a turning point, a crucial period increased vulnerability and heightened potential, and therefore, the ontogenetic source of generational strength and maladjustment . . . . different capacities use different opportunities to become full-grown components of the ever-new configuration that is the growing personality.

Evolution has made man a teaching as well as a learning animal, for dependency and maturity is guided by the nature of that which must be cared for. Generativity, then, is primarily the concern for establishing and guiding the next generation. There are of course, people who, from misfortune or because of special and genuine gifts in other directions, do not apply this drive to offspring of their own, but to other forms of altruistic concern and indeed, the concept of generativity is meant to include productivity and creativity, neither of which, however, can replace it as designations of a crisis in development. For the ability to lose oneself in the meeting of bodies and minds leads to a gradual expansion of ego-interests and to a libidinal investment in that which is being generated . . . .

As to the institutions which reinforce generativity and safeguard it, one can only say that all institutions by their very nature codify the ethics of generative succession. Generativity is itself a driving power in human organization. And the stages of childhood and adulthood are a system of generation and regeneration to which institutions, such as shared households and divided labour strive to give continuity. Thus the basic strengths enumerated here and the essentials of an organized human community have evolved together as an attempt to establish a set of proven methods and a fund of traditional reassurance which enables each generation to meet the needs of the next in relative independence from personal differences and changing conditions.

Psychosocial strength, we conclude, depends on a total process which regulates individual life cycles, the sequence of generations, and the structure of society simultaneously: for all three have evolved together.

1.2 *Four Adult Transitions*[4]

DANIEL J. LEVINSON

There is usually moderate or great discontinuity between the pre-adult world in which a man grew up and the adult world in which he forms his first life structure.

[4] From Daniel J. Levinson, with Charlotte N. Darrow, Edward B. Klein, Maria H. Levinson, Braxton Mckee, *The Seasons of a Man's Life*, Ballantine Books, New York, 1978, pp. 58–63.

The Age Thirty Transition: Changing the First Life Structure

This transition, which extends from roughly 28 to 33, provides an opportunity to work on the flaws and limitations of the first adult life structure, and to create the basis for a more satisfactory structure with which to complete the era of early adulthood. At about 28 the provisional quality of the twenties is ending and life is becoming more serious, more 'for real'. A voice within the self says: 'If I am to change my life—if there are things in it I want to modify or exclude, or things missing I want to add—I must now make a start, for soon it will be too late'.

Men differ in the kinds of changes they make, but the life structure is always different at the end of the Age Thirty Transition than it was at the beginning. Some men have a rather smooth transition, without overt disruption or sense of crisis. They modify their lives in certain respects, but they build directly upon the past and do not make fundamental changes. It is a time of reform, not revolution.

But for most men, our study reveals, this transition takes a more stressful form, the age thirty crisis. A developmental crisis occurs when a man has great difficulty with the developmental tasks of a period; he finds his present life structure intolerable, yet seems unable to form a better one. In a severe crisis he experiences a threat to life itself, the danger of chaos and dissolution, the loss of hope for the future. A moderate or severe crisis is very common during this period

The shift from the end of the Age Thirty Transition to the start of the next period is one of the crucial steps in adult development. At this time a man may make important new choices, or he may reaffirm old choices. If these choices are congruent with his dreams, talents and external possibilities, they provide the basis for a relatively satisfactory life structure. If the choices are poorly made and the new structure seriously flawed, he will pay a heavy price in the next period. Even the best structure has its contradictions and must in time be changed.

The Second Adult Life Structure: Settling Down

The second life structure takes shape at the end of the Age Thirty Transition and persists until about age 40. This structure is the vehicle for the culmination of early adulthood. A man seeks to invest himself in the major components of the structure (work, family, friendships, leisure, community—whatever is most central to him), and to realize his youthful aspirations and goals.

In this period a man has two major tasks: (*a*) He tries to establish a niche in society: to anchor his life more firmly, develop competence in a chosen craft, become a valued member of a valued world; (*b*) He works at making it: striving to advance, to progress on a timetable. I use the term 'making it' broadly to include all efforts to build a better life for oneself and to be affirmed by the tribe.

Until the early thirties, the young man has been a 'novice' adult. He has been forming an adult life and working toward a more established place in adult society. His task in the Settling Down period is to become a full-fledged adult within his own world. He defines a personal enterprise, a direction in which to strive, a sense of the future, a 'project' as Jean-Paul Sartre has termed it. The enterprise may be precisely defined from the start or it may take shape only gradually over the course of this period.

The imagery of ladder is central to the Settling Down enterprise. It reflects the interest in advancement and affirmation so central to this period. By 'ladder' we refer to all dimensions of advancement—increases in social rank, income, power, fame, creativity, quality of family life, social contribution—as these are important for the man and his world. The ladder has both objective and subjective aspects: it reflects the realities of the external social world, but it is defined by the person in terms of his own meanings and strivings.

At the start of this period, a man is on the bottom rung of his ladder and is entering a world in which he is junior member. His aims are to advance in the enterprise, to climb the ladder and become a senior member in that world. His sense of well-being during this period depends strongly on his own and others' evaluation of his progress toward these goals.

At the end of the Settling Down period, from about age 36 to 40, there is a distinctive phase that we call Becoming One's Own Man. The major developmental tasks of this phase are to accomplish the goals of the Settling Down enterprise, to become a senior member in one's world, to speak more strongly with one's own voice, and to have a greater measure of authority.

This is a fateful time in a man's life. Attaining seniority and approaching the top rung of his ladder are signs to him that he is becoming a man (not just a person, but a male adult). Although his progress brings new rewards, it also carries the burden of greater responsibilities and pressures. It means that he must give up even more of the little boy within himself—an internal figure who is never completely outgrown, and certainly not in early adulthood.

The Mid-life Transition: Moving from Early to Middle Adulthood

The late thirties mark the culmination of early adulthood. The Mid-life Transition, which lasts from roughly age 40 to 45, provides a bridge from early to middle adulthood. It brings a new set of developmental tasks. The life structure again comes into question. It becomes important to ask: 'What have I done with my life? What do I really get from and give to my wife, children, friends, work, community—and self? What is it I truly want for myself and others?' A man yearns for a life in which his actual desires, values, talents and aspirations can be expressed.

Some men do very little questioning or searching during the Mid-life Transition. They are apparently untroubled by difficult questions regarding the meaning, value and direction of their lives. Other men realize that the character of their lives is changing, but the process is not a painful one. They are in a manageable transition, one without crisis. But for the great majority of men this is a period of great struggle within the self and with the external world. Their Mid-life Transition is a time of moderate or severe crisis. They question nearly every aspect of their lives and feel that they cannot go on as before. They will need several years to form a new path or to modify the old one.

We need developmental transitions in adulthood partly because no life structure can permit the living out of all aspects of the self. To create a life structure I must make choices and set priorities. Every choice I make involves the rejection of many other possibilities. Committing myself to a structure, I try over a span of time to enhance my life within it, to realize its potential, to bear the responsibilities and tolerate the costs it entails. During a transition period—and especially in the Mid-life Transition—the neglected parts of the self more urgently seek expression and stimulate the modification of the existing structure.

Entering Middle Adulthood: Building a New Life Structure

The tasks of the Mid-life Transition must be given up by about age 45. A man has had his allotted time for reappraising, exploring, testing choices and creating the basis for a new life. The opportunity to question and search is present throughout middle adulthood and beyond, but at this point new tasks predominate. Now he must make his choices and begin forming a new life structure.

The end of Mid-life Transition, like all shifts from one period to the next, is marked by a series of changes rather than one dramatic event. It may be evident only as a man looks back a few years later that he was in fact committing himself to the choices around which a new life structure took shape.

In some lives the shift is signaled by a crucial marker event—a drastic change in job or occupation, a divorce or love affair, a serious illness, the death of a loved one, a move to a new locale. Other lives show no conspicuous change: life at 45 seems to be just as it was at 39. If we look more closely, however, we discover seemingly minor changes that make a considerable difference. A man may still be married to the same woman, but the character of his familial relationships has changed appreciably for better or worse. Or the nature of his work life has altered: he is quietly marking time until retirement; his work has become oppressive and humiliating; or seemingly small changes in his mode of work have made his work life more satisfying and creative. A man's life structure we have found, necessarily changes in certain crucial respects during the course of his Mid-life Transition.

The life structure that emerges in the middle forties varies greatly in its satisfactoriness, that is, its suitability for the self and its workability in the world. Some men have suffered such irreparable defeats in child-hood or early adulthood, and have been so little able to work on the tasks of their Mid-life Transition, that they lack the inner and outer resources for creating a minimally adequate structure. They face a middle adulthood of constriction and decline. Other men form a life structure that is reasonably viable in the world but poorly connected to the self. Although they do their bit for themselves and others, their lives are lacking in inner excitement and meaning. Still other men have started a middle adulthood that will have its own special satisfaction and fulfilments. For these men, middle adulthood is often the fullest and most creative season in the life cycle. They are less tyrannized by the ambitions, passions and illusions of youth. They can be more deeply attached to others and yet more separate, more centered in the self. For them, the season passes in its best and most satisfying rhythm.

1.3 *Giant Strides and Personal Costs in Developing Societies*[5]

SUDHIR KAKAR

Erikson says, 'There are . . . periods in history which are relative identity vacuums and in which three forms of human apprehension

[5] From Sudhir Kakar, *Identity and Adulthood*, Oxford University Press, Bombay, 1979, pp. 46–49, 53–55.

aggravate each other: fears aroused by discoveries and inventions (including weapons) which radically expand and change the whole world image, anxieties aggravated by the decay of institutions which have been the historical anchor of an existing ideology, and the dread of an existential vacuum devoid of spiritual meaning.' I submit that at present we are witnessing such an 'identity vacuum' in Indian history. This is manifested in manifold ways. Over the years we have seen in our clinical work a manifestation of depression which I feel is a phenomenon of 'anomie'. Typically these are of young people who come to us with complaints of inability to concentrate, a general feeling of loneliness with concomitant symptoms of loss of appetite, sleeplessness, etc. A typical young man of this genre comes from a village. He is a first generation student. His parents are illiterate farmers or artisans. His siblings may have gone through the exercise of going to school but have left school by the third or fourth grade and gone into the family occupation. Our client is an exception. He does well in school. After completing primary education he goes to the nearest town for secondary education. He is intelligent, and performs very well academically. He completes his high school creditably. All the family resources are pooled together to send him to college in the city. He has been brought up to believe that he is something special. His parents, his siblings and others in his home town go to great lengths in financing his education. He comes to the college in the city. His alienation from his roots has three distinct phases. When he first comes to the city he is full of self-confidence. Very soon he is very homesick. He visits his home at every available opportunity and looks forward to his vacations. By the time he has finished his second term he is not so enthusiastic about his visits home, and they are shortened. After a year he finds excuses not to go home. He feels very guilty but has enough rationalizations. But these are not convincing and the conflict emerges. From a situation where he was the star of the show he comes to an environment where he has to compete with many equals and even superiors to hold his own. Added to this is the fact that in comparison to his city peers he is seen as a country bumpkin. The sudden deflation of self-image is devastating. Initially he goes home to find comfort, security and a sense of belonging. But he is a stranger in his own environment. He is the educated, city-bred, sophisticated, all-knowing person. His uneducated parents cannot claim to advise him. They look up to him for enlightenment. There is a subtle message that he is superior and that they have invested all they have so that he succeeds. This is a burden which is a deadweight. He cannot tell them that he is lonely and comes back so that he can derive strength from them. But, alas, their image of him is that of a strong self-dependent person. He goes back to the city utterly helpless. He wants to justify their trust and confidence in him. He is angry that they have placed such a burden on him. He cannot afford to be angry because they have given him everything. These young people are defeated, helpless, lonely, looking for someone who will understand this dilemma, uncritically and without condescension. They are not ready to make decisions. Their elders, the decision-makers, feel that they are incompetent to make decisions for their 'educated son'. Thus they find themselves totally estranged from their own environment and they do not have a place in the environment which has fallen to their lot. This situation symbolizes a crisis occurring on a much larger scale and needs to be considered in a developing society like India where more and more people are migrating to the cities for education, where they find themselves isolated.

In Indian society the daughter-in-law–mother-in-law conflicts are well known. The fact which needs to be emphasized is that the traditional concept of mutual adaptation, at least tolerance, is not operating as well as it once did. Whenever this is expected, the price paid for maintaining a semblance of harmony is very high. It is generally believed that Indian women are passive. I would like to offer a different perspective on this so-called passivity. It has been repeated often enough that the woman is dependent on a male in all stages of life—a father in childhood, a husband during adulthood and a son during old age. This calls for remarkable adaptational capacities in any human being. If one's continued role status depends upon the whims of others, one has to guard it by all possible means. I feel the woman accomplishes this by very subtle manipulations. She is the passive one but she also determines the level of intimacy, gratification of affectional needs and assurance of relative harmony in the family. In this dynamic process the son has a pivotal role. The daughter has to marry and leave home anyway. Thus she cannot be counted upon to play a significant role, whereas it is the son who maintains the continuity of the mother's existence. She cannot alienate his sympathies. Dominance-submission is one coordinate of this interaction pattern. If this does not work, a more subtle and more sure method is the generation of the shame-guilt component. Working with male children we see that their sense of loyalty is so great that they reject any probing or interpretation of their anger towards their mothers. Sometimes it is relatively more readily accepted towards fathers. Behaviourally, aggression may be directed towards the mother but at a conscious level this is not acceptable. This is seen in a different context from the mother's point of view. She can tolerate aggressive behaviour but is shocked if a child verbally expresses hostility and wishes of death. The feeling towards the father is an ambiguous one. He is either idealized or perceived as an object of contempt for his passivity. He is seen to be a straw hero who struts about dominating vulnerable, defenceless children. This does not mean that he is not feared and obeyed, but the motivating factor is not respect for his authority. If these are the models for identification, one can well imagine what kind of integrated personalities will develop.

The consequences of this parental constellation are seen in adolescents perhaps a little less obviously than in adults . . . . In the clinical set-up we see paradigms of adult failure . . . the uncertainty, the dependence and incapacity to make independent decisions are all obvious. These comments are not meant to be denigrating but are in pursuance of my thesis that the social structure does not permit the emergence of a cogent adult role as perceived in western societies. Subordinating one's individual needs to the interests of the group, be it a family, a kinship group, a clan or a class, is upheld as a virtue. The linear structure of authority distribution reinforces and sustains this paradigm. Thus self-assertion becomes selfishness, independent decision-making is perceived as disobedience. The response from the in-group is tacit disapproval if not outright condemnation. Under such circumstances it is easier to play safe. The only way this can be accomplished is by passive aggressive behaviour or regression into total passivity. Up to a certain point passivity provides an escape but in the present day and age, life tasks demand a certain assertiveness and some capacity to make decisions. Inability to fulfill these requirements leads to frustration. Inevitably, frustration beyond a point results in ego disintegration in the individual and disorganization in the social structure. As Erikson points out,

> What I mean by this sinister reference is that there is a limit to a child's and an adult's individual endurance in the face of demands which force him to consider himself, his body, his needs, and his wishes as evil and dirty, and to believe in the infallibility of those who pass judgement. Occasionally, he may turn things around, become secretly oblivious to the opinion of others, and consider as evil only the fact that they exist: his change will come when they are gone or when he can leave them.

The above comments are prompted by the conviction that in India we have to do some fresh thinking about our whole value system. It is not that the traditional beliefs and the values on which they are based are totally irrelevant. These values should be seen in a historical perspective. In an agrarian, relatively less competitive social structure where kinship bonds had economic, social and moral justifications, the value systems certainly had a place. In the present day we have to ask if they still fulfil individual and social needs. The distress caused in individual lives and the fragility of a social structure which can get disorganized at the slightest stress, calls for social scientists to objectively evaluate the present situation.

1.4 *Knowledge, Practice and Values*[6]

ARTHUR N. TURNER AND GEORGE F.F. LOMBARD

According to one view of the relation between systematics, knowledge and practice, the process, in oversimplified terms, goes something like this. From an assumed existing body of knowledge (1), a great scientist develops a new theory made up of testable hypotheses (2), which lead to experiments (3), which generate findings (4), leading to methods of application (5), and finally to improved practice (6). According to this model the practitioner makes little contribution to the process of developing knowledge. He comes into the chain of events only at the end of the process and it almost seems as if it would all work better without him.

However the history of the development of the orientation we have been studying, and our own efforts to practice it, illustrate very clearly that this one-directional chain of events does not at all represent the actual development of knowledge and practice. A most accurate model of what takes place in the history of the development of any science requires a circular rather than a linear model, in which the role of the practitioner is central rather than that of a somewhat inconvenient last step. Some of the major phases of this development could be represented by Figure 2.

This conception of the development of knowledge and practice is not put forward as an adequate description of a very complex subject. Its purpose is only to call attention to the probability that what we discovered in our own study and practice of inter-personal behavior may have wider relevance. The observations which come from skillful practice and the hypotheses which derive from systematic knowledge contribute to each other. The ideas which make sense at the level of clinical uniformities and at the level of theory are the same ideas which make sense to the intuitions of a skillful, responsible practitioner. For this kind of balanced progress in both theory and practice to take place, scientific and practical viewpoints must remain in effective communication with each other. To

⁶ From George F.F. Lombard, ed., *The Elusive Phenomena*, by Fritz J. Roethlisberger, Boston, MA: Division of Research, Harvard Business School, 1977.

Figure 2

SYSTEMATIC
KNOWLEDGE

CLINICAL
UNIFORMITIES

OBSERVATIONS AND
EXPERIENCES OF THE
PRACTITIONER

maintain and improve this communication is becoming an increasingly important management challenge.

In this conception of the knowledge-practice relation, the intuitions, curiosities, and feelings of the practitioner remain important contributors to the development of systematic knowledge, which in turn is useful to the practitioner as a framework for the organization of the observations and reflections he draws from this experience. Thus any theory of human behavior is useful to a manager—not when he believes it tells him what to do, but when it helps him order the phenomena he experiences in useful ways and test out for himself the consequences of differences in his own behavior. This kind of relationship between knowledge and practice requires that the practitioner remain curious about and sensitive to what he experiences when he interacts with another person. To benefit from and contribute to useful knowledge the practitioner has to learn to respond ever more skillfully to the total situation in which he is involved and to recognize that his own feelings are an unavoidable part of that situation.

Listening to Oneself

This is what this book has really been about to us: the administrator's ability to increase his awareness and understanding of how he feels about events in which he is involved and other people with whom he interacts. Sometimes in the midst of my involvement, at other times when I reflect on what has taken place, I have to ask myself this question and listen with skill to my answer: How is what I am aware of experiencing outside of myself being affected by what I may not be aware of experiencing inside?

Sometimes I can ask for help on this question from colleague, friend, or counselor, but often I will have to work on it alone . . . . For too long, it seems to us, there has been a sort of collusion between administrator and 'behavioral scientist' (a label as misfortunate in our opinion, and as fashionable, as 'change agent') to avoid open and forthright expression of the central value position on which their work together is based. Thus one popular model for the development of the field of interpersonal behavior in organizations sees it as an exchange between the practitioner committed to the improvement of organizational performance and the researcher committed to the improvement of scientific knowledge about human behavior. As new 'findings' are discovered they become the means by which the practitioner increases his organization's efficient production of goods and services. This model says nothing about how and by whom improved skill is to be developed, and it seems to sanction no open communication about fundamental values.

To us, increased knowledge about human behavior in organizations (improved 'behavioral science') is important, and we feel equally committed to the efficient utilization of human resources in the production of material goods and services. These two goals are both important, and each contributes to the other. But they are not enough. In addition, our world needs, desperately as we see it, improved skill in applying to organizational life what is already known about human behavior (and has been known for centuries), and it needs more clear commitment to the development of those kinds of human organizations within which each member is able to realize his potential as a thinking, feeling, growing human being.

1.5 *Experiential Learning*[7]

DAVID A. KOLB

Today's highly successful managers and administrators are distinguished not so much by any single set of knowledge or skills but by their ability

[7] From David A. Kolb, Irwin M. Rubin and James M. McIntyre, *Organizational Psychology: An Experiential Approach to Organizational Behavior*, Prentice-Hall, Inc., New Jersey, USA, 1984, pp. 45–46.

to adapt to and master the changing demands of their job and career, that is, by their ability to learn. The same is true for successful organizations. Continuing success in a changing world requires an ability to explore new opportunities and learn from past successes and failures. So stated, these ideas are neither new nor particularly controversial. Yet it is surprising that this ability to learn, which is so widely regarded as important, receives little explicit attention by managers and their organizations. There is a kind of fatalism about learning; one either learns or one does not . . . .

Part of the reason for this fatalism lies in a lack of understanding about the learning process itself. If managers and administrators had a model about how individuals and organizations learn, they would better be able to enhance their own and their organization's ability to learn . . . .

Differences in learning styles need to be managed in management education. For example, managers who come to the university for midcareer education experience something of a 'culture shock'. Fresh from a world of time deadlines and concrete specific problems that they must solve, they are suddenly immersed in a strange slow-paced world of generalities, where the elegant solution to problems is sought even when workable solutions have been found. One gets rewarded here for reflection and analysis rather than concrete goal-directed action. Managers who 'act before they think—if they ever think' meet the scientists who 'think before they act—if they ever act'. Research on learning styles has shown that managers on the whole are distinguished by very strong active experimentation skills and are very weak on reflective observation skills. Business school faculty members usually have the reverse profile. To bridge this gap in learning styles, the management educator must somehow respond to pragmatic demands for relevance and the application of knowledge, while encouraging the reflective examination of experience that is necessary to refine old theories and to build new ones. In encouraging reflective observation, the teacher often is seen as an interrupter of action—as a passive 'ivory tower' thinker. Indeed, this is a critical role to be played in the learning process. Yet if the reflective observer role is not internalized by the learners themselves, the learning process can degenerate into a value conflict between teacher and student, each maintaining that theirs is the right perspective for learning.

Neither the faculty nor student perspective alone is valid. Managerial education will not be improved by eliminating theoretical analysis or relevant case problems. Improvement will come through the integration of the scholarly and practical learning styles. One approach to achieving this integration is to apply the experiential learning model directly in the classroom. This workbook provides games, role plays, and exercises (concrete experiences) that focus on central concepts in organizational psychology. These simulations provide a common experiential starting point for participants and faculty to explore the relevance of psychological concepts for their work. In traditional management education methods, the conflict between scholar and practitioner learning styles is exaggerated because the material to be taught is filtered through the learning style of faculty members in their lectures or presentation and analysis of cases. Students are 'one down' in their own analysis because the data are secondhand and already biased. In the experiential learning approach, this filtering process does not take place because both teacher and student are observers of immediate experiences which they both interpret according to their own learning style. In this approach to learning, the teachers' role is that of facilitator of a learning process that is basically self-directed. They help students to experience in a personal and immediate way the phenomena in their field of specialization. They provide observational schemes and perspectives from which to observe these experiences. They stand ready with alternative theories and concepts as students attempt to assimilate their observations into their own conception of reality. They assist in deducing the implications of the students' concepts and in designing new 'experiments' to test these implications through practical 'real-world' experience.

There are two goals in the experiential learning process. One is to learn the specifics of a particular subject matter. The other is to learn about one's own strengths and weaknesses as a learner (i.e., learning how to learn from experience). When the process works, participants finish their educational experience not only with new intellectual insights, but also with an understanding of their own learning style. This understanding of learning strengths and weaknesses helps in the back-home application of what has been learned and provides a framework for continuing learning on the job. Day-to-day experience becomes a focus for testing and exploring new ideas. Learning is no longer a special activity reserved for the classroom, but becomes an integral and explicit part of work itself.

The Organization as a Learning System

As do individuals, organizations learn and develop distinctive learning styles. They, as do individuals, do so through their transactions with the environment and through their choice of how to relate to that environment. This has come to be known as the open systems view of organizations. Since many organizations are large and complex, the environment they relate to becomes highly differentiated and diverse. The way the organization adapts to this external environment is to differentiate itself into units, each of which deals with just one part of the firm's external conditions. Marketing and sales face problems associated with the market, customers, and competitors; research deals with the academic and technological worlds; production deals with production equipment and raw materials sources; personnel and labor relations deal with the labor market; and so on.

Because of this need to relate to different aspects of the environment, the different units of the firm develop characteristic ways of thinking and working together—different styles of decision-making and problem solving. These units select and shape managers to solve problems and make decisions in the way their environment demands. In fact, Lawrence and Lorsch define organizational differentiation as 'the difference in cognitive and emotional orientation among managers in different functional departments'.

If the organization is thought of as a learning system, each of the differentiated units that is charged with adapting to the challenges of one segment of the environment can be thought of as having a characteristic learning style that is best suited to meet those environmental demands. The Learning Style Inventory should be a useful tool for measuring this organizational differentiation among the functional units of a firm . . . .

1.6 Reframing the Problem: Practitioner Dialogue with the Situation[8]

DONALD A. SCHON

Each move is a local experiment which contributes to the global experiment of reframing the problem . . . . As architect Quist reflects on the unexpected consequences and implications of his moves, he listens to the situation's back talk, forming new appreciations which guide his further moves. Most significantly, he becomes aware that the gallery he has created, the 'soft back area' to the L-shaped classrooms, has become 'in a minor way . . . the major thing'. Seizing on the gallery's potential, he 'extends it here so as to look down into here'. Later, he carefully avoids placing the administration building on the site in a way that would spoil 'the whole idea'.

Thus the global experiment in reframing the problem is also a reflective conversation with the situation in which Quist comes to appreciate and

[8] From Donald A. Schon, *The Reflective Practitioner: How Professionals Think in Action*, Basic Books, Inc., New York, 1984, pp. 94–95, 140.

then to develop the implications of a whole new idea. The reframing of the problem is justified by the discovery that the new geometry 'works slightly with the contours,' yields pleasant nooks, views and soft back areas, and evokes in the situation the potential for a new coherence. Out of his reframing of Petra's problem, Quist derives a problem he can solve and coherent organization of materials from which he can make something that he likes.

Three dimensions of this process are particularly noteworthy: the domains of language in which the designer describes and appreciates the consequences of his moves, the implications he discovers and follows, and his changing stance toward the situation with which he converses.

It would be a mistake to attribute to the inquirer at the beginning of such a process the articulated description which he achieves later on—to say, for example, that Quist must have known unconsciously at the beginning just how this site is screwy and just how the geometry of parallels can be successfully imposed on it. To do so would be to engage in instant historical revisionism. The perception of similarity and difference implicit in Quist's initial description of the situation is, as Kuhn says, both logically and psychologically prior to his later articulation of it.

It is our capacity to see unfamiliar situations as familiar ones, and to do in the former as we have done in the latter, that enables us to bring our past experience to bear on the unique case. It is our capacity to see-as and do-as that allows us to have a feel for problems that do not fit existing rules.

The artistry of a practitioner like Quist hinges on the range and variety of the repertoire that he brings to unfamiliar situations. Because he is able to see these as elements of his repertoire, he is able to make sense of their uniqueness and need not reduce them to instances of standard categories.

Moreover, each new experience of reflection-in-action enriches his repertoire . . . . Reflection-in-action in a unique case may be generalized to other cases, not by giving rise to general principles, but by contributing to the practitioner's repertoire of exemplary themes from which, in the subsequent cases of his practice, he may compose new variations.

1.7 *Training for Leadership*[9]

A.K. RICE

The basic Tavistock conference method is to construct situations in which the conventional defences against recognizing or acting on

[9] From A.K. Rice, *Training for Leadership*, Tavistock Publications Ltd., London, 1965, pp. 25–27.

interpersonal and intergroup hostilities and rivalries are either removed or at least reduced. This permits examination of the forces at work. The method consists therefore of lowering the barriers to the expression of feeling, both friendly and hostile; of providing opportunities for a continuous check on one's own feelings, and for comparing them with those of others, about given situations. Or, to put it another way, it is to check fantasy against reality. It means that the anxiety of learning is enhanced, and that therefore the ways in which anxiety is generated and controlled become part of the learning opportunity.

How the conference is designed, how it is managed, how competently the staff carry out their tasks are all parts of the situation in which learning can take place. Everything that happens in the conference, therefore, whether by design or accident, is material for study.

The consultant's behavior is as important for learning as what he says: perhaps more so, since the words he uses to describe his feelings are symbols, of greater or less abstraction of the behavior they represent.

In addition, in the conference the staff represent authority. Apart from the other roles they take as consultants and lecturers, collectively they represent conference management. The members inevitably project upon them their fantasies, fears, and doubts about authority and its power, and the analysis of this projection requires the analysis of the relationships among the staff themselves to distinguish what is intrinsic to the staff group and what is projected onto them by the members. Hence the authority relationships within the staff, and the way staff members conduct themselves individually and collectively, provide further 'here and how' learning opportunities.

1.8 *The Creation of Settings*[10]

SEYMOUR B. SARASON

. . . . There is, on the surface at least, a bewildering array of attempts to create new settings. For example, when legislation was passed to set up the Peace Corps, it literally meant that scores of new settings would have to be created; the central setting in Washington and scores of others in countries around the world. In each of these instances people would be brought together in what were for them new relationships over a sustained period of time to achieve certain objectives . . . . The

[10] From Seymour B. Sarason, *The Creation of Settings and Future Societies*, Jossey-Bass, Inc., San Francisco, 1972, pp. 2–3 and 283–84.

creation of a new university, hospital, clinic, school, or community agency is another example of the creation of a setting, and within each of them there is almost always found instances possessing the characteristics of the creation of a setting. For example, when a hospital decides to set up a new intensive-care unit, or when a university launches a new department, or when a community initiates a new program for the inner city we are again dealing with the creation of a setting. And then there is the business and industrial sector, where one can safely assume that new settings are developed with a very high frequency. It may be a new company, factory, restaurant, or store, the labels, overt forms, purposes, and size may vary in the extreme, but almost always, they possess the defining provisional characteristics of the creation of a setting.

In the past decade or so, more new settings (leaving marriage aside) have been created than in the entire previous history of the human race. . . . . One cannot keep up with the new setting created daily to cope with one or another type of problem. The rate of setting creation is somewhat fantastic, and it is understandable, albeit incorrect, if we confuse this fact with real change. Such a confusion is analogous to one in which increases in Gross National Product are taken to signify the accomplishment of desired goals.

Creating a human setting is akin to creating a work of art. It is also different. It involves more than one artist; it involves different problems of function, materials, and organization; its products are different; its place and relationships to society are different . . . . Like a work of art the creation of setting requires of a group that it formulate and confront the task of how to deal with and change reality in ways that foster a shared sense of knowing and changing and allows it to regard its development as a necessary antecedent to and concomitant of its efforts to serve or please others. Like the artist, its problems are never solved once and for all, they are ever present and varyingly recalcitrant, they discourage and distract, but it knows that this is the way it is and has to be and there is no good alternative to trying and learning. It treasures feeling and reveres reflection and calculation; it knows that there is always a tension between the two from which something new may emerge.

Although there can be a kinship between the creation of a setting and the artistic process, there ordinarily is none because of heightened self-consciousness that clearly differentiates between routine and imitative thinking and innovative, imaginative thinking. To say that the creation of a setting can be like a work of art is to say that it can involve in an organized way the most productive attributes of the human mind. If it can be like a work of art, it will only be after we have been helped to change our categories of thinking.

Where new knowledge and understanding will take us is not predictable. It is hard to accept the fact that the more you know the more you need to know and that it is an endless process that does not end in a utopia. There will always be problems. This is the consequence of all new knowledge just as it should be part of the perceived reality of all those who create settings today and dream of future societies.

1.9 *Liberation Education*[11]

PAULO FRIERE

The central problem is: how can the oppressed . . . participate . . . in developing the pedagogy of their liberation? Only as they discover themselves to be 'hosts' of the oppressor can they contribute to the midwifery of their liberating pedagogy. As long as they live in the duality in which *to be* is *to be like*, and *to be like* is *to be like the oppressor*, this contribution is impossible. The pedagogy of the oppressed, which cannot be created by the oppressors, is an instrument of this critical discovery by the oppressed: that they themselves and their oppressors as well are both manifestations of dehumanization . . . .

In this situation the oppressed do not see the 'new man' as the man to be born from the solution of this contradiction through the transformation of the old concrete situation of oppression, which gives way to another situation-liberation. For them, the new man is themselves, now become oppressor of others. Their vision of the new man is individualistic; their 'adherence' to the oppressor makes impossible either their consciousness of themselves as persons or their consciousness of being an oppressed class. They want agrarian reform, not to become free men but to possess land and thus to become landowners—or, more precisely, possess over other workers. It is a rare peasant who, once 'promoted' to overseer, does not become more of a tyrant toward his former comrades than the owner himself. One might say, with reason, that this is due to the fact that the concrete situation of oppression remains unchanged. In this instance, the overseer, to make sure of his job, must be as tough as the owner—and more. This does not negate our previous assertion; that in these circumstances the oppressed find in the oppressor their example of 'manhood' . . . . The telltale shadow of the former oppressor dogs them. He continues to be their example of humanity.

---

[11] From a lecture by Paulo Friere at Harvard University in Spring 1961.

The 'fear of freedom' to which the oppressed are subject, a fear which may equally as well lead them to desire the status of oppressors or bind them to the 'status' of the oppressed, is another aspect worthy of reflection. One of the basic elements of the relationship between oppressor and oppressed is *prescription*. Every prescription represents the imposition of one man's choice upon another, transforming the receiving conscience into one which 'houses' the oppressor's conscience. Thus, the behavior of the oppressed is prescribed behavior. It is based on alien guidelines—the guidelines of the oppressor. The oppressed, who internalize the image of the oppressors and follow their guidelines, are fearful of freedom. Freedom would require them to eject this image, to fill the resulting 'emptiness' with another content, autonomy and responsibility, without which they cannot be free. Freedom is a conquest, not a gift. It must be constantly pursued, and this pursuit exists only in the responsible act of the pursuer. No one has the freedom to be free unless, in his freedom, he fights for it. Nor is freedom an ideal located outside of man, from which he may be alienated. It is not an idea which becomes a myth. It is the indispensable condition of the pursuit in which men, as uncompleted beings, are engaged . . . .

However, the oppressed who have become adapted and resigned . . . (for) long . . . feel incapable of running the risks it requires. They are also afraid because the struggle for freedom threatens not only those who have been 'free' to oppress, but also their own oppressed comrades who are fearful of still greater repression . . . . While dominated by the fear of fredom they refuse to appeal to others or to listen to the appeals of others or even to the appeals of their own conscience. They prefer gregariousness to authentic comradeship; they prefer conformity with their state of unfreedom to the creative communion produced by freedom or even the very pursuit of freedom.

The oppressed suffer from the duality which has established itself in their innermost being. They discover that, being unfree, they cannot exist authentically. They want authentic existence, but fear it.

Liberation is thus a childbirth, and a painful one. The main which emerges is a new man, viable only in and through the solution of the oppressor-oppressed contradiction; the humanization of all men. Or to put it another way, the solution of this contradiction is the childbirth which brings to the world this new man; no longer oppressor, no longer oppressed, but man in the process of freeing himself . . . it is necessary for the oppressed to commit themselves to the liberating praxis . . . .

'Banking' Education versus Problem-posing Education

The raison d'être of liberation education lies in its drive toward reconciliation. Education must begin with the solution of the teacher-pupil contradiction, by reconciling the poles of the contradiction so that both are simultaneously teachers and pupils.

This solution is not (nor can it be) found in the 'banking' concept, for which education is the act of depositing, transferring, and transmitting values and knowledge. On the contrary, reflecting the society of oppression, 'banking' education maintains and even stimulates this contradiction. In this type of education,

(*a*) the teacher teaches and the pupils are taught

(*b*) the teacher knows everything and the pupils know nothing

(*c*) the teacher thinks and the pupils are thought about

(*d*) the teacher talks and the pupils listen meekly

(*e*) the teacher disciplines and the pupils are disciplined

(*f*) the teacher chooses and enforces his choice, and the pupils comply

(*g*) the teacher acts and the pupils have the illusion of acting through the action of the teacher

(*h*) the teacher chooses the program content, and the pupils (who were not consulted) adapt to it

(*i*) the teacher confuses the authority of knowledge with his own professional authority, which he places in opposition to the freedom of the pupils

(*j*) the teacher is the subject of the learning process, while the pupils are mere objects

If the teacher is one who knows everything, while the pupils know nothing, it is obviously the role of the former to bring, deliver, transmit and impart his knowledge to the latter—knowledge which thus ceases to be living experience and becomes narrated or transmitted experience.

It is not surprising that in this 'banking' concept of education men are seen as adaptable, adjustable beings. The more the pupils work at storing the deposits entrusted to them, the less they develop the critical awareness which would result from their intromission in the world as transformers of that world. The more completely they accept their passive role imposed on them, the more they tend simply to adapt to the world (instead of transforming it) and to the fragmented reality of the 'deposits' they receive.

This 'banking' concept of education, which minimizes or annuls the creative power of the pupils, stimulating their credulity instead of their critical faculties, serves the interests of the oppressors, who are interested neither in having the world revealed nor in seeing it transformed. The (non-humanist) humanitarianism of the oppressors aims at preserving a situation from which they benefit and which permits them to maintain their false generosity. For this very reason they react, almost instinctively, against any attempt at an education which stimulates authentic thought, one which does not become ensnarled in partial visions of reality but always seeks out the ties which link one point to another and one problem to another.

Indeed, what the oppressors have in mind is changing the mentality of the oppressed, not the situation which oppresses them; for the more the oppressed are adapted to that situation, the more easily they can be dominated. To do this, the oppressors use the 'banking' concept of education, to which they annex a paternalistic social action apparatus. In the latter, the oppressed receive the euphemistic title of 'welfare recipients'. They are treated as individual cases, as marginals who deviate from the general configuration of society, which is 'good, organized and just'. From this viewpoint, the oppressed represent the pathology of the healthy society, which must therefore adjust these 'incompetent and lazy' men to its own patterns by changing their mentality. As marginals—men 'outside' or 'on the margins' of society—the solution would be their 'integration, their incorporation' into the healthy society which they had formerly 'forsaken', like renegades renouncing a happy life. The solution would be for them to stop staying 'outside' and to come 'inside'. The truth, however, is that the oppressed, the so-called 'marginals', never were 'outside'. They were always 'inside'—inside the structure which changed them into 'beings for others'. Accordingly, the solution is not to 'integrate' them, not to 'incorporate' them into this structure of oppression, but to transform that structure so that they can become 'beings for themselves'. This solution, however, is obviously not the objective of the oppressors; hence, the 'banking education' which serves the interests of the latter can never orient itself toward the conscientizacao of the pupils. 'Problem-posing' education, responding to the essence of consciousness—*its intentionality*—rejects communiques and embodies communication.

Accordingly, education which liberates cannot consist of 'depositing', narrating, transferring, or transmitting 'knowledge' and values to pupils— mere 'receivers—in the style of 'banking' education; it must be an act of cognition. It is a learning situation in which the cognizable object, instead of being the object of the cognitive act, is the intermediator between the cognitive actors; teacher on the one hand and learners on the other. Thereby, problem—posing education immediately requires that the contradiction between the teacher and the taught be resolved. Dialogical relations—indispensable to the capacity for cognition of cognitive actors with regard to the same cognizable object—are otherwise impossible . . . . It is through dialogue that this solution is achieved; the teacher-of-the-pupils and the pupils-of-the-teacher cease to exist and a new thesis emerges; teacher-pupil with pupil-teacher. Now the teacher is no longer merely the-one-who-teaches but one who is himself taught in dialogue with the pupil, who in turn while being taught also teaches. Both become agents responsible for a process in which they both grow. In this process arguments based on 'authority' are no longer valid. In this process, authority, in order to exist, must be *on the side of* freedom, not *against* it.

At this level, no one teaches another, just as no one is self-taught. Men teach each other in fellowship, intermediated by the world. They are interlinked by the cognizable objects. In this way the problem-posing educator constantly re-forms his cognitive act in the capacity for cognition of the learners. The latter—no longer docile recipients of 'deposits'—are now critical investigators in dialogue with the educator, who is also a critical investigator. When the educator presents to the learners, for their consideration, the content of the study to be made, he reconsiders his earlier considerations as the learners make their own considerations.

Since this educational method constitutes a learning situation, the role of the problem-posing educator is to create, together with the learners, the conditions under which knowledge at the level of the *doxa* is replaced by true knowledge, at the level of the *logos*.

1.10 *Double Binds*[12]

NATASHA JOSEFOWITZ

If I'm assertive
I'm seen as aggressive
If I'm aggressive
I'm a bitch
I won't be promoted
Let's try it again
If I'm non-assertive
I'm seen as a patsy
If I'm a patsy
I won't be promoted

[12] From Natasha Josefowitz, 'Good Management Potential', in *Paths to Power: A Woman's Guide from First Job to Top Executive*, Addison–Wesley, Reading, Massachusetts, 1980.

1.11 *Personal Thoughts on Teaching and Learning*[13]

CARL R. ROGERS

I wish to present some very brief remarks, in the hope that if they bring forth any reaction from you, I may get some new light on my own ideas.

I find it a very troubling thing to think, particularly when I think about my own experiences and try to extract from those experiences the meaning that seems genuinely inherent in them. At first, such thinking is very satisfying, because it seems to discover sense and pattern in a whole host of discrete events. But then it very often becomes dismaying, because I realize how ridiculous these thoughts, which have much value to me, would seem to most people. My impression is that if I try to find the meaning of my own experience it leads me, nearly always, in directions regarded as absurd.

So in the next three or four minutes, I will try to digest some of the meanings which have come to me from my classroom experience and the experience I have had in individual and group therapy. They are in no way intended as conclusions for some one else, or a guide to what others should do or be. They are the very tentative meanings, as of April 1952, which my experience has had for me, and some of the bothersome questions which their absurdity raises. I will put each idea or meaning in a separate lettered paragraph, not because they are in any particular logical order, but because each meaning is separately important to me.

a) My experience has been that I cannot teach another person how to teach. To attempt it is for me, in the long run, futile.

b) It seems to me that anything that can be taught to another is relatively inconsequential, and has little or no significant influence on behavior. That sounds so ridiculous I can't help but question it at the same time that I present it.

c) I realize increasingly that I am only interested in learnings which significantly influence behavior. Quite possibly this is simply a personal idiosyncrasy.

d) I have come to feel that the only learning which significantly influences behavior is self-discovered, self-appropriated learning.

e) Such self-discovered learning, truth that has been personally appropriated and assimilated in experience, cannot be directly communicated

[13] From Carl R. Rogers, *On Becoming a Person*, Houghton Mifflin Company, Boston, 1961.

to another. As soon as an individual tries to communicate such experience directly, often with a quite natural enthusiasm, it becomes teaching, and its results are inconsequential. It was some relief recently to discover that Soren Kierkegaard, the Danish philosopher, had found this too, in his own experience, and stated it very clearly a century ago. It made it seem less absurd.

f) As a consequence of the above, I realize that I have lost interest in being a teacher.

g) When I try to teach, as I do sometimes, I am appalled by the results, which seem little more than inconsequential, because sometimes the teaching appears to succeed. When this happens I find that the results are damaging. It seems to cause the individual to distrust his own experience, and to stifle significant learning. Hence I have come to feel that the outcomes of teaching are either unimportant or hurtful.

h) When I look back at the results of my past teaching, the real results seem the same—either damage was done, or nothing significant occurred. This is frankly troubling.

i) As a consequence, I realize that I am only interested in being a learner, preferably learning things that matter, that have some significant influence on my own behavior.

j) I find it very rewarding to learn, in groups, in relationships with one person as in therapy, or by myself.

k) I find that one of the best, but most difficult ways for me to learn is to drop my own defensiveness, at least temporarily, and to try to understand the way in which this experience seems and feels to the other person.

l) I find that another way of learning for me is to state my own uncertainties, to try to clarify my puzzlements, and thus get closer to the meaning that my experience actually seems to have.

m) This whole train of experiencing, and the meanings that I have thus far discovered in it, seem to have launched me on a process which is both fascinating and at times a little frightening. It seems to mean letting my experience carry me on, in a direction which appears to be forward, toward goals that I can but dimly define, as I try to understand at least the current meaning of that experience. The sensation is that of floating with a complex stream of experience, with the fascinating possibility of trying to comprehend its ever changing complexity.

I am almost afraid I may seem to have gotten away from any discussion of learning, as well as teaching. Let me again introduce a practical note by saying that by themselves these interpretations of my own experience may sound queer and aberrant, but not particularly shocking. It is when

I realize the implications that I shudder a bit at the distance I have come from the commonsense world that everyone knows is right. I can best illustrate that by saying that if the experiences of others had been the same as mine, and if they had discovered similar meanings in it, many consequences would be implied.

a) Such experience would imply that we would do away with teaching. People would get together if they wished to learn.

b) We would do away with examinations. They measure only the inconsequential type of learning.

c) The implication would be that we would do away with grades and credits for the same reason.

d) We would do away with degrees as a measure of competence partly for the same reason. Another reason is that a degree marks an end or a conclusion of something, and a learner is only interested in the continuing process of learning.

e) It would imply doing away with the exposition of conclusions, for we would realize that no one learns significantly from conclusions.

I think I had better stop there. I do not want to become too fantastic. I want to know primarily whether anything in my inward thinking as I have tried to describe it, speaks to anything in your experience of the classroom as you have lived it, and if so, what the meanings are that exist for you in your experience.

2. THE PERSONAL DIMENSION: INSIGHT, OPENNESS, COMPETENCE (AND GOOD FORTUNE)

'Plenty of people can draw, but you . . . have observation.'

John Millais to **Beatrice Potter**

I believe men's minds to be largely, perhaps all, classable according as they act, as some are instinctively pushed out to the margins of things and there they remain restless and dissatisfied unless and until they there perceive, or think they perceive, clear lines of demarcation. Such minds see truth, reality of all kinds—or what they take to be such—as so many geometrical figures: within these luminous lines all is true, 'safe', 'correct'; outside them at once begins error, 'danger', incorrectness.

Then there are other minds which see truth's realities as intensely luminous centres, with a semi-illuminated outer margin, and then another and another, till all shades off into outer darkness. Such minds are not in the least perturbed by each having to stammer and to stumble. When they have moved out some distance, they fall back upon their central light. They become perturbed really, only if and when minds of the geometrical type will force them for the time into their own approach and apprehension.

Baron von Hugel

In order to lose one's identity one must first have one, and in order to transcend, one must pass through and not bypass ethical concerns . . . not generating short (what one) could not or did not wish to take care of.

Erik H. Erikson

INTRODUCTION

The creative, open, energetic, interactive nature of learning for action calls for persons to match, persons who reach out realistically and who can stimulate others to similar learning and can facilitate it. Their modelling gives life to what they profess and faces others with demanding and also liberating opportunities for learning.

We start with some readings about the personal dimensions of training and consulting. The all-round competence that trainer consultants bring to assessing real life situations in order to contribute best to them draws on important personal qualities. Among these are self-understanding—preferences, limits, strengths, weaknesses—and the acceptance of that self; so that while, he is at work with others, the trainer does not distract himself with internal dialogue—about how he appears to others, for instance, or how safe he is as he explores new areas. Thus he or she can give his attention totally and wholeheartedly to the present moment and company, be they participants, clients or colleagues.

A second personal characteristic of effective consultant trainers is that they are reflective: after the encounter is over they seek to understand how the situation developed and what their part in it was, and how they might be more effective in a similar situation in the future. They build time for such reflection into their schedules, away from the pressures of the interactive situations themselves. This continuing learning through reflection often becomes the trainer consultants' most telling contribution of all as others working with them notice this openness and in their turn 'unfreeze'. Not making time for reflection is self defeating.

Competence, Personality and Culture

That we need to go back to the 1960s for our readings on the essentially personal basis for training shows how close our profession may be to that 'forgetting of being', which is the German philosopher's Heidegger's eerie caution for professionals in all spheres.

The first reading by Irwin Weschler *et al.*, discusses this interweaving of personality and competence in one setting: sensitivity training. 'Personal dynamics' is 'undoubtedly a key determining factor' for one trainer preferring to concentrate attention on group processes while another concentrates on individual development. Clearest in sensitivity and other highly personal training, a good match of trainer with setting and techniques is important over the whole range of training and consulting, even in 'distance learning' and instrumented instruction. Behind every instrument is a person who has designed it, chosen it for *this* purpose with *these* participants, uses it, monitors and assesses its use. Lynton then describes how different, and differently-disposed, trainers worked in the same twelve week residential programs with participants from several cultures.

What is this 'fit'? What does it really mean to 'start where the participants, villagers, children *are*', to share their experience, to 'feel' with them? Anthropologist Clifford Geertz[1] takes off from Bronislaw Malinowski's *A Diary in the Strict Sense of the Term*. The distinction he uses, between the 'experience-near' concepts that practitioners habitually use in their fields and the 'experience-distant' concepts trainers and other specialists seek to impart is reminiscent of Elton Mayo's—of the Hawthorne Experiments in the late 1920s—between 'knowledge of acquaintances' and 'knowledge about', following William James. 'To grasp concepts that (for participants) are experience-near, and to do so well enough to place them in illuminating connection with experience-distant concepts theorists have fashioned to capture the general features of social life, is clearly a task at least as delicate, if a bit less magical, as putting onself into someone else's skin'.

The other end of the fit, the participants' in *their* culture, time and place, also stands out clearest in the most personal kinds of training but is likewise important in *all* training. Clients seek a trainer or consultant who suits them, who fits. How the partners view each other is therefore also important. The reading by Kakar deals with this correspondence in the contexts of healing in both Eastern and Western cultures. The musical metaphor serves him best: 'With his self as the musical instrument whose many strings have been tuned to the required pitch . . . the choice of the [healer] is determined by the fit between the actual man and the ideal image'—ideal that is, in the eyes of the seeker.

Personal growth is Jerome Bruner's metaphor for learning at this deeper level. 'Growing is becoming different, not better or faster. You may become better or faster at accomplishing certain external feats . . . but the accomplishment is achieved by processes that are qualitatively different, not simply quantitatively improved'. For growing, the distinctions between 'therapy', 'tutoring', 'teaching' and 'training' may be very thin, Bruner writes, and he has always been bemused by attempts to draw them.[2] We turn to Jung and Buber for passages on the development of personality and the nature of dialogue with life: 'awareness'. 'Only acute necessity is able to rouse it . . . brute necessity . . . the motivating force of inner or outer fatalities' (Jung). Observations and onlooking

[1] Clifford Geertz, *Local Knowledge: Further Essays in Interpretive Anthropology*, Basic Books, New York, 1983.

[2] Jerome Bruner, *In Search of Mind*, Harper, New York, 1983.

are not enough, engagement is required, what Buber calls 'answering': awareness. The Lynton reading (2.2) recounts such growing in a residential training center in South East Asia and examines some practical implications and pitfalls for trainers in it.

Basically important in personal growth is an increasing awareness about ethical and value issues and clarity about one's positions on them. On choosing fields of work and clients, we hold that, on both personal and philosophical grounds, a consultant trainer must avoid work in situations that are likely to overwhelm him and render him impotent or which run intrinsically counter to important values he holds. Avoiding professional settings roles and activities in which the consultant trainer knows he has serious blind spots, for whatever reasons, is part of this responsibility. Far-reaching social issues have also come to the fore on which he takes a stand, openly or by implication. Work to improve the production or use of atomic weaponry or of unethical drugs is so unacceptable to many consultant trainers in industrially developed countries that they decline to work there and so avoid going to war against themselves.

Inclusion/discrimination issues—whether and on what basis client organizations and associations of professionals themselves ensure the participation of women, poor, handicapped, tribal and other heretofore ignored or oppressed people as a matter of policy—have become prominent, and ecological safeguarding, a responsible concern for future generations adds others. We include extracts from a twelve page printed *Statement of Values and Ethics for Organization Development Professionals* based on the work of twenty professional associations in Europe, Japan and North America.

Evidence is accumulating that many trainer consultants, having chosen to enter and stay in this stimulating profession, then stress themselves with the multiple and conflicting pressures in it. It has generally been reported that their stress levels are, in general, 'much higher than those of the clients they serve.' Genetic constitution and supporting relationships account for some of the variance in stress levels but 'poor life style habits account for more than 50 per cent of the risks to one's health' and, we would add, to the implications of this for work with clients. 'Sufficient challenge, control how one does things . . . and activities to which one feels committed' are the three important dimensions to manage. Timeliness, good fit, may determine when a person of fitting competence 'does or says something which happened to need doing or saying at the moment' and so succeeds. To judge time and fit well takes, besides competence, some venturing, certainly some wisdom and also a dash of luck.

A Practitioner of Conviction—and Skill

. . . but conviction with competence is less than liberation . . . a new identity will be very much attached to an intimate mastery of a set of skills', Erik Erikson's piece is a good lead into the final set of readings in this section which is about skill—any skill—and its acquisition. It can throw light on what skill *is* (the consultant trainer's in this case) and how it can be developed.

The notion of skill is from mere technique. 'All skills are complicated . . . an acquired integral response to a many-faceted situation . . . or it is not skill but bungling incompetence'. Roethlisberger, of the Hawthorne experiments' fame, treats this more fully and ends with a tabular statement of 'the knowledge enterprise'. For *developing* knowledge, the concrete situation is the starting point, the source, whereas for practicing it the situation is the target.

2.1 *From Personal Dynamics to Interventions*[3]

IRWIN R. WESCHLER

The nature of trainer-intervention is based on something more than intellectual considerations. The personality dynamics of the trainer undoubtedly are a key determining factor. A trainer who chooses the self-in-process direction must be willing and able to face, at least on occasion, intense emotional encounters which involve strong expressions of hostility, anger, love, fear, anxiety, hope, and the like. He must be able to face such feelings and deal with them, both as they occur in others and in himself, without becoming blocked, anxious, or confused. He must be able, on occasion, to share his own feelings with the group.

It is our hypothesis that many trainers who have a strong intellectual commitment to the group orientation have it because they cannot deal comfortably with intense personal feelings. The group focus reasonably insures for them that the interpersonal encounters are not likely to become too deep and too intense. On the other hand, there is no doubt that some trainers who strongly prefer the individual orientation do so on neurotic grounds. The individual focus generates an interpersonal

[3] From Irwin R. Weschler and E.S. Schein (eds.), *Issues in Human Relations Training*, National Training Laboratories, Washington, D.C., 1962 (Reading Number 5).

milieu which provides the trainer with an opportunity to experience and work through some of his own unresolved problems. Further, it provides the somewhat personally alienated trainer with an opportunity to experience close and intense interpersonal encounters of which he usually may be deprived.

These trainer issues concerning the relation between his interventions and his dynamics are real—but often side-stepped. We feel they can no longer be ignored if we are to understand, as objectively as possible, the full meaning and implications of the self-in-process orientation to sensitivity training.

In distinguishing the seven successive stages of personal growth which involve primarily a change in the manner of experiencing Rogers describes progress from the lower end of the continuum—where people view their feelings as remote and not now present, where there exists a maximum-incongruence, where the individual is unwilling to communicate to the self, where his experience is construed in a rigid way perceived as external facts where problems are unrecognized and there is no desire to change, where close relationships are avoided—to the other end of the continuum—where feelings are now allowed to bubble into awareness and full experience, where an individual becomes able to live freely in a fluid process of experiencing, where incongruences between experience and awareness are merely temporary shocks requiring no special need for defense, where life appears rich in meaning and is modified by each new experience where there is increasingly a sense of self-responsibility for problems and where interpersonal relations are lived openly and freely as part of a satisfying, integrative process of life.

. . . training requires practitioners with a high professional and clinical competence, a dedication of purpose, a genuine interest in the well-being of peeople, a constant commitment toward experimentation and evaluation and an appreciation of the potential risks inherent in this type of activity . . . . Yet risk and progress go hand in hand, as we try new approaches to make it possible for many more to see, hear, feel, and experience life fully and effectively.

2.2 Close/Personal or Distant/Impersonal Faculty in Residential Settings[4]

ROLF P. LYNTON

Teaching is a very personal, individual activity. As with the members, so with a teacher: what he is sets the limits to what he does. The implications

[4] From Rolf P. Lynton, *The Tide of Learning: The Aloka Experience*, Routledge and Kegan Paul, London, 1961, pp. 141 and 204–9.

for training are not in terms of what a faculty member knows but what he is; not what he can do but what he can be; not what he can train others to be but what he can permit others to become . . . .

The part the faculty as a whole play in the course is determined by one need; that they cease to be seen by the members primarily as people holding positions of authority and come to be seen primarily as people with arms and legs, that is, as persons not institutions . . . .

Some faculty members at Aloka choose to limit their relations with the members essentially because of this refusal to occupy the traditional authority positions. They make this refusal explicit whenever they see the danger that some members are reverting to the subordinate roles with which they are familiar. In pursuit of their aim they avoid getting involved in activities with the members outside the formal programme or occasions immediately related to it, such as a private talk on a professional basis. They choose one role and one kind of relationship with the members, and, while a residential programme does not allow them to stick 100 per cent to such a limitation, they are as rigid about it as they can be. They are concerned often with clarifying and safeguarding their role.

Their inclination to limit and define their role has much professional support, particularly from the groups that are influenced by psycho-analytic theory and are interested in the role of the therapist. The clarity of relationship and of the consistently unmistakable signal that members cannot expect the faculty member to step into the shoes of their authority figure at home can be very valuable. To the faculty member this limited orientation simplifies the clues and choices by which he can decide on his behavior in any situation and gives him the certainty that he can limit his involvement and control the time he spends with the members.

But limitation of role and relationship leave the faculty member distant from the members and this has serious disadvantages. Our experience suggests that though the faculty member is distant, he yet continues to be very much the focus of the members' for a long time, like a door through which an important person is expected to enter. And every interpretation he makes from this distance puts him back on stage and confirms his presence as an important person. Repeatedly a faculty member who tried to limit his role in this manner came to be regarded as manipulative and his contributions feared and resented. His very distance from them is familiar to the members and allows them to identify the faculty with the authority figures of their past. The same distance, of course, also means that his interpretations are based on few clues. The only clues he has to guide his understanding of a member and the group are from the discussions and other parts of the formal programme when the members are guarded and deliberate.

The members in their turn see the faculty member's behavior, based on only a very limited range of situations, as distant; they see him not only as unresponsive but as consistent to a predetermined line of action rather than as a person pursuing the general aim of helping them to his best ability in any particular situation. In short, while the members come to understand that the faculty member who limits his role in this way will on no account become the traditional authority figure, they cannot also see him as a person. The more the faculty is regarded by the members as external to their organization, the more his interpretations can be 'written off' as related to purposes of his own which do not concern them. Particularly in view of their short association at Aloka it may appear to be an advantage that no personal attachments are likely to be formed as a result of this impersonality of the faculty. But this advantage is offset by the refusal of the members to take their eyes off him and to do what he wants to achieve by this limitation; to concentrate their attention on one another and on themselves.

The alternative which other faculty members prefer is to value a freer association with members, to come close and become personal; indeed as close and as personal as they can while maintaining professional standards of work. The limitations on this are essentially set by the faculty member's understanding of himself. For an individual can teach from closeness and remain effective at it only so long as his need to be close to the members and accepted by them does not prevent him from seeing and making the unsettling comment when it is necessary or withholding the support which the member wants but does not need. In this regard, the faculty do on occasion for one another what they try to do consistently for the members: they help one another to recognize and face up to the personal needs which are finding their way into his behavior.

These faculty members choose to have several roles in relation to the members. In unstructured discussions in the formal programme they may be resource people, contributors in line with the topic being discussed, as well as interpreters of what is going on in the group. In the field they will share the work conditions with the members on a footing of equality. They join in games, week-end trips, and other informal activities of the group. They may have administrative responsibilities. They joke and generally have an easy relationship with the members. In short, they seek to teach through closeness to the members. Beyond refusing to behave in the traditional manner of authority they go on, in effect, to demonstrate how people can relate to one another effectively and find in it much satisfaction as persons.

This attempt has its own many difficulties. By virtue of the very quantity of his contacts with members, the faculty member will sometimes be ineffective. His free behavior may come to be regarded as the

key element in the development of the group, making the Aloka experience unique and apparently irrelevant in the rigid relationships of traditional communities. And there are the real dangers that members see
this free behavior of a faculty member not as personal to him but as
deliberately and consistently opposite to the behavior of others they
know in authority, 'a line', the rebellion that many of them have been
itching to express for a long time. When the consistency in this picture
fades in the light of experience of further contact, they may go on to find
in the faculty members the benevolent father whom they have missed
and whom they would like to emulate in their families and communities
at home.

Most faculty members at Aloka prefer to have the advantages of
closeness more or less at the cost of these difficulties. Professionally, it
allows them a quicker understanding of the members and a familiarity
with the behavior of each over a wide range of situations. The many
informal contacts increase the chances that the members in turn will
profit from their observations of the faculty member as he goes in and
out of many situations. His occasional errors of judgment and ineffective
behavior shrink his halo. The disadvantages of the attempts of some
members to copy the faculty member's behavior, to 'use it' and 'apply it'
themselves, may be offset by the many possibilities of learning which
find fertile ground in the identification from which both possibilities
spring.

In the last analysis the faculty members will do what they feel comfortable doing and will find grounds to support it. One faculty member
enjoys closeness, informality and free association and, over and above
the professional advantages and disadvantages which follow his choice,
his joy will communicate itself to the members and find resonance
among them. Another faculty member prefers a less exposed, more
certain relationship and, along with the professional advantages and
disadvantages which follow his choice, his joy will communicate itself to
the members and find resonance among them. Another faculty member
prefers a less exposed, more certain relationship and, along with the
professional advantages and disadvantages which follow from that
choice, his values, too, will be communicated to the members.

While the faculty team has a common orientation and are pretty
consistently one on the clues they observe and their understanding of
the clues, they respond differently. Each has his own style of working
and living. Members often remark how widely different they see the
ways of teaching of different faculty members. Some prefer one, some
another. It is the same with the ways the different faculty members walk
and talk informally, with the members, with their own wives and children,
with staff, with others. And assuming the maturity and professional

competence for which faculty members are chosen to come to Aloka, each style has a value precisely as a comprehensive expression of a person. It has value as soon as there is 'system in the madness', and as this system makes sense in terms of the persons who are involved. So that, at Aloka the emphasis is off the fearful notion that there may be 'one best way' to lead, to discipline, to show initiative, and to do any of the other things the young leaders and administrators who come to Aloka wish to do well, and is on themselves and developing their characteristic personal styles of living and working as expressions of themselves.

Finally, whatever the advantages and disadvantages of the different styles of working and living which the members of the faculty team display to the members, the very fact that they are different has a clear and important advantage in that the faculty at Aloka does not tend itself to be institutionalized. It does not remain the monolithic superstructure of authority which members want to attach importance to when they come, consisting of some people whom they suppose to be only just short of omniscient, omnipresent, and omnipotent. These words have been on the blackboard several times at Aloka to make explicit the assumptions underlying some statements made by members in a discussion. That different faculty members behave so differently ensures that the members do personalize them. And with that a major goal is achieved.

2.3 *Healer and Client*[5]

SUDHIR KAKAR

'Every sickness is a musical problem,' Novalis once said, 'and every cure a musical solution'. The musical metaphor is indeed much more apt for Muslim Psychotherapy than the scientific metaphors of biology, psychology or information processing that govern contemporary Western psychotherapy. With his self as the musical instrument whose many strings have been tuned to the required pitch, when Baba plays the healing raga he is not practicing a science but what Auden called 'the intuitive art of wooing Nature'. The success of the 'wooing' depends much more on the person of the healer than on the depth of his knowledge or the technique he employs. In Baba's world view, shared

[5] From Sudhir Kakar, *Shamans, Mystics and Doctors*, Oxford University Press, New Delhi, 1982, pp. 38–39.

by his patients, a pir must develop certain essential qualities if he is to be a successful wooer of nature and a musician of healing. First, he must cultivate certain virtues of character—purity of mind and body, truthfulness, a definite detachment. Second, he must be what we may call a 'boundary man'—someone who chooses to live at the margin of his society, where he is in the world but not of it. Third, he needs to pass through an inner transformation that would connect him with, and make him receptive to, what the Sufi mystical tradition calls the soul force. Needless to say, none of these requirements can hope to find a place in the graduate training of a clinical psychologist or in the medical education of a psychiatrist. In fact, the only counterpart of 'inner transformation of the healer' in the Western psychotherapeutic tradition, namely the mediative procedures of a long personal analysis that every aspiring psychoanalyst must go through, has now become an old-fashioned rarity among the burgeoning number of Western psychotherapists and psychiatrists who are crusaders for one or more techniques of mental healing.

The belief that it is the person of the healer and not his conceptual system or his particular techniques that are of decisive importance for the healing process is also an unquestioned article of faith for most Indian patients. One of Baba's patients, who had successively consulted an Ayurvedic physician, a psychiatrist, a sayana, a tantrik, a bhakta and a pir (i.e., Baba) before he had settled on the choice of his therapist, looked at me uncomprehendingly when I asked him as to how he reconciled in his own mind the different explanations for the cause of his illness. It had seemed to me that his selection of a therapy from those being offered by the various healers—whose conceptual systems derived from traditions as diverse as ancient Indian medicine and Western psychological medicine. Muslim sorcery, Hindu shamanism, Hindu devotional mysticism and Sufi spiritualism—must have been especially difficult. 'It is the vishwas a healer inspires which is crucial', he had said, using a Hindi word that denotes both trust and confidence. And how did a healer inspire the vishwas? From his groping attempts at putting into words what is clearly a matter of feeling, he conveyed that, whereas one level of a patient's interaction with the healer is the talk about symptoms, their etiology, the possible therapy and the prognosis, there is another and perhaps more significant exchange taking place simultaneously. In this other conversation carried out without words and below the threshold of consciousness, the patient is busy registering whether and how well the doctor opposite him fits into his culturally determined image of the ideal healer. The choice of the therapist is then determined by the fit between the actual man and the ideal image whose main features I have sketched above. It was also obvious that not only the healer but the healing process too is located at the edge of the society, in the sense that religious restrictions and social taboos tend to be suspended for the duration of the healing encounter.

2.4 *The Development of Personality*[6]

CARL JUNG

. . . what is usually meant by personality—a well-rounded psychic whole that is capable of resistance and abounding in energy—is an adult ideal. It is only in an age like ours, when the individual is unconscious of the problems of adult life, or—what is worse—when he consciously shirks them, that people could wish to foist this ideal on to childhood. I suspect our contemporary pedagogical and psychological enthusiasm for the child of dishonourable intentions: we talk about the child, but we should mean the child in the adult. For in every adult there lurks a child—an eternal child, something that is always becoming, is never completed, and calls for unceasing care, attention and education. That is the part of the human personality which wants to develop and become whole. But the man of today is far indeed from this wholeness. Dimly suspecting his own deficiencies, he seizes upon child education and fervently devotes himself to child psychology, fondly supposing that something must have gone wrong in his own upbringing and childhood development that can be weeded out in the next generation. This intention is highly commendable, but comes to grief on the psychological fact that we cannot correct in a child a fault that we ourselves still commit . . . . If as children they were brought up too strictly, then they spoil their own children with a tolerance bordering on bad taste; if certain matters were painfully concealed from them in childhood, these are revealed with a lack of reticence that is just as painful. They have merely gone to the opposite extreme, the strongest evidence for the tragic survival of the old sin—a fact which has altogther escaped them.

If there is anything that we wish to change in our children, we should first examine it and see whether it is not something that could better be changed in ourselves. Take our enthusiasm for pedagogics. It may be that the boot is on the other leg. It may be that we misplace the pedagogical need because it would be an uncomfortable reminder that we ourselves are still children in many respects and still need a vast amount of educating.

At any rate this doubt seems to me to be extremely pertinent when we

[6] From Carl Jung, *Collected Works, Vol. 17*, Princeton University Press, 1982, pp. 169–73.

set out to train our children's 'personalities'. Personality is a seed that can only develop by slow stages throughout life. There is no personality without definiteness, wholeness, and ripeness . . . as the fruit of a full life directed to this end. The achievement of personality means nothing less than the optimum development of the whole individual human being. It is impossible to foresee the endless variety of conditions that have to be fulfilled. A whole lifetime, in all its biological, social, and spiritual aspects, is needed. Personality is the supreme realization of the innate idiosyncrasy of a living being. It is an act of high courage flung in the face of life, the absolute affirmation of all that constitutes the individual, the most successful adaptation to the universal conditions of existence coupled with the greatest possible freedom for self-determination. To educate a man to this seems to me no light matter. It is surely the hardest task the modern mind has set itself . . . . Only the autumn can show what the spring has engendered, only in the evening will it be seen what the morning began . . . .

Clearly, no one develops his personality because somebody tells him that it would be useful or advisable to do so. Nature has never yet been taken in by well-meaning advice. The only thing that moves nature is causal necessity, and that goes for human nature too. Without necessity, nothing budges, the human personality least of all. It is tremendously conservative, not to say torpid. Only acute necessity is able to rouse it. The developing personality obeys no caprice, no command, no insight, only brute necessity; it needs the motivating force of inner or outer fatalities . . . .

. . . the development of personality from the germ-state to full consciousness is at once a charisma and a curse, because its first fruit is the conscious and unavoidable segregation of the single individual from the undifferentiated and unconscious herd. This means isolation, and there is no comforting word for it. Neither family nor society nor position can save him from this fate, nor yet the most successful adaptation to his environment, however smoothly he fits in. The development of personality is a favour that must be paid for dearly . . . . It also means fidelity to the law of one's own being.

2.5 *On Becoming Aware*[7]

MARTIN BUBER

The onlooker and the observer are similarly orientated . . . neither demands action from them nor inflicts destiny on them . . . .

[7] From Martin Buber, *Between Man and Man*, MacMillan, New York, 1985, pp. 8–13.

It is a different matter when in a receptive hour of my personal life a man meets me about whom there is something, which I cannot grasp in any objective way at all, that 'says something' to me . . . speaks something that enters my own life . . . . The effect of having this said to me is completely different from that of looking on and observing . . . in each instance a word demanding an answer has happened to me.

We may term this way of perception becoming aware.

It by no means needs to be a man of whom I become aware. It can be an animal, a plant, a stone. No kind of appearance or event is fundamentally excluded from the series of the things through which from time to time something is said to me. Nothing can refuse to be the vessel of the Word. The limits of the possibility of dialogue are the limits of awareness.

. . . living means being addressed . . . . And when such a moment has imposed itself on us, we then take notice and ask ourselves, 'Has anything particular taken place? Was it not of the kind I meet every day?', then we may reply to ourselves, 'Nothing particular, indeed, it is like this every day, only we are not there every day'.

The signs of address are not something extraordinary . . . . What occurs to me addresses me . . . it remains the address of that moment and cannot be isolated, it remains the questions of a questioner and will have its answer . . . .

Faith stands in the stream of 'happening but once' which is spanned by knowledge . . . . Lived life is tested and fulfilled in the stream alone.

I know as a living truth only concrete world reality which is constantly, in every moment, reached out to me. I can separate it into its component parts, I can compare them and distribute them into groups of similar phenomena, I can derive them from earlier and reduce them to simpler phenomena; and when I have done all this I have not touched my concrete world reality. Inseparable, incomparable, irreducible, now, happening once only, it gazes upon me with a horrifying look . . . .

The true name of concrete reality is the creation which is entrusted to me and to every man. In it the signs of address are given to us.

2.6 *Values and Ethics for Organization Development Professionals*[8]

CERTIFIED CONSULTANTS INTERNATIONAL

1. Understand their purposes and interdependence with one another.

[8] From Certified Consultants International, Draft Statement, Nashville, Tennessee, USA, 1986, pp. 3–9.

2. Review their purposes and revise them over time as conditions and their awareness of conditions change.
3. Clarify and refine their relationships so they can align themselves.

Helping individuals within the system to:

1. Accept responsibility for their lives.
2. Recognize both the extent of and the constraints on their freedom, their power to choose how they live their lives within the system, and the impact of the system on their lives.
3. Recognize the possibilities for promoting social justice, helping each higher order subsystem (team, department, division, and so on), understand its purpose and interdependence and accept its responsibility for fulfilling its role within the system.

Providing for equitable distribution of the fruits of the system's productivity.

Creating and supporting a climate within which freedom, equality, mutual trust, respect, and love prevail.

Helping people align both individual and system purposes with:

1. The needs and purposes of all the system's stakeholders.
2. The welfare of all the people of Earth, all living things, and their environment.

A human system whose parts are integrated and consciously aligned with the system's overall purpose; and its environmental context will function more effectively and efficiently because:

1. The system will avoid wasting energy on counterproductive behavior.
2. The environment will support the system if the system is aligned with the environment.

(Note: This does not deny the possibility of productive behavior by the system directed at changing the environment in order to achieve more enduring alignment.)

OD/HSD Professionals

1. Acknowledge the important and pervasive influence of values and ethics on the effectiveness and potential for growth of individuals, organizations, and more inclusive human systems and consider them in the process and content of their OD/HSD practice.
2. Place high value on:
   a) Consciousness of values—knowing what they consider most important/desirable/worthy.
   b) Excellence—people doing the best they can with their potential, individually and collectively.

    c) System effectiveness and efficieny—achieving desired results (purposes, goals and objectives) at minimum cost.

    d) Holistic, systemic view—understanding human behavior from the perspective of whole system(s) which influence and are influenced by that behavior and conceiving of the dynamics of systems in terms of the interdependent parts/subsystems which comprise them and of the macrosystem(s) within which the systems are parts.

    e) Stakeholder orientation—recognizing the interests that different people have in the system's results and valuing those interests equitably.

    f) Human potential—viewing people as having unique potential that can be realized through contribution to collective achievement and valuing the full realization of that potential.

    g) Quality of life—recognizing that the whole experience of life is important (not only those uses of life that serve system purposes) and that work life should serve both system and personal purposes.

    h) Individual dignity, integrity, worth and fundamental human rights.

    i) The dignity, integrity, and worth of organizations, communities, societies, and other human systems.

    j) Authenticity in relationships and openness in communication.

    k) Wide participation in system affairs, confrontation of issues leading to effective problem solving and democratic decision-making.

3. Realise that they are in a service profession in which they make available their expertise and personality, and are prepared to discuss the way they do this with colleagues and participants in the consulting process.

4. Recognize the responsibilities of individuals to the groups, organizations and other human systems of which they are members.

5. See themselves as members of a global professional community and accept their responsibilities to that community; recognize that the accomplishments of the OD/HSD profession are the results of both individual and collective effort.

6. Recognize that choices which may seem unethical in short run may be ethical in the longer run, such as not responding to a request for a quick fix in order to allow conditions to emerge under which more authentic help is possible.

7. Recognize that along with respecting the right of free choice goes the responsibility for discussing with clients the consequences of their choices and how those choices might be changed to yield different consequences.

8. Recognize the need for balance in cases where the above values conflict and recognize further that practice according to the values and ethics described in this Statement may be precluded by certain cultural conditions.

Ethical Guidelines for an OD/HSD Professional

As an OD/HSD Professional, I commit to supporting and acting in accordance with the following guidelines:

1. Responsibility for Professional Development and Competence.

a) Accept responsibility for the consequences of my acts and make every effort to ensure that my services are properly used.
b) Recognize the limits of my competence, culture, and experience in providing services and using techniques; neither seek nor accept assignments outside those limits without clear understanding by the client when exploration at the edge of my competence is reasonable; refer client to other professionals when appropriate.
c) Strive to attain and maintain a professional level of competence in the field, including:
  i) Broad knowledge of theory and practice in:
    a. applied behavioral science generally.
    b. management, administration, organizational behavior, and system behavior specifically.
    c. multicultural issues, including issues of color and gender.
    d. other relevant fields of knowledge and practice.
  ii) Ability to:
    a. relate effectively with individuals and groups.
    b. relate effectively to the dynamics of large, complex systems.
    c. provide consultation using theory and methods of the applied behavioral sciences.
    d. articulate theory and direct its application, including creating of learning experiences for individuals, small and large groups and for whole systems.
d) Strive continually for self-knowledge and personal growth; be aware that 'what is in me' (my perceptions of myself in my world) and 'what is outside me' (the realities that exist apart from me) are not the same; be aware that my values, beliefs, and aspirations can both limit and empower me and that they are primary determinants of my perceptions, my behavior, and my personal and professional effectiveness.
e) Recognize my own personal needs and desires and deal with them responsibly in the performance of my professional roles.
f) Obtain consultation from OD/HSD professionals who are native to and aware of the specific cultures within which I work when those cultures are different from my own.

2. Responsibility to Clients and Significant Others

a) Serve the short- and long-term welfare, interests, and development of the client system and all its stakeholders; maintain balance in the timing, pace, and magnitude of planned change so as to support a mutually beneficial relationship between the system and its environment . . . .

b) Help all stakeholders while developing OD/HSD approaches, programs, and the like, if they wish such help; for example, this could include workers' representatives as well as managers in the case of work with a business organization.

c) Work collaboratively with other internal and external consultants serving the same client system and resolve conflicts in terms of the balanced best interests of the client system and all its stakeholders; make appropriate arrangements with internal and external consultants about how responsibilities will be shared.

d) Encourage and enable my clients to provide for themselves the services I provide rather than foster continued reliance on me; encourage, foster, and support self-education and self-development by individuals, groups and all other human systems.

e) Cease work with a client when it is clear that the client is not benefiting or the contract has been completed; do not accept an assignment if its scope is so limited that the client will not benefit or it would involve serious conflict with the values and ethics outlined in this Statement.

f) Avoid conflicts of interest . . .

g) Define and protect the confidentiality of my client-professional relationships . . .

h) Provide for my own accountability by evaluating and assessing the effects of my work . . .

3. Responsibility to the Profession . . .

a) Be aware of the possible impact of my public behavior upon the ability of colleagues to perform their professional work; perform professional activity in a way that will bring credit to the profession.

b) Work actively with ethical practice by individuals and organizations engaged in OD/HSD activities and, in case of questionable practice, use appropriate channels for confronting it . . .

c) Contribute to continuing professional development by:
   i) Supporting the development of other professionals, including mentoring with less experienced professionals.

ii) Contributing ideas, methods, findings, and other useful information to the body of OD/HSD knowledge and skill . . .

4. Social Responsibility

a) Strive for the preservation and protection of fundamental human rights and the promotion of social justice.
b) Be aware that I bear a heavy social responsibility because my recommendations and professional actions may alter the lives and well-being of individuals within my client systems, the systems themselves, and the larger systems of which they are sub-systems.
c) Contribute knowledge, skill, and other resources in support of organizations, programs, and activities that seek to improve human welfare; be prepared to accept clients who do not have sufficient resources to pay my full fees at reduced fees or no charge . . .
d) Recognize that accepting this Statement as a guide for my behavior involves holding myself to a standard that may be more exacting than the laws of any country in which I practice . . .
e) Serve the welfare of all the people of Earth, all living things, and their environment.

2.7 *Conviction and Competence*[9]

ERIK H. ERIKSON

Identity is safest, of course, where it is grounded in activities . . . a new identity will be very much attached to an intimate mastery of a set of skills dictated by the state of science and technology as well as the arts, and no attempt to humanize life should belittle or bedevil this mastery itself. Competence without conviction, to be sure, is not more than a form of fact-slavery; but conviction without competence is less than liberation.

. . . New facts, demonstrated by men who can play with facts with utmost sincerity, and who, in their competence and certainty have the courage to stand alone and can thus risk both sanity and acceptance, often seem to shatter what we continue to think must be real. The

[9] From Erik H. Erikson, *Dimensions of a New Identity*, W.W. Norton, New York, 1974. p. 105.

paradox is that these facts and theories increase human power over nature (and human nature) enormously, but create a lag between what we know and what we can 'realize'—a dangerous situation, indeed.

2.8 *Skillful Behavior*[10]

FRITZ J. ROETHLISBERGER

A description of skill from an external point of view emphasizes clearly that skill deals with the concrete (but) it falls short of specifying the nature of skill from the point of view of a skilled person . . . . Viewed from this perspective, skill becomes the way by which man begins to improve his relation to his surroundings. It becomes the response of the whole organism, acting as a unit, that is more or less adequate to a particular point in a given situation. This response of the total organism, acting as a totality or unit, implies something different from a technique. Instead of being a technique to be learned, skill becomes a way of learning, a way of assimilating and ordering experience by which one's relation to one's surroundings can be improved. It becomes something intrinsic and not something extrinsic to the learner-practitioner.

Looked at from this point of view, the woodcarver is not learning, in the first instance, techniques of wood carving. He is learning slowly and gradually about the properties of the woods from which he can fashion certain objects. He is learning about the tools he needs in order to assist him. He is learning about the utilities of the objects he fashions. None of these elements is highly differentiated.

. . . Skill, conceived in this way from the point of view of a practitioner, has three characteristics from which in time systematic knowledge about the nature of the phenomena may develop.

The first characteristic is the organic character of the skilled response. There is a balanced development between the outward and inward aspects of what is being learned. On the outward side the skillful practitioner learns something about the natural phenomena to which his responses are addressed. On the inward side he learns how to improve his responses to what he encounters in the environment. These two processes go hand-in-hand . . . he gains growing and developing awareness of the complexity of relationships in the phenomena as well as a growing and developing confidence in his capacity to deal with them.

[10] From George F.F. Lombard (ed.), *The Elusive Phenomena* by Fritz J. Roethlisberger, Harvard Business School, Boston, MA, 1977, pp. 350–53, 392–93.

The second characteristic of this organized system of a capacity for response in skillful behavior is that it improves slowly and gradually, step by step, through time. An individual learns to creep before he learns to walk; he learns to talk before he can make speeches and becomes a politician . . . .

The third characteristic of skill is that it develops through attention to the phenomena at the point of interaction with them. Although this seems obvious, it is often overlooked by the knowledge-seekers and by those who try to develop skill by reading a book or in ten easy lessons. This capacity of the practitioner to attend to the phenomena at the point of interaction with them is a necessary prerequisite for making the first elementary, useful discriminations about the phenomena as well as about his relation to them. Without the capacity to attend, there is little capacity to observe and discriminate. Without the capacity to observe and discriminate, there is little capacity to develop an organized system of response to the phenomena. And without a capacity to develop an organized system of response, there is little capacity to attend, observe, and discriminate among phenomena. As a result of this ring-around-a-rosy, no skill develops. Individual behavior becomes a 'signal response' to an external stimulus. For me this is not skill but its opposite.

The Knowledge Enterprise

In these three characteristics of a skillful response reside, in rudimentary form, all the elements from which the knowledge enterprise develops. This response contains the roots of more effective observation of the phenomena, more effective ways of learning about them, more effective ways of dealing with or 'controlling' them and thus of improving one's relation to them. Through its exercise the practitioner gains a sense of competence, achievement, and mastery and begins to exercise some intuitive judgments about them.

To these products of skill the word knowledge may be given. This knowledge is of a limited kind. It is not knowledge about things in a sophisticated or scientific sense. It is the kind of knowledge which William James called knowledge of acquaintance; which Henderson called an intimate, intuitive familiarity with the phenomena; which Mayo referred to as first-hand observation; and which Piaget called syncretistic—an apprehension of wholes without sharp delineation of parts.

This kind of knowledge is limited in space and time. Because skill deals with the concrete, its practitioner can use it only somewhere and sometime in particular. What is learned is extremely local. One may learn, for example, something about the ways of a buffalo and become a skillful buffalo hunter without knowing anything about the ways of the elephant and without becoming a skillful elephant hunter; and this skillful buffalo or elephant hunter is far from being a 'zoologist'.

In this lowly stage of knowledge there are no sharp distinctions between the descriptive and the normative. The skillful practitioner is not interested in describing the phenomena as they are for their own sake. He is no disinterested seeker of the truth; rather he is action-oriented. Nevertheless, in his endeavor to improve his relations to his surroundings, he does not ignore the properties of things as they are. The woodcarver, whether he is carving a bowl or, for that matter, an ornament (the outcome of the practice of skill does not have to be something practical), is attending to the properties of the particular wood he is using. In a syncretistic fashion he knows that to do his carving he needs an instrument harder than the wood he is carving; he may not know precisely how much harder it needs to be, but he knows it must be harder.

He has no strong notions about how things should be. He is not trying to make wood have the properties of stone, nor bamboo have the properties of pine or maple, if by some unlikely chance these different woods exist in his locality. He accepts the fact of these differences; the recognition does not throw him into despondency or get him 'hung up' or 'uptight'. He feels that he can improve his relations to things as they are. In fact, in a syncretistically optimistic fashion he feels he can fashion things as they might be from things as they are. He feels that by taking into account the properties of things as they are, he can fashion things that never existed before. He can fashion necklaces, earrings, bowls, and so on, objects that were not growing in a natural state in his own backyard. In this sense he is being descriptively prescriptive or normative but, as I have said, in a syncretistic way. He is so naive, or should I say so intellectually non-obsessive, that the distinction between things as they are or might be or should be is no issue for him—as we would say in the 1970s, 'no problem'.

For the intuitive practitioner of skill, the distinction between theory and practice is also no problem. He practices his skill with no explicit theory about the nature of the phenomena with which he is dealing. Neither is he seeking to explain them. He just makes use of the uniformities in the phenomena he is observing.

How Skill Develops

Although I am arguing that higher forms of knowledge are derived from skill and that skill is derived from a certain kind of experiencing of, learning about, or responding to, phenomena in order to improve one's relation to them, a question can be raised about how skill develops in the first place. After all, many games different from the one I call skill can be played with the phenomena. Why should this one have been cultivated, or as would be said today, 'reinforced'?

I assume that skillful behavior develops because it is a rewarding experience and that the phenomena themselves do the rewarding; in the sense that the phenomena allow themselves, so to speak, to be manipulated or controlled better by the skillful practitioner than by someone who plays other kinds of games with them. A woodcarver, for example who knows that some woods are harder than others, even though he does not know how much harder, is able to fashion articles accordingly. He thus achieves a mastery over his physical environment and feels competent to deal with it.

I would not say that the phenomena are pleading to be understood, explained, or manipulated.

If a knowledge seeker is satisfied with the stage of knowledge at which he is working, there is nothing which requires him to proceed to the next higher level of the knowledge enterprise. If he nevertheless proceeds to the next stage, he has to abide by the rules of the game at that level. Each knowledge seeker may become enamored with the tools and methods of his level, so long as he does not think these tools alone will get him over the hump to the next level. If he does not realize that by themselves they are not enough, he becomes 'hung up' at the lower level. There is no more serious mistake than for a knowledge seeker who is at one level of the knowledge enterprise to think that he is at another; that is, he should not think he is applying a scientific theory before he has achieved one. If he does, he is not only kidding himself; he is also confusing others. It is equally serious when a knowledge maker becomes overcommitted to the tools of one level and takes a polemical stance with regard to their value in explaining the phenomena. The following are some examples of this mistake: the clinician who plasters descriptions of situations with diagnostic concepts into neat logical bundles; the correlation seeker who thinks his significant correlations explain something; the casual hypothesis seeker who thinks he has the tools for getting hold of propositions that will explain themselves by stating what the causes of the phenomena really are; the general-proposition maker who is so enamored with scientific explanations that he ceases to understand the phenomena with which he deals.

Figure 3 : The Knowledge Enterprise*

LEVELS	CHARACTERISTIC STATEMENTS (Theories)	METHODS	PRODUCTS
Analytical (scientific) Knowledge	General propositions	Creative and inductive leap of imagination	Deductive systems
	Empirical propositions	Operational definitions rigorous measurement	Statements of the form x varies directly or indirectly with y under given conditions
	Elementary concepts	Definition of concepts and variables Elementary measurement	Statements of the form x varies with y
Clinical Knowledge	Conceptual schemes	Observation and interviewing Classification	Descriptive cases and syndromes Taxonomies
Skill	Knowledge of acquaintance	Practice and reflection	How-to-do-it statements and aphorisms
		The phenomena.	

*For the development of knowledge, read from the bottom up;
for the practice of knowledge, read from the top down.

3. COLLEAGUESHIP

INTRODUCTION

A live example of reflective practice:

Just when I sat down to write this introduction, I was in dire need of the collegiate support I wanted to write about. I was leading a consulting team in a large developing country. Over a period of four years we had helped get under way a provincial strategy of training system development as a strategic next step to greatly increasing the number of well-trained and well-used health workers in the national system. Four provinces had got under way. The Training Unit in the Central Ministry, originally set up and still staffed, structured and organized for planning and implementing training programs itself rather than for managing a national system with dispersed resources, was beginning to participate significantly in these provincial developments. It had begun to upgrade its assessment of new provincial capabilities and, in the light of this, to revise its own functions in managing national networks of trainers and materials, planning programs, securing resources, maintaining quality, etc. The final year of technical assistance was just starting with the addition of practical internships for twenty-five top staff of proven competence and commitment to become technical and system consultants for continuing our functions after we left. At this moment it became clear that the funding agency had not completed its part of the work and, though warmly supporting these developments and forewarned about the high cost of delaying, did not have the necessary funding mechanisms actually in place. This threatened an immediate two-to-three months' 'hold' on needed short-term technical consultants, the abandonment of some inputs and fearsome losses of momentum and credibility for the whole effort.

I had three long-term colleagues. One was in town and due to continue developing one technical capacity in a country which was now threatened. The two other colleagues, each residing in a province, were due to come to headquarters in the pre-planned course of regular duties. What, I asked myself, did I expect from them by way of colleagueship and support in this predicament? And, by implication, what light did these needs of mine in this situation throw on the choice of readings for this section?

Supports Needed for Development

An opportunity to air my frustration and my anxieties for one: I needed to avoid keeping these bottled up, to avoid their bedevilling and short changing my assessments of the complex situation and its prospects and so limiting my options for action. An understanding person was required for this in an open, unguarded relationship, and readily available. My local colleague filled this bill admirably.

Then, secondly, in the ensuing moments of calm, I needed help with assessing the situation most fully and truly and identifying 'all' possible options for actions. Additional pairs of eyes, in short, and additional assessors and creators of possible scenarios.

Thirdly, I needed a sense of togetherness in what we—together, out of this joint assessment—decided it was best to do: what, with whom and by whom, and so on. We would proceed together, supplementing each other's strengths, personal and situational, and also communicate appropriate sureness to all with whom we needed to deal—provinces, Control Unit, funding agency and more widely.

And fourthly, I wanted an honest feed-back about my part in it all. Retrospectively too, what had I missed doing that this impasse had come about at all? And also, how I was to play my part from here on.

One-Sidedness of Current Literature

With these thoughts, I turned to the folder for this section into which I had for many months slipped readings to consider for inclusion. This folder was one out of the whole set in my desk at home, one folder for each section in which I simply accumulated readings and references as I came across them in my current reading or retrieved them from memory and bookshelf. When, as now, I was ready to turn my attention to a section, these items were there for sorting, to be examined against our mental picture of what needed to be included in a particular section and could then be augmented through purposeful visits to libraries to fill any gaps.

I was in for an unpleasant surprise: the folder was very slim. It contained very few items. This struck me doubly hard because it was so very contrary to my long-term interests in what has come to be known as the epidemiology of support—in contrast to the epidemiology of diseases and the pathological status of population. In a series of studies Dr. John Cassel and his colleagues showed that population groups as varied as immigrants, school children from deprived homes, mothers delivering first babies, unemployed men and others caught in adverse, stressful circumstances and 'high life change' remained much healthier if they had social supports ('psycho-social assets'). The differences between their health and the health of similar cohorts without adequate support was so marked that these scholars recommended 'a radical change in the strategies used for preventive action', away from finding and treating sick individuals to improving and strengthening social supports, concentrating on people at risk. 'Support', the studies operationalized, comes with commitment—to shared objectives, working consensus on issues and problems, ability to identify and weigh alternatives, participation in a collective process and reliable feedback about one's own part and standing in the immediate group.[1] On this basis, I had developed and taught a graduate course in stress and support, and connected it with my professional practice. I was alive to the issues, had a fair library on the matter, had continued reading, and had gone right on accumulating cuttings and references and also acquiring new books.

Worse was to come: as I read the few items in the folder, I discarded them one after another as too general, too academic for practising trainers and consultants,or as belonging more properly to other sections. At the end, just one reading was left after that first sorting: a lengthy extract of 'Building trainers into a team'—from Lynton's *The Tide of Learning* (1961) and included in the original edition of *Training for Development* (1967). Surely, surely that could not be the field!

Back I went to my shelves: to scan *all* books with 'support' in the title, e.g., self-support and support-groups (an expanding literature). Also to all the books there on 'stress', on 'coping' and on 'transitions'. Then to the psychologists and analysts, especially the humanistic ones, such as Erik Erikson and Sudhir Kakar.

The result, now included in this section, is still thin and disappointing as a collection, though we of course warmly recommend the individual items. Preoccupation with pathological situations and therapeutic encounters continues to dominate the literature. A striking recent example is the special double issue on support in the *Journal for Social Issues*.[2]

---

[1] A particularly good overview of the approach findings and implications of this work is John Cassel's own Wade Hampten Frost Lecture to the American Public Health Association, 'The Contribution of the Social Environment to Host Resistance', published in the *American Journal of Epidemiology*, Vol. 10, No. 2, 1975, pp. 107–23.

[2] 'Social Support: New Perspectives in Theory, Research and Priority', Vol. 40, No. 4, 1984 and Vol. 41, No. 1, 1985.

Not a single piece in it is on support needs in developmental situations or on collegiate support. A second aspect of the literature focusses on situations of high stress. These are usually situations that can be classified sharply, as on a battle-field: special, extraordinary events. It also focusses on how strongly a whole host of forces, colleagues included, converge to maintain sameness and to discourage practitioners from developing themselves and changing their situations. Medical practice provides many examples. Studies show, for instance that there are large locational differences in the amounts of surgery undertaken to mend the same pathologies and that these differences have most to do with 'individual physicians following' what is considered standard and accepted practice in the community . . . . A physician who follows the practices of his or her colleagues is safe from criticism, free from having to explain his or her actions.[3] Of course, physicians also choose to live and practice in communities with standards that they find congenial. So the circle is closed.

Yet some changes do take place and the same studies list 'new ideas brought to the community by new physicians' among the top sources for them. These innovators tend to be inveterate pioneers; they persist even without support and often in isolation. How many give up and stop half way is not known. From scanning a broad range of professions another study concludes that 'the piece . . . missing for all of them [is] some mechanism for providing on-going learning and support to the individual . . . embarked on humanizing his or her organization'.[4]

Matching Support with Situations

For a general description of collegiate support for creative, developmental activity we turn first, once again, to the 1961 account of 'Building trainers into a team' at Aloka, an international training center in Sri Lanka, later established in India. Careful structural arrangements and many spontaneous interactions are both involved. One leads to differential assignments and their coordination through sufficient and reliable mechanisms. Within that structure there is high openness, informality and dispersed agenda setting. The next reading is about work teams. Team 'resources (including emotional resources) lie in the individual differences of team members' and became available only as individuals differentiate themselves 'actively and openly'. In periodic meetings, of government committees for instance, only the beginnings of this

[3] Eddy, David M.D., 'Variations in Physician Practice: The Role of Uncertainty', *Health Affairs*, Summer, 1984.

[4] Kirschenbaum, Howard and Barbara Glaser, *Developing Support Groups*, University Associates, La Jolla California, USA, 1978, p. 2.

differentiation occur—over and over again, writes inveterate meeting goer Lewis Thomas (3.3) and then he is all ready to be intrigued by that new method of listening *without* meeting, the Delphi technique of serial iterations and sharings by mail.

The next reading pursues the structural component more broadly. It is about support systems and about building them so that any trainer consultant can expect to provide for his support needs in all foreseeable situations, in his personal as well as professional life. Ensuring a sufficient range and variety of support is one issue, and doing so in a personally congenial setting and style is another. On the latter, trainer consultants are probably like the sailors Laurens Van der Post journeyed with, in that, some 'preferred small ships and the greatly increased feeling of companionship and common identity which they gave to all who served in them; [others] would select the biggest ships of both Navy and Merchant Marine, perhaps, because they found there a kind of anonymity which enabled them, in the midst of many, to be more their own men than they could have been locked into the close family circle of those who served in the smallest ships'.[5]

Seashore points to the subsets in every sound support system. Each is 'a small group of people from a large population to suit my needs at a particular time. My support system [sub-system, in our terminology here] to deal with family stress is quite different from the support system I need on the job'. He tabulates seven common needs along with the types of support relevant to those feelings and situations. He goes on to identify and discuss some common problems in building support systems. Among them are conflicting motivations and developing dependencies on the system at the cost of 'your own sense of autonomy and independence'. Problems with *maintaining* support systems and with *renewing* them from time to time could be added.

Support Mechanism and Processes

The largest set of readings samples mechanisms of support which are widely available, e.g., meetings, peer consultation and professional support groups, guru and member relationships; ways of securing feedback and forward guidance besides discussion, e.g., 'nominal groups', observer and feedback roles and, reaching outside immediate colleagues, getting outside help with problems that hinder the smooth functioning of collegiate groups, and professional support groups. Last but surely not least in importance is individual alone time, for reflection, for drawing on support from within.

[5] From Van der Post, *Yet Being Someone Other*, The Hogarth Press, London, UK, 1982, p. 53.

The final set of readings focusses on the internal dynamics of support-giving, receiving and structuring. 'An individual facing a need to make a transition' writes Phyllis Silverman, 'feels an enormous aloneness . . . [when he/she] finds a community of like-minded people . . . who share his "stigma" [he] feels part of humanity again'.[6] Both the fear of alone-ness and the relief on becoming 'part of humanity again' are vividly understandable in the light of the next reading, from Berger and Luck-mann. A major transition the kind that leads to 'enormous aloneness', involves foregoing the 'subjectively crystallized' *only* outer and inner reality acquired through 'primary socialization': *the* world. The basic structure of all secondary socialization(s), i.e., for acquiring and com-mitting oneself to a new reality has to resemble that primary socialization: 'emotionally highly charged', 'semi-automatic', 'quasi-inevitable'. It means making a new 'home' and a new 'identity', '. . . community . . . provides the indispensable plausibility structure for the new reality . . . .'

Berger and Luckmann label such changes of realities and 'displacing all their worlds', 'alternation' and the quality of community required to sustain it 'religious'. Reed (3.9) uses 'oscillation' to describe the needs of individuals to mix times for social support with times to be alone. Both are necessary, especially to venturesome, creative persons. In the company of the likeminded he and she recapture a sense of personal worth and of the worthwhileness of his/her endeavors and goals, and renews the courage to persist in them. Alone he/she ventures, and integrates new inner and outer realities. Communal worship, for Reed, has the primary function of providing for this necessary depend-ence. Van der Post describes the equally necessary time alone. Little steps, quietly persisted in and supported by colleagues in numerous places, are the effective modality. Lewis Thomas adds a note on our 'conjoined intelligence', and 'collective power'.

3.1 *Building Trainers into a Team*[7]

ROLF P. LYNTON

It was common for two faculty members to be at the same session . . . to use the break-time and after class for checking with one another how it

[6] Silverman, Phyllis R. *Mutual Help Groups: A Guide for Mental Health Workers*, National Institute of Mental Health, Rockville, Md., 1972, p. 17.

[7] From Rolf P. Lynton, *The Tide of Learning: The Aloka Experience*, Routledge & Kegan Paul, London, 1960, pp. 182–96.

was going. Faculty members used to go in and out of each other's living quarters, sharing ideas, talking of some experience they had just had, expressing the feelings they had controlled during contact with the members, exchanging written assignments, and enjoying the close personal relationship. Traditions grew up according to which faculty members congregated in the office or had tea together regularly, without necessarily anything specific to talk about. So with their very different backgrounds and varied professional training, and their different styles of teaching, they yet achieved a consistency in their orientation and in the kinds of cues they used and their reactions to them.

Their consistency cut across the faculty assignments to different parts of the programme. All faculty members taught some case sessions, and several took turns with the work programme and field visits. But for the most personal discussions, those in which members reviewed their own experience, the same faculty member stayed with a group. That was one important division which faculty meetings needed to bridge. A second division existed between those faculty members who lived very closely with the members, sharing a cottage and meals, and those who lived in separate cottages with their families. This division was not just one of convenience. . . . faculty who lived most closely with the members were junior faculty, people who had been outstanding members of . . . [earlier] courses and who had been brought back to develop further their considerable promise as trainers. Thus their age and recent experience as well as their living arrangements and professional assignments put them nearer to the members.

[These] faculty were in positions of particular stress, since they were closer to the members but not of them, and at the same time members of the faculty but apprentice members, so to speak. One of the things we have learned is the value of bringing junior faculty in pairs, just as the members were chosen in pairs in order to give them a colleague with whom to share continuously their questions, their anxieties, and their moments of triumph.

Faculty Meetings

The scheduled meetings of the whole faculty put some certainty into the picture of spontaneous consultation and exchange. They ensured that enough time was indeed set aside for discussing everything necessary, for the timetable of a residential course tends to be overful and overlong . . . . Without scheduled faculty meetings some points would perhaps not have received consideration, particularly such long term matters as training design. The meetings were useful also to ensure that all faculty members were familiar with what had been of significance in the sessions, not merely the two or three who were present at the sessions or checked with one another on the spur of the moment . . . the scheduled meetings also protected faculty members from each other . . . . If there had been no meeting, faculty members would have interrupted one another even more than kindred spirits naturally do and cut up everybody's day into little bits until nobody could have called any part of it his own.

There were six faculty meetings in the days just before that course began and forty-two more during the three months, lasting an average of one hour and a quarter each. Half the meetings took place in the first four weeks, when meetings were daily with only very few exceptions and each lasted longer than the average. During the second four weeks there were twelve meetings; during the last four weeks, nine.

Though they were scheduled in advance and all four faculty members were expected to take part, the meetings were quite informal. They usually took place in the evening over after-dinner coffee in the director's cottage. They had no set agenda. Faculty members spoke about what was important to them from the day's work and for looking ahead . . . . The atmosphere of free talking and listening, some of it in disappointment, some in joy, much of it in fun, and all in close and growing fellowship, that was of its essence. Here was the professional base of operations; the emotional base, too, where faculty members found support and encouragement, tried out first thoughts, and relaxed. And from which they emerged refreshed and reassured.

The faculty meetings were full of . . . spontaneous reviewing of the programme: a suggestion for this, adjustment there, a thought filed for future reference, a prediction on how something would work out. The concern which underlay these detailed considerations and action questions was with fitting all the pieces together into a unified experience for the members. The whole programme was to convey the stimulation and reflection conducive to learning. It was one, though it had many pieces . . . the unity had to be maintained. Its communication was to go on learning. There is no escape from that. It is wherever you look, all around you and most of all inside you. In this shifting and changing it was the faculty's business to maintain this unity, this balance, this totality.

Worrisome concern may seem from these recordings to have set the tone of the faculty meetings . . . . But the impression is due more to their deliberate choice of what to talk about at the meetings, and this emphasis has not been adjusted here. Elation and statements of something having gone well do not occupy much time. But they are very real and important and provide the refreshment with which the faculty members turn back to the problems which must occupy their attention.

General Reflections

What also stands out clearly from the recordings is the apparently limitless capacity the faculty members had to be intrigued in their work and to learn much from it that was relevant to future courses and to larger issues.

Informally and unpredictably, the faculty meetings ranged over what was immediate to what was distant, what was personal to one member in the course, to what threw light on the kind of community he came from, what had happened that day in the discussion, to the personal basis within himself from which the faculty member responded. In these meetings the faculty members stretched and exercised their capacities, explored and examined their own limits and practiced their ability to work as equals, as cooperative people, as people able and inclined to reflect and learn from their experience. Essentially they could only communicate to the members the value of care by themselves caring, of cooperation by themselves cooperating, of learning and developing oneself by themselves learning and developing as persons. In the faculty meetings the faculty members had the same unified experience that they sought to provide for the members in the course.

3.2 *Individual Differences and Team Development*[8]

SUZANNA FINN EICHHORN

. . . interdisciplinary teams exist because complex problems require a mix of resources and by increasing the resource base of knowledge, skills and information, problem-solving will be more effective. In order for inter-disciplinary teams to fulfill their raison d'être, the resources must be actualized. Those resources reside in the individual differences of team members and their diversity is the totality of their individual resources.

In this study, an attempt was made to explore team development specifically related to the actualization of those individual differences. It was discovered that when individual differences were suppressed, conflict resulted, and team resources remained unknown and not fully utilized.

[8] From Suzanna Finn Eichhorn, *Becoming: The Actualization of Individual Differences in Five Student Health Teams*, Institute for Health Team Development, Montefiore Hospital & Medical Centre, Bronx, New York, 1974, pp. 78–80.

When individual differences were suppressed, team structures for mission, roles and relationships tended to be protective of unspoken individual needs and, consequently, more defensive than actualizing of resources. When conflict was openly confronted and individual differences acknowledged and legitimized, team resources became utilized in mutual problem solving and in building new structures for mission, roles and relationships. Forces were identified that hindered or facilitated phased movement.

In these teams, this actualizing of individual differences was necessary for integration. Individuals had to differentiate actively and openly before they could integrate. Individuals did not become linked to each other until they had knowledge of, and experience of (through interaction), their individual differences. Utilization of each other as resources toward accomplishment of their team mission was thus facilitated by a differentiating process. Similarly, utilization of each other as resources in working the human issues of team life, was facilitated by an open sharing of individual needs. Thus, an ongoing process that openly acknowledged and legitimized individual differences in building a mission, in defining roles and in developing relationships, became facilitative of team integration . . . .

. . . both the differentiating and the integrating of individual differences are important aspects of team development . . . they allow individual resources to flourish and to link together . . . .

. . . the assumptions individuals in these five teams brought with them about equality, harmony and 'togetherness' are not unique to them; the early covert protection of individual needs, the early fears of conflict and the concerns about individual differentiation are likewise common issues in beginning groups . . . interventions that help teams focus on the forces working for or against actualization will help provide movement toward more satisfying structures and processes. Specific skill building in conflict confrontation is essential . . . missions that evolve through the joining of known individual differences, . . . roles that evolve through the acknowledgement of different individual skills and knowledge, the human understanding potential that evolves through the acknowledgement and valuing of individual human needs are the pay-offs.

3.3 *On Meetings as Collective Monologues and Listening without Meeting*[9]

LEWIS THOMAS

The marks of selfness are laid out in our behavior irreversibly, unequivocally, whether we are assembled in groups or off on a stroll alone
. . . .

Thus when committees gather, each member is necessarily an actor, uncontrollably acting out the part of himself, reading the lines that identify him, asserting his identity. This takes quite a lot of time and energy, and while it is going on there is little of anything else getting done. Many committees have been appointed in one year and gone on working well into the next decade, with nothing much happening beyond these extended, uninterruptible displays by each member of his special behavioral marks.

If if were not for such compulsive behavior by the individuals, committees would be a marvellous invention for getting collective thinking done. But there it is. We are designed, coded, it seems, to place the highest priority on being individuals, and we must do this first, at whatever cost, even if it means disability for the group . . . . Integrity is the most personal of qualities; groups and societies cannot possess it until single mortals have it in hand. It is hard work for civilization . . . .

Because of the urgency of the problems ahead, various modifications of the old standard committee have been devised in recent years, in efforts to achieve better grades of collective thought. There are the think tanks, hybrids between committee and factory, little corporations for thinking. There are governmental commissions and panels, made up of people brought to Washington and told to sit down together and think out collective thoughts. Industries have organized their own encounter groups, in which executives stride around crowded rooms bumping and shouting at each other in the hope of prodding out new ideas. But the old trouble persists: people assembled for group thought are still, first of all, individuals in need of expressing selfness.

The latest invention for getting round the disadvantages of meetings is the Delphi technique. This was an invention of the 1960s, worked out by some RAND Corporation people dissatisfied with the way committees laid plans for the future. The method has a simple, almost silly sound. Instead of having meetings, questionnaires are circulated to the members

[9] From Lewis Thomas, *The Medusa and the Snail: More Notes of a Biology Watcher*, The Viking Press, New York, 1974, pp. 115–20.

of a group, and each person writes his answers out and sends them back, in silence. Then the answers are circulated to all members and they are asked to reconsider and fill out the questionnaires again, after paying attention to the other views. And so forth. Three cycles are usually enough. By that time as much of a consensus has been reached as can be reached, and the final answers are said to be substantially more reliable, and often more interesting, than the first time around. In some versions, new questions can be introduced by the participants, at the same time as they are providing answers.

It is almost humiliating to be told that Delphi works, sometimes wonderfully well. One's first reaction is resentment at still another example of social manipulation, social-science trickery, behavior control.

But, then, confronted by the considerable evidence that the technique really does work—at least for future-forecasting in industry and government—one is bound to look for the possibly good things about it.

Maybe, after all, this is a way of preserving the individual and all his selfness, and at the same time linking minds together so that a group can do collective figuring. The best of both worlds, in short.

What Delphi is, is a really quiet, thoughtful conversation, in which everyone gets a chance to listen. The background noise of small talk, and the recurrent sonic booms of vanity, are eliminated at the outset, and there is time to think. There are no voices, and therefore no rising voices. It is, when you look at it this way, a great discovery. Before Delphi, real listening in a committee meeting has always been a near impossibility. Each member's function was to talk, and while other people were talking the individual member was busy figuring out what he ought to say next in order to shore up his own original position. Debating is what committees really do, not thinking. Take away the need for winning points, leading the discussion, protecting one's face, gaining applause, shouting down opposition, scaring opponents, all that kind of noisy activity, and a group of bright people can get down to quiet thought. It is a nice idea, and I'm glad it works.

It is interesting that Delphi is the name chosen, obviously to suggest the oracular prophetic function served. The original Delphi was Apollo's place, and Apollo was the god of prophecy, but more than that. He was also the source of some of the best Greek values: moderation, sanity, care, attention to the rules, deliberation. Etymologically, in fact, Apollo may have had his start as a committee. The word apollo (and perhaps the related word apello) originally meant a political gathering. The importance of public meetings for figuring out what to do next must have been perceived very early as fundamental to human society, therefore needing incorporation into myth and the creation of an administrative deity; hence Apollo, the Dorian god of prohecy.

The Pythian prophetess of Delphi was not really supposed to enunciate clear answers to questions about the future. On the contrary, her pronouncements often contained as much vagueness as the I Ching, and were similarly designed to provide options among which choice was possible. She symbolized something more like the committee's agenda. When she collapsed in ecstasy on the tripod, murmuring ambiguities, she became today's questionnaire. The working out of the details involved a meticulous exegesis of the oracle's statements, and this was the task of the exegetai, a committee of citizens, partly elected by the citizens of Athens and partly appointed by the Delphic oracle. The system seems to have worked well enough for a long time, constructing the statutory and legal basis for Greek religion.

Today's Delphi thus represents a refinement of an ancient social device, with a novel modification of committee procedure constraining groups of people to think more quietly, and to listen. The method seems new, as a formal procedure, but it is really very old, perhaps as old as human society itself. For in real life, this is the way we've always arrived at decisions, even though it has always been done in a disorganized way. We pass the word around; we ponder how the case is put by different people; we read the poetry; we mediate over the literature; we play the music; we change our minds; we reach an understanding. Society evolves this way, not by shouting each other down, but by the unique capacity of unique, individual human beings to comprehend each other.

3.4 *Building Support Systems*[10]

CHARLES SEASHORE

What kind of support do people need? The answer to that is, of course, they need different things at different times depending on what the particular stage in the transition they are managing. Figure 4 describes seven needs and the type of relevant support which is responsive to those feelings.

The composition of a support system ought to be looked at in terms of what kind of difficulty or problem situations you find yourself in at any given moment. I look at a support system as pulling together a small group of people from a large population to suit my needs at a particular

[10] From Gerald Caplan and Maria Willilea (eds.), *Support Systems and Mutual Help*, Grune & Stratton, Florida, 1976.

Figure 4

	Need	Relevant Type of Support	Solution
1.	Confusion about future	Models	Clarity
2.	Social isolation	Referent group identity: share concerns	Social integration
3.	Personal isolation	Close friends	Intimacy Caring
4.	Vulnerability	(Crisis) Helpers who can be depended on in a crisis	Assistance
5.	Low self esteem	Respectors of my competence	Higher esteem
6.	Stimulus isolation and deprivation	Challengers	Perspective energy
7.	Environmental isolation (Resources unknown)	Referral agents	Connect with Resources

time. My support system to deal with family stress is quite different from the support system I need on the job.

Looking at the needs side of Figure 4, if the crisis is one of confusion about the future, then appropriate support would come from locating models who could serve as clarifiers of future roles. If you are experiencing social isolation and you feel a need to be part of a larger group of people—where are the people like me?—you want to look for people who share common concerns with you. On the other hand, you might be feeling very vulnerable and out of touch and you want to move towards a place where you can get assistance and in that sense you may want to look at people you can depend on in a crisis. For that function, new parents of a new child might want to look for a pediatrician as opposed to other parents who are having the same trouble with colic on that given night. If you are feeling not social isolation, but personal isolation, you know that there are lots of people like you but your primary feeling is one of aloneness and you are looking for some kind of intimate warm contact. You would be looking for people you can count on as close friends. You may be feeling a sense of powerlessness and wanting some additional feelings of self worth. One of the most frequently left out categories of people in support systems as we have analyzed them, especially with women and with people who are not employed, has to do with locating people who respect your competence. It's the kind of gratification that a craftsman gets from a returning customer. Reaffirmation of one's self worth can be an extremely important aspect of a support system.

Another kind of isolation is called stimulus isolation . . . if you put a person in a situation without any auditory or visual stimulation, within a short period of time (48–72 hours) they will begin hallucinating and go crazy. Some people experience that right on the job with a lot of noise around them. The opposite of that is to build into your support system somebody who is bumping up against you, somebody who is pushing and abrasive to you—abrasive in the sense that you get a perspective challenger. You will find that some people systematically leave out of their support system any notion of abrasion. Their notion of abrasion is a head-on collision between a dripping can of molasses and a razor sharp marshmallow; it doesn't have a whole lot of impact. And lastly, to the degree that you feel disconnected from what is available in the environment, you need to have access to other resources. What you are looking for is people who can be good referral agents. They don't have to know how to do it themselves. You will find that kind of person floating through a lot of organizations. They know exactly where to have something mimeographed. They know where the gasoline is, they know where the toilet paper is stored. It is appropriate to think about these kinds of categories as you consider what types of people to have available in your system.

In an informal survey of some people at entry levels in a large clerical organization, over 20 per cent identified no one they felt they could count on for support, no one in any immediate sense.

What size should a support system be? What's right for one person may be a little different than what's right for another. We tend to think that there may be a general pool, of twenty or more people available from which, at any given time, you can quickly mobilize three to six. That is when you feel settled in a situation.

Three Typical Problems in Building Supports

What are some typical problems in building support systems? One problem encompassing support systems is that people tend to get individuals with conflicting motivations in their support systems. Adolescents tend to try to include their parents as support system members as they are rebelling out of the home and wanting to move into their own apartment. There is no way that most parents can approach that with anything like unambivalent feelings of support. You may find similar difficulty in the work setting if you happen to be a prized employee, by inquiring of your boss, does he know of any places that you can be transferred to a better job. That kind of support is a little difficult to come by.

Another problem in building an effective support system is that people tend to isolate their support system members. We've been doing a study on a small group in Washington on the degree to which people isolate the professional resources available to them. They actually tell one story to the doctor, another story to the lawyer, another story to the minister, another to the neighbor, and another to the spouse. We got these people together, which is how we discovered that this was going on. Getting a support system together can be an electrifying experience.

A final danger in building a support system is the tendency to create dependence on the support system so that you lose your own sense of autonomy and independence. You find yourself looking for them to come up with the answers as opposed to them being resourceful to your answering your own question. That is not totally inappropriate. In some situations you may want to create a lot of dependence. Over the long haul, however, it can be very debilitating.

3.5 *The Professional Support Group*[11]

HOWARD KIRSCHENBAUM AND BARBARA GLASER

. . . The distinction between personal and professional growth is central to the success of any given group . . . .

Some people have found great help in a personal growth workshop, a human relations laboratory, an encounter weekend, a religious retreat, or other kinds of personal growth experiences . . . . Other kinds of personal growth experiences can be more continuing and systematic in their focus—couples' groups, ongoing human relations groups, women's consciousness-raising groups, therapy, Re-evaluation Counselling Communities, and the like . . . .

[11] From Howard Kirschenbaum and Barbara Glaser, *Developing Support Groups: A Manual for Facilitators and Participants*, University Associates, San Diego, California, 1978, pp. 3–5.

Ideally, individuals would be involved in both types of growth and learning. One's personal growth (if it is real and integrated into one's personality and not merely the reflection of some current personal growth fad) can do nothing but enhance one's professional effectiveness. Professional effectiveness can also contribute importantly to one's sense of personal well-being. Although personal and professional growth are both needed, it is usually difficult for both to take place simultaneously in the same group. There seems to be a tug-of-war between the personal and professional focus in small learning groups. If the focus is not clarified, the group usually vacillates back and forth, with neither goal being realized effectively. While it may be argued that this need not be the case, in practice it almost always is, even when the group members are knowledgeable about group dynamics. Many groups have floundered and even disbanded over this issue. The 'encounter-group Syndrome' . . . . can be a major pitfall of the professional support group if the group is not clear about its primary purpose . . . .

But it is not totally an either-or . . . if personal issues are excluded entirely, professional goals will break down (as those who have experienced staff meetings can attest to). The support groups advocated here meet many personal needs. They are safe places, places where the members like to be, where there is support, caring; concern, laughter, and camaraderie. These are not sterile learning situations, but the primary goal is never obscured. It is a matter of priorities and balance.

If you are considering joining an existing support group, it is important to ask yourself the following questions:

.. Are the interests of the group similar to mine?
.. Do I feel that I am compatible with most members of the group?
.. Are the time and place of the support-group meetings convenient for me?

If your answer is no to one or more of these questions, or the group is filled, or you are not aware of any existing groups, then the alternative is to start your own support group.

- One choice is to identify a group of colleagues in your organization whom you already know and feel good about and invite them to join you in a support group.

- A second approach is to select people in a similar vocational endeavor; e.g., teacher trainers, women who work professionally with other women, community organizers, managers, consultants, parents, etc.

- A third option is to identify a particular topic that a group of people might be interested in, e.g., models of management.

3.6 *Differentiating the Observation-for-Feedback Function*[12]

DAVID H. JENKINS

. . . Sometimes groups bring in a specially trained person to serve as their observer, especially to get the observer role started and adequately identified. This permits the total group to participate in the problem discussion. Frequently the observer job is rotated among the members of the group to give each a chance for the experience and to keep no one from contributing to the general subject matter which is discussed from meeting to meeting.

Non-participation of the observer is necessary to keep him from thinking about the subject matter rather than about the behavior of the group. To become involved in what is being said prevents focussing on the questions how, it is being said, its relation to the direction of the discussion, etc. The observer needs to maintain his vantage point of objectivity at almost any cost, yet without losing his feeling of membership in the group.

The attention of the observer may be directed at a variety of behavior in the group. He notes the general level of motivation, the general work atmosphere of the group, the orientation of the group, leadership techniques, and other factors which affect productivity. Here is an example of the kind of observation sheet used in several recent discussion groups with some sample notes of the kind an observer makes.

Group Discussion Observation

A. Direction and Orientation

1. How far did we get?
Covered only half of agenda. Spent too much time on details.
2. To what extent did we understand what we are trying to do?
Several members not clear on goals. Some continual disagreements on purposes.
3. To what extent did we understand how we are trying to do it?

[12] From Warren Bennis *et al.* (ed.), *The Planning of Change*, Richard & Winston, Inc., New York, 1961, pp. 760–61.

Almost no discussion about procedure, resulting in confusion at times.
4. To what extent were we stymied by lack of information?
None. Relevant information at hand in group.

B. *Motivation and Unity*

1. Were all of us equally interested in what we are trying to do?
No. Two or three not sure problem is worth the time.
2. Was interest maintained or did it lag?
Slowed down during time leader made lengthy contribution.
3. To what extent were we able to subordinate individual interests to the common goal?
Rather low feelings of any unity. Two or three not feeling united with group at all.
4. To what extent were we able to subordinate individual interests to the common goal?
Antagonisms between R.K. and L.M. outside of group tended to show up here.

C. *Atmosphere*

1. What was the general atmosphere of the group?
   a. Formal or informal?
   Fairly formal, although some first names used.
   b. Permissive or inhibited?
   Fairly permissive except for period after leader lectured.
   c. Cooperative or competitive?
   Little competition, some positive evidence of cooperative feelings.
   d. Friendly or hostile?
   Lukewarm friendly.

Observations on the Contributions of Individual Members of the Group:

A. *Contribution of Members*

1. Was participation general or lopsided?
All participated at least to some extent. Some monopolization by B.C. and W.U.

2. Were contributions on the beam or off at a tangent?
Hard to determine as goals not clear.
3. Did contributions indicate that those who made them were listening carefully to what others in the group had to say?
At points of higher interest in the discussion some were not listening to others.
4. Were contributions factual and problem-centered or were the contributors unable to rise above their preconceived notions and emotionally held points of view?
Some tendency towards bias, especially during first hour.

B. Contributions of Special Members of the Group

1. How well did special members serve the group?
a. *Leader*: A little tendency to dominate, but catches himself before group reacts negatively. Tried unsuccessfully to get group to draw conclusions.
b. *Recorder*: Asked for clarification occasionally. This seemed to help group to clarify for itself.
c. *Resource person*: None in group today.

Other Observations

J.R. and B.J. criticized solutions while they were being suggested. Is that why so few suggestions came out?

Although an alert, untrained observer can sometimes be sensitive to many of the obvious difficulties in the group, training can greatly increase the value of the observer. This is especially true of the ability of the observer to detect the causes or relationships which produce the symptoms which he notices. For example, there may be no apparent reason for the sharp remark one member passed to another unless one recalls that earlier in the meeting the second member had criticized unnecessarily one of the contributions of the first member. There may have been some antipathy that developed which had not yet been resolved. With improved sensitivity the observer becomes increasingly valuable to the group in helping them go behind the symptoms and recognize the causes of the difficulty.

A group need not assume that lack of a trained observer prohibits use of this technique for improvement, for the tactful, objective member who is alert to problems of interpersonal relations can function satisfactorily in this role. Increased sensitivity will undoubtedly come with continued experience. The responsibility for self-analysis to which the group commits itself by establishing the role of group productivity observer extends to include assistance to the untrained observer to help him do the best job possible for the group.

The observer is a resource which is available to the group at any time. Sometimes groups set aside ten to fifteen minutes at the end of each meeting to discuss their progress and skill with the observer. Sometimes effective use is made of the observer by calling for his help at a crucial or difficult point in the discussion, using his analysis to assist in untangling the difficulty in which the group finds itself. Only infrequently does the group spend any large amount of time on this kind of discussion, and they only as it is felt to be profitable.

3.7 *Consulting Help with Problem Solving*[13]

CHARLES SEASHORE AND ELMER VAN EGMOND

Communication with the staff was the problem area selected for training by the members of the group. This included many kinds of specific problems ranging from the sending of messages to the attitudes and feelings of individuals which were blocking or facilitating communication. We have selected three problems which are closely interrelated in their effect upon the organization but distinct in the sense that a different training design was appropriate for each of them.

1. The Blocking of Communication Due to Unwarranted Attitudes and Feelings of Staff Members Toward One Another

Where there is infrequent contact between members of a organization who are dependent upon one another for efficient work, it is quite likely that unwarranted opinions and feelings will develop since all the facts are neither available nor freely communicated. These opinions and feelings can then serve as a screen through which behavior of the other person is interpreted, causing distortion of the communication which does take place.

---

[13] From Charles Seashore and Elmer Van Egmond, 'The Consultant-Trainer Role', in Warren Bennis *et al.*, *The Planning of Change*, Richard & Winston, Inc., New York, 1961, pp. 663–65.

We were aware of this kind of problem in listening to various persons talk about the factors which helped or hindered them in their jobs. It became clear that both the intentions and the behavior of co-workers were being misunderstood and distorted. This generated attitudes which further inhibited communication.

Utilization of a group setting which included all of the relevant persons enabled three activities to take place: catharsis, reality testing, and problem solving. Frustrations had grown up over a period of time and we found that it was necessary for these to be expressed before better channels of communication could be set up. In the process of catharsis, it was also possible to do some reality testing to see if the attitudes and feelings were warranted or whether they had arisen out of lack of communication and resulting frustrations. Following reality testing of attitudes and opinions, those which did seem to be warranted were examined in terms of whether or not they were functional to the achievement of the goals of the individuals and organization, and if not, what conditions needed to be changed to make them functional.

Our attempt here was to first 'unfreeze' the old attitudes and feelings and move toward a more realistic and functional set of beliefs on the part of individuals. Our next concern was to 'freeze', at least temporarily, these new perceptions. Thus, our link to the future operation of the organization was the immediate establishment and maintenance of new attitudes which would allow us to move ahead on other facets of the communication problem.

2. The Lack of Corrective Methods for Altering Maladaptive Patterns of Behavior

New information is constantly generated in an organization and this requires further alterations in feelings, attitudes, and behavior. As new things are tried, evaluation is needed to assess the helpfulness of changes. There is also the possibility that misunderstandings and misconceptions may develop since perfect communication does not exist at all times. This is particularly true of high status persons in the organization who do not ordinarily receive information from lower status members without . . . some screening process. For a superior to desire feedback on how his behavior affects others is not enough; those who are able to give the information must see his willingness to listen and feel that the transmission of information can result in a desirable change in the superior's attitudes and behavior.

Following a request by the superintendent for feedback from the staff, a meeting which included representatives from different staff levels was planned. In this small group setting, staff members were able to express to the superintendent how they felt his behavior related to specific problem situations. As consultant-trainers, our function included setting the standards of the meeting, acting as initiators, and either probing, remaining passive, or providing emotional support to individuals, as it seemed appropriate. The attempt here was to provide an opportunity for the status person to discover how specific behaviors on his part affected others, and to relate these feelings to his intentions. Discrepancies between one's intentions and the reactions one evokes in others can then be used as the basis for change. A summary of this meeting was given to the entire training group at their next meeting.

This served as a learning method which might continuously be used by the staff in assessing discrepancies between their intentions and the way their behavior is seen by those with whom they are interacting. The link between our activity as consultant-trainers and future change in the organization was to provide a model of a corrective mechanism which could be used for continuous evaluation and change after we terminated our relationship with them.

3. Lack of Direct Communication Channels between Different Parts of the Organization

One of the major problems of the top men in organizations concerns the demands that are made upon their time by others. Everybody wants to talk to the top management, but this, usually, is an impossibility. Although much of the responsibility and authority had been delegated to assistants in this organization, there still remained a real need for those on the staff to have direct communication on matters about which only the superintendent was fully informed. The problem was to devise a method which would meet the needs but not put undue demands upon his time.

When this problem became apparent to members of the group, it was decided to try out some different approaches to solving the difficulty by taking actual areas where staff members felt the need for communication. A meeting was designed to meet this need while keeping within the realistic limits of the amount of available time the superintendent would actually have. Training involved setting up a model which could be evaluated and revised on the basis of some trial runs.

Many of the factors which were present in the real situations were built into the training model so that it could be easily adapted and transferred to the existing structure of the organization. So a third link between consultant-trainer activity and organizational change is setting up a model which involves as many of the real elements of the normal daily operation as possible with the group members then having responsibility for transferring the model into the routine operation of the institution either during or after the consultant-trainer activity.

3.8 *Constraints on Significant Learning*[14]

PETER L. BERGER AND THOMAS LUCKMANN

'The basic structure of all secondary socialization has to resemble that of primary socialization. Significant others are in charge of his socialization . . . their definitions of his situations are posited for him as objective reality . . . highly charged emotionally . . . . Society, identity *and* reality are subjectively crystallized in the same process of internalization . . . what is real 'outside' corresponds to what is real 'within'. Objective reality can readily be 'translated' into subjective reality, and vice-versa . . . [There is] no *problem* of identification (since) no choice of significant others . . . his identification with them is quasi-automatic . . . his internalization of their particular reality is quasi-inevitable . . . . He internalizes it as *the* world, the only existent and only conceivable world.

[But] the symmetry between objective and subjective reality cannot be complete. The two realities correspond to each other, but they are not coextensive. There is always more objective reality available than is actually internalized in any individual consciousness. [Also], there are always elements of subjective reality that have not originated in socialization . . . (so) the symmetry between objective and subjective reality is never a static, once-for-all state . . . the relationship . . . is like an ongoing balancing act . . . . Building from the 'home' reality, linking up with it as learning proceeds and only slowly breaking this linkage, appertain to learning sequences in secondary socialization.

The facts that the processes of secondary socialization do not presuppose a high degree of identification and its contents do not possess the quality of inevitability can be pragmatically useful because they permit learning sequences that are rational and emotionally controlled. But because the contents of this type of internalization have a brittle and unreliable subjective reality compared to the internalizations of primary socialization, in some cases special techniques must be developed to produce

---

[14] From Peter L. Berger and Thomas Luckmann, *Social Construction of Reality: A Treatise in the Sociology of Knowledge*, Doubleday, New York, 1966.

whatever identification and inevitability are deemed necessary. The need for such techniques may be intrinsic in terms of learning and applying the contents of internalization, or it may be posited for the sake of the vested interests of the personnel administering the socialization process in question . . . . A professional revolutionary . . . needs an immeasurably higher degree of identification and inevitability than an engineer . . . the necessity comes not from intrinsic properties of the knowledge itself, which may be quite simple and sparse in content, but from the personal commitment required of a revolutionary in terms of the vested interests of the revolutionary movement. Sometimes the necessity for the intensifying techniques may come from both intrinsic and extrinsic factors. The socialization of religious personnel is one example.

The techniques applied in such cases are designed to intensify the affective charge of the socialization process. Typically, they involve the institutionalization of an elaborate initiation process, a noviuiate, in the course of which the individual comes to commit himself fully to the reality that is being internalized. When the process requires an actual transformation of the individual's 'home' reality it comes to replicate as closely as possible the character of primary socialization. But even short of such transformation, secondary socialization becomes affectively charged to the degree to which immersion in, and commitment to, the new reality are institutionally defined as necessary. The relationship of the individual to the socializing personnel becomes correspondingly charged with 'significance', that is, the socializing personnel take on the character of significant others vis-à-vis the individual being socialized. The individual then commits himself in a comprehensive way to the new reality. He 'gives himself' to music, to the revolution, to the faith, not just partially but with what is subjectively the whole of his life. The readiness to sacrifice oneself is, of course, the final consequence of this type of socialization . . . .

. . . To have a conversion experience is nothing much. The real thing is to be able to keep on taking it seriously; to retain a sense of its plausibility. This is where the religious community comes in. It provides the indispensable plausibility structure for the new reality . . . . The plausibility structures of religious conversion have been imitated by secular agencies of alternation. The best examples are in the areas of political indoctrination and psychotherapy.

The plausibility structure must become the individual's world, displacing all other worlds, especially the world the individual 'inhabited' before his alternation . . . . Alternation . . . involves a reorganization of the conversational apparatus. The partners in significant conversation change. And in conversation with the new significant others, subjective reality is transformed. It is maintained by continuing conversation with them, or within the community they represent . . . . People and ideas that are discrepant with the new definitions of reality are systematically avoided. Since this can rarely be done with total success, if only because of the memory of past reality, the new plausibility structure will typically provide various . . . procedures to take care of 'backsliding' tendencies. These procedures follow the general pattern of therapy . . . . What must be legitimated is not only the new reality, but the stages by which it is appropriated and maintained, and the abandonment or repudiation of all alternative realities . . . .

In addition to this reinterpretation in toto, there must be particular reinterpretations of past events and persons with past significance. The possibility of 'individualism' (that is, of individual choice between discrepant realities and identities) is directly linked to the possibility of unsuccessful socialization . . . . The 'individualist' emerges as a specific social type who has at least the potential to migrate between a number of available worlds and who has deliberately and awarely constructed a self out of the 'material' provided by a number of available identities.

3.9 *Attachment and Autonomous Activity: 'Oscillation'*[15]

BRUCE D. REED

. . . all human beings act from time to time in ways which restore their sense of inhabiting a world of meanings, rather than being objects at the mercy of other objects . . . adaptation to, and mastery of, the physical and social world, is maintained by periodic disengagement to renew contact with a source of meaning and confidence . . . . Periods of attachment normally alternate with periods of autonomous activity in adult life . . . . We have called this alternating process 'oscillation'. We have also suggested that each world in which the individual moves—his home, his job, his local community, for example—offers occasions in which he has the opportunity to renew and reorder the way he construes that world and his place in it. They provide opportunities for him to regress to extra-dependence upon figures or objects which are representative of that group, institution or society . . . annual conferences, regimental parades and inspections, weekly staff meetings and daily

[15] From Bruce D. Reed, *The Dynamics of Religion*, Darton, Longman & Todd, London, 1978, pp. 12–14, 41–56.

ward-rounds, all have some actual or vestigial utilitarian function, but in each case what people do, and the significance with which their actions are invested, goes beyond this function. A prison governor described a regular meeting of the senior staff of his prison which was known to everyone as the knitting circle. As the name indicated, they did not seek to make many decisions; it was a time to sit around and chat. Yet no one could seriously contemplate abolishing the meeting. It made more sense to him to suppose that it was a ritual, the function of which was to enable the staff to hold in their minds an idea of the institution and its management as a totality, when they were carrying out their responsibilities in different parts of the establishment.

The life of many institutions may be observed to include ritual occasions of this kind. Activities which appear aimless, ineffective or repetitive become meaningful if it is assumed that they serve to remind people of the nature of the institution they are in, what its aims and values are, who its key figures are (past, present or future), and what is their own status in it. We have reached the conclusion that such occasions are essential for the coherence of any institution. If no such occasions are observed, there is reason to doubt whether the institution holds together as a totality in the minds of its members . . . .

Implicit in this interpretation of behaviour in institutions is a theory about . . . what constitutes reality for any individual. Institutions are not physical objects. They are constituted by . . . a shared idea, held in the minds of individuals, whose ideas includes a reference to their own position with respect to the institution, as members or non-members, owners, employees, consumers, competitors or merely observers . . . the shared ideas which constitute institutions have to be reinforced, repaired and updated. This requires occasions on which they are not taken for granted, but become the focus of attention. One such occasion is the ritual occasion . . . .

It is useful to divide members of any community into three types. There are first those who engage in what we describe as *personal oscillation*. These participate regularly in acts of worship; collectively they experience the process of oscillation for themselves, and are often aware of the point of transition from extra-dependence to intra-dependence as they engage in the various rituals . . . .

The second type are those who engage in *representative oscillation*. These seldom or never attend worship but it is important for them that a member of their family, an acquaintance, or a significant person in the community such as their doctor, goes to church, as it were, on their behalf. They come anxious if that person does not go, and even if they apparently criticise them . . . it is done in such a way that the . . . goer is reinforced in his behavior.

The third type are those who engage in *vicarious oscillation*. This group does not identify themselves with any individual worshipper, but it is important for them that church buildings should remain standing, that they hear the church bells ringing, and that they see people going to church. This group has no apparent interest in church-going, but our studies have indicated that they constitute a considerable group in society which may not be made manifest until the church building is threatened with closure. For many of them, the church is a place to stay away from, but upon which they covertly depend, like the adolescent who apparently abandons his parents when he runs away from home, but likes to think they are still there if he should ever want to come back to them.

3.10 *Alone Time for Reflection*[16]

LAURENS VAN DER POST

I awoke early and went at once, just before an impatient dawn was at the rails outside our cabin, to look out over the sea. I had done it as if it were a most immediate task. From then on I continued to do so daily, on board all the ships I have ever travelled in. It was as if I had to begin my day with the reassurance that the sea had not vanished in the night. Perhaps it was a relic of some ancient rite left over on the scorched scene of our contemporary spirit . . . .

Primitive people often act or dance their prayers to creation, and this might well have been something similar. All I can say for certain is that never yet, after this silent contemplation of the day breaking over the sea, has the reassurance failed to carry me through the day as it did on this first morning on the Canada Maru . . . .

Somewhere between the ages of three and five I became aware of a frontier between the immense past, which was the hidden source of the meaning I sought, and the short term of life I had in which to live it and which would involve me in another act of painful and conscious birth of an individual self within. As a result, the boy that grasped that revelation remained ageless within me and became the tutor as well as examiner of the active knowledge I acquired of such a charge and potentiality of being and becoming, and still the sternest judge of how well I had

[16] From Laurens Van der Post, *Yet Being Someone Other*, The Hogarth Press, London, 1982, pp. 125, 318, 319, 394.

discharged so sacred a trust. He still remained my severest critic and mentor, and in those days at Um Idla it was as if I were meeting him again after a sojourn of many years, in a strange land and he took me, without rebuke, warmly by the hand. Implicit in this meeting between my grown-up self and this someone other, was an absence of any feeling of defeat, and it sent me with a strange peace and confidence at heart to take my camel train into the sleeping-sickness bush.

[Later, in prison camp], it raised my own predisposition of character and temperament to be aware of the importance of the small in life into a highly conscious and cardinal imperative. Creation, it seemed to me, was even more active in the apparently humble, often despised, rejected and insignificant detail of the immediate life of the individual, than on the melodramatic and grandiloquent stage on which the establishments and authorities of the world sought it. No life, however humble, the parable started plainly, was ever without universal importance if it truly followed its own natural gift, even if it was only to plough a straight furrow and plant potatoes well. Out of sight of heart and mind of their world, as prisoners were naturally predisposed to think, and even in their dreams, unconvinced that saving intervention from without was possible, it had a decisive element of reassurance for me and in due course, for all. Whatever chance remained of survival, it proclaimed, depended on a creative attention and positive response to the daily trifles of imprisonment, living an imperilled 'now' as if it were a safe and assured 'forever'.

Accordingly, I gave myself and all the reason I possessed, to this 'other person'. I came to listen to what it had to say with the utmost care. More and more, it was always there like some kind of guardian angel over us, not just to resolve the petty but painful daily confrontations with the Japanese, but to defuse the major crises which convulsed their relationship with the prisoners in a rhythm of a monotonous regularity, it seemed to me, with the appearance of every full moon and first few days of its waning, and which could have resulted either in selective killing or indiscriminate massacre. It gradually helped to create an atmosphere of behavior, of example on our part, and of dealing with Japanese authority, . . . that made the negative marginally less active than the positive, on our prison earth. It says something for the Japanese that, totally deluded and collectively and archaically possessed as they were, nonetheless, somewhere they remained part of the Japan I had known and loved, to make them not unresponsive to atmosphere of this kind. And in order to maintain this atmosphere, . . . I always started with myself and an assumption of a special responsibility and obligation ultimately invested in me by life for just such an occasion. More and more it seemed that being and doing involved not just myself and this other but a foursome: myself, and the other, and, through the greater awareness create as a result, the finding of two more senses: one of special awareness for my own and our men's sake, and another, to all those less aware, like our captors. To be aware and to contain the less aware seemed to be the beginning of morality and a true dynamic of change, and the way to meaning and truth of one's own.

It was not always as easy as it might sound. I had no comfort or reassurance in my own appreciation of these intangible feelings. I had, for instance, over many years, tried to be obedient to my own intuition; and I knew how necessary it was to begin by learning to separate what was truly objective intuition from the personal fear and hope that so often usurped its role. I tried harder than ever to observe the distinction in prison and often discussed it with Nichols. He had little doubt that the chances for survival were almost non-existent, . . . which made his conduct all the more impressive. But I could find nothing definite, either way, in my hunches. Right to the end, my intuition, later re-enforced by the kind of intelligence . . . was that the issue was daily in the balance, and daily we had something of our own to put in the scales of fate to keep the balance even . . . .

What mattered was that without these voyages, I would not have seen so clearly into the nature of my own confusions, a culpable lack of self-knowledge which injured myself and others and added, however min-utely, I was certain, to the general alienation and desperation of the time in which I live. Somehow I had to start with myself, disband and re-group in a new way. These moments determined that I would have to begin all over again and start with what was on the doorstep of my own mind, with what was nearest, and where I saw clearest, and not where some ideal collective vision called like a siren on the horizons of imagi-nation. I was acutely aware of an amassing of the forces of doom, and though I had an inkling of their true nature, this apparently was not shared by others. I would have, therefore, to begin by warning in the best way I could. Thereby, I would at the very least recover some continuity of purpose.

3.11 *With a Teacher, Guru, Mentor*[17]

LAURENS VAN DER POST

. . . What was about to happen between us was to be not an act of will and mind so much as a growth from roots deep in the dark and mysterious

[17] From Laurens Van der Post, *Yet Being Someone Other*, The Hogarth Press, London, 1982, pp. 128–29.

earth. The very first word I learnt from him was 'sensei': master or teacher. And it is as both master and teacher, in the indivisible connotations they had for the ancient Chinese and architects of the Japanese Renaissance, that he remains in my grateful memory. That classical concept had innumerable implications of great significance. It presupposed that a person could be a master to others only through continued seeking of the truth and humility of his own teaching. Someone could only teach others through what he had taught and mastered in himself. So ultimately, of course, he taught even more by living example than by words. It was a concept, therefore, concerned with the act and meaning of knowledge; and the heightening of responsibility of the human being, in proportion to the increase in his knowledge. It was never just an uncommitted acquisition of knowledge for knowledge's sake, which passed as 'education' in my own world. So, though without dogma or doctrine, it had profound religious undertones. Also, through the nature of both Chinese and Japanese writing, the fact that it was a vast system of a condensed and highly evolved picture-writing, not related to sound and word but designed directly to express whole ideas, situations and complexes of feelings, one could not study it without being involved throughout, with the growth of human consciousness.

All this was confirmed by some brief words with my teacher just before we went down for our midday meal. He joined me briefly, his large brown eyes strained with overwork and yet inwardly illumined as with a refreshed emotion. Did I remember, he asked me, how at the beginning of our voyage he had been compelled to correct me when I took 'Maru' to be the Japanese for ship? He had tried to explain that it was a kind of suffix of the most ancient origin, and was intended to remind man that certain material things of his own fashioning were more than matter and carried a charge of spirit and symbolic meaning all on their own. In this way some of Japan's greatest knights and warriors had given names to their swords with this suffix of 'Maru' added, to remind them that their swords too were instruments of spirit which should be accordingly used. This practice was most profound and appropriate, applied to ships, because the ship was perhaps the most evocative symbol of spirit of all and deserving of the 'Maru' after its name. He hoped we would not be put through the ultimate test of having to go through the eye of the looming storm but, if we did, would I remember all the feelings and definitions associated with 'Maru' because he had a feeling I would have the best possible definition of the word since I would then see 'Maru' in action?

I was much moved because all this was so in keeping with the spirit which had made me designate him as the plenipotentiary of religion in the ship, and I could not help discussing with him the matter of the 'unpredictable bend' in the nature of typhoons, which the Chief Engineer had mentioned to me. He suggested with unusual quietness that the voice of nature, as uttered through the spirit of ancestors so much closer and dependent on it in their day, should not be ignored in these matters. Their voice, however, remote, never failed to help regulate one's behavior even when asked to bear the unbearable. Then he added an afterthought, intent on removing any hint of rebuke to the Chief Engineer. It was not surprising, he said, that a new generation of Japanese raised in contemporary and especially Western scientific ways, should have forgotten the ancestors, their 'kami' and all that which was above them, their trees and mountains, and so their links with the gods.

3.12 *Conjoint Intelligence*[18]

LEWIS THOMAS

Although we are by all odds the most social of all social animals—more interdependent, more attached to each other, more inseparable in our behavior than bees—we do not often feel our conjoined intelligence. Perhaps, however, we are linked in circuits for the storage, processing, and retrieval of information, since this appears to be the most basic and universal of all human enterprises . . . . The circuitry seems to be there, even if the current is not always on.

The system of communications used in science should provide a neat, workable model for studying mechanisms of information-building in human society. Ziman, in a recent Nature essay, points out, 'the invention of a mechanism for the systematic publication of fragments of scientific work may well have been the key event in the history of modern science'. He continues:

> A regular journal carries from one research worker to another the various . . . observations which are of common interest . . . . A typical scientific paper has never pretended to be more than another little piece in a larger jigsaw—not significant in itself but as an element in a grander scheme. This technique, of soliciting many modest contributions to the store of human knowledge, has been the secret of Western science since the seventeenth century, for it achieves a corporate, collective power that is far greater than any one individual can exert.

[18] From Lewis Thomas, *The Lives of a Cell: Notes of a Biology Watcher*, The Viking Press, New York, 1974, pp. 12–15.

It is fascinating that the word 'explore' does not apply to the searching aspect of the activity, but has its origins in the sounds we make while engaged in it. We like to think of exploring in science as a lonely, meditative business, and so it is, in the first stages, but always, sooner or later, before the enterprise reaches completion, as we explore, we call to each other, communicate, publish, send letters to the editor, present papers, cry out on finding.

4. THE CONSULTANT TRAINER AT WORK

INTRODUCTION

Actual work settings, roles and styles come now into focus, with practitioners in action. The eight pieces—yes, even the opening one, by Benjamin Franklin two hundred years ago—are by practitioners who have long and wide-ranging experience and also reflect and write (a rare species!). They write here about their approaches to all manner of assignments and the different roles they take, and also about the changes they have made (as Juanita Brown puts it in her reading) in 'the underlying set of assumptions which guide [my] work . . . [as] a result of changes in my inner world or in the demands of the larger environment within which organizations must operate today . . . probably some of both'. The inner and outer worlds—the trainer consultant as instrument and her field of action—are clearly connected in these pieces.

To exemplify how this integrity permeates professional work and how professionals develop it further in their practice, even to the extent of shifting their world view to a fresh paradigm and making *that* explicit, strikes us as most important. Readings about particular aspects of a consultant trainer's competence will come in later sections. Only if competence is properly rooted can particular roles and work designs, methodologies and techniques be well-chosen and used reliably. Unrooted and/or unexamined, their choice and use are chancy and irresponsible. The first reading, reporting a well-meant offer of development assistance and its courteous, reasoned refusal and counter offer, is a vignette of unexamined assumptions and consequences.

Two extracts from Cyril Sofer follow. The first and longer piece summarizes work on management training with a technical college to which industrial companies send staff. Multiple settings are involved, each with sets of relationships, many interlocking. Sofer played two distinct roles. As a consultant he stimulated, initiated next steps, proposed new resources, restructured, evaluated and so on. As a trainer, he organized and led meetings and staff development programs. A system with at least six constituencies was in simultaneous play: consultant/ trainer, the College faculty, the participants, their firms (the college's 'clients'), the administration, and the community and local authorities (which linked formally into the college as its Board of Governors). The extract conveys well, the rich and quickly expanding scope of work and contacts involved when following through a request for assistance, and the mixed feelings, complex implications, interconnections and broad range of demands on the consultant any such request makes, even the simplest. In the second extract, Sofer categorizes and discusses his major functions as consultant across three different system consultations: this same college, a hospital and a manufacturing enterprise. 'Perhaps more important than "factual" findings', he concludes, 'was the *manner* in which my colleagues and I defined and reconceptualized the problems with which we were presented'.

With Miles we then turn specifically to the trainer's role within a program. As he sees it, it combines planning, guiding, and evaluating. Shortened by taking out references to group training (Miles' particular concern), this piece seems useful for facilitating most kinds of learning for action through formal programs.

What both consulting and training for action require most of all is a relationship with clients and participants that differs basically from the traditional 'expert' model of consulting and teaching. While the 'expert' knows, decides, tells, often carries out 'to demonstrate', the development consultant stimulates, joins in exploring, gives feedback and supports client staff, and so builds the client organization's capacity for effective planning and managing itself. Champion, Kiel and McLendon have particularized consultant roles further and matched each with desired outcome(s). Each denotes an emphasis, a primacy, not a severe separateness, but at the far ends of the range they set out, the differences are sharp. Juanita Brown in the next reading tabulates paradigm shifts from 'traditional' to 'emerging' in terms of how she sees the client, focusses her time and attention, and chooses an appropriate role. Next, Schoen then embodies this different relationship in a 'reflective' contract. For both consultant and client, the new relationship makes different demands on competencies and each gains satisfaction from different sources than before. The change-over is difficult. Clients and consultants can minimize and resolve these by creating a 'behavioral world' for their work together. Indeed, one of them may initiate such a change and gradually gain the other's support in bringing it about.

Development tasks calling for awareness in new directions, new 'paradigms', 'change-overs', are carried out more surely and safely with careful monitoring. This section ends with piece by a practitioner as monitor/researcher of his own practice: he maps 'his world of work', scores his interactions with it and categorizes them on key dimensions, keeps fuller notes on particular items, and summarizes patterns in the development from time to time, to guide next steps and further plans. A simple instrument can aid this.

4.1 Two Different Worlds[1]

BENJAMIN FRANKLIN

At the treaty of Lancaster, in Pennsylvania, anno 1744, between the Government of Virginia and the Six Nations, the commissioners from Virginia acquainted the Indians by a speech, that there was at Williamsburg, a college with a fund for educating Indian youth; and that if the chiefs of the Six Nations would send down half a dozen of their sons to that college, the government would take care that they be well provided for, and instructed in all the learning of the white people.
The Indians' spokesman replied:

> We know that you highly esteem the kind of learning taught in those colleges, and that the maintenance of our young men, while with you, would be very expensive to you. We are convinced, therefore, that you mean to do us good by your proposal and we thank you heartily.
>
> But you, who are wise, must know that different nations have different conceptions of things; and you will not therefore take it amiss, if our ideas of this kind of education happen not to be the same as yours. We have had some experience of it; several of our young people were formerly brought up at the colleges of the northern provinces; they were instructed in all your sciences; but, when they came back to us, they were bad runners, ignorant of every means of living in the woods, unable to bear either cold or hunger, knew neither how to build a cabin, take a deer, nor kill an enemy, spoke our language imperfectly, were therefore neither fit for hunters, warriors, nor counsellors; they were totally good for nothing.
>
> We are, however, not the less obligated by your kind offer, though we decline accepting it; and to show our grateful sense of it, if the gentlemen of Virginia will send us a dozen of their sons, we will take care of their education, instruct them in all we know, and make men of them.

[1] From Benjamin Franklin, *Remarks Concerning the Savages of North America*, Passey, Private Press of Franklin, 1784.

4.2 *In Multiple Roles and Settings²*

CYRIL SOFER

It was a major strain on the department staff [of the Technical College with which Sofer was consulting] to tolerate the criticism of themselves by firms and students, and to know that we thought much of this justified. Through our close contact with the teachers and their work context, we could understand some of their difficulties (unequal abilities of students, unreality of their demands, shortage of trained staff, opposition of colleagues, and so on). But we made it clear that we thought they could do more to improve matters than they were in fact doing.

The major strain for us was toleration of their ambivalence towards us. We felt rather like guests invited to dinner, who settle down to criticize their hosts and to authenticate the criticisms.

A substantial contribution to a constructive outcome of this early crisis was made by the fact that we showed ourselves prepared to be corrected. Even more important, we were ready to help to seek remedies for the defects we had commented on.

There were many subsequent occasions on which the staff questioned our judgement, corrected us, or disliked our findings or advice (and on which we corrected our information). But it became more or less accepted that we brought information (even unpopular information) into the department and commented on its practical implications, while the department made selective use of our knowledge, experience, and advice. And we had learned to voice our impressions while they were being formed, however tentative they might be, rather than let tension mount as staff waited for formal written statements . . . .

As the project progressed, tension slackened in relations between the older members of the department and ourselves. One important reason was that our growing knowledge of firms and students led us to the conclusion that the pace of innovation was too drastic, that the new staff members were introducing new teaching techniques before they had adequately mastered them, and that they needed to conserve much of what was positive and useful in the older, more conventional tradition. When we made this clear, the older members of the department began to see us as 'objective' people, who would take a balanced view of a situation rather than side with one or other faction. Another major contribution to amicable relations came from the collaboration with me

² From Cyril Sofer, *The Organization from Within*, Tavistock Publications, London, 1961, pp. 84–91.

of Mr. Cook, the senior lecturer in the department, in a short study of the training needs of a firm that approached the department for help, for its supervisory staff. During the course of this study. Mr. Cook and I had much the same role with regard to the firm's staff as my [Tavistock] Institute colleague and I had in our relations with the department staff.He and his colleagues were able to see even more clearly now, that in the course of such an investigation, one scrupulously respected individual confidences; concentrated on questions of structure, roles and relationships, rather than on individual personality or individual competence, and had as one's central aims the understanding of the organization, and the provision of help in the constructive use of this understanding . . . .

Since many of the problems depended ultimately on what a full-time teacher could and could not do, we undertook a detailed analysis of the teacher's post as it was and could be. This was done mainly through repeated group discussions with the staff. After every two or three such discussions we prepared a set of notes which were further developed on the next occasion . . . .

We continued to pass on to the teachers, selected material from our studies of the students, the firms, and themselves, and to discuss practical implications for current and projected work with industry. There was considerable sensitivity about many of the points raised, especially where these indicated, as they frequently did, a need for changes in staff behavior.

But changes occurred in what both we and they considered a positive direction.

The department critically reviewed its teaching programme. It pruned those of its conventional management courses which appeared to confer paper qualifications rather than to develop managerial ability. It exercised greater discretion in the acceptance of students. Mainly through the use of guided group discussion, the staff improved their techniques of teaching emotionally charged material. They made their teaching more practical by wide use of project methods. A tutorial system was instituted to personalize responsibility for students, and bring part-time teachers into closer contact with the full-time staff through more frequent consultations about students. Three new appointments were made, and the operating efficiency of the department was visibly improved.

It became clear that the department had to lower its sights in work with firms and to safeguard its core of conventional, acceptable work . . . .

We worked with the staff towards the greater realization that they had to cooperate with firms in a way that showed they could tolerate circumscription of their efforts and develop new opportunities. This was best done on limited and well-defined tasks . . . [and] to concentrate on the development of links with a relatively small number of firms. Apart from training surveys, some small-scale field research began and joint teaching programmes began to develop.

Through the very fact of our investigations, significant changes occurred in relations between the department and surrounding firms . . . . We convened a one-day conference—to which representatives of examining institutions, the County Council, and the Ministry of Education were also invited—to discuss our findings and their implications. This was followed by another more action-oriented meeting convened by the chairman of the governing body of the college. At this meeting the chairman, the head of the department, and I, suggested that a development panel be formed between the department and a few representatives of local firms, to consolidate and expand the direct links formed between them during the research . . . . Anxiety about the effectiveness of the college was, however, low enough to permit constructive suggestions to be made as to the exact functions and operations of the panel, and to enable members to arrange for representatives of firms, the department, and the college principal to present concrete proposals to the governing body . . . .

As they developed their plan for work with students and firms, and studied the criticisms which we voiced or reported, members of the department felt it would be an advantage to have more training in research and training techniques.

The head of the department asked whether we could arrange this advanced training at the Tavistock Institute. We agreed [and] gave a course attended by all departmental staff, at which my colleagues and I led seminars on Institute projects and case conferences on problems brought . . . members of the department seemed to profit from the fact that they could observe at close range how Mr. Hutton and I, as social scientists . . . went about our work and could evaluate with us the modes of approach we adopted

We kept the County Council in touch with findings and developments through regular discussions of progress reports with the liaison committee, and through the official responsible for technical college education . . . .

4.3 *Fact-finding or New Perspectives*[3]

CYRIL SOFER

. . . provision of help to the organization . . . consisted of:

[3] From Cyril Sofer, *The Organization from Within*, Tavistock Publications, London, 1961, pp. 98–101.

1. The assembly and analysis of facts, and reconceptualization of problems.
2. Redefining assumptions and expectations.
3. Participation in planning and action.
4. Introducing, monitoring and evaluating innovations.

1. The Assembly and Analysis of Facts, and Reconceptualization of Problems

The importance of fact-finding in this work can . . . be over-stated. For one thing, the facts I collected were often new only to me—the organization knew about them already. For another, the mere collection of facts may well be found to give little help; indeed, it has been shown in experimental work, that an individual's capacity for making sound judgements about complex situations may even be impaired by providing him with a mass of data (which he believes should be relevant) unless he understands quite clearly how it influences or should influence his behavior. Thirdly, when boiled down to 'findings, the types of factual conclusions or leads for action with which a social consultant emerges are apt to seem obvious, commonsense or trivial. This is partly because people know many truths' intuitively, and partly because they retain simultaneously several broad theories about cause and effect, one of which may well be supported by research.

Often, it was the process of analysis, the redefinition of the problem, the character of the material mustered, the weights which different items were given, which provided the most help for the administrators. These did not necessarily provide fresh answers or conclusions, but contributed more usefully and lastingly to the deepening and extension of capacity for judgement, to the birth of new conceptions of how human problems should be defined, and to the clarification and explication of the logical basis for conclusions already suspected.

Perhaps more important to the administrators than 'factual' findings was the manner in which my colleagues and I defined and reconceptualized the problems with which we were presented; made existing assumptions explicit and examined their validity; assessed which of the contradictory and equally 'obvious' conclusions about situations were in fact true; illuminated the social and psychological forces at work, accepting feelings and attitudes as social facts which had to be included in any overall appreciation; and drew attention to role and culture conflicts previously defined wholly as inter-personal issues. Indeed, it would be legitimate to regard much of what was done in the three projects as a

special sort of training experience for administrators, based on sociological and psychological expertise.

2. Redefining Assumptions and Expectations

The assumptions about human behavior, on which directorates operate,
commonly underestimate the extent to which people are willing to take
responsibility and to make their resources available to the organizations
to which they belong. In all three cases, my presence and method of
work increased my confidence that colleagues could agree on a common
set of organizational objectives and adopt them on their own. Looking
back, I should say that I communicated my belief in this possibility by
beginning, in each case, by finding key groups with which I could
concentrate my work. Although there existed at the same time a central
person to whom I acknowledged a special responsibility—the managing
director of the Davidson Company, the director of the research unit, the
head of the management department—the relationship with the key
group of organizational leaders conveyed my belief that they had unused
capital available to them as a collectivity.

The established expectations of groups of staff concerning particular
colleagues often functioned to restrict the contribution they made. The
expectations had become a set of self-fulfilling prophecies . . . in each
case my work brought the established systems of reciprocal expectations
into question, and enabled participants to set slightly higher standards
for each other in a way which called forth not only a more cooperative
atmosphere but also somewhat better contributions.

3. Participation in Planning and Action

As an outsider the consultant provides a relatively objective and independent viewpoint. I brought an extra mind of a different sort to the
problems of the groups with which I worked, and information about the
way other organizations tackle similar or related problems. From my
general training in social science and practical experience with organizations, I was able to contribute ideas for solving operational problems
of selection, appraisal, communication, and training; and for collecting
information about the character of the environment.

My presence helped the groups to be more objective, as it provided
them with an opportunity to project themselves into my position to try

to see themselves as I saw them. This is the complement of the insight which derives from the consultant's capacity to project himself into the position of members of the group.

My interest and the involvement themselves acted as forces helping the groups to achieve their objectives . . . . They were helped by my apparent willingness to tolerate solutions at the level that was really possible for them, however defective these might be by ideal criteria . . . there was still another sense in which client groups were helped to form policy, i.e., by the fact that we could open routes for them to resources which they did not know beforehand or which they would not normally realize were available for their purposes . . . .

4. Introducing, Monitoring, and Evaluation Innovations

All three projects involved some changes in, and by, the project groups. There were shifts in perceptions and definitions of problems, in the contexts in which particular questions were examined, in the way in which decisions were taken, in the character of organizational decisions, and in the manner and timing of their execution. These changes can be summed up in the statement that in the course of each project, there was some movement by each group towards the discovery of its primary task and towards the establishment of better means for attaining this.

My colleagues and I were partly responsible for these changes, to which we contributed information, frames of reference, moral support, experience, 'feedback' from the environment, ideas, and suggestions. We also helped through providing formal and informal occasions for the review and evaluation . . . .

4.4 *In the Trainer Role*[4]

MATTHEW B. MILES

The trainer's responsibility is to facilitate learning . . . . When the training group gets bogged down, or becomes apathetic, or is full of fight, the trainer's job is not necessarily to help the group 'get out of this

---

[4] Matthew B. Miles, *Learning to Work in Groups*, Teachers College Press, New York, 1980, pp. 237–47.

mess', but to help them learn from the mess. Doing this may at times require that the trainer act differently from a teacher, a member or a leader.

In brief, the trainer must act as a planner prior to a training activity, as a guide during the operation of the activity, and as an evaluator during the planning of new activities.

The Trainer as Planner

During the planning stages of a program—or a specific training activity— the trainer's role is primarily to help produce practical, promising plans for learning. During early diagnostic work, the trainer may help others in assessing needs for training and in launching formal planning. Then he helps the program planning group . . . in further diagnosis of needs, and in the construction of a set of learning experiences that meet these needs for specified participants . . . .

The major contribution of the trainer during planning is probably methodological. He can supply technical help to the planners ('If the issue is practice in handling irrelevancies, we could use a fishbowl coaching session,' or 'Videotape playback really helps people be more sensitive to what's happening').

Beyond providing immediate technical help, the trainer also needs to be sensitive to the training process in general . . . .

Are real dissatisfactions . . . worked on?
Is the training climate psychologically safe—does it allow
  people to unfreeze their old ways of doing things?
Are members getting an oppotunity to practice new kinds of
  behaviors and learn how well they succeeded?
Are people getting a chance to think about what they are going
  through and how it applies to their own future behavior?
Is the training group developing as a group?
Does the situation support and aid each member's own private
  quest for improvement?

. . . training functions may be shared through the group, even though one person is designated as trainer. If learning is to become a self-operative process, each member of the training group must, in some part, come to take responsibility for guiding her own learning. The trainer role, like the chair role, is thus a kind of 'safety net'—the trainer will fill needed training functions in the group, but only if no one else does. If trainer and group see the trainer role as a supportive one, it helps to reduce the worries of the beginning trainer, that he must be omniscient and omnipotent . . .

The Trainer as Guide: Building Group Norms

During the actual operation of a training activity, the trainer's basic role is to help things keep moving so that people learn as much as possible. The trainer's behavior during training sessions helps to set group norms, that is, informal standards, ways of behaving that are highly valued by the members of a group. In a training group, certain norms are needed . . . . Here are some of these training-relevant norms.

People are Important

The trainer has a basic feeling of respect for the worth of persons. She does not interrupt, she listens; she rejects ideas but not people. She shows that she believes that persons are ends and all else is means . . . and the norm of basic respect for persons gradually becomes established in the training group.

It's Safe to Try Things Out Here

The trainer also indicates by her actions that . . . trying something new is not only permissible but desirable. She permits and invites discussion of her own behavior. She does not criticise anyone for expressing any feelings or ideas. Gradually, willingness to experiment becomes a group norm too.

Feelings are Important

The trainer takes expressions of feeling seriously. When people say they feel mad, sad, bad, glad, he helps the group see that these are basic data from which to work. Feelings of group members tell us how well progress on the task is going—whether people are interested and involved, whether the goal is clear, how well a particular leader's approach is working. Frank expression of feeling is essential if the group members are to understand the processes going on.

Things are Not Taken 'Personally'

The trainer responds 'objectively' to expressions of feeling. Feelings are facts, her behavior says to the group . . . Joe gets mad at me, that tells us something about what has been happening, and so does my impulse to lash back at him. The trainer does not inhibit her own feelings, but reports them for discussion and analysis. The trainer does resist the temptation to actually lash back, to get caught by the ebb and flow of interaction, wound up in the content of group discussion rather than attending to its process.

This sort of objectivity . . . aids considerably in learning about what leads to what in groups . . . .

The trainer also encourages objectivity through work procedures, such as tape playback, a process observer, or post-meeting reaction sheets. The implicit message is: 'We can look at ourselves and learn from this'. As the group moves along, members come to share a work-centered objectivity in the midst of their feelingful life.

We Learn from Doing Things and Analyzing them

From the start, the trainer indicates by his actions that he sees learning as beginning with concrete experience. He does not lecture or exhort the group, and he does not encourage windy discussions of 'leadership', or 'how to handle the blocker'. In fact, he is likely to trip people up when they start doing this, asking how the topic relates to what is happening in the group. He helps group members set up trials of particular approaches to problems, and help people think carefully about what they have done. In addition, he supplies coherent conceptual frameworks to aid in analysis . . . .

We Plan Together

. . . the trainer shows the group members that he believes the training group is basically a shared, planful enterprise. He does not spring things on the group. He does not attempt to pull his rank on others. He does not take a *laissez-faire* attitude: he invites cooperative planning. And he refuses to take sole responsibility for the success of the group.

The trainer communicates his belief in these norms for effective training group operation, by everything he does. At the outset of the group, he may outline and discuss proposed group norms explicitly. As the group proceeds, he 'models' the norms through his behavior. And members, more and more, have successful experiences with analyzing how the group works, . . . members' acceptance of these norms will aid them in continued independent learning after the training program is over.

It is far more important that the trainer accept these norms in her own set of personal values than it is that she be especially proficient in the specific methods and techniques of training. This is not said as exhortation, but simply as a fact of life the trainer must face . . . . Good trainers can be aggressive or docile, outgoing or reserved, jovial or serious—but the trainer's personality must almost certainly include some commitment to values underlying norms like those just described.

Of course, no trainer exemplifies these norms to the nth degree. The trainer's belief in these norms is revised and deepened as she experiences many different training-group situations . . . .

The Trainer as Guide: Specific Behaviors

The trainer . . . must also supply certain functions in the training group during a training activity, or see that they are supplied: providing methodological help, guiding analysis, giving support, confronting and stimulating, encouraging group growth, controlling group movement, and maintaining his own membership in the group. The basic skill of the trainer lies in being able to decide when a particular function is needed—and when it is not. Whatever his specific behavior (including the behavior of keeping quiet), the trainer always has one basic purpose—helping to set conditions for effective learning.

. . . the trainer must be open to continuous and thoughtful analysis by the training group, of such matters as, the effectiveness of her own role, the value of the activities she has helped to plan, and trouble spots in the activities that need to be reduced or eliminated through new planning. Without such session-by-session evaluation, even the best of trainers will do a poor job.

4.5 *Choosing a Consulting Role*[5]

D.P. CHAMPION, DAVID H. KIEL AND
JEAN A. McLENDON

Consultants—internal and external—often talk about getting 'burned'. Usually, it happens when the way the consultant's role has been structured

[5] From D.P. Champion, David H. Kiel and Jean A. McLendon, 'Choosing a Consulting Role', in *Training & Development Journal*, February 1990, Vol. 44, No. 2, pp. 66–69.

leads to no-win situations. There isn't much clear guidance for the consultant and client as to whether the role being played is the right one.

In order to do this kind of practical assessment and to facilitate collaborative agreements between clients and consultants, we need three things:

- a clear understanding of the purposes of a consulting relationship;
- a language for talking about consulting roles;
- criteria for determining which role is appropriate in a given situation.

GOALS AND ROLES

In any consultation, the clients will have two types of needs:

The Need for Results

Refers to concrete outcomes associated with a project. These might include changes in the bottom line, organizational structure, information transmitted, skills learned, or behavior and attitudes.

The Need for Growth

Means increased capacity to perform new functions or behaviors on a continuing basis. In other words, if a high level of growth is achieved in the consultation, then the client will be able to do the job next time with less or no outside help.

The need for results and the need for growth will vary depending on the nature of the consulting project. For example, in performing a one-time service with which the client is unfamiliar, the consultant's major focus is likely to be 'getting the job done' for the client.

However, in helping the client perform an important and recurring—but new—task, the appropriate emphasis is on helping the client learn how to perform that task over the long haul, instead of merely producing an immediate result.

When project outcomes are specified in that way, it is easier to determine what services are needed from the consultant and what contributions are needed from the client system to bring about the desired changes.

By constructing a grid model of consultings using as the two axes

Figure 5 : Typical Roles Statements for the Consulting Role Grid

Counselor	Coach	Partner
'You do it; I will be your sounding board.'	'You did well; you can add this next time.'	'We will do it together and learn from each other.'
Facilitator	**Teacher**	**Modeler**
'You do it; I will attend to the process.'	'Here are some principles you can use to solve problems of this type.'	'I will do it; you watch so you can learn from me.'
Reflective Observer	**Technical Adviser**	**Hands-on Expert**
'You do it; I will watch and tell you what I see and hear.'	'I will answer your questions as you go along.'	'I will do it for you; I will tell you what to do.'

Copyright © 1985, Champion, Kiel, and McLendon

Figure 6 : The Consulting Role Grid

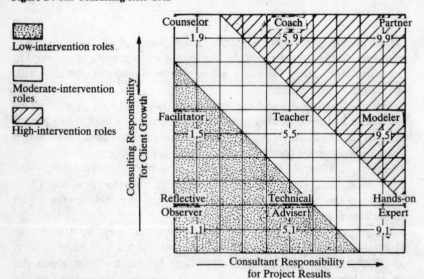

Adapted from Champion, Kiel, and McLendon
Copyright © 1985.

consultant responsibility for growth and consultant responsibility for results, we can identify the specific consulting roles appropriate for the mix of services that the consultant is expected to provide.

The nine roles of the consulting role grid (Figures 5 and 6) reflect the options the consultant has in a given situation. Presumably, if a consultant correctly assesses the situation, he or she is likely to choose the role that will be the most effective.

NINE ROLES

The consultant who takes on the hands-on expert role (9,1) actually undertakes the task on behalf of the client. In this role, the consultant has most, if not all, of the responsibility for producing good results. The client is not expected to grow in capacity very much. He or she will need the consultant again, next time, in order to perform the task equally well.

The modeler role (9,5) implies that the consultant is highly responsible for results in the current project, but also that there is some value in the client system building its own capacity. The modeler carries out the task for the client system, but does so in a way that makes his or her approaches and techniques apparent. The consultant is available for answering questions about what he or she is doing, and why. The implication is that sometime in the future, the client may carry out the task.

The partner role (9,9) implies high responsibility for results and growth. It assumes that both the client and the consultant have the capacity to successfully perform aspects of the task, and that both will share responsibility for the results. It also assumes that a big jump in the client's capacity to do the task, is an important goal. The partner role means that the client is ready to learn in a hands-on way and that the consultant can teach effectively in this mode, as well as guide the task to successful completion.

In the coach role (5,9), the consultant does not have direct responsibility for performing the task. Instead, he or she may observe the performance of the task and provide feedback. The coach uses highly directed instructional techniques to improve the client's performance: providing feedback, prescribing and observing practice sequences, and giving advice and support during actual job performance. The coach is indirectly involved in carrying out the task, but highly involved with the client and his or her growth.

The teacher or trainer role (5,5) is even more removed from the scene of the action. The trainer or teachers unlike the coach, is concerned with general performance rather than performance in a specific situation. For example, the teacher is concerned that the client knows the basic principles and has mastered the skills of managing a meeting, while the coach may actually observe the client leading meetings and discuss the results afterward.

The technical adviser role (5,1) is a back-up role. In this role, the consultant has moderate responsibility for results; the client uses the adviser's expertise for specific purposes. The technical advisor may have close or distant personal relations with the client, but his or her concern is not the growth of client capacity, except in an incidental sense. The focus is on helping the client get over a specific problem that the technical adviser's knowledge and experience can solve.

In the counsellor role (9,1), the consultant's concern is almost entirely for the capacity of the client to perform the task. The counsellor tries constantly to help the client clarify and set goals, maintain positive motivation, and develop and implement effective plans. The counsellor often is removed from the performance of the situation. He or she may have to rely on the client's data about what is happening in the project. Hence, much of the counsellor's skill is in helping the client to gather, analyze, and develop conclusions from his or her own experience.

The facilitator role (5,1) consists largely of helpful but process-oriented activities, such as, convening, agenda building, recording, collating and displaying data, providing techniques such as problem analysis or brain storming, and planning and leading meetings. Through the facilitator's intervention, clients may absorb the helpful techniques and processes the facilitator uses. That leads to moderate growth of the client's capacity in these areas. One main reason the consultant is an effective facilitator, is that he or she has a low stake in the task at hand and, is neutral within the client group. This is a low task-responsibility role.

With the reflective observer role (1,1), the client is most responsible for results and capacity building; the consultant is least responsible. The consultant's task is limited to feeding back observations and impressions. In spite of the low activity level of the consultant, this role can have a dynamic effect on a client system that is skilled in using such assistance. The reflective observer can help clients monitor themselves on such ambiguous but crucial indicators, as trust, teamwork, and openness.

A consultant may play multiple roles simultaneously within a client system, but with different clients. He or she might be a counsellor to one manager, a trainer for the team the manager leads, and a coach for a task-force of other managers. In this framework, the consulting role is always defined situationally with a specific client or client group.

Ideally, roles will be defined and clearly understood by both the client and consultant. Many consulting errors arise from the consultant's attempt to play more than one role simultaneously with the same client without a clear contract to do so.

How to Choose

The process of role choice and transition is obviously a critical area of judgement and skill for the consultant. What guidelines can we go by to make informed choices?

We can identify four key areas, building on Robert Tannenbaum and Warren Schmidt's classic formulation of criteria in determining behavioral choice for leadership roles. 'How to Choose a Leadership Pattern', *Harvard Business Review*, March–April, 1958.

The Organizational Situation

The roles in column 9 on the grid (partner, modeler, and hands-on expert) are likely to be appropriate in cases where there is immediate need for results and for client capacity development. If client capacity is already moderate to high, then the low-intervention roles (counsellor, facilitator, reflective observer, and technical adviser) may make more sense.

Characteristics of the Client

In determining an acceptable role relationship, the client ought to ask the following questions: Will the proposed consulting relationship be likely to achieve the results that the organization needs? Will I be helped to grow in the process, in a direction that is in my long-term interests? Will the skills that I already possess be used to their fullest extent? Are the skills that the consultant possesses being used in the best way?

Characteristics of the Consultant

The capacity of the consultant is the most obvious limiting factor in determining a consultant role. Consultants cannot take on the more results, or growth-oriented roles if they lack the experience, knowledge, and confidence to do so. But if the consultant is competent to take on various roles, how should he or she choose among them? Willingness, interest, and time are factors. The consultant needs to ask him, or herself, not only 'Can I do this?' but 'Do I want to serve in this role?'. A role that is unwanted will probably not be well performed.

The Client/Consultant Relationship

A relationship of trust and openness permits collaborative determination of the appropriate client-consultant role. Too often, the client's unwillingness to ask for help leads to an insufficient consulting role, or the consultant's need for business results leads to an unhealthy dependency. But most relationships don't begin with the necessary trust to permit open discussion and negotiation of roles. The grid model, by providing a common language for clients and consultants, may help overcome some initial barriers.

4.6 *A Shifting Paradigm*[6]

JUANITA BROWN

My own world view—the underlying set of assumptions which guide my work—has changed over the last several years . . . . Taken as a unified whole, the left-hand column of the outline reflects the way I was socialized to use the tradition of Organization Development, a profession based on very effective problem-solving techniques and human interaction processes. The right-hand column represents the direction of my 'emerging self' as a practitioner. Of course, this is a continuum, and I find that I move back and forth along it depending on the needs of the situation, my own comfort with risk-taking, and my increasing skill in designing effective interventions based on a new set of underlying beliefs. I have certainly not discarded my 'old skills', but they are now being employed in a new context.

[6] From Juanita Brown, 'A Shifting Paradigm for Organizational Consultation', *Vision/Action*, The Journal of the Bay Area OD Network, San Francisco, June 1987, pp. 1–3.

How I See the Client and the Organization

Traditional Paradigm	*Emerging Paradigm*
* The Client is not healthy, has problems, and needs help in fixing what's wrong.	* The client is whole and well, and needs my collaboration to discover and fully express that which already exists but may not yet be fully visible in daily operational life.
* Workplace as an institution business establishment	* Workplace as a neighborhood, community, family.
* Workplace as center, primarily for meeting economic and social needs.	* Workplace as center for creation of meaning and renewal of the human spirit.

How to Focus My Primary Time and Attention as a Consultant

Traditional Paradigm	*Emerging Paradigm*
* Diagnosing and fixing the broken parts which have been presented to me for repair. By focusing on the parts, I will be able to help the whole.	* Apprehending the potential of the whole. By focusing on the systemic *connections* among the parts I will increase the likelihood of the 'presenting problems' in the parts being 'solved'.
* Knowing what went wrong and how to improve it. Focus on past and present Problem–solving.	* Knowing what's going right . . . . Focus on what people really want to see happen in the future. Images of potential and plans to reach it.
* Internal Issues (within the team, department, organization).	* Boundary relationships (between groups, departments and between the organization and environment).
* Process (behaviors/interactions of people and groups).	* Structure and Results (configuration of the parts themselves and the effect of these on behaviors and desired outcomes).
* Interpersonal/Functional (Team Building, Communications, Goals, Objectives—Enhancing the present).	* Metapersonal/Strategic (Mission, Vision, Values—Creating the future).
* Group and organization level as focus.	* Individual person (creativity, health, personal vision, spirit) included as part of larger systemic focus.
* Human resource development as core.	* Interaction of technology, social structure, and individual psyche as core.
* Finding the right answers solutions—Knowing.	* Discovering the right questions issues—Learning.
* Rational understanding. Action Research. Linear techniques.	* Reason & intuition as a team. Active Sensing. 'Evocative Technologies'.
* Pre-planned intervention strategy (completed work plans, overall time lines, proposals).	* Iterative planning of interventions. Successive approximations. (Clear starting points, Criteria for success.)

(*Continued*)

Traditional Paradigm	Emerging Paradigm
* Agreement/Acceptance.	* Alignment/Attunement.

My Appropriate Role as Consultant

Traditional Paradigm	Emerging Paradigm
* Change Agent.	* Evocateur.
* Master Mechanic.	* Artist/Craftsperson.
* Process Facilitator.	* Overall Design Engineer.
* Pragmatic Problem–solver.	* Practical Idealist—Catalyst for 'Dreaming and Scheming'.
* Helping professional 'In Search of Excellence' (provide methods to help the client 'do' better).	* Co-Navigator on a joint 'Search for Essence' (provide collaborative support for client to discover what both doing and 'being' better mean).
* Process Consultant.	* Context Creator.
* Designer and facilitator of structured events/activities.	* Creator of space and contexts for 'good conversations'.
* Team-builder.	* Community Development Specialist.
* 'Middle Grounder'. Maintain professional stance within the norms of the existing culture to gain credibility. Use only the 'consultant' part of myself.	* 'Edge Walker'. Look *very* professional but be a caring iconoclast. Gain credibility by being effectively different. Use my whole person.
* Allow the client to set the pace. Follow the client's lead.	* Be a constructive nudge—a loving irritant (pearls may develop!).
* Encourage open client expression of needs, feelings, values and beliefs. Minimize sharing mine unless asked.	* Encourage open client expression of spirit—a sense of large meaning and purpose. Sensitively share my values and beliefs along with others.
* Be objective. Don't get involved in the content. Avoid over-engagement. Success is client responsibility.	* Care deeply. Appropriately share relevant expertise. Co-create success. Full effort is full victory.

Einstein said that our significant problems cannot be solved at the same level of thinking we were at when we created them. Thinking about our work as practitioners from this perspective allows us to ask whether we are focussing on solving problems within the current framework (first order change), or whether the situation demands a shift of context altogether (second order change). For example, are we using a Western model of linear cause-effect reasoning to guide our diagnosis and intervention strategy, or do we find ourselves exploring a more holistic (albeit messy and paradoxical) systems perspective which may place an entirely different light on the issue. Or perhaps the 'problem' is not interpersonal conflict at all, but a crisis of meaning or organizational spirit, manifesting itself in the behavior we label as conflict. As consultants I believe we have a responsibility to be clear and intentional, at least with ourselves, about how we are using our skills.

4.7 *The Reflective Contract*[7]

DONALD A. SCHON

In situations which are neither emergencies nor routine cases, the establishment of a reflective contract is possible and may seem worthwhile; but as compared with the traditional contract, it is difficult. The difficulty lies in the different demands on competence, and the different sources of satisfaction that are presented both to the professional and to the client.

Let us consider, first, the situation of the professional. When he is a member of a 'major' profession, whose role carries a strong presumption of authority and autonomy, then the problem of moving to a reflective contract involves giving up his initial claim to authority and sharing the control of the interaction with the client. When the professional's initial position is weak, when he tends to be regarded as a mere service provider rather than an authority, then the problem is reversed. I think, for example, of the principal of a school anguished by her inability to confront what she believes to be the unreasonable demands of parents; of engineers in large companies who feel coerced by the directives of general managers too ready to sacrifice product quality or safety to immediate commercial advantage; of human service personnel in public bureaucracies who feel that agency procedures prevent them from attending to the clients they are supposed to serve. It is not unusual in such cases to find that individuals aspire to a professional status that they are only tenuously, or partially, given. Their difficulty in establishing a reflective contract with their clients is to acquire enough voice in the situation, to be able to do so.

Whether the professional occupies a position of initial strength or weakness, the reflective contract calls for competences which may be

---

[7] From Donald A. Schon, *The Reflective Practitioner: How Professionals Think in Action*, Basic Books, Inc., New York, 1983, pp. 298–303.

strange to him. Whereas he is ordinarily expected to play the role of expert, he is now expected from time to time, to reveal his uncertainties. Whereas he is ordinarily expected to keep his expertise private and mysterious, he is now expected to reflect publicly on his knowledge-in-practice, to make himself confrontable by his clients.

As the professional moves toward new competences, he gives up some familiar sources of satisfaction and opens himself to new ones. He gives up the rewards of unquestioned authority, the freedom to practice without challenge to his competence, the comfort of relative invulnerability, the gratifications of difference. The new satisfactions open to him are largely those of discovery—about the meanings of his advice to clients, about his knowledge-in-practice, and about himself. When a practitioner becomes a researcher into his own practice, he engages in a continuing process of self-education . . . the practice itself is a source of renewal. The recognition of error, with its resulting uncertainty, can become a source of discovery rather than an occasion for self-defense.

Indeed, it can be liberating for a practitioner to ask himself, 'what, in my work, really gives me satisfaction?' and then, 'How can I produce more experiences for that kind?'.

These differences in sources of satisfaction and demands for competence might be expressed as follows:

Expert	Reflective Practitioner
I am presumed to know, and must claim to do so, regardless of my own uncertainty.	I am presumed to know, but I am not the only one in the situation to have relevant and important knowledge. My uncertainties may be a source of learning for me and for them.
Keep my distance from the client, and hold onto the expert's role. Give the client a sense of my expertise, but convey a feeling of warmth and sympathy as a 'sweetener'.	Seek out connections to the client's thoughts and feelings. Allow his respect for my knowledge to emerge from his discovery of it in the situation.
Look for deference and status in the client's response of my professional persona.	Look for the sense of freedom and of real connection to the client, as a consequence of no longer needing to maintain a professional facade.

Just as the reflective contract demands different kinds of competences and permits different sources of satisfaction for the practitioner, so it does for the client.

For one thing, the problem of choosing a practitioner presents itself to the client in a new way. He must choose not only on the basis of the practitioner's reputed expertise (always a, more or less, 'black box') but on the basis of his amenability to the reflective contract. Is the practitioner willing to talk about the issue at hand, to consider it from more than one point of view, to reveal his own uncertainties? Is he interested in the client's perceptions of the issue? Is he open to confrontation, without defensiveness? Is he willing to carry out experiments on the spot and to be open about such experimenting, including the conditions under which he would regard his views as confirmed or refuted? What is his stance toward his own knowledge? Does he claim only to 'know', or is he interested in, rather than threatened by, alternative ways of seeing the phenomena that do no fit his models?

The competences and satisfactions appropriate to clients in the reflective contract can be summarized and contrasted with the traditional contract roughly, as follows:

Traditional Contract	Reflective Contract
I put myself into the professional's hand. In doing this, I gain a sense of security based on faith.	I join with the professional in making sense of my case, and in doing this I gain a sense of increased involvement and action.
I have the comfort of being in good hands. I need only comply with his advice and all will be well.	I can exercise some control over the situation. I am not wholly dependent on him; he is also dependent on information and action that only I can undertake.
I am pleased to be served by the best person available.	I am pleased to be able to test my judgements about his competence. I enjoy the excitement of discovery about his knowledge, about the phenomena of his practice, and about myself.

For any professional or client who wishes to move from traditional to reflective contract, there is the task of reshaping the norms and expectations which the other part brings to the interaction. If one party to an institution wishes to begin acting in a nontraditional way, he is apt to create new sorts of dilemmas for himself. Should a professional, for example, risk losing his patient's confidence in order to create the possibility of reflective contract? Should he risk exploring the client's meanings when the client might regard such exploration as intrusion? Should he reveal the complexity of the situation at the risk of frightening or confusing the client?

The way in which such risks present themselves is a function of the sort of behavioral world in which professional and client encounter one another. Their behavioral world may be conducive to the avoidance of risks, the suppression of dilemmas, the exercise of mystery and mastery, and in these ways may foil a practitioner's efforts to establish a reflective contract with his client. But the behavioral world is an artifact which professional and client jointly create. They can change it in the directions required by the reflective contract if they have the will and competence to do so. Indeed, one of them may initiate such a change and gradually gain the other's support in bringing it about.

4.8 *As Monitor/Researcher of his own Praxis*[8]

ROLF P. LYNTON

Data on scientific activities and programs, says an article in *Science* (1977), 'are frustratingly deficient. Record-keeping by science agencies has been designed primarily to account for money rather than to provide first for analyses of who went where and when'. And for what; and what happened when he/she/they did what they did that mattered to the purpose? My recording is a craftsman's tool in the first place, a researcher's, only in the distant second. It helps me do the best work I can under the very exposed conditions of developing innovative institutions. I could not live with myself if, seeing the high risks that go with the high promise of building a truly community-oriented school (of public health), I did not do everything I could to sharpen my perception of current events around me, use the best conceptual formulations of what to anticipate, and monitor my own behavior in very orderly fashion. Most of all is this done with close colleagues, members of my 'core group', and a special consultant hired for the purpose from outside. But recording both stimulates my reflective self and feeds it. It also acknowledges that, as dean, I ultimately face my part in this innovative enterprise alone, that I, indeed, carry an individual responsibility.

By recording I mean not the daily log or journal that I also keep, but the systematic underpinning of data for it . . . .

The antecedants of the present form (see figure) take me back to 1961 in India, when I started work as a Ford Foundation consultant to a new institution, following a period of six years as founder-director of an international training center (Aloka). It was my wife, Ronnie, who suggested

---

[8] From Rolf P. Lynton, *Boomerangs and Alligators: Professional Education in the Public Interest*, Unpublished manuscript 1978, pp. 75–84.

that it might be wise to keep track of this strategic change of role, to sustain an extra consciousness of it and so, presumably also an extra capacity for sensitive behavior in the change-over from director to consultant and from director-in-charge to team member (between four and eight international consultants were attached at various times to the new institution, a staff college).

I started, simply enough, with keeping all documents—of those I sent I made sure to keep a copy—and a note of every contact I had with each work colleague, Indian and foreign. This produced a diary, and a more systematic one than most, in that every contact had some notation.

Before long, this simple method threatened to become overwhelming and, for increasing numbers of contacts, also unnecessary: many contacts were brief and their contents routine and well-known. It was then that I developed a simple time/relationship matrix. It itemizes my colleagues in their main structural groups across the top of the page, leaving room for some 'other' and 'visitors' categories. Down the side on the left, it divides the day into half hours. With a simple red mark I can, as I go through my day, score every transaction on the matrix. I can also indicate by simple successive numbering any that I particularly want to make a diary note about when I have time.

As a result, my diary became selective—and manageable—while the basic recording—of *all* interactions—also continued. The time-matrix allows me to distinguish, very simply, between long and short, large and small, meetings, and what colleagues (inside and outside the Institute) were involved in them. I can *see* patterns easily, including blanks (omissions).

This mode of scoring and diary keeping I kept up for the five years I worked with the Institute in India, half of it as team leader of the consultants. I valued the opportunity it offered to live my work life twice over. Usually, I wrote my diary notes first thing in the morning and then felt well prepared to face the new day. There were certainly times when the whole relentless business felt like a straight-jacket; happily these were also the times when recording was most rewarding because so much was going on. I ended the five years with 4,500 pages of personal diary, all documents into and out of my office, and the complete interaction scores day by day.

Research into that whole body of data came later. Analysis anchored in more comprehensive conceptual schemes showed up a massive flaw in our work, an imbalance: we had concentrated attention on program development and the internal affairs of the Institute and neglected the Institute's external relationships. With that recognition, my interest in organization-environment linkages became vivid, systematic and lasting.

For my more recent institution-building programs, the matrices

comprehend more external relationships. The first step towards constructing the matrix (for the new school) was to identify the main
classifications of colleagues, students, agencies and other constituencies
with which the school needed to relate. Most of these were obvious. For
instance, the composition of an Advisory Committee determined one
set of classifications in the general constituency of 'other colleges,
schools and departments'. It would clearly be important to monitor
contacts with each of these eight academic units in USC, whereas
grouping contacts with others together would suffice. It would also be
important to track contacts with the heads of these units separately from
contacts with their representatives on the Committee; so each of these
units received three sub-classifications—dean or chair, committee
representatives and others. Similarly, three major State agencies were
separately identified and room provided for specifying particular Divisions in each, with which the school was to work most closely.

Such constituencies and subsets, liberally interspaced with spaces for
'other', that is emergent, constituents had columns across the matrix,
the half hours of the day downwards. Five additional columns allowed
for some rough and ready categorization of each contact as it took place.
Figure 1 reproduces extracts of the completed matrix for one rather
typical day.

This five categories I chose to categorize were: which party initiated
the contact, the main contents and purpose of it, and my estimates as to
the achievement of the immediate purpose and—very different, this—the
estimated effects of this contact on the longer-term relationship with the
constituent. The diary for this day (15 Jan 1976) has eight notes (for the
contacts numbered in the margin on the left).

The matrix lay on my desk for marking up during the day, in the course
of my contacts with people or just after. A vertical line in the column
shows a meeting, face to face, its length, the duration of it; T stands for
telephone, M for a verbal message; four or five simple signs and letters
fill the columns on the right. The full key is shown here. Each contact
took about as much time to mark, as saying hello. The result is a daily
record which covers all kinds of personal contacts; and documents cover
the rest. Making the marks in red made for easy scanning.

Key for Five Classificatory Columns

1. *'Initiated'*
   self = s
   other(s) = o
   joint = j
   unclear = blank

Figure 7 : Relationship-Time Matrix For Monitoring Own Practice

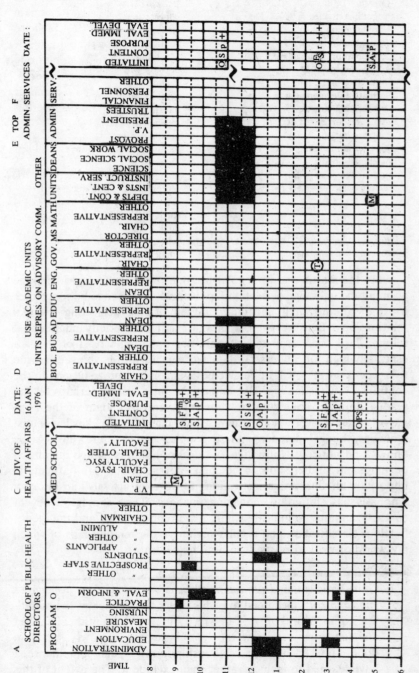

2. '*Content*'
   Program *A*ctivities = A
   *Ad*ministration = Ad
   *Col*leagueship = Col
   *C*onfrontation, conflict = C
   *D*iffuse linkage = D
   *F*uture, scanning, long-term = F
   *N*ormative development = N
   *O*rganization structure = O
   *O*ther *R*esources = OR
   *Pol*icy = Pol
   *R*elationship building = R
   *S*anction, support = S
   *S*tudent *S*election = SS
   *F*aculty *S*election = FS

3. '*Purpose*'
   *a*llocate = a
   *ad*vise = ad
   *c*onfront, for example,
      differences = c
   *d*evelop = d
   *e*xplore = e
   *f*irm up, set = f
   *i*nform = i
   *imp*lement = ım
   *m*aintain = m
   *mo*nitor/evaluate = mo
   *o*btain = o
   *p*lan = p
   *r*epresent = r
   *s*can/visualize future = s
   *t*each = t
   *th*ink = th

4. '*Evaluate—immediate*': +, −, blank = no comment
5. '*Evaluate—developmental*': +, −, blank = no comment

What the matrix and its regular use does most for me is to keep me aware of the full range of relationships with which I need to be concerned. Most of all they help me guard myself against neglecting external relationships. Because even if they are left only briefly unattended, relationships soon drop out of sight for good. The risks of this are especially high for 'underserved' constituencies who have every reason to expect that they will be neglected again, initial protestations to the contrary notwithstanding. But among the unintrusive, perhaps all too readily dormant contextual relationships, are also some of the most important and powerful for the new schools mandate, e.g., key legislators, university budget planners—these people, agencies, etc. have to be known and noticed. Normative and diffuse linkages, which institution development studies show to be commonly neglected, are particularly important for innovative institutions to develop actively. So my own emphasis has shifted to managing linkages. Time and frequency of contacts continue to indicate where my attention flows, and the identification, classification and regular review of the relationships of which my world of work consists have become central.

To sum up:

1. Quite basic is the *identification of the components of the institution's environment* which need to be included: this delineates the boundaries of my world of work to which I must pay attention. To offset any tendencies to draw the boundaries too narrowly, when in doubt about including a relationship in my regular surveillance, I have learned to include rather than exclude it. The extent of this

world needs to be regularly reviewed because new components do emerge, for instance, through legislation of subtler processes: 3 to 4 monthly intervals seem right in the first year, twice a year after that. At least refinements in some categories will be required.

2. For proper *management and for letting this type of data influence action*, the matrix can be programmed for machine scanning, so it can reveal trends in the data for early discussions and use on a regular basis.

3. *Some characterizations of the contacts* is useful, even if it is rough. For instance, important dimensions of commitment and reciprocity in relationships are indicated by the pattern of initiatives in the contacts. I, therefore, score, and periodically summarize, the balances of initiatives in each relationship. I also summarize the purposes for which a particular relationship is most often used.

4. Along with the scoring of all interactions, I keep up my *diary* for selected items daily. When because of too many meetings and travel the diary falls behind more than a day, I use the occasion for a systematic review of all relationships, ranging over recent events, and for assessing the quality of them for now and for the future (the diary for developing the new School includes five such systematic summaries in the three years).

Keeping the diary up to date takes me a little over an hour a day, a half-hour some days, as much as two hours, on others. That time includes making notes for actions that come to mind while I write the diary and scan the record to see where I am this morning and what I need to focus on for the day.

With the meticulous recording of my institution building experience, I am also in the position to make a small contribution to filling the data gap that *Science* points to, in the quote reproduced at the start of the piece. But that is a by-product. The primary objective of the recording effort is self-monitoring. It keeps me in top form, such as that is, helps me live my life twice in quick succession, an examined life, and so raises my critical awareness of the world around me and of myself in it . . . .

PART II

Specific Roles, Functions and Methods

5. PLANNING: STRATEGY AND DESIGN

INTRODUCTION

Any lingering suggestion that we have selected readings for this volume for comprehensive coverage, even light scanning, or for conceptual completeness, will surely evaporate now, in this part. We are concerned with highlighting some important areas, issues and useful ways of making progress. We have, therefore, chosen pieces in which widely recognized practitioners present the maps and guidance they have distilled from their own work. Of these, several are from lectures and other summary statements which compel maximum clarity in little space. Some are seminal: classics from twenty or more years ago.

Strategic Planning

The first area we want to highlight in this section, because it is commonly neglected (avoided?), at great cost, is the strategic dimension of consulting and training. What is the particular assignment to contribute to the intended line of development as a whole and how will it fit into the overall development plan? Issues that this order of questions raise are not, in the first place, tactical but strategic, not primarily about how to cause least disturbance in the on-going routine operations but about envisaging, mapping, identifying and then acting, so that relevant constituencies inside and outside the organizations become involved and orderly processes, initiated for shaping the specific intervention to its purpose. That strategic planning is still very rare or only very slight, can have many reasons. Fears of getting into complexities beyond one's understanding are least necessary among them. With these readings, we want to make strategic planning at least more tractable. If consulting/training is to aid change—as distinct from replication—then a certain range of considerations (not an infinite number nor unthinkably complex combinations of them) must be taken into account and brought into effective play. The dimensions to be included make up complex patterns and the data for parts of them *will* be soft, or perhaps bridged by conjecture, but they *can* be ordered.

Political scientist Karl Deutsch[1] has warned that all human systems have inherent tendencies to shut themselves off from information that does not fit readily the perceptions, relationships and social/organizational arrangements of the people in it: 'Self-closure'. An essential function of consultants and trainers, therefore, is to open clients' 'eyes' and become more alert to, as also competent to act on, information relevant to the development they intend.

Developmental action is different from crisis management, even of a series of crises. The first reading by Lynton lays out the differences. Briefly if, in line with the tendencies to self-closure, decision makers see needs for changes as minor and temporary, they will ask the consultant trainers to provide brief, discrete, once-for-all 'solutions'. Which is fine when that is all that the situation warrants. If, on the contrary, the situation calls for help with *development*, then settling for this simple stimulus-response model is not effective; worse, it does harm, for it confirms the client in his inadequate assessment—and, ironically, this is almost certainly the case if the intervention 'succeeds', in terms of its original limited formulation. A consultant/trainer has then, in effect, colluded with the client/participant in avoiding the *transformation* that true development requires.

As changes in society accelerate and interplay in exponentially complex ways, as in developing societies, situations that can be dealt with by specific, temporary interventions, are quite rare. The second reading consists of extracts from Emery and Trist's seminal work on 'turbulent', i.e., unpredictable environments and socio-technical constructs to cope with them. Increasingly, the task of consultants and trainers is to help clients—individuals, groups, organizations, communities—to set themselves up for continuing (as well as all-round) learning, for foreseeing and managing development as an on-going process. External linkages to these complex changing environments can be categorized into just five sets, according to the purposes they serve. The next reading does this.

Time can be a great orderer. Though much needs to be envisaged and mapped, not everything needs attention all at once. Priority settings, actions and actors can be orchestrated in useful sequences. William Foote Whyte does this in the next reading. 'Overcoming (some identified) obstacles (for a start) builds momentum so that the field of forces at later stages may be markedly changed . . .' (Whyte).

[1] Karl W. Deutsch, *The Nerves of Government*, Free Press, New York, 1966.

Program Assessments and Intervention Designs

'Needs Assessment', as the term is commonly used, refers to information on which to design particular units rather than overall strategy. Joe Thomas' piece with that title focusses on 'three common pitfalls in diagnosing' needs of this order: too few sources of information, too few ways of securing information and too few people involved in considering the information and deciding about the program.

Thomas' piece bridges over to readings about three particular training interventions. All have a competent practice in view, not mere increases in knowledge or in instrumental or conceptual dexterity. In the first, Betty Mathews and K. Pisharoti describe, in orderly detail, how to draw training designs directly from job specifications and settings, in their case villages near Gandhigram, South India.

The other two readings in this set deal with process-focused 'laboratory' strategy and with programmed learning for individuals. Many specific items of standard information and skill can be effectively and economically programmed for learning by individuals in their own place and at their own time and pace *if* detailed instructions and step-by-step feedback are provided and participants want to learn. Access to trainers during the program is for resolving residual difficulties. The rigorous approach and meticulous detailed designing that characterize individualized programmed learning are the basis, also, of modular strategies which aim to match each component of what needs to be learned, with an appropriate set of training arrangements, methodologies and materials. Even the basic tool kit for modular programming is very varied. It includes designs and materials for individual work as well as for sessions with others, active and also quietly reflective components, time at work alternating with concentrated training sessions, and attitudinal knowledge and skill components. Trainers choose components to facilitate any particular learning(s) and fit them into optimal sequences and overall designs. Modular strategies depend on heavy investments of staff time for planning and preparing a program.

The final pair of readings capture something of the underlying shifts in approach, direction and resource allocation, which all the newer, more meticulously designed strategies depend on. The first, based on experiences with developing competency-based curricula for medical education, is mostly about preparing teachers, students and the institutions for these far-reaching changes. The second is an overview of 'the instructional process', in the widest sense, which makes these strategies work.

5.1 *Innovative Subsystems²*

ROLF P. LYNTON

This paper focuses on systems . . . which have outgrown the possibility of attaining optimal integration through interpersonal, spontaneous, face-to-face contact, and therefore require formal integrative devices.

In classical organization theory the dominant criterion for this classification was size: a system greater than a given size required formal devices, a smaller system did not. Recent empirical research findings indicate that the degree of differentiation, and therefore the need for integration, correlates much more closely with the degrees of uncertainty in technology and markets, than with absolute size. The focus . . . is on systems (1) that need to cope with high degrees of uncertainty, and (2) that have developed sub-systems to develop innovations for the system.

Assessment of Uncertainties

The accuracy with which decision makers in the system assess uncertainties for the system guides formal differentiation within the system, as well as the design of integrating devices. There are two basic models for this assessment. One model treats uncertainties as a succession of discrete stimuli to which the system needs to respond with appropriate innovations. In this model differentiation and integration are functions of the frequency and force of the expected stimuli. It is a model that has affinities with familiar stimulus-response models in learning theory and with the early formulations of an administrator's functions in terms of weight and frequency of decision-making. The integrative devices appropriate to this assessment are linkages of minimal complexity and duration. As stimuli for innovative responses increase in frequency, temporary and informal devices may become permanent and formal, but the kinds of devices and their limitations will not change unless the model of assessment changes. The other model treats uncertainties as a continuous general state requiring a continuously varying response from the whole system. This model treats the system and its environment as a continuous interaction in uncertainty and as aiming to achieve and

² From Rolf P. Lynton. 'Linking an Innovative Sub-system into the System', in *Administrative Science Quarterly*, Vol. 14, 1969, pp. 398-400.

maintain a steady state in and through this interaction. Emery uses the word 'turbulence' to describe the environment in this model.

The spontaneous response to a turbulent environment is to reduce the turbulence. The first model aims at reducing the complexity and uncertainty by segmentation or dissociation, which are essentially the defense mechanisms that lead to passive adaptation. The second model aims at establishing hierarchies of goals, which may then serve as guides to behavior, i.e., to allocating attention and other resources to causal strands on the basis of established priorities. Through the development of such codes, the field is no longer perceived as turbulent . . . .

. . . In the first model, the cost of the responses is a permanent ceiling on the rate of innovation; in the second model, costs occur from the slower rate of innovation due to various rigidities associated with the acceptance and revision of codes.

The empirical data . . . show a heavy incidence of failure for ad hoc and temporary linkage devices. They refer to situations in which linkages were designed to perform some specific function(s) and failed to do so. Actually an unrecorded kind of failure may be more serious, namely the system rigidities that the introduction of the inadequate linkages reinforced. The basic weakness of the discrete stimulus-innovation model shows up most sharply when the intended linkage succeeds. For, there is no evidence that the successful integration of two or three sub-systems increases the degree of integration of the system as a whole; on the contrary, commonly, a well-integrated sub-system (or a set of sub-systems) may become isolated, and then it and the rest of system become rigid separately, in defense against one another. Katz and Kahn . . . state that 'the major error is to disregard the systemic properties of the organization and to confuse individual change with modifications in organizational variables'. Very little of the growing literature on innovation and its diffusion has been attentive to this problem. The prevailing focus of attention is on the individual innovator when he adopts an innovation, why, etc. (Rogers, 1962), not on the organizational setting in which innovation takes place. The early sociological role studies may have unwittingly supported this orientation. In the rural economy, the typical adopter was an individual farmer rather than a collectivity, such as an organization. Even in later studies, the influence of the larger social setting on the farmer-innovator tended to be underestimated. Studies of innovation in educational systems, like schools of various kinds and school districts, either show a lack of available knowledge about the functioning of organizations and communities or suffer from a kind of great-man orientation . . . .

. . . The currently widespread emphasis on the importance of 'dissemination of research findings' seems to continue the popular view that the content or demonstrated efficacy of a particular innovation, as such, is crucial in determining whether it will be adopted and used effectively. In short, to use an image from Gestalt psychology, specific planned change attempts have most typically been 'in figure', occupying the focus of attention, while the organization itself has remained 'the ground'. That this model commonly persists in the face of growing experience of its inadequacy, indicates its long antecedents in history and also the deep reluctance many decision-makers seem to feel about making major system changes that may be required to interact effectively with a turbulent environment. They prefer to assess the uncertainty as small and the response to it as routine, whereas it might be more useful to take as a primary target the improvement of system dynamics, specifically the linkage design . . . turbulent environments require the linkage of dissimilar sub-systems whose goals correlate positively, i.e., sub-systems which are not in competition cannot take over the role of the other. Therefore, linkages between them will tend to maximize cooperation. As Thompson (1967) has shown, such a matrix can take several shapes, but all provide for two aspects: (1) that which links the system to the environment, through which broad social sanctioning is secured and the system is attuned to the needs of the environment and (2) that linkage which enables sub-systems to engage in effective joint search for common ground rules, while retaining the degree of privacy, protection, and autonomy they need to carry out their distinctive functions.

The strategic objective then has to be formulated in terms of institutionalization. As institutionalization becomes a prerequisite for achieving a steady state in a turbulent environment, then sub-system goals have to be found and formulated, which accord with system goals and which offer a maximum convergence between its sub-systems.

5.2 *Organizational Environments*³

FRED E. EMERY AND ERIC L. TRIST

Four Types of Causal Texture

. . . We have now isolated four 'ideal types' of causal texture, approximations to which may be thought of as existing simultaneously in the

³ From Fred E. Emery and Eric L. Trist, 'The Causal Texture of Organizational Environments', in *Human Relations*, Vol. 18, 1965.

'real world' of most organizations—though, of course, their weighting will vary enormously from case to case . . . . Together, the four types may be said to form a series in which the degree of causal texturing is increased, in a new and significant way, as each step is taken. We leave, as an open question, the need for further steps . . . .

The simplest type of environmental texture is that in which goals and noxiants ('goods' and 'bads') are relatively unchanging in themselves and randomly distributed. This may be called the placid, randomized environment . . . under random conditions . . . the optimal strategy is . . . to do one's best on a purely local basis . . . . The best tactic, moreover, can be learnt only by trial and error and only for a particular class of local environmental variances . . . . While organizations under these conditions can exist adaptively as single and indeed quite small units, this becomes progressively more difficult under the other types.

More complicated, but still a placid environment, is that which can be characterized in terms of clustering: goals and noxiants are not randomly distributed but hang together in certain ways. This may be called the placid, clustered environment . . . .

The new feature of organizational response to this kind of environment is the emergence of strategy as distinct from tactics. Survival becomes critically linked with what an organization knows of its environment . . . . In the clustered environment, the relevant objective is that of 'optimal location', some positions being discernible as potentially richer than others.

To reach these requires concentration of resources, subordination to the main plan, and the development of a 'distinctive competence' . . . . Organizations under these conditions, therefore, tend to grow in size and also to become hierarchical, with a tendency towards centralized control and coordination.

The next level of causal texturing we have called the disturbed-reactive environment . . . the existence of a number of similar organizations now becomes the dominant characteristic of the environmental field. Each organization does not simply have to take account of the others when they meet at random, but has also to consider that what it knows can also be known by the others. The part of the environment to which it wishes to move itself in the long run is also the part to which the others seek to move. Knowing this, each will wish to improve its own chances by hindering the others, and each will know that the others must not only wish to do likewise, but also know that each knows this . . . .

If strategy is a matter of selecting the 'strategic objective'—where one wishes to be at a future time—and tactics, a matter of selecting an immediate action from one's available repertoire, then there appears in

type 3 environments to be intermediate levels of organizational response—
that of the operation . . . . One has now not only to make sequential
choices, but to choose actions that will draw off the other organizations.
The new element is that of deciding which of someone else's possible
tactics one wishes to take place, while ensuring that others of them do
not . . . . The flexibility required encourages a certain decentralization
and also puts a premium on quality and speed of decision at various
peripheral points . . . .

It now becomes necessary to define the organizational objective in
terms not so much of location, as of capacity or power to move more or
less at will, i.e., to be able to make and meet competitive challenge
. . . .

Yet more complex are the environments we have called turbulent
fields. In these, dynamic processes, which create significant variances
for the component organizations, arise from the field itself. Like type 3
and unlike the static types 1 and 2, they are dynamic. Unlike type 3, the
dynamic properties arise not simply from the interaction of the component
organizations, but also from the field itself. The 'ground' is in motion.

Three trends contribute to the emergence of these dynamic field
forces:

1. The growth to meet type 3 conditions of organizations, and linked
   sets of organizations so large that their actions are both persistent
   and strong enough to induce autochthonous processes in the environment . . . .
2. The deepening interdependence between the economic and the other
   facets of the society. This means that economic organizations are
   increasingly enmeshed in legislation and public regulation.
3. The increasing reliance on research and development to achieve the
   capacity to meet competitive challenge . . . .

For organizations, these trends mean a gross increase in their area of
relevant uncertainty. The consequences which flow from their actions
lead off in ways that become increasingly unpredictable: they do not
necessarily fall off with distance, but may at any point be amplified
beyond all expectation; similarly, lines of action that are strongly pursued
may find themselves attenuated by emergent field forces . . . .

Values and Relevant Uncertainty

What becomes precarious under type 4 conditions is how organizational
stability can be achieved. In these environments individual organizations,

however large, cannot expect to adapt successfully simply through their own direct actions . . . . Nevertheless, there are some indications of a solution . . . . This is the emergence of values that have overriding significance for all members of the field. Social values are here regarded as coping mechanisms that make it possible to deal with persisting areas of relevant uncertainty. Unable to trace out the consequences of their actions, as these are amplified and resonated through their extended social fields, men in all societies have sought rules, sometimes categorical, such as the ten commandments, to provide them with a guide and ready calculus. Values are not strategies or tactics; as Lewin (1936) has pointed out, they have the conceptual character of 'power fields' and act as injunctions.

So far as effective values emerge, the character of richly joined turbulent fields changes in a most striking fashion. The relevance of large classes of events no longer has to be sought in an intricate mesh of diverging causal strands, but is given directly in the ethical code. By this transformation, a field is created which is no longer richly joined and turbulent but simplified and relatively static. Such a transformation will be regressive, or constructively adaptative, according to how far the emergent values adequately represent the new environmental requirements . . . .

Matrix Organization and Institutional Success

. . . turbulent fields demand some overall form of organization that is essentially different from the hierarchically structured forms to which we are accustomed. Whereas type 3 environments require one or other form of accommodation between like, but competitive, organizations whose fates are to a degree negatively correlated, turbulent environments require some relationship between dissimilar organizations whose fates are, basically, positively correlated. This means relationships that will maximise cooperation and which recognize that no one organization can take over the role of 'the other' and become paramount. We are inclined to speak of this type of relationship as an organizational matrix. Such a matrix acts in the first place by delimiting on value criteria the character of what may be included in the field specified—and therefore, who . . . . Professional associations provide one model of which there has been long experience . . . . The strategic objective [is that] . . . organizations become institutions through the embodiment of organizational values which relate them to the wider society. '. . . the executive becomes a statesman as he makes the transition from administrative management to institutional leadership' (Selzuick, 1957, p. 154).

The processes of strategic planning now also become modified. In so far as institutionalization becomes a prerequisite for stability, the determination of policy will necessitate not only a bias towards goals that are congruent with the organization's own character, but also a selection of goal-paths that offer maximum convergence as regards the interests of other parties . . . .

Such organizations arise from the need to meet problems emanating from type 4 environments. Unless this is recognized, they will only too easily be construed in type 3 terms, and attempts will be made to secure for them a degree of monolithic power that will be resisted overtly in democratic societies and covertly in others. In the one case they may be prevented from ever undertaking their missions; in the other one may wonder how long they can succeed in maintaining them.

An organizational matrix implies what McGregor (1960) has called Theory Y. This in turn implies a new set of values. But values are psychosocial commodities that come into existence only rather slowly. Very little systematic work has yet been done on the establishment of new systems of values, or on the type of criteria that might be adduced to allow their effectiveness to be empirically tested . . . in the large corporation or government establishment, it may well take some ten to fifteen years before the new type of group values . . . could permeate the total organization. For a new set to permeate a whole modern society, the time required must be much longer—at least a generation, according to the common saying . . . .

Managing an Open System

Arising from the nature of the enterprise as an open system, management is concerned with 'managing' both an internal system and an external environment. To regard an enterprise as a closed system and concentrate upon management of the 'internal enterprise' would be to expose the enterprise to the full impact of the vagaries of the environment.

If management is to control internal growth and development, it must in the first instance control the 'boundary conditions'—the forms of exchange between the enterprise and its environment. As we have seen, most enterprises are confronted with a multitude of actual and possible exchanges. If resources are not to be dissipated, the management must select from the alternatives a course of action. The causal texture of competitive environments is such that it is extremely difficult to survive on a simple strategy of selecting the best from among the alternatives immediately offered. Some that offer immediate gain lead nowhere, others lead to greater loss; some alternatives that offer loss are avoidable, others are unavoidable if long-run gains are to be made. The relative size of the immediate loss or gain is no sure guide as to what follows. Since the actions of an enterprise can also improve the alternatives that are presented to it, the optimum course is more likely to rest in selecting a strategic objective to be achieved in the long run. The strategic objective should be to place the enterprise in a position in its environment, where it has some assured conditions for growth ... . Achieving this position would be the *primary task* or overriding mission of the enterprise.

5.3 *Institution Building Theory for Use in Consultation*[4]

ROLF P. LYNTON AND JOHN M. THOMAS

. . . A review of current formulations reveals at least three major prerequisites for further development of the organization-environment framework in consultation:

1. One is a more objective focus on the environment in specific instances . . . specificity (is needed) in conceptualizing what is meant by environment (and) as to the nature and types of exchange and processes.

2. A useful organization-environment framework should attempt some integration of three key variables: the nature of the environment; internal structure and processes such as leadership, specific programmes and decision-making; and a concept of the organization's primary purpose [with] explicit focus on the organization's strategic goal.

3. A third prerequisite for a valid 'organization environment' framework is . . . a more specific 'exchange' typology . . . .

. . . two conditions which are increasingly common make a proactive stance of organizations, *vis-à-vis* their environment, particularly desirable. One is the high turbulence . . . in the environments of an increasing number of organizations. Increasingly, even the most powerful organizations have to come to 'terms with their environments' . . . . Even where power and active influence are most limited, a proactive stance can still increase the flow of information and support to the organization and so increase its ability to predict environmental conditions.

[4] From Dharni P. Sinha (ed.), *Consultants and Consulting Styles*, Vision Books, New Delhi, 1982, p. 83.

The second condition which makes a proactive stance important for an organization is high autonomy of the units in the environment on which the organization depends for its outputs or for its resources or for both. Here organizational success depends on 'outreach'. This is most obviously the case for service organizations, e.g., health systems and political organizations. Autonomies in the environment are especially high where the organization receives its funds from one source, e.g., the government, in order to deliver services to a third party, e.g., people in the slums; where the culture of the organization is sharply different from the culture of the people for whom the services are meant; and where intended recipients of outputs are unorganized. High autonomy also characterizes the organizational members of coordinating and inter-agency mechanisms and, less obviously but, importantly, innovate sub-systems within many kinds of organizations, including industrial ones.

. . . developing a self-evaluating organization in consultation is related to the desirability of maintaining organizational autonomy *vis-à-vis* the environment. And, in turn, this points to the significance of a diagnostic methodology which emphasizes the diverse resource and support ex-changes the organization must develop and manage. The institution-building theory is most useful for precisely this type of organization since it defines institutions as organizations with innovative purpose.

External Linkages

. . . the institution-building model distinguishes between linkages for different purposes: 'Enabling' linkages provide the institution with legit-imate authority to start and to operate, and to give it access to the funds and other support it needs. 'Functional' linkages provide for substantive exchanges with the environment. 'Normative' linkages deal with the establishment of standards in the institution and with its attempts to influence norms in the environment. 'Diffuse' linkages are for building widespread understanding and support for the institution . . . a fifth type of ('collegial') linkage provides at the institutional level what colleagueship does at the individual level, through exchanging experi-mental information and developing common strategies and common resources.

Beyond its use for overview and planning, the classification of linkages has practical values for the detailed designing, management, and evalu-ation of linkages. It facilitates checking existing linkages for appropriate-ness to purpose and for mutuality; both are required for effectiveness and stability of each linkage. Beyond this, if linkages are mapped and examined jointly, they reveal unattended or neglected relationships and other aspects of patterns important for institutional policy and planning. Such maps provide valuable data for decisions on institutional leadership, notably governance, internal structure, resource allocation, and operations.

5.4 *Limiting Factors Strategy*[5]

WILLIAM FOOTE WHYTE

The strategy of limiting factors intervention takes advantage of the principle that it is not necessary to eliminate all limiting factors before starting an action program. Overcoming obstacles builds momentum so that the field of forces at later stages may be markedly changed from when the program was begun.

Limiting factors are not fixed elements in the environment. They vary according to the situation the change agent is trying to affect, and according to resources (including information) with which he has to work. Therefore, the first task is to make a diagnosis to determine whether, with the resources the change agent has at his command and might be able to mobilize in later stages of the program, there is a good probability of success. If the diagnosis leads to a favorable conclusion, the next step is to identify the immediate limiting factors that could prevent the program from getting started and developing some early momentum. As the change agent acts against the first limiting factors, he should think of the limiting factors he will face farther down the road, so that he and his program participants are not surprised by these obstacles and are ready to cope with them.

Multi-objective planning translates into social theory certain ideas of economists and city and regional planners. While economists have given more attention to the analysis of scarcity, comparing objectives in terms of trade-offs and opportunity costs, they also recognize 'externalities' (Samuelson, 1967): the additional valuable outcomes produced in carrying out a project aimed at one principal objective. City and regional planners necessarily must think in terms of more than one objective (Haith and Loucks, 1973), but often their analysis involves estimating how much of one objective must be sacrificed to reach another or how much additional cost must be incurred to reach both objectives.

[5] From William Foote Whyte, 'Potatoe Peasants and Professors: A Development Strategy for Peru', *Sociological Practice*, Vol. 2, No. 1, 1977, pp. 20–23.

Sociologists in the past, backed into this problem through considering 'latent functions' (Merton, 1949) and 'unanticipated consequences of purposive social action' (Merton, 1936) but without drawing the action implications from such notions. Now, if sociologists are so smart in finding these latent functions and unanticipated consequences in the actions of other people, why cannot we apply this same analysis, in advance, to the actions we ourselves plan to take? In other words, why cannot we plan so as to make the latent functions explicit and to make intentional the otherwise unanticipated consequences? . . .

5.5 Needs Assessment[6]

JOE THOMAS

. . . needs assessments are not being performed appropriately. They tend to be performed on a periodic, program-oriented, 'crisis management' basis, with little attempt to coordinate the assessment with other organizational activities. Blake and Mouton (1980) have stated that 'responding to felt needs rather than real needs might be the number one problem facing HRD professionals today'.

. . . Individuals who conduct needs assessment often tend to reduce the scope of their assessment by looking only at a limited number of sources of information and by using only one or two favorite techniques for collecting and analyzing the data. In a typical assessment program, the program designer meets with the department manager and they determine that the supervisors seem to be having trouble explaining the new cost-control system to their subordinates. They agree that it looks like a communication problem and that a communication program would probably be useful.

This scenario may be oversimplified, but it does illustrate three common pitfalls in diagnosing program needs. First, the source of information about the need for a program is limited—in this case, the source is the department head and program planner's perception of the problem. Other sources of information could have been explored. Second, the interview was the only technique that was used to diagnose the problem. Again, other techniques such as questionnaires, observation, and critical incidents may have been more appropriate. Finally,

[6] From J. William Pfeiffer and Leonard D. Goodstein (eds.), *The 1984 Annual for Facilitators, Trainers and Consultants*, University Associates, San Diego, CA, 1984, pp. 195–205.

the decision was made by only the two individuals. Other means of data analysis obviously could have been helpful . . . .

Sources of Information

A needs assessment is conducted to determine the extent of a specific organizational problem and to design a program to resolve that specific concern. The first step of the program designer is to try to acquire an understanding of the problem. This understanding usually is achieved by collecting information. Individuals, groups, public sources, and organizational records all are potential sources of information, as shown in Figure 8.

Figure 8: Sources of Data

Individuals	Internal sources External sources
Groups	Committees Constituents
Public Sources	Government publications Trade associations Indexes Business services Public statements
Organizational Records	Company reports Performance records Task analyses

Data-Collection Techniques

The next problem faced by the diagnostician is to determine how to collect the needed data from the various sources available. Many methods can be used. Some of them require the involvement of individuals or groups. Others such as observation and review of existing data require less direct involvement. Figure 9 is a partial listing of techniques for collecting information . . . .

Figure 9: Data-Collection Techniques

Individually-Oriented Methods	Interviews Questionnaires Tests
Group-Oriented Methods	Sensing interviews Committees Delphi technique Nominal-group technique Brainstorming
Observation	Systematic observation Complete observation Participant observation
Review of Existing Data	Sensitivity Originality

Data Analysis

After the sources of needed information are identified and the data collected, it is necessary to analyze and interpret the data. The procedures that are frequently used include some form of gap analysis, scaling methods, weighting formulas, and consensus. These procedures can be used to analyze data collected by a variety of techniques and more than one procedure can be used to analyze a group of data. These techniques are listed in Figure 10.

Figure 10: Methods of Data Analysis

Gap Analysis

Scaling Methods: Rating scales
       Rankings
       Nominal-group technique

Weighting Formulas
Consensus: Voting   Compromise

. . . The three dimensions of needs assessment indicate an ongoing, systematic process. The accuracy of the needs assessment will be improved if all three elements of the diagnostic process are considered simultaneously.

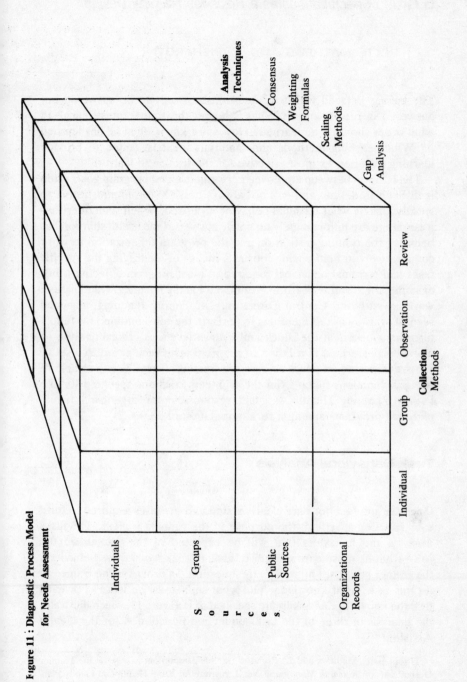

Figure 11 : Diagnostic Process Model for Needs Assessment

5.6 *Job Specifications as a Basis for Training Design*[7]

BETTY MATHEWS AND K. PISHAROTI

The trainer is faced with four questions not only to be answered but answered in precise order: What is it that the trainee must learn? In what order should it be learned?. How will I know when he has learned it? What teaching methods and materials are best suited to provide learning experiences most effective for the trainee to learn it?

The relation between employee performance and program goals often is difficult to define, and it is not always possible for administrators to specify exactly what terminal behavior is desired. When such questions arise, there are unfortunately no magic answers. One useful solution has been for the training institution and the program organization to work cooperatively in field testing jobs as a means of identifying the specific tasks and terminal behaviors required to meet program objectives. For example, the Institute of Rural Health and Family Planning, Gandhigram, working with the Central Directorate of Family Planning, assigned several of its own staff members to perform the roles outlined for family planning workers at the Block and Village levels. A critical analysis of activities performed in relation to program achievement led to a set of job specifications on which to base job training. Figure 12 is a sample of two job functions taken from the eighteen functions specified for the Family Planning Health Assistant responsible for organizing family planning programs among a rural population of 20,000.

Task Behavioral Analysis

Once the job functions are clearly stated and the tasks required to fulfil each function specified, the purpose of the training is clear. The tasks describe the behaviors that will be expected of the trainee on the job—what he must learn to do. To further break down these behaviors, the trainer addresses himself to the question: In order for the trainee to do this task, what knowledge and what skills must he learn? For each task the knowledge and skills are specified as in Figure 13, which illustrates the analysis of three of the tasks under job Function A for the Health Assistant.

[7] From Betty Mathews and K. Pisharoti, in 'Job Description as a Basis for Training Design', *Action Research Monograph No. 2*, Institute of Rural Health and Family Planning, Gandhigram, India, 1966, pp. 208–14.

Figure 12
*Example of Two Functions Taken from Job Specification of Health
Assistant, Family Planning*

Job Functions	Specific Tasks
A. Make a general survey of each village chosen for initiating the Family Planning Program including a village map, study of social structure and group relationships.	1. Visit the village to meet concerned leaders and explain the activities he wishes to carry out in the village.
	2. Collect information from leaders and officials, re-number of households, location of caste groups, relations between castes, vital statistics for village for the previous year.
	3. Prepare outline map of village showing important landmarks, streets, numbers of houses, caste groupings and their relationships, *panchayat* leaders' houses, other leaders.
B. Identify health and family planning leaders in the program village.	1. Select every tenth house and interview the male spouse using a standard interview schedule.
	2. Help the Auxiliary Nurse Midwife to select another sample of every tenth house to interview a female spouse with the same schedule.
	3. Interview each person named by respondents as a leader to health and family planning to ascertain his willingness to serve on a family planning committee.
	4. Conduct a group meeting of those accepting the leader role to fix a time and place for a one-day training camp.

Organizing the Data for Learning Purposes

From the job description for any one worker, there may be as many as two or three hundred separate tasks specified and five to ten times as many specifications of the knowledge and skills to be taught. From these specifications, the trainer knows what the trainee must be taught. He wants to organize these data into a pattern that will be most meaningfully related to the learning process. To do this, he needs to analyze again the job functions and tasks to determine whether the tasks are performed in a sequential chain, that is, are all the tasks for Function A to be

Figure 13
Job Function A—Knowledge and Skill Specifications

Tasks	Knowledge	Skills
1. Visit the village to meet the concerned leaders and explain the activities he wishes to carry out.	The specific activities that are to be explained, how they are to be carried out.	How to explain his role and the activities in a way that enlists the interests and cooperation of the leaders.
	Methods for finding out who are the concerned village leaders.	How to approach village leaders and what to say.
2. Collect information from leaders and officials and records { About number of households, caste groups, and group relations.	Method of preparing interview plan. Types of relationships between caste groups and their indicators. What officials to contact.	How to interview individuals of groups for general information. How to elicit indicators of caste relationships.
{ About vital statistics for previous year.	What vital events are needed.	How to work with a village registrar, how to read, and how to record, needed data.
3. Prepare outline map of village showing streets, numbers of houses, caste groupings caste relationships, locations of *panchayat* leaders and other leaders.	Why a map is needed, and how it can be used as a tool in getting job done.	How to tour a village to draw outline map and mark relevant data.

performed before the tasks for Function B can be performed? In the Illustration of the Health Assistant job, the tasks do form a sequential chain of events to be repeated by the worker for each new program village. With such a chaining pattern built into the job itself, the trainer need only order the knowledge and skills for each task . . . .

As jobs become more complex, however, less chaining of tasks occurs. For example, the tasks of a shop foreman, who supervises a number of workers, serves as technical expert and as liaison with upper management, will have much less chaining than the tasks performed by a lathe operator. When the tasks defined for a particular job have only minimal chaining, the trainer, in order to transpose the data into teaching-learning experiences more effectively, may need to impose an order on them. For this purpose, the knowledge and skills themselves can serve as a basis for organizing the data into subject blocks. That is, all the tasks, knowledge, and skills that relate to community education and working with community groups are grouped together in one block . . . .

Grouping the tasks, knowledge, and skills by subject areas, however, does create a new set of problems for the trainer. First of all, the total job, although it may lend itself to subject groupings, is to be performed by the graduated trainee as an integrated whole. Ultimately, he will be required to use technical skills and knowledge, supervisory skills and knowledge, problem-diagnosis and problem-solving skills together, in a single event. Although to teach specific knowledge and skills may require this temporary separation of functions, the training design needs to specify how these separately taught areas are to be reintegrated. Some ways of doing this include (*a*) close team work and coordination by trainers teaching different areas so that students are guided to relate these different subject areas to the same practical problems day by day; (*b*) case problem analysis involving the multiple dimensions found on the job; and (*c*) field practice in the real job situation followed by review sessions.

Framing the Objectives

To address himself to the question of how to know when the trainee has learned, the trainer needs to think in terms of the required terminal behaviors to be expected from the trainees. To be useful, an objective must specify what the learner is doing when he demonstrates that he has learned, that is, the terminal behavior that is to be observed and measured. Also, the objective must specify the minimum level of performance that is acceptable evidence of learning . . . .

Such specifications of the expected outcomes of teaching and learning are not as difficult at it might seem at first because the job-task for which the knowledge and skills are to be learned has already been specified and serves as a focus for the learning objectives. For example, the objectives for Task 1 in Figure 13 might look something like this:

> To be able to write a description of all the activities for making a village survey (that appear on the study-discussion list) in the order in which they are to be performed.

The terminal behavior is specified as, *to write a description of all the activities for making a village survey*, is a specification of the content area; the words *all*, and *in the order in which they are to be performed*, is a statement of the minimum level of acceptable performance and, finally, the conditions under which the performance is to be carried out are indicated by the identification of a particular *study-discussion list*. This objective, then, may be said to meet the criteria for framing an objective, but is it adequate to fulfil the requirements of Task 1? Further examination of the task, the knowledge, and skills required suggests that at least two additional objectives are needed:

> To be able to describe orally these activities that are to be carried out in a village in a classroom setting simulating the village situation (role playing) so that the listeners feel that they want to cooperate.

> To be able to describe orally these activities to village leaders in the field and actually gain evidence of their support and cooperation for carrying out the activities in their village.

These three objectives lead the trainee step by step in the learning process so that by the time he carries out the third objective, he has demonstrated his ability to perform that task successfully in terms of a performance standard.

The Training Design

. . . To complete the training design, one further operation is usually required. The trainer may find, as he reviews all of the learning experiences for a chaining job, that some rearrangement of their order is required to adapt them to local conditions. For example, rather than sending the student for field practice in relation to each task, he may want to group a number of tasks together for field practice to prevent fragmenting the field program itself. When the trainee carries out the third objective under actual job conditions, perhaps he should be able also to begin carrying out the survey activities and involve the village leaders in this process. If so, then the trainer would schedule all the classroom experiences first, to be followed by a block of time for all the field practice experiences related to a series of tasks. Whatever the rearrangement, it will depend directly upon the action program operations carried out by the training institution and the variety of field laboratories it has developed or is able to develop in cooperation with the organization requesting job training.

For job specifications with minimal chaining, it will be recalled that the tasks, knowledge, and skills were grouped into subject blocks . . .

being prepared requires him to conduct a village community survey that involves study of community sanitation, family planning, health knowledge, and attitudes of people and the social interaction of the community as well as survey technique . . . . The trainer . . . has the task of ordering the learning events to a calendar of time in such a way that the trainee has the opportunities to learn the knowledge and skills from each subject block that are relevant to a given task before he is required to demonstrate his mastery of that task.

With the learning experience organized in a timetable that makes the best use of the training institution's resources, the trainer has before him a training design that answers the four questions (in the first paragraph).

This may seem, at first, to be a rather difficult and complex process for answering these questions. It is difficult! Training is difficult and demands the highest quality of skill and effort from trainers if it is to be freed from the elements of chance and waste. And training is costly! . . .

Training is successful only to the extent that trainees are provided opportunities for learning that are relevant to the tasks they are expected to perform on the job. To plan for less is to plan for waste!

5.7 *A Laboratory Strategy*[8]

LELAND P. BRADFORD

A training approach directed toward bringing about desirable changes in the way people work and relate to others must analyze five major areas. These are:

1. The aspects of individual learning necessary for change in the total individual.
2. The optimum condition under which change can be encouraged—the training plan.
3. The psychological atmosphere conducive to change.
4. The ways of handling the personal problems arising from efforts to change.
5. The support necessary to enable the individual to maintain the change.

[8] From Leland P. Bradford, 'Human Relations Training', a Paper Partially Based on *Explorations in Human Relations Training*, Washington, D.C., National Training Laboratories, 1954, pp. 54–59.

The Training Design

The training plan or design which can reach this target requires certain basic parts.

1. Opportunity to interact with others in a training group and to analyse the experience and gain insight into oneself and others.
2. Opportunity to gain an awareness of inadequacy and of the potentiality for improvement.
3. Opportunity to hypothesize about the consequences and effectiveness of new behavior and to test out the hypotheses in practice.
4. Opportunity to practice new skills until security in their use is gained.
5. Opportunity to foresee backhome resistances to new behavior and to plan and develop ways of overcoming such resistances and of maintaining the new behavior after it has been learned.

These conditions essentially add up to the following requirements for training:

1. Creating experience centered training groups in which curriculum content is derived from the behavior of the members. Essentially a feedback system is established in which the individuals and the group as a whole are collecting information about their own behavior in relation to their goals, bringing the information as input to create changes in the manner and direction of output.

   Methods of appropriate and adequate observation and collection of perceptions and feelings, as well as methods of feeding back data so they will be received and not resisted, should comprise some of the skills of the trainer.
2. Creating opportunities for the individual to test out hypotheses about changed behavior. The two basic principles of feedback and experimentation are adapted in a variety of ways to make up a training program.

Action and interaction, analysis, hypothesizing, testing and practicing, compose an effective training program in human relations. Lectures, research reports, films, demonstrations provide the cognitive basis to provide more meaning and direction to experientiai learning.

Two additional aspects of an effective training program are needed. Because much of leadership and membership in all areas of life—the workplace, the trade union, the social organization and the home—takes place in group processes, group methods are needed. These can only be learned through participation in group situations under training conditions and analysis of the group experiences.

Secondly, the training group, if it has been helped to develop strength and sensitivity, can help its members along the rough and sometimes painful road of change.

Change, whether in behavior or in related knowledge or attitudes, does not usually come easily if the change has any depth or importance for the individual. New ideas and attitudes frequently upset old ideas and attitudes that had comfortably 'explained' situations. The acceptance of new ideas and attitudes usually requires a reorganization of other ideas and attitudes and implies different approaches to planning and executing. Change in behavior is usually even more difficult, particularly in relationships among people. Change in behavior means that the individual will appear different from that which he has appeared to be to other people and this implies a host of anxieties the individual may have about the consequences of his being seen as different. He may not be successful. He may lose status with others, or may suffer ridicule. All of these factors may lower readiness for learning and change on the part of the individual.

Group influences can be strong in helping individuals develop readiness (overcome resistance) to learning and change. If the group is attractive to the individual, it can exert pressures on him to change as the other members of the group are changing. The fact that other group members face the same problems for which change is needed is comforting and reassuring. There is a lessening of feeling of guilt for having a problem and for needing to change old ways in order to solve it.

An Atmosphere Conducive to Change

. . . The task of creating a permissive atmosphere is not an easy one. Certainly, permissiveness is not created by passivity, but by sensitive action upon the part of leaders. Permissiveness is not the same as laissez faire leadership in which leadership is abdicated.

In developing an atmosphere of permissiveness, the training leaders attempt to accomplish the following aims:

1. To create an awareness of the similarity of the problems facing individual group members. A problem census collected by going around the table, or by sub-groups of two or three, exploring problems among themselves and reporting them to the group is a means of discovering similarity among problems.

2. To relate these problems to the set of forces producing them, including the actions of the individual trainee. However, when the trainee sees his behavior as only one among many forces, he may tend to have reduced feelings of guilt and defensiveness.
3. To prevent, in early stages of discussion, quick answers or judgements from others about the importance of any individual's problems.
4. To prevent interpersonal attacks under the guise of discussion of the problems, and efforts to gain status through lowering the position of others by ridiculing their problems.
5. To establish objective methods of examining problems such as role-playing, careful examination of the problem as a case study, etc.
6. To develop group concern for each individual and emotional support for the group member in the process of change. As the training leaders, in continuous interpretation of the process of the group, relate members' behavior to what the group is really requiring in terms of needed roles, there comes a greater tendency for the entire group to be concerned with each person and to provide support and reinforcement to him.

5.8 *Programmed Instruction*[9]

H. OLIVER HOLT

. . . Four characteristics are typical:

Small steps—The subject matter is broken down into a large number of small steps organized into an instructional sequence. The student masters these steps one at a time.

Continued responding—As he works through the program the learner responds to each step and in most cases either fills in blanks with missing words or makes a choice among given alternatives.

Immediate knowledge of results—Programmed books and teaching machines are designed so that the learner can turn a page, move a slide or turn a knob and know immediately whether the response he has just made is correct.

Self-pacing—Each learner works with his own book or machine and

[9] From H. Oliver Holt, 'Programmed Self-instruction', *Bell Telephone Magazine*, USA, 1973 (Spring), pp. 168–72.

works through the program at his own pace. As a result of this, the teaching environment is quite different from the usual classroom situation . . . .

Some Advantages

There are several important interacting advantages of programmed instruction.

One advantage is the flexibility this allows both the learner and the course administrator. Individuals often can work through programs in their own offices, thus accomplishing two things: they save travel and living expenses which would be necessary if they went away to school; they can work on their program part-time, without total disruption of their jobs . . . .

In addition, some Plant Department schools have found it advantageous to suspend rigid scheduling of their basic . . . courses since the use of programmed textbooks has been introduced. Each trainee now stays in school only as long as it takes him to demonstrate his proficiency in the subject matter. He then goes back to his job immediately, without waiting for the rest of the group. In addition, since students do not learn together, there is no need for them to begin together . . . .

Self-pacing and individual learning also constitute major reasons given by trainees for preferring programmed self-instruction to more conventional methods. It offers advantages to both slow and fast learners. Slow learners, who may drop farther and farther behind in the conventional class, have the extra time they need to grasp the elements of the subject. Faster students, often bored or even frustrated by the slow pace of typical group instruction, retain their interest by progressing quickly through the material in the course . . . .

Uniform Quality

. . . several advantages of programmed self-instruction . . . fall under the category of 'quality control'. Under conventional lecture-discussion conditions . . . there can be no assurance that one is getting a high quality product across several lecture-discussion classes.

The situation is quite different with a properly developed self-instruction program. In the first place, the standard procedure for producing a high quality product is to 'cut and try' a program throughout its development.

Specifically, this means that it is subjected to empirical trials on sample groups of the trainees for which it is intended. It is tested and revised as many times as necessary to make it meet training objectives. The final product, then, not only has been demonstrated to be effective, but remains constant. That is, all students who take a particular programmed course take the same course . . . .

Evidence of one type of quality is offered by several research studies. These studies report a higher homogeneity of final examination scores than is the case with conventional instruction. That is, scores are clustered toward the high end of the scale and there are few, if any, failing students (see Figure 14).

Figure 14 : Performance in Lecture Discussion and Programmed Instruction Groups

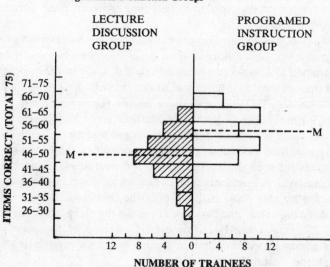

Popular articles about programmed study often promise spectacular savings in time. Certainly, there are many occasions when a great deal of time is saved, but these do not, by any means, always occur. A programmed course may, in fact, take as much time or more than its conventional counterpart . . . .

Some Limitations

While programmed instruction has substantial advantages, it also has several limitations which must be considered:

An appropriate program is hard to find. There are many programs on the market, but they are primarily academically, not industrially, oriented.

A good program—one that does an efficient teaching job—is difficult to identify . . . .

Program writing is also time-consuming and often requires the efforts of several people to produce an extensive program . . . it takes four kinds of knowledge and skill: program development methods, knowledge of the subject matter, frame writing, and technical and copy editing.

Good programs are expensive . . . . There are several other conditions which might limit the use of this method. For example, when the subject matter is so unstable that continual expensive revisions would be necessary; when there are so few students that the expense of a program may not be justified; when the self-pacing characteristic cannot be exploited and may, in fact, be detrimental.

5.9 *Competency-based Curricula*[10]

WALTER C. McGAGHIE, G.E. MILLER, A.W. SAKOD AND T.V. TELDER

Medical education that is competency-based differs from the subject-centred and the integrated course models in three fundamental ways. First, such a curriculum is organized around functions (or competencies) required for the practice of medicine in a specified setting. Secondly, it is grounded in the empirically validated principle that students of the intellectual quality found in medical schools, when given appropriate instruction, can all master the prescribed basic performance objectives. Thirdly, it views education as an experiment where both the processes of student learning and the techniques used to produce learning are regarded as hypotheses subject to testing. The intended output of a competency-based programme is a health professional who can practise medicine at a defined level of proficiency, in accordance with local conditions, to meet local needs . . . .

. . . The principles of learning for mastery, i.e., entry-level testing, stepwise instruction, flexible time scheduling, and frequent assessment, describe the operational characteristics of the competency-based curriculum model, which leads to cumulative learning along a continuum of increasing medical sophistication. A frequent bonus in such a system is

---

[10] From W.C. McGaghie, G.E. Miller, A.W. Sakod, and T.V. Telder, *Competency-based Curriculum Development in Medical Education*, WHO, Geneva, 1978, pp. 18–21 and 90–91.

that the rate of learning accelerates as the student's experience grows, thus reducing the time needed to achieve programme goals. For example, when a combination of clinical problems, independent study, audiovisual materials and computer-based mastery testing was used . . . one group of medical students was able to satisfy basic science requirements, usually achieved after two years, in only one year.

Defining professional competence is the cornerstone upon which a competency-based programme of medical education is built. Unless this task is approached both thoughtfully and systematically, the medical curriculum is more likely to be a reflection of faculty interests than of student and public needs . . . .

General Considerations in Defining Competence

The desirable attributes of a health professional, whether physician or nurse or basic medical scientist, are determined by many influences. Expert opinion, the practice setting, the types of patients or the health care problems to be encountered, the nature of a discipline or a speciality, the stage of socio-economic development of a community or nation (present as well as future), all deserve consideration. In reaching a decision about the competence goals for a specific curriculum, planners may examine all or select only a few of these essential determinants, depending upon the type of health professional being trained, the curriculum level, or simply the time and resources available. Whatever sources are employed, the primary consideration in planning must always be the nature of the professional role a graduate must play, not merely the information that faculty experts are most comfortable in teaching . . . .

Those who endorse the assumptions and purposes of competency-based education, must also recognize that implementation will alter the usual modes of institutional operation. Educational activities, record-keeping systems, and time schedules may all have to change, but the most significant modification will be those of faculty and student attitudes and practices, which must shift in a manner that emphasizes learning rather than teaching. Such changes are not easy to bring about. One prominent student of organizational development has said that 'trying to reorganize a university is like trying to reorganize a graveyard'. . . . even those curriculum changes that show great initial promise are often abandoned after a few years, largely because of the institution's failure to make those changes in its structure and functioning that will support and promote, rather than oppose, a dynamic process of curriculum development.

If it is to be lasting, educational change must be regarded as a continuous process of institutional and professional renewal. It has no discernible end-point. It grants tentative acceptance to today's innovations while being committed to improvement tomorrow. It is experimental in the true sense, regarding approaches to learning and teaching, even those that have won long acceptance, as hypotheses worthy of testing rather than as empirical laws . . . .

The Teacher

. . . three new roles for teachers can be identified. The first is that of planner, probably the most difficult and time-consuming of the functions which must be embraced if a competency-based curriculum is to be successful. Teachers have always been expected to plan their instruction, and often spend long hours doing so. It is not the quantity but the character of the effort which must change.

. . . In a programme directed at mastery of defined competencies, time becomes a variable that will be determined by individual progress toward the goals; and content, in the sense of subject matter courses, must be replaced by a system of organization that focuses on professional problems whose solution depends on knowledge and skills derived from many disciplines . . . .

The second new role is that of manager of instructional resources. The usual course outlines, which identify lecture topics, reading assignments, laboratory exercises or clinical experience for all students, are incomplete in a competency-based programme. In such a curriculum, it is essential to list the specific competency objectives, to indicate the alternative learning resources that are available to assist students toward those objectives, and to define the assessment procedures that can be used to determine individual progress. There must also be an indication of specific time periods when teachers are available to assist individual students or groups in surmounting whatever learning problems they may encounter. In these meetings, the teacher's task is to encourage and not to dominate, to guide rather than to tell, to suggest sources rather than to provide directly all the knowledge students must acquire.

The third role is that of evaluator. The skill with which this function is carried out will probably be a major determinant of programme success . . . teachers genuinely concerned with helping [students] to assess their own progress toward defined competency goals, no matter what learning path is chosen, and without communicating judgement but merely identifying the nature of that progress, independence and personal responsibility for learning, without which a mastery-based system cannot succeed, will be nurtured.

These new roles are not easy for teachers to adopt when they have themselves been educated in a more conventional way and have developed a style of teaching that is comfortable, as well as consistent with a personal percer'ion of professional responsibility. Yet such personal perceptions are rarely uniform within any medical school . . . .

The Student

. . . One necessary change is . . . a willingness to join with teachers in thoughtful discussion about learning objectives and instructional strategies. Just as the teaching staff must use new sources to determine educational goals that are consistent with community needs, so must students learn that their personal opinions must be replaced by systematic delineation of the competencies to be acquired. Demands for a stronger voice in planning will probably produce a favourable response from teachers only when students show willingness to engage in a disciplined examination of alternatives, not merely emotional espousal of beliefs.

5.10 *The Instructional Process*[11]

STEPHEN M. COREY

In as much as this paper is intended to bring to bear on teaching and the teaching process a scientific and disciplined rather than a literary point of view, I want at the outset to suggest this operational definition of instruction: Instruction is the deliberate manipulation of the environment of an individual in order to get him to emit or engage in specified behavior in response to specified situations.

The first implication of this definition is in the word 'deliberate'. Instruction is neither whimsical nor accidental. Instruction is a planned activity. The quality of the planning may leave much to be desired in that the consequences of the instructional plan may not materialize. It is my view, nevertheless, that by being deliberate, instruction requires some plan, some strategy, some design. Not all activity that might be referred to as teaching is deliberate in this sense. Some teaching involves

[11] From Stephen M. Corey, *Programmed Instruction*, the 1967 Yearbook of the National Society for the Study of Education, 1967, pp. 215–24.

providing the learner with a very lush environment (a long bibliography?). What he chooses to learn is up to him.

The second cluster of implications is in the phrase 'manipulation of the environment'. These manipulations may and actually do become extremely various. The learner may be talked to, requested to read, requested to listen, asked to do things with apparatus, to move objects, to look at pictures, or to go some place to observe things and events. All of these represent planned or deliberate manipulations of the learner's environment in our sense. The assumption is, of course, that these environmental manipulations are attended to, or better, responded to, by the learner. The lecture must be heard, the pictures seen, the directions followed, and so on. Taking such responding for granted rather than attempting to determine its actuality is a common cause of unsuccessful instruction. The instructor may manipulate what he thinks is the learner's environment. He may speak and gesture and demonstrate and give directions, but unless the learner responds, there is no telling whether or not it is his environment, in contrast with an environment that has been manipulated.

The third implication, and one that may not be at all obvious, is the separation this definition of instruction suggests between curriculum planning and the process of instruction. Curriculum planning is the process whereby the ultimate behaviors to be taught are established. Instruction is the process whereby the learning of these behaviors is facilitated. Curriculum planning is replete with value judgements of a philosophical type. It is this curricular planning that results in decisions that various populations at various times should be taught to appreciate certain kinds of literature, to master accounting skills, to spell conventionally, to understand national history, and so on. The process of instruction starts with the 'givens', preferably stated as behaviors rather than as vague aspirations, and develops programs that are designed to achieve them. This means several things to me. First, it suggests that instruction is empirical in that its effects must be determined and these effects used to improve the process that generated them. Second, like any distinction between ends and means, separating curriculum planning as the process of determining educational ends or objectives from instruction as the process of achieving these objectives or ends, cannot be carried to extreme lengths. Ends and means are in general too interdependent to warrant more than a separation of convenience for conceptualizing. It probably should be noted here that differentiating between curriculum planning and instruction, with almost exclusive attention to the latter, leaves the bases for curricular decisions unattended to. These decisions are, of course, of great importance in the development of any course of study or program of courses.

The final implication of this definition of instruction is that the consequences of instruction must be known, must be observable, for the process to continue and to become more effective. The planning of instruction is based upon the prediction, often unformulated, that certain types of manipulations of the learner's environment will have certain effects upon him as manifested by his behavior. These 'hypotheses' can only be confirmed by observing whether the anticipated consequences of the instruction actually result from it. This means, to me, that whatever is intended to result from an instructional plan must be observable to those who planned and/or implemented the instruction. If the consequences of instruction are not observable, it is impossible to establish any 'cause and effect' relationship between instruction and learning. In order that these consequences of instruction be observable, they must be described as behaviors or the products or behaviors—something that is written, recorded, constructed, etc. No instructor has access to the mind of the learner. The only consequence of his instruction he can observe is what the learner does.

Given the above definition of instruction and its implications, I now turn to a consideration of the several activities that seem to me to constitute instruction. The contention is that any instance of instruction involves making a choice among alternative activities in respect to each of a sequence of identifiable operations. The quality of these decisions determines the efficiency of instruction. While instructional efficiency is not often made the explicit focus of attention in any type of institutionalized instruction, some efficiency considerations seem to me always to be implied. Admittedly these considerations are more often implicit than explicit, but I can remember no instances of a deliberate choice on the part of instructors to employ the less efficient of alternative instructional procedures each of which is judged to be generally effective in reaching stipulated objectives. Time seems always to be a factor in instruction as it is in life. If the same things can be accomplished in less rather than more time, the former is chosen. This assumes, of course, that efficiency data of some appreciable degree of reliability and validity are at hand. Such is often, or even usually, not the case in instruction. Strong opinions are held regarding the consequences of this or that instructional procedure, but the bases for the opinions are rarely verifiable.

My reason for commenting below and at such length on the several aspects of instruction is the belief that an analytical approach to the process may provide a useful conceptual framework for describing and evaluating specific instances or specific programs of instruction, irrespective of their purposes or auspices. It is quite likely that the extent of my analysis would try the patience of the practitioner whose work assignments, so far as the planning of instruction is concerned, have been based upon traditional and common sense notions of what is involved.

Seven Tasks

Developing or planning instruction requires that the instructor, or as may more often be the case, the several persons responsible for the instruction, accomplish a number of separate tasks. While these tasks generally come in a roughly predictable sequence, there are many interactions. This point is elaborated later. I want now, however, to describe the several things that anyone responsible for instruction must do.

(a) He must describe (i) the behaviors intended to be the ultimate outcomes or objectives of the instruction as well as (ii) the situations or stimuli to which these behaviors are considered to be appropriate responses. The ultimate behaviors or ultimate instructional objectives are, as I have said, the result of decisions made by curriculum planners in contrast with instructional planners. The behaviors described as the intended outcomes of instruction might be verbal or nonverbal or a combination. I am thinking of nonverbal or sensorimotor behavior as that which operates directly on the environment in some fashion. An illustration of a symbolic instructional objective for a very limited instance of instruction might be: 'Says "Christopher Columbus" in response to the oral question (auditory stimulus)': 'What person subsidized by Spain is generally believed to have discovered America?' An illustration of a nonsymbolic or sensorimotor instructional objective might be, 'Adjusts the lathe to a tolerance of .008 inch when directed to do so by his supervisor'.

Several points may need emphasis here in connection with any description of the terminal behaviors that define the purpose of an instance of instruction. First, it is not sufficient, although it is certainly necessary, for the persons planning and/or implementing the instruction to be the only ones who are clear and explicit regarding its intended outcomes. It is important, too, for the learners to be clear and explicit in their understanding of the behavior the instruction is planned to get under their control. Few instances of academic instruction are planned to get under their control. Few instances of academic instruction designed to result in modification of verbal behavior, pay much attention to acquainting the learner with the ultimate behaviors the instruction is designed to result in.

A second implication of the 'terminal behavior description' aspect of instruction is that the situations to which these behaviors are judged to be appropriate responses, must also be specified. For a pupil to behave by saying 'Christopher Columbus', for example, in response to the stimulus, 'Whom do Americans often call the Father of their country' would not be acceptable.

The third point needing emphasis in regard to stating instructional objectives as behavior is that there must be some indication of the minimum quality of this behavior that will be accepted as evidence of successful instruction. This designation of quality, or standard of acceptability, would be included, of course, if the description of the instructional objective were sufficiently complete. Usually, however, it is not. For example, this statement of an objective for instruction in shorthand is not adequate in this respect:

Translates oral speech into shorthand symbols and subsequently reconstructs the speech by translating the symbols orally.

This statement is better:

Translates 30 minutes of nontechnical speech delivered from manuscript at an average rate of 100 words per minute into shorthand symbols and subsequently reconstructs the speech without error so that it conforms to the original MS.

Finally, these instructional objectives must be so stated and described as to make it possible to get evidence of their existence [see item (c) below]. In other words, whatever it is that the instruction is intended to accomplish must be observable.

(b) He must identify and describe the characteristics of the population to be instructed. For efficient instruction, these characteristics often need to be stated in considerable detail and may involve a range of conditions and behaviors. A specified chronological age might be one condition for admission to a particular instructional situation. An illustration of a more academic behavior that might be stipulated for the population to be instructed is, 'Has mastered the multiplication tables through 15'. What I am referring to here is the need to make clear the assumptions an instructor makes about what the persons to be instructed must already know that is relevant to the instructional objectives or what physical conditions they must meet. These 'entering' behaviors or characteristics must be present before the individual 'enters' the instructional system or instance of instruction being planned. These 'entering' behaviors or conditions represent those components or aspects of the terminal behaviors (terminal objectives) that have resulted from a disciplined behavioral analysis of these objectives but will not be taught.

One important aspect of the establishment and description of the behaviors and conditions that should be obtained, in respect to the population to be instructed before instruction as such starts, has to do with the learner's readiness to do what the instructional plan demands of him. These demands—that he put forth effort to attend, to read, to listen, to respond, to manipulate objects, and so on—as they are assumed in any program of instruction are often incompatible with the learners' actual readiness or willingness to engage in such activities. When this appears to be the case, those who have planned the instruction generally blame the learner for his limitations. They rarely view their own instructional plans as being at fault.

Describing the requisite conditions and characteristics of the population for which the instruction has been designed, is, of course, closely related to the formulation of terminal objectives or behaviors. The latter must be considered in relation to the population that will acquire them.

(c) He must construct a terminal test for determining whether or not the terminal behaviour representing the instructional objectives can be engaged in at the specified level of quality and in response to the appropriate situations or stimuli. The responses to the terminal test are the evidence that the person instructed has under his control the behaviors the instruction was designed to teach. The construction of a good terminal test is usually a major task. First, and of extreme importance, it must be valid in the sense that the behavior required to cope with the test successfully is the same behavior the instruction was designed to teach. If instruction has been designed, for example, to teach the correct spelling of words a learner chooses in order to express his own ideas in an essay, and the terminal tests consists of spelling words dictated by the teacher, the test may not be valid. The reason is that the test was not constructed so as to determine the existence of the behaviors the instruction was designed to teach.

A second requirement of a good terminal test is that the number of responses and situation sampled by the test must be sufficient. To illustrate this requirement, consider a test to determine whether or not the following terminal behavior has been brought under the control of the learner by instruction:

Responds with the correct answer to problems involving the determination of cube root.

The terminal test question this behavioral objective raises has to do with providing a sufficiently extensive sample of cube root problems to enable the learner to cope with all of the exigencies such problems present.

In developing a program of instruction, it is helpful to work on the 'terminal behaviors' and the 'terminal test' at the same time. The need to devise a method of getting evidence that the behavior presumably taught will actually be emitted in response to given situations often reduces the tendency to state terminals vaguely or to have unrealistic expectations in regard to them. As a matter of fact, one way to define instructional objectives operationally is to describe the testing situations to which a learner must respond appropriately if the objectives have been achieved.

(d) He must analyze the 'terminal objectives' or the 'terminal behaviors' of the instruction into their elements or components. This is often a complicated and demanding task and one to which relatively little explicit attention is paid in many instances of instructional planning. This is noticeably the case in connection with instruction designed to result in the verbal behavior identified with knowledge. Principles are taught with inadequate attention to teaching the concepts upon which the principles are based. Concepts are taught with inadequate attention to the basic discriminations the concepts require.

The careful analysis of an instructional objective that has been stated in behavioral terms may result in a long list of component behaviors. Various ones of these components will be assumed to be known before instruction and will be designated as entering or prerequisite behaviors. The remaining behaviors may either (a) be taught in the instructional program or (b) controlled through effective directions (manualized). The behavioral analysis of instructional objectives has as its eventual purpose the identification of the instructional units.

(e) He must construct tests or other procedures to determine whether or not the prerequisite behaviors and/or conditions (readiness, normal eyesight, etc.) obtain in respect to the population to be instructed. This screening is done so that only the learners for whom the instruction is designed will be expected to undergo it. Generally, and for reasons of efficiency, an instructional program should be planned and developed for a relatively specific and homogeneous population of learners. When characteristics of the population to be instructed, such as its general educational level and its command of the subject matter considered prerequisite, are stipulated and enforced, this substantially reduces population heterogeniety. Given current teaching and promotion practices, however, it is very hazardous to assume background knowledge if the assumption is based on the fact that the persons for whom the instruction is intended have completed and 'passed' certain grade levels or even certain specific courses. There are many data to support this caution. Failure of instruction to do what it was designed to do, often results because the entering characteristics and behaviors that were assumed were not in fact present. The construction of screening tests to determine the existence of prerequisites involves the same validity and sampling problems that were noted under (c) above in relation to the terminal test.

(f) He must develop an effective sequence for teaching the behaviors which resulted from an analysis of objectives and were put in the category 'to be learned'. The sequencing of instructional units so as to result in the most efficient establishment of behavior control, verbal or otherwise, has been subject to little careful study. There are many bases for establishing sequence—chronology, as in history; from simple to more complex, as in spelling; from easy to more difficult, from the specific to the general, from the general to the specific, according to the wish of the learner; and so on and on. Choices among sequencing possibilities are usually made without much supporting data.

(g) He must create environments that will elicit and reward the behaviors represented by the instructional objectives. Creating these environments represents the central task of instruction and is accomplished by the use of instructional stimuli of great variety. In the broadest sense, and within the general context of instruction, instructional stimuli are those stimuli that are consciously used in the instructional process to describe, elicit and reinforce the behaviors to be learned. When these instructional 'stimuli' exist in some 'stored' form, as is the case with books, models, simulations, charts, maps, films or tapes, they are instructional materials. Advocating the use of a 'variety of instructional materials' is a generalized recognition of the fact that some instructional stimuli are more likely to elicit specific desirable behaviors than are other instructional stimuli. Appropriate responses to situations involving automobile driving are more apt to be elicited by actual steering wheels than by symbolic stimuli (words) referring to steering wheels.

(h) He must arrange for an appropriate practice and reinforcement schedule so that the desired behaviors once under the learner's control will continue to be elicited by the appropriate stimuli for as long as is deemed desirable. This aspect of instruction has received little direct attention. Arranging for 'review' is common, but when the desired terminal behavior once appears to be under the learner's control, and by this is meant that he can respond appropriately when he is requested to do so, the ravages of forgetting are either completely overlooked or it is assumed that they will be dealt with in other than an instructional context. One of the expensive and pervasive sources of waste in institutionalized education results from the almost complete lack of attention to postinstructional reinforcement. The learner is discharged from the instructional situation as soon as there is evidence that the terminal behavior has just been learned. Little is done to increase the likelihood that the learner's control of his responses will continue.

Flexibility for Adjustment

While there is some operational logic to the sequence of the activities described above that seem to be necessary for instruction as I am conceiving of it, the sequence is not to be viewed as rigid and there is considerable interaction among the various aspects of the total task. Work on the terminal test, for example, often forces a reformulation of the objectives. Similarly, identifying 'prerequisite behaviors' often requires a reconsideration of other aspects of the instructional plan.

As I have said, aspects of instruction (e) through (h) above are always subject to modification in the light of their consequences. This conception of instruction as an empirical process, that is constantly made more effective by having its consequences taken into account, is inherent in the concept of instruction that has been developed. It is perfectly clear, however, that in the vast majority of instances of instruction, no precise or comprehensive evidence of consequences is sought and the failure to do so is interestingly rationalized. The rationalization most commonly used, whenever even a slight bit of evidence seems to question instructional procedures that are familiar to, and valued by, the instructors, is that the ones being instructed are not living up to their obligations.

The consequences of instruction can be observed in at least two different ways. First, as the various instructional situations are being developed, they can be tested by having two or three learners respond to them in order to determine whether or not they are effective. Second, when the instructional plan is completed, it can be field tested with the populations and under the circumstances with which it was designed to deal. Needless to say, neither procedure is used with any frequency as instructional plans and programs are developed by most institutions providing instruction.

Required Competences

The various tasks that have been described as constituting instruction can be accomplished with varying degrees of care, discipline and objectivity. The point I would like to stress, however, is that to the degree the planning and implementation of the instruction represents careful systematic and objective action and evaluation, the purpose of the instruction is more apt to be achieved. In order for there to be discipline and objectivity, it seems to me that instructional planning and the implementation of instructional plans require the following kinds of competencies:

1. A specialist in the behaviors that constitute the objectives of the instruction. This means someone who knows a great deal about whatever behavior the instruction is designed to result in.
2. A behavioral analyst. This analysis of the gross behavioral objectives is undertaken to identify the singular components and elements of instruction and to establish a tentative sequencing of these behaviors. This aspect of instruction is widely neglected.
3. An 'instructional environment' or medium specialist who is able to make good decisions about the kind of stimuli (oral, written, pictorial, three dimensional, etc.) that promise to be most effective given the task to be achieved by the instructional program.
4. A perceptive interviewer who will arrange for procuring an interview-type reaction to the instruction by a few subjects of the type who will benefit from it as the instruction is being developed.
5. An expert in the experimental [field] testing of instances or programs of instruction.

Needless to say, these kinds of competence exist in all degrees of quality and several of them may be represented in the qualifications of a single person.

Summary

The conception and analysis of the instructional process that has been elaborated at some length in the preceding pages suggests that the basic instructional unit or module consists of stimuli that:

1. Describe or otherwise make clear to the learner the behavior he is to acquire control over.
2. Describe or otherwise make clear the situation to which this behavior is an appropriate response.
3. Attempt to elicit this behavior as a response to the appropriate situation.
4. Reinforce or reward the behavior as soon as possible after it is emitted.

Speaking generally, and being aware of the risks such generalizing entails, it seems clear to me that the great majority of instances of institutionalized instruction bear down heavily and almost exclusively on the first aspect of instruction as listed above. By this is meant that the instruction emphasizes to the effective exclusion of almost everything else, the description of, or statement of, the ideas, concepts, principles, definitions, and so on that the learner is subsequently expected to emit as verbal behavior. Much less attention is directed to making clear the situations for which these verbal behaviors are judged to be appropriate responses, to trying continuously to elicit these behaviors or give practice in their emission, or to reinforcing the correct behaviors as soon as possible, after they are emitted.

6. GUIDING: METHODS AND INTERACTION STYLES FOR TRAINERS

INTRODUCTION

The readings in this section are for trainers, and for consultants when they perform training functions. There are three sets of them: on selecting training method(s), on a small sample of particular methods themselves, and on managing the transition from training to work situation. That, unplanned, four of the seven readings in this section come from the University Associates' *Annual Handbooks for Group Facilitators*, Trainers and Consultants over the years show their special value for practitioners.

The opening reading presents an eightfold typology of methods to choose from and briefly discusses major clusters of them. The following reading then identifies four important considerations into the selection: organization's commitment to having the intervention succeed, the degrees of accuracy and of complexity involved in particular methods, and the 'learner resistance' likely to be met. 'The key principle . . . is that methods are chosen according to their ability to address the identified conditions'. The third reading adds considerations of 'learning style' and 'trainer behavior'. When these two match well and suit 'the identified conditions', trainers have maximum scope for behaving helpfully in the myriad events that constitute training.

The next set of reading start with a discussion of the Case Method, 'one of many attempts to get more of real life into classrooms and training programs'. 'Real' here means real in somebody *else's* life: creating that distance has advantages and also limitations. Role playing, the next topic, has wide utility. Though it is structured from a situation other than the participants' own, their attention—and learning—becomes rivetted on their own behavior, and it can often lead to high involvement and quite personal learnings. For maximising learning, the program and the staffing of role playing sessions must allow enough time for reflection and discussion of the play, and skillful facilitating.

Modern technologies of recording have become inexpensive and available enough to include a discussion of 'self-modeling and behavior rehearsal' with the aid of video cameras and playback. This reading focusses on their use in human relation training but is illustrative of improving practice in many areas.

The final reading presents a conceptual tool for helping participants plan for their re-entry into their work and home situations after training. This is just one of many 'cultural transitions' for which the tool may be useful. Participants transformed by significant learnings necessarily head into conflict and disconfirmation when they return 'home'. Advance work in making the expectations of the different parties realistic and on visualizing what behaviors will be useful and which not, can pay off handsomely. Processes can be instituted to assure participants that they will be welcomed back and that their fresh learnings will influence their work.

6.1 *A Classification of Training Methods*[1]

UDAI PAREEK

[For] a broad understanding of . . . modalities and methods three dimensions [may] be kept in view.

   a) the amount of participant activity allowed . . . .
   b) the amount of emphasis on cognitive learning, and
   c) the amount of emphasis on providing experience to, and scope for, experimentation by the participants.

. . . participant-activity is not necessarily in conflict with trainer activity. The trainer's role remains central; he directs and controls . . . . Even then the participant-activity can be either high or low . . . .

Using these three dimensions results in a typology of eight sets of methods:

1. *Inspirational methods:* These methods are primarily based on high activity on the part of the trainer. Giving a sermon or a pep talk to . . . participants in the hope that this will change their attitudes and behavior is a good example of this methodology. In this methodology all the three dimensions are low.

---

[1] From Udai Pareek, 'The Pedagogy of Behavior Simulation', *Indian Educational Review*, Vol. 16, 1981, pp. 1–24.

2. *Expository methods:* In these methods, cognitive emphasis is very high, while participant activity and emphasis on experiences is low. A good example of expository is the lecture method . . . .

3. *Natural learning methods:* . . . Learners are left on their own, with free and unplanned activity. The emphasis on learner activity is high, whereas it is low on planned experience or on cognitive inputs. The following modalities are worth mentioning in this regard.

  a) *Trial and error learning*: . . . no planned activity . . . the learner is left to try on his own—learning from the mistakes and then trying out new ways, until he has learned . . . .

  b) *On the job training*: . . . the participant is put on the job . . . and he learns from whatever experience he gains . . . no emphasis on planned experiences or planned experimentation . . . .

  c) *Discussion methods*: . . . Natural groups . . . discuss various topics and people express their views, share several things with each other, and learn whatever they can from . . . .

4. *Individualized methods:* These methods . . . are low on providing experience or experimentation by the learner and high on both participant activity and cognitive emphasis.

Programmed instruction: . . . takes the participant at his own pace. The materials . . . prepared with great care . . . [take] the learner step by step, have questions to be answered by the learner, give immediate feedback whether the answer is right or wrong and why, minimize chances of learners making mistakes, and provide enough practice for correct responses . . . mass media [often] supplement training.

5. *Behavior control methods:* [These] are very low on the cognitive dimension and on active participation of learners. The main emphasis is on helping the learner experience, and experiment with, some behavior. Two methods are worth mentioning here.

  a) *Behavior reinforcement*: This method, based on theories of learning Pavlov's (conditioned reflex) or its further development and refinement by Skinner (called operational conditioning) [relies on] a schedule of reinforcement (reward) [so that] each act of desired behavior is reinforced or rewarded . . . . This training does not produce cognitive understanding nor [is] the learner actively involved in generating learning situations. However, the learner is certainly experiencing various phenomena, and indirectly is encouraged to experiment.

  b) *Modelling*: . . . participants learn many things from [their] experiences . . . of the trainer, the total group of faculty in an institution, . . . the head of the institution, the general climate prevailing in the institution, and norms of behavior which are practised rather than taught or talked about. The conscious efforts of presenting desirable behavior . . . [are] called modelling.

6. *Controlled exposure methods:* A low level of participation by the trainees and a high emphasis on experience and cognitive learning characterize these methods.

Demonstration: . . . very widely used, . . . can range from a very simple one in the class-room, when a teacher shows some action and the participants observe, to complex demonstrations . . . in a controlled area where experiments have been going on . . . (and) participants are taken . . . to see . . . the results of (e.g.) the new seed or other practices . . . and helped to understand why the experiment succeeded.

7. *Encounter methods:* These methods emphasize both experiencing by the learner as well as learner-activity . . . [They] are not high on cognitive learning. In fact, the main aim of these methods is to help the participant learn new behavior and practise it . . . .

a) *Laboratory training*: An intensive experience about how participants work together, compete, . . . and learn from each other . . . . T (for Training) or L (for Learning) groups . . . small, between 8 to 15 . . . deal with authority, experience various methods of leadership development in the group, and experiment with their own behavior . . . . This method seems to be very effective for producing basic attitudinal changes and . . . further learning.

b) *Assertion training*: . . . used to help people learn to assert themselves without being aggressive or immodest, and at the same time not yield to the ideas and pressures of others . . . value clarification training is similar. Exercises . . . for cognitive restructuring, behavioral rehearsal, modelling and assessment are used.

c) *Motivation development*: helps participants analyze their motivation by taking samples of their imagery and . . . increase a particular content . . . (e.g.) achievement motivation (concern for excellence) or extension motivation (concern to serve and develop other people), power motivation (concern to influence and make an impact on others) . . .

d) *Creativity training*: . . . (helps) people recognize their level of creativity and develop an insight into the blocks which prevent them from being [more] creative . . . [Then] they experiment with the help of various techniques to become more creative in general, and in particular on their jobs. Creativity in work situation takes the form of non-conformative behavior . . .

8. *Discovery methods:* When the emphasis is high on all the three dimensions, i.e., cognitive learning, activity by the learner, and experience and experimenting by the learner, we have methods in which people discover knowledge for themselves. These methods are very effective in producing change in behavior. The rationale of these methods is that change in behavior does not occur only by new experience and reinforcement, but also by the development of proper cognitive framework so that people learn why certain things happen and may be able to understand and advance their insight further. Several such methods are available:

a) *Experiments*: . . . verifying . . . is only a form of demonstration. [In] real experiment . . . [participants] develop experiments [to] question some hypotheses and set-up new hypotheses. Experiments can be conducted in . . . fields like administration.

b) *Field training*: . . . . Helping the participants work in actual work setting, for example in a factory or in a village community, with a plan to record their learning from such experience.

c) *Case teaching*: . . . A case describes an actual situation and its dynamics . . . (and) participants discuss the various dimensions.

d) *Role playing*: [rehearse] to deal with a particular situation.

e) *Behavior simulation*: a game, or an exercise (e.g., through the use of computers) to experience [an entire situation] in a controlled way . . .

f) *Instrumented training*: Instruments . . . usually used to test abilities, attitudes, personality, styles or behavior . . . can also be used for training . . . provide significant data which participants can use to enhance their insights, and to prepare plans to experiment with new behavior . . .

6.2 *Selecting Appropriate Methods*[2]

DONALD T. SIMPSON

The key principle . . . is that methods are chosen according to their ability to address the identified conditions. Adhering to this principle keeps the trainer from inappropriately designing personal biases into the program. For example, many trainers favor experiential methods

[2] From J. William Pfeiffer and Leonard D. Goodstein (eds.), *The 1983 Annual for Facilitators, Trainers and Consultants*, University Associates, San Diego, CA, 1983, pp. 223–30.

Figure 15: Training Methods that are Appropriate Under Specific Circumstances
A Appropriate Methods

Emphasis or Knowledge Components		
	Low Complexity	*High Complexity*
Low Resistance	Reading Lecture/panel discussion Film/slide/tape	Interactive case study Interactive instruments Simulation/game
High Resistance	Group discussion	Programed instruction Case study/analysis Experiential/lecture

Emphasis on Skill Components		
	Low Complexity	*High Complexity*
Low Resistance	Demonstration (e.g., film) +practice	Modeling On-the-job training feedback Instruments
High Resistance	Structured experience Group role play Modeling	Role play Psychodrama Simulation/game

Figure 16 : Example of Ways to Use a Case Study to Accommodate Different Conditions

Identified Conditions	Suggested Learner Activities
Emphasis on Knowledge Components	
Low complexity, low resistance	Fead the case as an example of some concept described earlier.
High complexity, low resistance	Read and analyze the case, perhaps by responding to summary questions or by-writing essays.
Low complexity, high resistance	Reading and discuss the case.
High complexity, high resistance	Read, analyze, and discuss the case, perhaps developing a group analysis or recommendation.
Emphasis on Skill Components	
Low complexity, low resistance	Read the case as an example of a skill such as problem identification
High complexity, low resistance	Read and analyze the case, perhaps working out a problem-analysis sequence
Low complexity, high resistance High complexity, high resistance	Read the case, analyze it, and develop a role play or simulation from it that includes interaction with others.

because of their particular applicability in fostering the learning of interpersonal skills. But to apply such methods to a simple knowledge component might be inappropriate; a precourse or intersession reading assignment might not only suffice for this purpose, but also save group time for a more suitable use, such as skill practice. Figure 15 presents methods that are appropriate under specific circumstances.

The use of many training methods or tools can be varied in accordance with specific conditions. For example, a case study can be used in several ways, as illustrated in Figure 16.

6.3 *Learner and Trainer Styles*[3]

RONNE TOKER JACOBS AND BARBARA SCHNEIDER FULFRMAN

In designing learning experiences, teachers/trainers need to account not only for learner preferences but also for their own experience and preferences. Figure 17 details the relationships between learner styles and teacher/trainer roles.

Figure 17: Learner-Teacher/Trainer Descriptors

Learner Style	Learner Needs	Teacher/Trainer Role	Teacher/Trainer Behavior
DEPENDENT (May occur in introductory courses, new work situations, languages, and some sciences when the learner has little or no information on entering the course.)	Structure Direction External reinforcement Encouragement Esteem from authority	Director Expert Authority	Lecturing Demonstrating Assigning Checking Encouraging Testing Reinforcing Transmitting content Grading Designing materials
COLLABORATIVE (May occur when the learner has some knowledge, informa- tion, or ideas and	Interaction Practice Probe of self and others Observation	Collaborator Co-learner Environment setter	Interacting Questioning Providing resources Modeling Providing feedback

[3] From J. William Pfeiffer and Leonard D. Goodstein (eds.), *The 1984 Annual for Facilitators, Trainers and Consultants*, University Associates, San Diego, CA, 1984, p. 103.

Figure 17 (Continued)

Learner Style	Learner Needs	Teacher/Trainer Role	Teacher/Trainer Behavior
would like to share them or try them out.)	Participation Peer challenge Peer esteem Experimentation		Coordinating Evaluating Managing Observing process Grading
INDEPENDENT (May occur when the learner has much knowledge or skill on entering the course and wants to continue to search on his or her own or has had successful experiences in working through new situations alone. The learner may feel that the instructor cannot offer as much as he or she would like.)	Internal awareness Experimentation Time Nonjudgmental support	Delegator Facilitator	Allowing Providing requested feedback Providing resources Consulting Listening Negotiating Evaluating Delegating

6.4 *The Case Method*[4]

HARRIET RONKEN LYNTON AND ROLF P. LYNTON

The teaching of cases is one of many attempts to get more or real life into classrooms and training programs. Ideally, cases confront the member of the discussion group with situations which faced someone like himself somewhere, sometime. They present a chunk of somebody's real life, but not of the member's own life during training. As pieces of real life, they are full of people, not of abstractions, and too complex to be fitted into neat categories, generalizations, and other intellectual equipment. As somebody else's experience, a case can help the member explore his own attitudes and behavior as if by personal analogy, at moments when direct attention to his own experiences would provoke only fear and defence, not learning. Doing it by analogy instead of for

[4] From Harriet Ronken Lynton and Rolf P. Lynton, *Asican Cases*, Aloka Centre for Advanced Study and Training, Mysore, India, 1960, pp. 2–4.

himself in the commitments of real life, increases his freedom to explore more of the ins and outs of a problem which he might otherwise ignore, and to go beyond his habitual response into an exploration of second and third thoughts instead of settling for the first. This close but not insistently personal quality also allows some concepts to be explored and understood in case sessions which will help in understanding personal experiences.

Degrees of Identification

The place of cases in an educational program, the choice and sequence of cases and the emphasis the instructor can give in the discussion of them, all revolve around the degree to which members identify themselves with the people in the case. The ideal can be formulated readily enough: the greatest values are gained if a member can identify with one or more persons in the case but not so closely that he himself ceases to be a different person.

For working directly with member's attitudes, there are better ways than teaching cases. Cases are not even particularly good projective devices, though they certainly need some of this quality for effective use. Ideally, they serve primarily in helping members conceive that there may be several ways of looking at, thinking about, and acting in an identical situation, to wonder which they might choose if they had themselves been in it, to ask more effective questions of the data life throws up to them, and to go on to learn some generalizations and concepts from this study of field data. Without a limited identification there would be no learning. Without the remaining difference and distance there would be no systematic thought and understanding.

Stating the ideal is one thing; achieving it is another. The line between too much and too little identification is in practice very difficult to draw. Medicine, law, and social work, the disciplines in which reaching of cases has the longest tradition, have sought to limit identification and maintain the focus on the subject matter by abstracting the client into a conglomeration of standard symptoms: these conglomerations of symptoms, not the patient, the accused, or the substandard family, become 'the cases' and pose 'the problem'. The person recedes into the background; the problem occupies the attention.

This emphasis looks promising whenever cases are thought of primarily as vehicles for teaching subject matter rather than as anologies through whose examination and diagnosis members can review their own experiences . . . .

The other kind of cases limit identification and invite attention to their subject matter of human relations in the opposite direction to abstraction: they include a lot of personal details as persons in the case see them. They therefore lend themselves to learning the complex and manifoldly determined makeup of a 'point of view' and 'the concept a person has of himself'; to the study and understanding of personal feelings and how they can be seen to affect the behavior of a person; situations of rivalry and social change as they in fact come up to real people in real life, just as illogical and incomplete as it usually is. A member can see himself as like Mr. X in the case in many ways, and this may prompt him to reflect about himself. But with so many detailed differences and a different totality he will not see himself as Mr. X in disguise. He can learn from Mr. X without becoming him.

Our preference for this kind of case is related not only to the way we believe people learn but also to what we feel is most important for people to learn, at least at this time . . . . [Whereas] the abstraction in the other kinds of cases emphasizes what human affairs have in common, the convergent phenomena . . . [these] emphasize the differences . . . the divergent phenomena of human affairs . . . . Where capacities for development are straining fearfully at every resource, and most basic of all at the people themselves and the communities in which they live . . . the crying need is for the pioneer, the person who can conceive of diverging from his own and go on, both to take the initiative and then to maintain the new element in his society. But this pioneer must be as much a bridge as an innovator, for barring the occasional prophet, he can be effective only when he does not break so completely with the traditional society that he no longer has any relationships there.

This social innovator, this pioneer, is caught in his own feelings in the first place. These we work with directly . . ., in study groups and other interpretive sessions as well as in field work. What we expect a member to gain from the cases is a systematic way of thinking about people including himself, and the assurance that, though the emotional and other demands of change are quite personal to himself, others go through the same kind of throes and are in that sense his kin.

Which Case, and When?

The situations which leaders, administrators, and trainers have to understand and handle, are infinitely varied. Moreover, people gain their insights and their understanding of such situations along different routes and at different speeds. Therefore, a case which is suitable at some particular stage for one training group may not be suitable for another at the same stage. Ideally, the instructor would have available several cases suitable for the particular stage the training group has reached from which to select the most promising. These cases would be of recent date and present situations of the kind which members of the group might be expected to meet somewhat in the way they come up in the cases.

To guide him in selecting the right case at the right moment, the instructor needs an increasingly intimate understanding of his group, for it is primarily the members that he is teaching and not primarily the case.

The Instructor

Gauging the proper time and way to draw the members' attention now to their own experiences, now to other peoples, is the instructor's most difficult task. He cannot escape it if he thinks of himself as someone who helps people to develop themselves, to change their attitudes and their behavior. Both the personal referent and the learning from the experiences of others are valuable . . . . The experiences of other people are most prominent in the case discussions, where the instructor may even discourage references to personal experiences if they threaten to drain off the tensions that belong properly in the study groups and can be better handled directly there.

From minute to minute, the instructor is concerned with helping to make the work meaningful to the members. It must be stimulating, personal, disturbing, but not so much so that the members freeze. The instructor's task is to help them look instead of stare; understand instead of overthink; listen to other people's feelings instead of to the din of their own. What is at stake is learning that is made up of personal growth. So even when he brings in teaching material outside the group's own experience, the instructor still focuses first on the members, not on the cases. What will be most useful now, is the question which persistently occupies his mind.

6.5 *Simulating Reality: Role Playing*[5]

UDAI PAREEK

Role playing is an old method adopted by children to learn new social roles. Children may often be seen acting as parents or other adults. This

[5] Abridged from Udai Pareek, 'Role Playing as a Human Relations Training Technique', *Indian Journal of Social Work*, Vol. XI, 1960, pp. 251–59.

kind of play activity is a good learning device for children. However, this has been developed into a new technique for use with both children and adults.

Role playing is a method of adopting roles from real life, other than those being played by the person concerned, and understanding the dynamics of those roles. It is 'a method of studying the nature of a certain role by acting out its concrete details in a contrived situation that permits of better and more objective observation'. Role playing is a conscious attempt to examine the various roles played in actual life.

Role playing developed as a result of new developments in interpersonal techniques started by Moreno.[6] Later, this technique was adapted for its use in various situations in interpersonal relations like education, administration, industry, social work, therapy, etc. Various parallel names have been used for role playing, such as, leadership training, reality practice, experience practice, spontaneity training, etc. However, the term 'role playing' is the most accepted and is more expressive. The technique of role playing can be adopted for various purposes and the nature of the technique would differ for different purposes.

While planning role playing, one important factor to be considered is that of establishing rapport with the audience and the role players. The role players should clearly understand the purpose of role playing and should be agreeable to play the roles.

Considerable skill is required in the selection of a situation for a role-play session. The situation should be of challenging nature and should be of concern to those who are participating in role playing; for this purpose a conflict situation may prove better, but it should not involve areas of personal conflict.

Equally important is the technique of role briefing. Those who are to play roles should understand clearly the type of persons they are required to be during the role-play session. It is better to prepare written briefing sheets and distribute them to the persons concerned. In a group role playing situation, the whole group need be briefed regarding the general situation and group atmosphere. The individuals in the group situation should be briefed separately. Briefing should concern only emotional state and attitudes and should not contain details about the type of things the role player should say during the role-play session.

For good role playing, the role players should get involved in the

---

[6] In the early twenties of this century Moreno experimented with groups of role players in the theatre of spontaneity in Vienna (see J. Nehnevajsa, 'Sociometry: Decades of growth' in J.L. Moreno (ed.) *Sociometric Reader*, The Free Press, Glencoe, Ill., 1960, pp. 707–53. Moreno's major contribution in this regard is available in English in J.L. Moreno, *Who Shall Survive?* Beacon House, New York, 1953.

situation. This would depend much on the type of briefing. Involvement is necessary to make the role-play session as near to reality as possible.

The role of the role-play director is of great importance. He should see that role playing is proceeding according to the briefing. During the role-play session, he observes the progress of role playing and cuts the role-play whenever he feels that it is not proceeding properly and is not fulfilling the purpose for which it is arranged. He can also cut the role-play to explain the dynamics behind a particular statement. During the role-play, he can also interview the role players to show to the observers how the various persons have been feeling.

Sometimes role-play is done by one or more than one expert to demonstrate some principles or practices. In this case, the person may be in role for sometime and then may come out of the role to explain the dynamics behind the role being played. It is useful to develop this practice of stepping in and stepping out of the role by role players, to explain to the observers the relevant feeling they would like to report.

The final analysis of role playing is of great importance. After the role-play session is over, it should be thoroughly discussed. For this purpose it is necessary to do some audience briefing in the beginning. The observers may be asked to observe the dynamics of the group engaged in role playing, with the help of an observation sheet or form. Guided observation during the role-play session helps in making the purpose of role-play clear. At the end of the role-play session, the role-play director and the observers may interview the various role players to know the dynamics behind the role-play interrelationships. It is sometimes useful to use an *alter ego*—one of the observers who may identify himself with one of the role players to report to the observers the feelings of that player to see the difference between the reportings of the feelings by two persons. After analysis and evaluation of this type, the role-play session may be concluded.

Some Role-Play Procedures

Role playing is being increasingly used for human relations training. Various forms of role playing are being developed for this purpose. The main requirement in role playing is of assuming roles and playing them out. The following are some of the methods adopted in this connection. The utility of a procedure would depend on the purposes for which role playing is to be arranged, the type of audience, etc.

Simple Role Playing

The usual method adopted may be called simple role playing or what Maier calls 'Single Group Role Playing'.[7] In this procedure one role-playing group performs and all others act as observers. The role-play can be cut by the role-play director whenever there is a need of explaining the dynamics to the audience. This procedure is quite useful for purposes of demonstration, for developing skills in sensitivity to the feelings of others, for intensive training, and for use with the small groups. In this procedure role play is arranged before the audience, who at the end discuss for the final analysis and evaluation of the role playing. The analysis can be facilitated by the use of an *alter ego* for the major roles in a role play. This arrangement is especially useful to develop skill in sensitivity to the feelings of others by providing the chance to the *alter ego* to view the differences in the perception of feelings by the role player and *alter ego*. There are many advantages in Single Group Role Playing. First, it helps in the training of observation, as all the persons present in the role-play contribute to the observation of the session in progress. The various aspects of the role-play session are observed by different persons. Second, it helps in training in the analysis of behavior. Various observers present in the group try to find out the reasons of things said and done and the dynamics behind the behavior of the different roles.

Third, the advantages of feedback are effectively available to the role players, and this helps in developing their insight into the behavior they have been role playing. The feedback is more effective since it comes from various observers. And lastly, there is better training in sensitivity to feelings. This is specially so when an *alter ego* is used for the role-play situation.

Multiple Role Playing

When the purpose of role playing is to involve all the persons present in the group, the Multiple Role Playing procedure[8] can be adopted. In this procedure the audience is formed into convenient role playing groups and the various groups role-play simultaneously. A good procedure to divide the audience into groups is to have two or three persons sitting in

---

[7] N.R.F. Maier, A.R. Solem, and A.A. Maier, *Supervisory and Executive Development, a Manual for Role Playing*, John Wiley & Sons, Inc. New York, 1957.

[8] N.R.F. Maier and L.F. Zerfoss, 'MRP: A Technique for Training Large Groups of Supervisors and its Potential Use in Social Research', *Human Relations*, Vol. V, 1952, pp. 177–86.

the odd rows turn and face two or three others in the even rows, which would make small groups. Written instructions are distributed, and the various small groups start role playing on the same problem. After a specified time the role play is terminated and discussion is begun. It is always useful to have process observers in every smaller group.

The method of Multiple Role Playing has its own advantages. First, every member in the group gets practice in role playing. Second, the solutions arrived at by different groups can be discussed and compared with one another and useful conclusions can be drawn. Third, Multiple Role Playing is good for studying the process of group interaction. When process observers are working with the various groups, their report of the interaction processes are very helpful in developing insight in the participants. Although the same roles are being played by the various groups, the differences due to personality and group factors produce differences in approach.

Audience Role Playing

In this procedure[9] the audience is made sensitive through the use of a specially prepared situation and then is required to react to a change in the situation. Some details of a situation are read before the audience so that it is attuned to a particular emotional attitude. Later on new experiences are introduced and the actions of the members of the group are noted through specially prepared forms. The behavioral changes are measured in an artificial situation of attitude change. This kind of role playing is useful in finding out effective ways of changing attitudes.

Skit Completion Method

The procedures of role playing discussed above can be used in a variety of ways. It may sometimes be necessary to gear role-play sessions directly to the conflict problem. For this purpose, it may be necessary to cut out preliminary parts of the role-play and to introduce the problem direct for the purpose of role playing. To accomplish this, a skit is often presented before the audience, and the audience is required to observe it. When the point of problem conflict is reached, it is left and the role-play session starts. The Skit Completion Method[10] is meant to carry developments to a specific conflict area which becomes the starting point for role playing.

[9] N.R.F. Maier and A.R. Solem, 'Audience Role-Playing: A New Method in Human Relations Training,', *Human Relations*, Vol. IV, 1951, pp. 279–94.

[10] Maier, Solem, and Maier, *op. cit.*

Dramatized Case Method

A similar procedure is to present a dramatized version on the basis of written dialogues of a situation and then to introduce the role playing at the point where conflict reaches a climax.[11]

Various other changes have been made in the procedures of role-play to suit specific purposes. Hendry[12] introduced the idea of complacency shock by debunking his own lecture method and introducing the problem for the role playing. Zander[13] introduced what he called an 'Interawareness' discussion panel in which the panel discussion procedure was adopted after giving a detailed and specific statement of the problem to the panel and asking the members to assume specific roles during the panel meeting. A clarifier was required to interpret the process and the progress of the discussion to the audience. Other variations have been introduced by different workers in group dynamics and human relations training. The idea and basic process of role playing can be tailored to the needs of specific groups.

6.6 *Self-Modeling and Behavior Rehearsal*[14]

JERRY L. FRYREAR AND STEPHEN A. SCHNEIDER

Videotaped modeling in human-growth settings, which required participants to act both as learners and models, is a logical outgrowth of the documented effects of live modeling . . . . Much social learning is fostered by exposure to models who engage, intentionally or unintentionally, in patterns of behavior that are emulated by others . . . . In fact, the establishment of complex social repertoires is generally achieved through a gradual process in which people pass through an orderly, progressive learning sequence toward the final form of the desired behavior . . .

. . . a combination of verbal and demonstrational modeling procedures

[11] N.R.F. Maier, 'Dramatized Case Material as a Spring Board for Role Playing', *Group Psychotherapy*, Vol. VI, 1953, pp. 30–42.

[12] Maier, Solem, and Maier, *op. cit.*

[13] Alwin Zander, 'The Interaction-Awareness Discussion Panel', *Journal of Social Psychology*, Vol. XIX, 1944, pp. 369–75.

[14] From J. William Pfeiffer and Leonard D. Goodstein (eds.), *The 1983 Annual for Facilitators, Trainers and Consultants*, University Associates, San Diego, CA, 1983, pp. 203–6, 212.

is the most effective means of transmitting new patterns of behavior to those who are found to have behavior deficits. In addition, behavior is more likely to be learned from observing a model when the following conditions are met:

- The learners are given specific instructions on what to look for.
- Conflicting, competing, or irrelevant stimuli are minimized.
- In a succession of scenarios, different models are used, and the behavior they perform is vivid and novel.
- The model is attractive in an interpersonal sense.
- The model is seen as having expertise and as being similar to the observer.
- The model is visibly rewarded for engaging in the depicted behavior.
- The learners are given positive feedback and otherwise rewarded for their own modeling.

For the following reasons, video-enhanced human relations training, with a group, is well suited to meet these important modeling conditions.

- Through group discussion and guidance from the trainer, the group members are given specific guidelines for evaluating the effectiveness of their behaviors.
- Because the models work from a script, conflicting and irrelevant stimuli are minimized.
- Because the learners watch themselves, they are likely to give full, discriminative attention to the videotape. Furthermore, they actively evaluate their own performances with a view toward improvement.
- The group format, in which each member acts as a protagonist, automatically provides different models, each of whom acts out vivid and novel behavior from a script that is developed by the group.
- In as much as social skills contribute to interpersonal attractiveness, the participant models who act out such skills are seen as having that attribute.
- Because the script is designed to demonstrate maximally effective behavior, the model is perceived as having expertise. During the script-writing process, the group members contribute their own concerns, which tend to be similar to one another. Consequently, when the concerns are presented on a screen, the learner perceives the model as similar to himself or herself.
- The script is designed to ensure positive social responses from others.
- The group, the trainers, and the other actors in the scenarios all give positive feedback to the participant model.

An additional variable that has been shown to be crucial to the effective modeling of social behavior is the portrayal of a model who copes rather than one who has [already] mastered the behavior involved. The model who copes, performs in a progressively improving manner . . . . The self-as-model procedure is a coping-model program that involves the repeated practice of a behavior by an initially unskilled protagonist.

Self-Confrontation: The Special Case of Self-as-Model

. . . The self-as-model procedure is an excellent method for promoting self-understanding and growth: it depends on covert and overt imitation of one's own videotaped behavior. The imitation is followed by changes in self-perception and, subsequently, changes in social behavior outside the training setting.

It is important that the self-as-model procedure provide positive feedback so that the protagonists are not forced to focus only on their perceived mistakes . . . the self-image evokes strong arousal in the learner, 'priming' him or her for positive change.

The Training Program

Modeling, self-confrontation, and behavior rehearsal have all been shown to enhance human relations training. In addition, the advantages of group training are well documented. The video-enhanced group-training procedure combines what the authors believe are the best-supported elements of modeling, self-confrontation, and behavior rehearsal. By using a group structure, several positive elements are added: peer support, group problem solving, multiple models, a sense of universality, and group cohesiveness . . . .

6.7 *Re-entry from Training: A Concept*[15]

ART FREEDMAN

. . . Participants of a residential workshop often experience 'culture shock' when they pass from their predictable, 'real-life' worlds of family,

[15] From J. William Pfeiffer and John E. Jones (eds.), *The 1980 Annual Handbook for Group Facilitators*, University Associates, San Diego, CA, 1980, pp. 204–9.

work, social relationships, and religion into the temporary, artificial 'foreign' workshop world and then back . . . although participants derive a great many personal learnings from their workshop experiences, these learnings do not always hold up over time.

. . . the re-entering, culture-crossing travellers will have to be prepared to modify their recently acquired 'foreign' behavior . . . they will attempt to model their newly acquired behavior . . . inviting their native culture's citizens to tolerate, then accept, and then, maybe, experiment with the new behavior themselves. This is the process by which transcendental meditation, Tai Chi, the martial arts, Zen, acupuncture, and other aspects of Eastern cultures were probably introduced to the Western world.

The W-curve Hypothesis

In order to prepare people to leave a foreign culture and return to their native, back-home cultures of family, community, and work, it is helpful to explain the concept of transitions . . . (see Figure 18).

There are two points that the diagram illustrates that have not been discussed. One is hope. Without that, few people would bother to try anything new. They might be terribly dissatisfied with the current conditions of their lives, but without the hope that life does not have to be that way, people would tend to say something like 'Better to live with the devil I know than the devil I don't'. And they would sit dead still and endure chronic dissatisfaction or suffering.

The second point is that, in terms of levels of comfort, satisfaction, and effectiveness, the dips tend to be shallower and the peaks higher as people move from their foreign culture back to their native culture. It is this curvature that lends its name to this concept.

This model is especially helpful in providing workshop participants with some conceptual handles that they can use in re-entering their 'native' culture. This concept helps absorb a great deal of the tension and anxiety that participants tend to experience toward the end of a workshop when they begin to anticipate the re-entry process. They begin to ask themselves, 'How are my people back there ever going to understand me now? How can I let them know what I've been through here?'. This model allows participants to anticipate the re-entry 'dip' and develop a plan that will reduce its depth.

Figure 18 : The W-Curve Hypothesis Model

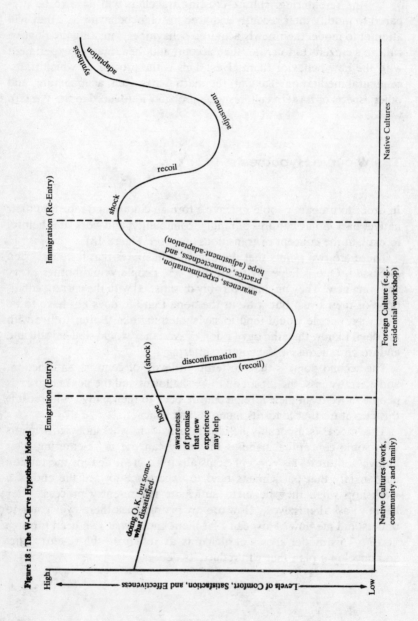

7. EVALUATION

INTRODUCTION

Evaluation is the third in the trilogy Mat Miles[1] offers of training and consulting functions, i.e., after planning and guiding. In it we here include monitoring, that is checking (even while the program or consultation is still going on) that an intervention is on course to achieve the intended results or needs mid-course correction. In the context of using training and consulting directly in order to improve action, monitoring assumes that practitioners are ready to modify a program and also able to adjust inputs and behavior. It is fine-grained, immediate evaluation. In this same action context, evaluation is only a part of the broader area of action research.

Evaluation is the kind of action research that deals mostly with questions set in advance of action, whether the goals stated in advance are likely to be feasible under prevailing conditions or, later, how far these goals have in fact been attained. Have all relevant constituents become sufficiently involved? How far have participants in fact learned the skills, etc., for which the training was instituted? Or, can the organization now cope with the tasks for which the consulting strategy and means were designed? Though set in advance of action, the criteria for evaluating are quite practical and evaluation can appropriately be seen as one kind of action research. The same motivation—to improve action—and the same practical approach characterizes it, as does all action research. It raises pertinent questions and urges collection of data for addressing those questions and finding tentative answers (one or more alternatives) for taking useful action. While special techniques and conceptual tools may be required for carrying it out, the bulk of evaluation is routine for practitioners. Certainly, it is their business to inspire evaluation and to focus it on specifications that matter in taking action in their particular situations. If this anchor to action is allowed to slip, evaluation tends quickly to become esoteric and ritualistic, i.e., to become focussed on conceptual or technical questions that do not matter

---

[1] From Matthew B. Miles, *Learning to Work in Groups*, Teachers College Press, New York & London, 1981, Chapter 7.

much for action, or to produce data for the record in order to satisfy routine administrative requirements.

Components and Processes

The first reading, one of two we include by Paul Nutt, tabulates key components and interactions in evaluation in four steps. Interpreting the findings is the last step in evaluation proper. Action (or inaction) on the findings, though 'a logical extension of the findings', is in its implementation, 'a judgmental process' that takes off from 'the sponsor's expectations and the way the findings are presented . . . . A personalized presentation geared to the needs of the recipient will convey more information than traditional data-centered reports'. A table contrasts these two ways of presenting evaluation findings.

Immediately (and urgently) following this agreeably neat overview comes Arturo Israel's important caution against the uselessness—worse, damage—of many increasingly elaborate evaluations now imposed on development programs. They have 'diverted management's attention to inputs, to the neglect of basic objectives . . . absorb an inordinate amount of scarce [staff] resources for no useful purpose . . . waste and distortion'. The risks of such perversions are particularly high in evaluating people-oriented programs, because they are least specific and develop best when service acquirers take creative (i.e., 'unprogrammed') decisions; and these are the very programs which may matter most to significant development.

Participant-observer evaluation, the subject of the next reading, is very promising for bridging the wide gap between development planners/ administrators and managers and the greatly different worlds of rural and urban communities. It 'makes sense (to planners *et al.*) out of the ways [people] normally talk and act'.

Evaluating Training and Consulting

Two readings follow on evaluating training in particular. Pareek's (7.4) fills the conceptual framework with four major categories—of clients, 'dimensions', evaluation designs and techniques—and makes the sets memorable by melodic anagrams (for trainers who remember things that way). The next step to detailing would be listing criteria for evaluating each category. For any particular situation, this involves choosing practical criteria from numerous possibilities of purpose and available resources, such as, records, time, expertise and funds. Choosing the most telling as well as the most economical criteria for illuminating action possibilities, is the strategic and often laborious early step in evaluation. Readers who need help expanding their range of possible criteria may find it useful to look at the long lists of examples (from business and industry) in W.R. Tracy's *Managing Training and Development Systems* (1974). There are separate lists for 'internal' and 'external' criteria, e.g., participant reaction, trainer team function, help with 'self-audits' for improving the quality of training. External criteria, broader and long-term, aim to throw light on the lasting impacts of training, e.g., on staff development to operate new technologies, or on institutional cohesion, strength and creativity. Similarly, A.C. Hamlin's *Techniques for Evaluating Training* (1974) includes long lists of techniques available for evaluating various dimensions among which are, individual learning, organizational changes and other developments. Included here, in the second reading about evaluating training, is the measurement plan for just one question from a recent evaluation in a Malaysian training institution. With nine criteria laid out for evaluating 'how well was the training carried out' and the 'procedures' attached to each criterion—how, when, by whom, information sources, basis for data analysis and instruments—a table with 54 cells results, some of these further subdivided. Crafting the plan to such detail, daunting as it looks, actually simplifies evaluation in practice.

For evaluating consulting, Swartz and Lippitt (7.6) propose three main areas: the client consultant relationship, the actual interventions (of which training may be one kind) and 'progress towards specific goals'. The reading shows these incorporated in a conceptual model.

Evaluators with Decision-makers

The last two readings focus more sharply on interactions between decision-makers (sponsors and clients) and evaluators. Patton's (7.7) is an overview of all the factors involved. He regards only two requirements as 'fundamental'. The first, that relevant decision-makers and information users must be identified and organized—'real, visible, specific, and caring human beings, not ephemeral, general, and abstract audiences, organizations or agencies. Second, evaluators must work actively, reactively and adaptively with these identified decision-makers and information users to make all other decisions about the evaluation'. Both require active negotiation and adaptation. In situations where the sponsors and funders of evaluation constitute a party different from operating clients, additional complexities arise. They are common in education, health and other public services, and also in many other programs and organizations that draw funds from banks, foreign governments or other third parties.

The last reading in this section, also from Nutt's work, pulls together characteristic experiences in the interactions between sponsors or clients and evaluators, and conceptualizes them. While clients often suffer from 'model mania', evaluators often show 'data mania'. Either can truncate an evaluation. They have different preferences, e.g., timeliness versus precision, and they often prefer different paths. Nutt identifies fourteen stages in evaluation where dialogue can be most useful and ways to avoid common traps for 'avoiding' sound evaluation.

7.1 *The Evaluation Process: Components and a Model*[2]

PAUL C. NUTT

An evaluation project begins when a sponsor seeks information that describes the merits of an intervention. As shown in Figure 19, evaluation proceeds through several stages and each stage is connected by a particular activity. As a first step, the sponsor makes assumptions which define the intervention [cause] and/or specify its effects. The initial model is an abstraction of the intervention and/or its effects, as seen by the sponsor. Assumptions are refined (implicitly and explicitly) by the sponsor until the abstraction confirms the sponsors's perception of reality.

The arrow linking the model and the stimulus is bidirectional. The two-way relationship suggests an interplay between the model and the stimulus. Either the emergence of new information needs or reflection, may cause the sponsor to change the model. Thus causal models, which describe the merits of an intervention, are 'fine turned' by insuring that the model can provide information for decision making.

Evaluation methods are linked to the causal model by proxies selected to measure the intervention's effects. The causal model forms the basis to select an initial set of proxy measures of cause-and-effect factors. Measures are also dictated by evaluation methods. The initial set of

[2] From Paul C. Nutt, *Evaluation Concepts and Methods: Shaping Policy for the Health Administrator*, Robert B. Luce, Bridgeport, CT.

Figure 19: The Evaluation Process

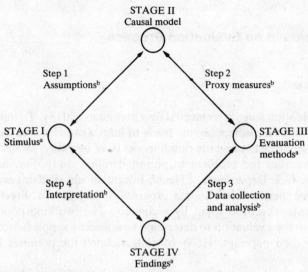

STAGE II
Causal model

Step 1
Assumptions[b]

Step 2
Proxy measures[b]

STAGE I
Stimulus[a]

STAGE III
Evaluation
methods[a]

Step 4
Interpretation[b]

Step 3
Data collection
and analysis[b]

STAGE IV
Findings[a]

[a]Major outcomes of an evaluation project

[b]Evaluation activities that have people acting out *roles,*
following cognitive *styles,* and applying select *tools.*

proxy measures may restrict the range of evaluation methods that can be applied. The causal model can be changed to incorporate measures believed to be more diagnostic.

Evaluation methods (e.g., experimental or quasi-experimental designs) dictate data collection and analysis procedures which, in turn, specify the internal and external validity of the findings . . . . The expected precision of the findings may suggest that a change in evaluation methods is desirable. Again, the two-way arrow demonstrates that data collection and analysis are controlled by evaluation methods and by the projected level of validity in the evaluation findings.

Findings are linked to the stimulus through an interpretation. The interpretation can take several forms. The sponsor may just check to see if the findings confirm his expectations, ignoring any other interpretation. In other instances, the findings may require elaborate explanations which complicate the interpretation. The sponsor's problem may have changed during the evaluation, calling for an interpretation of the findings in the light of recent developments. These developments may involve conditions or circumstances considered only obliquely by the project. Conflict between the evaluator and the sponsor often results when evaluation findings cannot be clearly interpreted, or when the findings cannot be related to changed conditions.

The Steps in an Evaluation Process

Assumptions

Each evaluation stage is connected by a dominant activity. To initiate an evaluation effort, assumptions are made to form a causal model. Assumptions are required because the causal model is, of necessity, an abstraction which simplifies the problem to permit detailed study. For instance, HEW (the U.S. Department of Health Education and Welfare) evaluated a proposed 'negative income tax program' to detect how direct dollar supplements would be spent by recipients. The 'working poor' were included in the evaluation to determine how income supplements would influence their earnings. HEW officials dictated the premises for the study.

Another set of assumptions would have dramatically altered the study. For instance, the preoccupation of economists with tax rates could have been dropped in favor of including female-headed families in the study. This would relax the rather tenuous assumption that female-headed families exercise few labor market choices . . . . Assumptions are rarely made conspicuous by sponsors.

Proxy Measures

Measures link the causal model and the evaluation approach. The causal model provides a list of program variables, block variables, and constraints, as well as objectives for the intervention . . . . Some of the causal factors in the model may resist measurement or manipulation when using an experimental or quasi-experimental design, dictating a change in the causal model and its assumptions.

Data Collection and Analysis

Findings stem from analysis which is dictated by the data collection device [design] that is applied. The precision of findings varies, depending on the evaluation method that is applied. Precision, and the ability to make diagnostic judgements, decline as quasi-experimental methods are substituted for experimental methods, and drop precipitously when nonevaluative methods are used . . . . Simple stratifications of data can dramatically enhance the explanatory power of an evaluation . . . . The internal and external validity of the findings should be projected considering the particulars of the evaluation project. The expected precision, scope, and other features of the findings may dictate which evaluation method should be used.

Interpretation

Evaluation findings are tied to the stimulus by an interpretation. To complete the cycle, the results of evaluation are presented to the sponsor. The findings are often generalized or extrapolated to suggest recommendations for action.

There are many very real problems in interpreting the findings of an evaluation. Polgar points out four examples of how program administrators can misunderstand evaluation information:

1) *Empty Vessel*: based on the assumption that nothing preceded the service or intervention program. The administrator ignores prior efforts, failing to build on positive features of past efforts, revealed by the evaluation.
2) *Separate Capsule*: limits or alters evaluation findings based on the sponsor's beliefs and past practices. If evaluation confirms the sponsor's views, the likelihood of adopting evaluation information increases.
3) *Single Pyramid*: assumes homogeneity of behavior in target groups. Clients may have different views and samples must reflect the proportion of these views in the evaluation . . . . Members of minority groups seldom seek out these services, even when they are free of charge.
4) *Interchangeable Faces*: values which cause consumers to behave in radically different ways must not be ignored. OEO (the U.S. Office of Economic Opportunity) exploited cultural motifs and used local residents as employees to make their health centers conform to local values. Many contended that cultural sensitivity was a major factor in the health center's ability to get minority groups to use health care services when many other efforts to promote health sensitivity among these groups had failed.

Interpretation is a judgemental process relying on the logical extension of evaluation findings . . . . Because interpretation is judgemental, the

policy guides that stem from evaluation findings are often challenged
. . . . The reactions to evaluation findings are based on the sponsor's
expectations and the way the findings are presented . . . . To be well
received, a presentation must stress recommendations and policy guides.
Details and the methodological gyrations needed to make these recommendations and policy guides, should be skipped. Sponsors have little
time for details and seldom appreciate their significance. Reports and
presentations that dwell on technical details are poorly received because
sponsors often lack technical skills and/or because of the pressure of
other tasks. Implications are stressed for administrators while extra-
polations tend to be shunned in academic circles. As a result, evaluation
reports stress dramatically different information from the preferred in
academic circles.

A personalized presentation geared to the needs of the recipient will
convey more information than traditional data-centered reports. Evaluation findings are seldom fully appreciated until they are translated from
scientific into personalized terms. Mitroff, Nelson and Mason call this
type of information 'mythic', and call for 'myth information' systems to
replace traditional reporting mechanisms. Figure 20 provides some distinctions between evaluative and mythic information.

Figure 20: Comparing Mythic and Evaluative Information

Mythic Information	Evaluative Information
Partial, personal, interested	Impartial, impersonal, disinterested
Anecdotal, stressing cultural motifs and images	Generalizable, stressing logic or experimental inquiry
Stirs emotions in a drama	Suppresses emotions by avoiding the dramatic
Bias accepted	Bias eliminated
Repetitive and redundant	Coherent and sequential
Implicit and intuitive	Explicit and precise
Takes moral stands	Amoral

Adapted from Mitroff, I.I., J. Nelson and R.O. Mason, 'On the Management of Myth
Information Systems,' *Management Science*, Vol. 21, No. 4, December 1974.

Evaluation findings tend to be impersonal, amoral, and precise, and
eliminate drama and emotion when most people prefer presentations
that are personal and stir emotions, using repetitive arguments and
taking a moralistic tone. According to Mitroff and Kilmann, a mythic
presentation incorporates the evaluation findings into a story that has
meaning to those who need the evaluation information.

7.2 *Distractions and Distortions*[3]

ARTURO ISRAEL

Since the mid-1970s, the increased interest in monitoring and evaluation has pushed managers toward greater concentration on measurable aspects—. . . effects on management or on operations are unclear, as is the extent to which they have diverted management's attention to inputs, to the neglect of basic objectives. A detailed evaluation of monitoring and evaluation systems would probably find they have done little to improve the quality of decision-making by management . . . . [In] the not uncommon situation, in which managers do not know and are not interested in learning how to use their monitoring and evaluation system or any other management information system available, the systems . . . generate no benefit. The availability of computers, however, generates a demand for information. Scarce, skilled personnel devote their time to gathering data and writing reports instead of working directly in operations. Data gathering is a bottomless pit which, if unchecked, can absorb an inordinate amount of scarce resources for no useful purpose . . . . The dilemma is that quantitative techniques are the most direct and obvious method of stimulating, at least partially, the discipline of specificity, but they are not automatically useful, and there is a good chance that they might have a negative effect. The introduction of these techniques should proceed with extreme caution . . . . Managers should be encouraged to define as early as possible the information that they are most likely to use, and the institution should adapt the choice of techniques to those requirements. Managers or professional staff should periodically review the use . . . reorientation in their application may well be needed so that the techniques are used to measure effects instead of inputs.

Beyond this initial point, the analysis becomes increasingly complex because a judgement about which techniques to use is contingent on many variables. One is the distinction between programmed and unprogrammed decisions. Programmed decisions typically, rely on quantitative techniques, but unprogrammed decision-making requires judgements for which only a limited amount of quantitative data is actually useful. How does one give this quantitative input only the proper weight and not

[3] From Arturo Israel, *Institutional Development: Incentives to Performance*, Published for The World Bank by The Johns Hopkins University Press, Baltimore/London, 1987, pp. 162–63.

more? . . . in high-specificity activities the relationship between programmed and unprogrammed decisions is like an inverse pyramid, in which the highest proportion of unprogrammed decisions is at the top and the lowest, at the bottom. In people-oriented activities, the shape changes into a rectangle because the proportion of unprogrammed decisions *should* increase at the lower levels.

In low-specificity activities that provide services that are very decentralized, and have low-level staff scattered over wide geographical areas, it is necessary for the management system to include a strong set of internalized norms because of the latitude that field staff have in making day-to-day decisions. Every day, field-workers face complex situations with little managerial supervision or control and few mechanisms for communication. The quality of their performance will depend on their having internalized the 'right' values and learned how their discretionary powers should be applied. In this respect, internalized norms are a surrogate for specificity and can ensure an adequate institutional performance. In order for staff to internalize the institutional norms, there need to be standardized rules that have been tailor-made for the activity.

7.3 *Participant-Observer Evaluation*[4]

LAWRENCE F. SALMEN

Participant-observer evaluation of development projects is an attempt to blend qualitative and quantitative methods of analyses so as to be useful to decision-makers and ultimately beneficial to the poor majorities for whom development assistance is carried out. Implicit in this approach, is an attempt to move beyond conceptual and methodological barriers created by evaluation typologies (formative or summative, process or impact) and to transcend dichotomies (we-they, subject-object, anthropologist-economist, professional-beneficiary). Participant-observer evaluation methods must closely follow those of ethnography, the field of social anthropology that has been referred to as 'neither "subjective" nor "objective"' but 'interpretive, mediating two worlds through a third', making sense out of the way informants naturally talk and act when they are doing ordinary activities rather than activities imposed by a researcher.

[4] From Lawrence F. Salmen, *Listen to the People: Participant-Observer Evaluation of Development Projects*, published for The World Bank by Oxford University Press, New York, 1987, pp. 121–27.

. . . The two basic methods—conversational interviewing and participant observation, including residence with beneficiaries—are intended to increase the reliability and relevance of evaluation and hence its utility to decision-makers in the development field. The basic problem with questionnaires is the artificiality of the interview setting. People are simply not apt to disclose important information about themselves to someone they do not know, regardless of the stated purpose of obtaining the information . . . they are not comfortable about disclosing certain aspects of their lives to middle-class interviewers standing at their door with pencil and paper in hand. The poor are least ready to be open about their health and sanitation practices, attitudes and behavior regarding birth control and, as is well known, income topics that are particularly important to developmental decision-makers.

Conversational interviewing, with its more natural setting, and where possible, on-site residence among project beneficiaries has been shown . . . to provide project managers with useful, timely and low-cost information with which to make project improvements. Participant-observer evaluation also includes reviews of second-hand sources of information, such as the minutes of meetings or correspondence, direct observation, and even minimal socioeconomic questionnaire surveys. It consciously blends qualitative and quantitative methods of analysis.

. . . The participant-observer evaluator acts as a broker, he or she attends to the effectiveness of the project in view of its goals in a particular context rather than to either beneficiaries or managers as distinct interest groups. The underlying assumption of participant-observer evaluation is that managers do not normally have an adequate understanding of the world they are trying to change. This understanding is found primarily among the people who inhabit that world. To gain this understanding, managers need to seek assistance from third parties who can relate the operational needs of the project to the social environment being affected . . . . Participant-observer evaluation recognizes the need to reach out to the people in such a way that they may speak freely about their own concerns. Openness is the stance. Closeness to the people is the position. The methods of participant-observation and conversational interviewing are tools to derive understanding. Often the most useful insights come more from the observer's proximity to the people, his acceptance by them and openness to them, than from the application of the tools themselves. The numbers come after the listening, not before. For participant-observation evaluation, numbers are not abstractions; they emerge from, and help to illustrate what a project means to, the people for whom it is intended.

The partial reliance of this approach on qualitative methods opens it to charges of subjectivity and distortion because of the presumed biases of the individual conducting the evaluation . . . . Bias can be diminished in participant-observer evaluation by the selection of sound, experienced observers, the use of triangulation . . . and the participation of project management at all key points in the design and execution of the investigation.

The information elicited by this directed listening has led to project improvements wherever participant-observer evaluation has been conducted . . . .

Participant-observer evaluation is widely applicable because it may be conducted by host-country nationals . . . men and women trained in a variety of disciplines.

7.4 *A Comprehensive Framework for Evaluating Training*[5]

UDAI PAREEK

Providing feedback for improvement and control is the essence. Two questions then come next: feedback to whom and improvement of what? The first question relates to the main client groups, and the second to the main dimensions to evaluate. Two additional questions are: how should evaluation be designed and in what specific ways should it be carried out: methods.

1. Main Clients

There are four main partners in training, and all of them are potential clients of evaluation. Their needs for feedback and use of feedback naturally differ, with some overlapping. The partners/clients are:

1. The participants or learners (L)
2. The training organization or institute (I) including, as sub-groups:
   a) Curriculum planners
   b) Program designers and
   c) Program managers
3. The faculty of facilitators or trainers (F)
4. The client organization, the ultimate user and financier of training (O)

[5] From R.K. Misra and S. Ravishankar (eds.), *Management Development and Training in Public Enterprises*, Ajanta, New Delhi, 1983, pp. 353–68.

The anagram LIFO may help recall all four.

2. Major Dimensions

Most models are based on four main dimensions: context, inputs, outputs are reaction. The last is not in the same category as the other three, since reaction can be to any of the three. Neglected has been the training process. The climate of the training organization, the relationship included in this are not only the interactions between participants and trainers and training methods, but also the general attitudes and relationships of trainers and participants, the 'climate' of the situation and other important determinants of the effectiveness of training which are not usually included in inputs.

The four major dimensions we evaluate therefore are: contextual factors (K), training inputs (I), training process (P), and evaluation of training outcomes (O), i.e., KIPO.

3. Evaluation Designs

Evaluation designs can be classified in various ways. One important dimension is the time when data are collected . . . only once after the training is over, or on two [or several] occasions, before training and again later, e.g., at the end and/or once or periodically 'at home', well after the training is over. A second dimension [is] the people, groups and institutions from which to collect data . . . .

In longitudinal designs (L) data are collected from the same group on several occasions. If it is done twice, it is usually a 'before-after-training' design. In *ex-post facto* designs (E), data are collected from the group only after the training is over; . . . this design has severe limitations for drawing conclusions [but where] this is all that is possible. . . is a challenge to develop design and methods to extract the most from it. Comparative survey design (S) may involve collection of data from other groups in addition to the group exposed to training. In this design also, there is no control and this sets other limitations to drawing conclusions.

The design with a great deal of control and sophistication is the matched group design (M). Several variations of this design can be used. Second group, matched on significant dimensions with the group exposed to training, can be identified and data be collected from both. Or, matched sampling can be selected for a comparative or cross-sectional survey (S). LEMS, for short.

Design can vary from simple to very sophisticated. A sophisticated design may call for several matched groups, one with training 'treatment', another with a different type of treatment, and a third with no treatment; combine this with *ex-post-facto* and longitudinal designs; and make the study 'blind', so that investigators do not know which group is in what category. Experimental or quasi-experimental designs may be used. If evaluation is to find out what changes have occurred, how much, and whether these are sustained over time, the design is bound to be complex. The choices depend on the main clients; what they want to know and what they can afford.

4. Evaluation Techniques

Various techniques can be used. One set is for using secondary data (S) and are 'unobtrusive' measures. Hamblin calls them 'keyhole' techniques, thereby expressing his disapproval of them, but there is really no reason to consider unobtrusive measures in general unethical. . . . [They] make use of available data or secondary source data. All indicators and indexes, for instance, are such measures. For example, to measure whether general morale has improved in a unit, it may be more useful to use secondary source data, such as records of absenteeism or productivity rather than ask questions. Similarly, an obtrusive measure of interrole linkage may be an increase in the number of voluntary meetings to solve common problems. In fact, identifying and using unobtrusive measures and secondary source data can be highly creative and effective and they need to be discovered and used more often for evaluation. However, if data are collected about individuals' behavior, whether by asking others or unobtrusively, without their knowledge and approval, it may be unethical. But this applied as much to interviews and other responsive techniques as to unobtrusive ones.

The greatest contribution to the development of evaluation techniques has been made by advances in scaling techniques. Techniques based on well prepared instruments (I) to measure various dimensions are being increasingly used. Various methods of scaling can be used to develop effective evaluation techniques and the three best known scaling techniques (associated with Thurstone, Likert, and Guttman) can be imaginatively used in preparing new evaluation tools. Recent developments have opened new vistas for sophistication in evaluation work.

Methods for collecting data directly from participants may include interviews, written reactions (questionnaires, scales, open ended forms), and projective techniques. These are responsive techniques (R). An additional method in this set worth mentioning is group discussion and consensus reports. In many cases, if the group consists of individuals with appropriate experience and knowledge, group evaluation may yield better results than figures calculated from individual responses. Another important technique, a very old one, is that of observation (O). Observation can also be a reactive technique if the persons being observed know that they are being observed.

Together then, four sets of techniques can be remembered as SIRO.

Seven Aspects of Training Evaluation

The seven major aspects of training to evaluate are listed below, with three parts for each. The sets are also matched with their 'dimensions'— KIPO. And the diagram orders these aspects into a conceptual scheme of training.

Coverage of Evaluation

Areas of Evaluation	*Dimension*
1. *Pre-training Factors* a. Preparation b. Learning motivation c. Expectations	Context
2. *Training Inputs* a. Curriculum including strategy (sequencing) b. Specific events c. Specific sessions	Input
3. *Training Management* a. Areas of satisfaction/dissatisfaction b. Training facilities c. Other facilities	Context
4. *Training Process* a. Learning climate b. Training methods (pedagogy) c. Other facilities	Process
5. *Participant Development* a. Conceptual development b. Learning of skills c. Change in values/attitudes d. Change in behavior e. Application	Outcome

Areas of Evaluation	Dimension

6. *Organizational Development*
  a. Job effectiveness
  b. Team effectiveness
  c. Organizational effectiveness
	Outcome

7. *Post-training Factors*
  a. Cost
  b. Organizational support
  c. Organizational factors hindering or
    facilitating use of training
	Context

Figure 21 : A Conceptual Model of Training

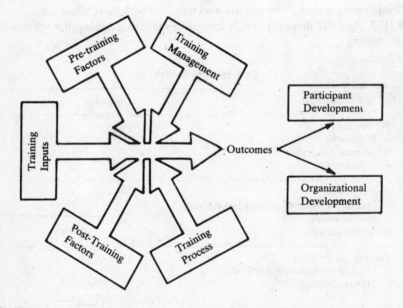

7.5 *Evaluating Training Programmes: A Case from Malaysia*[6]

UDAI PAREEK AND T.V. RAO

During early 1980, the Institute Latihan Pegawai Pelayaran Malaysia (MESTI) organized a twenty-seven day training programme for principals

[6] From Udai Pareek and T.V. Rao's *Handbook for Trainers in Educational Management*, UNESCO, Bangkok, 1981, pp. 129–32. The manual was based on the Evaluation Report No. GBA-II-80, Institute Latihan Pegawai Pelayaran, Malaysia, 1980.

of schools. The programme was designed on the basis of a survey of the training needs of sixty school principals. A total of forty-six trainers were involved in developing the course content covering six competency areas . . . . The course was attended by thirty primary and thirty secondary school principals.

The evaluation of this course was conceptualized as the process of delineating, obtaining and applying descriptive and judgemental information concerning the merit of the training courses, goals, plans, activities and results for the purposes of decision-making and some degree of accountability. The evaluation aimed at catering to the needs of various agencies including the training institutions, course developers, programme implementors, trainees, professionals in other divisions and funding agencies. The areas of evaluation included: soundness of the design, adequacy of programme materials, implementation, attainment of course outcomes, and applicability of skills acquired to on-the-job effectiveness. For each of these areas, a number of questions have been listed that point out the indicators of effectiveness of the training in that area. For example, in the area of implementation of training, the following indicators of effective implementation were listed: conducting the training according to schedule, conducting it as planned, cooperativeness of trainees, their motivation, adequacy of resources and facilities, extent of administrative problems, appropriateness of background of trainees, competence of programme planners and administrators.

Based on these indicators (called judgemental criteria by the evaluators), a set of questions called 'criterion questions' were formulated. Based on these questions, a measurement plan was drawn. The measurement plan indicated the measurement procedures. A part of the measurement plan for the area of 'implementation of the training programme' is presented in the figure.

Detailed instruments were developed . . . in the evaluation plan for each aspect. The detailed instruments are available in the detailed technical report of the project from MESTI.

The evaluation methodology, . . . the results . . . [and the] evaluation report . . . provide several insights for policy makers, trainers, and trainees to improve the quality of training. For example, on one of the criterion questions (EQ3d in the evaluation plan mentioned above) the following information and judgements were obtained after an analysis of data obtained through the instruments used as suggested in the plan:

EQ3d Criterion Question

Are available resources and facilities adequate and used?

Figure 22
Measurement Plan for Evaluation on Question EQ3
How well was the training carried out?

Criterion Questions	Measurements Procedures					
	How	When	By whom	Information Source	Data Analysis	Instruments
Are scheduled activities and events implemented in time?	The progress of the training will be checked against the official timetable.	Beginning and end of each session.	Evaluator	Activities and events of training.	Comparison	Official record timetable.
Is training carried out as planned?	Activities as they occur will be checked against the official timetable.	During each session.	Evaluator	Activities and events of training.	Comparison	Official record timetable.
To what extent are trainees co-operative, motivated, and satisfied with the training?	All training sessions will be observed.	During each session.	Evaluator	Trainees' behaviour.	Frequency	
	MESTI trainers will rate trainees' initiative and effort.	During group work.	MESTI trainers	Trainees' behaviour.	Means, variance.	Trainer rating questionnaire
	Trainees will use rating scales to indicate their feeling about each session.	End of each session.	Evaluator	Trainees' feelings.	Medians	Trainee rating questionnaire
	Incidents, complaints and grievances will be recorded.	During the course.	Evaluator	Incidents, complaints, grievances.	Frequency	Evaluation observation sheet
	Trainees' suggestions for the improvement of the course will be collected.	End of each session.	Evaluator	Trainees' perceptions.	Frequency	Trainee questionnaire
Are available recourses and facilities adequate and used?	On-course observation.	During training.	Evaluator	Resources, facilities.	Frequency	Evaluation sheet
	Trainers and trainees will use rating scales.	During training	Trainers Trainees	Trainer and trainee perceptions.	Frequency	Rating by Trainees and Trainers

Question	Method	When	Who	Focus	Measure	Instrument
Are administration problems small and under control?	Training sessions will be observed, incidents will be recorded.	During the course.	Evaluator	Incidents, events.	Frequency	Evaluation observation sheet
	Trainers will record what they have observed.	During training	MESTI trainers	Incidents, events.	Frequency	Trainers questionnaire
Do trainers seem to know their subject matter and have expertise as trainers?	Trainees will record what they have observed.	End of each session.	Trainees	Trainee perceptions	Frequency	Trainees questionnaire
	All training sessions will be observed.	During each session.	Evaluator	Trainers	Ratings	Evaluation sheet.
	Trainees will use rating scales.	End of each session.	Trainees	Trainers	Median	Trainee questionnaire
Are products of training sessions produced as scheduled?	Trainers will make records	During group sessions.	Trainers	Products of training.	Product status.	Trainer questionnaire
Do course administrators seem competent in managing the course and handling of unforeseen events.	Specific complaints will be noted.	During the course.	Evaluator Trainers	Complaints	Frequency	Evaluator and trainer notes
	MESTI administration will be rated by trainees.	End of each session	Trainees	MESTI administration.	Median	Trainee rating
Are the delivery methods used the most suitable for the particular topic or content area?	The appropriateness of the delivery method used will be rated by trainees. (Alternatively, trainees will record for each topic the delivery method that would be more appropriate)	End of each session.	Trainees	Delivery methods.	Median	Trainee rating

Information: The overhead projector was fully used. However, trainees sitting toward the back could not see well, especially the writings.

The microphone was also fully used. For most trainers, the microphone was necessary . . . . However, several trainers had the tendency to move about in front of the blackboard while they explained something. For these trainers, the fixed microphone was not suitable . . . .

Only one trainer handed out both Bahasa Malaysia and English versions of his handouts. This may be expensive but desirable . . . .

White chalk on the blackboard could not be clearly seen from the back of the class. The illumination on the blackboard was too low.

The main lecture room was suitable for the purpose although perhaps a little too narrow. The space used for small group work was not so suitable because trainees' voices from one group disturbed others in another group.

Lighting was sufficient expect for the blackboard surface. The rooms were air-conditioned.

A secretariat provided efficient support services throughout the course.

Board and lodging for trainees were looked after. No major problems were encountered.

Judgement

It can be said that the available resources and facilities at the Fakulti Pendidikan, University Malaya as well as those brought along from MESTI's office were fairly adquate and fully used.

7.6 *Evaluating the Consulting Process*[7]

D.SCHWARTZ AND G.LIPPITT

Figure 23 summarises a conceptual model. Brief explanations and definitions of the four independent elements of the diagram follow.

[7] From D. Schwartz and G. Lippitt, 'Evaluating the Consulting Process', *Journal of European Training*, Vol. 4, No. 5, 1975.

Research and Evaluation Areas

Client/Consultant Relationship: This area relates to the evaluation of the personal and professional relationships between client, client system and consultant. These relationships often have a major impact on the final outcome of the consulting process.

igure 23

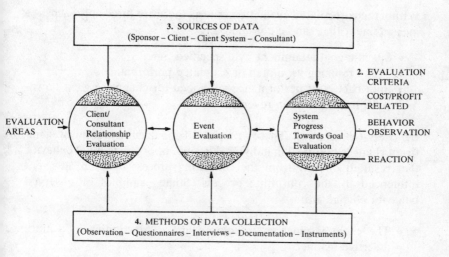

Evaluation of Consulting/Training Events: This evaluation area covers significant consulting interventions, such as survey-feedback meetings, skill training conflict-resolution meetings, and other important milestone activities. Assessing the impact and contribution of each of these types of event on the overall project can provide important information, both for designing future projects with the client and for improving similar events that will take place in the current project.

Progress Toward Specific Goals: This area relates to the client system's progress toward achievement of prestated goals and the contribution made by the consultation toward this progress. Evaluation of overall results helps to answer the client's question, 'Was the money I invested in consultation returned, at least, by the results achieved?'

Cost/Profit Related: Some 'hard-measure' criteria are developed to determine as directly as possible the effect of consultation on the achievement of specified results. Some examples of specified results related to cost/profit are:

- Consulting time and expense (estimate vs. actual);
- Consulting-event outcomes that result in increased sales, decreased costs;
- Trend changes in safety record, grievances, turnover, absenteeism, theft.

Within the cost-related evaluation criteria there are three approaches to measurement that can be considered:

- Specific goal attainment by a specified time;
- Trend tracking vs. a plan or estimated performance;
- Spot checks of performance vs. hoped-for change, e.g., a downward trend has been reversed.

Behavior Observation: These criteria call for documentation of significant changes observed in individual, group, or organizational behavior that resulted directly from the consulting process or from an event influenced by the consulting process. Some examples of observed behavior change are:

- The client is much more relaxed and is functioning in a more assertive manner.
- A change has occurred in the organization structure, simplifying lines of communication.
- Event participants demonstrate that they can plan for and conduct problem-solving meetings.

Reaction: These criteria relate to the reactions of the clients and the client system to the consulting process. They report feelings, attitudes and points of view as these change over time. Some examples of reaction criteria measurements are:

- The client's expressed feelings about the consulting relationship;
- The participant's evaluation of a training event;
- The reactions of the client system as expressed through a series of attitude surveys during the course of the consulting process.

Sources of Data

There are four sources of data for an evaluation system. Each of them is defined as follows:

The Sponsor is a person (or persons) who can significantly influence the consulting process and who has a strong interest in the instigation progress and final outcome of the consulting process. In some instances, the sponsor is the client's supervisor. Many times, particularly when working at the top of the organization, the sponsor is the client, e.g., the president. The sponsor also could be a group of people such as a city council, advisory board, executive committee or board of directors.

The Client is the person who makes the 'go or no go' decision about events and directions within the sphere of the project.

The Client System is any person or group directly involved in, or affected by, the consulting project.

The Consultant is the helper (or helpers) whose expertise has been contracted for, by the client. The helper may be internal to the client system or external to it. There may also be a combination of internal and external helpers.

Methods of Data Collection

Data can be collected in a wide variety of ways. The following are five methods that are most frequently used to collect data for evaluation of the consulting process.

Observation: Individual and group behavior is observed and recorded as it relates to the job to be done. Also observed and recorded are the ways in which systems are functioning, e.g., flow charting, decision trees, PERT charting.

Questionnaires: Formats are specially designed or standardized, asking for individual written responses concerning attitude, viewpoints, opinions, and perceptions.

Interviews: Individuals or groups are interviewed face-to-face or by telephone to gain their in-depth perceptions, sepcific examples, ideas, and feelings.

Documentation: Archival records, current records, and specially recorded data are used to show trends and changes resulting from the consulting process.

Instruments: Devices are specially designed for data collection with the purpose of stimulating individual feeback about a situation and to provide a framework for evaluation discussions between client, client systems, and consultant.

7.7 *Utilization-focused Evaluation*[8]

M.Q. PATTON

Utilization-focused evaluation is not a formal model or recipe for how to conduct evaluative research. Rather, it is an approach, an orientation, and a set of options. The active-reactive-adaptive evaluator chooses from among these options as he or she works with decision-makers and information users throughout the evaluation process. There is no formula guaranteeing success in this approach—indeed, the criteria for success are variable. Utilization means different things to different people in different settings, and is an issue subject to negotiation between evaluators and decision-makers.

The outline that follows, pulls together and organizes some of the critical elements and considerations in utilization-focused evaluation. This outline is not meant as a recipe, but only as a brief overview of some of the major points made above.

There are only two fundamental requirements in this approach; everything else is a matter for negotiation, adaptation, selection, and matching. First, relevant decision-makers and information users must be identified and organized—real, visible, specific, and caring human beings, not ephemeral, general, and abstract 'audiences', organizations, or agencies. Second, evaluators must work actively, reactively, and adaptively with these identified decision-makers and information users to make all other decisions about the evaluation—decisions about research focus, design methods, anlaysis, interpretation, and dissemination.

An Outline of the Utilization-focused Approach to Evaluation

I. Identification and Organization of Relevant Decision Makers and Information Users

A. Criteria for Identification: the Personal Factor

[8] From M.Q. Patton, *Utilization-Focused Evaluation*, Sage, Newbury Park, 1978, pp. 284–88.

1. People who can use information;
2. People to whom information makes a difference;
3. People who have questions they want to have answered; and
4. People who care about and are willing to share responsibility for the evaluation and its utilization.

B. Criteria for Organization
   1. Provision can be made for continuous direct contact between evaluators and decision makers for information users;
   2. The organized group is small enough to be active, hard working, and decision-oriented (my own preference is for a task force of fewer than five, and certainly fewer than ten, people);
   3. The members of the group are willing to make a heavy time commitment to the evaluation (the actual amount of time depends on the size of the group, the size and scope of the evaluation, and the members' ability to work together).

II. The Relevant Evaluation Questions are Identified and Focused

A. Criteria for Identification of Questions
   1. The members of the evaluation task force (i.e., identified and organized decision makers, information users, and evaluators) agree on the purpose(s) and emphasis of the evaluation. Options include:
      a Information for program improvement (formative evaluation);
      b Information about continuation of the program (summative evaluation); or
      c Both formative and summative evaluation but with emphasis on one or the other (equality of emphasis is not likely in practice when a single evaluation is involved)
   2. The members of the task force agree on which components and basic activities of the program will be the subject of the evaluation (the point here is simply to delineate what aspects of the program are to be discussed in detail as specific evaluation questions are focused).

B. Alternative Approaches for Focusing Evaluation Questions
   1. The evaluation question can be framed in terms of the program's mission statement, goals and objectives.
      a Evaluators must be active-reactive-adaptive in goals clarification exercises, realizing that the appropriateness of

generating clear, specific, measurable goals varies depending upon the nature of the organization and the purpose of the evaluation;

b Goals clarification provides direction in determining what information is needed and wanted—goals do not automatically determine the content and focus of the evaluation which depend on what task force members want to know;

c Goals are prioritized using the criterion of information need, not just that of relative importance to program.

2. The evaluation question can be framed in terms of program implementation. Options here include:

a Effort evaluation;

b Process evaluation; and

c The treatment identification approach.

3. The evaluation question can be framed in terms of the program's theory of action.

a A hierarchy of objectives can be constructed to delineate the program's theory of action, wherein attainment of each lower level objective is assumed necessary for attainment of each higher level objective;

b The evaluation might focus on any two or more causal connections in a theory of action;

c The theories or causal linkages tested in the evaluation are those believed relevant by evaluation task force members; and

d The evaluation question links program implementation to program outcomes, i.e., determines the extent to which observed outcomes are attributable to program activities.

4. The evaluation question can be framed in terms of the point in the life of the program when the evaluation takes place. Different questions are relevant at different stages of program development.

5. The evaluation question is framed in the context of the organizational dynamics of the program. Different types of organizations use different types of information and need different types of evaluation. Programs vary in organizational terms along with the following dimensions:

a The degree to which the environment is certain and stable versus uncertain and dynamic;

b The degree to which the program can be characterized as an open or closed system; and

c The degree to which a rational goal maximization model, an optimizing systems model, or an incremental gains model best describes decision-making processes.

6. The active-reactive-adaptive evaluator works with decision makers and information users to find the right evaluation question(s). The right question from a utilization point of view has several characteristics:

  a It is possible to bring data to bear on the question;

  b There is more than one possible answer to the question, i.e., the answer is not predetermined or 'loaded' by the phrasing of the question;

  c The identified decision makers want information to help answer the question;

  d The identified decision makers feel they need information to help them answer the question;

  e The identified and organized decision makers and information users want to answer the question for themselves, not just for someone else;

  f the decision makers can indicate how they would use the answer to the question, i.e., they can specify the relevance of an answer for their program.

7. As the evaluation question is focused, the fundamental, ever-present questions that underlie all other issues are: What difference would it make to have this information? How would the information be used and how would it be useful?

III. Evaluation Methods are Selected that Generate Useful Information for Identified and Organized Decision Makers and Information Users

A. Strengths and weaknesses of alternative methodological paradigms are considered in the search for methods that are appropriate to the nature of the evaluation question. Options include consideration of:

1. Quantitative and qualitative methods;
2. Hypothetico-deductive objectivity or subjectivity versus holistic-inductive objectivity or subjectivity;
3. Distance from, versus closeness to, the data:
4. Fixed versus dynamic designs;
5. Relative emphases on reliability or validity;
6. Holistic or component units of analysis; and
7. Inductive versus deductive procedures.

B. Decision and measurement decisions are shared by evaluators and decision-makers to increase information users' understanding of, belief in, and commitment to, evaluation data.

1. Variables are operationalized in ways that make sense to those who will use the data; face validity, as judged by decision makers and information users, is an important instrumentation criterion in evaluation-measurement.
2. Evaluation designs are selected that are credible to decision makers, information users, and evaluators.
3. Major concepts and units of analysis are defined so as to be relevant to decision makers and information users; the long-term relevance of difinitions and units of analysis are considered to increase the potential for continuous, longitudinal evaluation (where appropriate).
4. Multiple methods are used and multiple measures employed as much as possible to increase the believability of findings.
5. Decision makers and information users are involved in continuous methods, design, measurement, and basic data gathering decisions as changed circumstances, resources, and timeliness force changes in methods. Recognizing that initial proposals are poor predictors of final designs, active-reactive-adaptive evaluators seek involvement of relevant decision makers in design and measurement questions as they arise.
6. Decision makers weigh with evaluators the methodological constraints introduced by limited resources, time deadlines, and data accessibility problems. All task force members must be highly knowledgeable about the strengths and weaknesses of data collection procedures.
7. The utilization assumption guiding methods discussion is that it is better to have an approximate and highly probabilistic answer to the right question than a solid and relatively certain answer to the wrong question.

IV. *Decision Makers and Information Users Participate with Evaluators in Data Analysis and Data Interpretation*

A. Data analysis is separated from data interpretation so that decision makers can work with the data without biases introduced by the evaluator's conclusions.
B. Standards of desirability are established before data analysis to guide data interpretation; the nature of the standards of desirability will vary along a continuum from highly crystallized to highly ambiguous.

C. Data analysis is presented in a form that makes sense to decision makers and information users. Decision makers are given an opportunity to struggle with the data as they become available, so that surprises are avoided.

D. Evaluators work with decision makers and information users to make full use of the data.

1. Realizing that 'positive' and 'negative' are perceptual labels, the responsive evaluator avoids characterizing results in such monolithic terms. Most studies include both somewhat positive and somewhat negative findings, depending upon one's point of view. Analysis and interpretation focus on specific results, relationships, and implications rather than general characterizations of the program.

2. Both strengths and weaknesses of the data are made clear and explicit.

E. Evaluators work with decision makers and information users to develop specific plans for action and utilization based upon evaluation findings and interpretation.

1. Evaluation ultimately necessitates making leaps from data to judgement, from analysis to action.

2. Utilization-focused data analysis and interpretation includes the judgements, conclusions,and recommendations of both evaluators and decision makers.

V. *Evaluators and Decision Makers Negotiate and Cooperate in Dissemination Efforts*

A. Dissemination of findings is only one aspect of evaluation utilization, and a minor aspect in many cases. The primary utilization target consists of relevant decision makers and information users identified and organized during the first step in the evaluation process

B. Dissemination takes a variety of forms for different audiences and different purposes.

C. Throughout dissemination efforts both evaluators and decision makers take responsibility for the evaluation from initial conceptualization to final data analysis and interpretation. Options include:

1. Both evaluators and decision makers are present at dissemination presentations; and

2. Both evaluators and those for whom the evaluation was conducted are identified in all reports and presentations.

7.8 *Characteristic Impasses and Ways to Manage*[9]

PAUL C. NUTT

Figure 24 illustrates two ways that the evaluation process can be cut short. Sponsors and evaluators who attempt short cuts often exhibit stereotyped behavior which will be referred to as 'model mania' and 'data mania'. Each creates problems which limit the effectiveness of an evaluation.

Figure 24 : Some Truncated Evaluation Processes

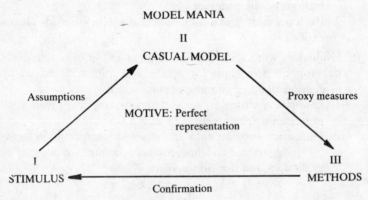

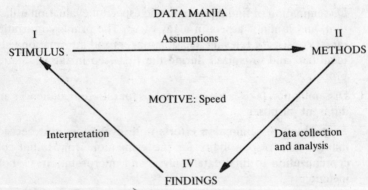

Reprinted with permission from Nutt, P.C., 'On Managed
Evaluation Processes,' *Technological Forecasting and
Social Change*, Vol. 17, No. 4 (1980).

[9] From Paul C. Nutt, *Evaluation Concepts and Methods: Shaping Policy for the Health Administrator*, Robert B. Luce, Bridgeport, CT.

Model Mania

The ideal evaluation process can be shortened by following an 'assumption-measures-confirmation' path. The motive behind this process is precision in the representation of the evaluation problem, provided by the causal model. It is termed model mania because the causal model and the proposed method of evaluation are repeatedly tested against perceived reality.

Model mania occurs when causal models are very difficult to construct or when the model proves to be contentious, raising many controversial questions. For example, a state mental health department with twenty or so custodial institutions sought to develop an evaluation scheme to measure the effectiveness of its institutional administrators. The task of devising a causal model for the process of mental health administration proved to be difficult. Each proposed model provided a unique conception of the administrator's role, which suggested a particular set of measures. Each of the models proved to be unacceptable to particular mental health reference groups. Cost and efficiency measures were criticized by psychiatrists and psychologists who treat patients. Quality care measures were seen as vague and nondiagnostic and thus unacceptable to executives in the State Department of Mental Health. The controversy led to many changes in the model in their attempts to find one that matched the implicit perceptions of the sponsor. In short, model mania led to no appreciable action in assessing the managerial competence in the institutions.

Evaluation that is focused on vague questions like measuring care quality in a hospital, or controversial issues such as the negative income tax evaluation, often results in iterative model building where model construction becomes an end in itself.

Data Mania

The evaluation process (Figure 24) can also be shortened by following an assumption-data-interpretation path. It is termed data mania because a preference for data supersedes all other considerations. The motive fuelling this process is speed.

Data mania stems from gathering data with little (if any) notion of causality and from ritualistic data accumulations. For instance, the health industry has lamented the lack of data to the point where legislation often mandates certain types of data accumulation. A recent example of data mania is the Health Planning and Resource Development Act of 1975, which requires a careful inventory of all health delivery resources.

Apparently, the resource profile is thought to have diagnostic value, helping planning agencies identify deficiencies in patterns of care delivery.

Sponsor and Evaluator Preferences

Figure 25 provides a schematic representation of sponsor and evaluator behavior when conducting an evaluation. The sponsor dominates the left side of the diagram. Administrators, who often become the sponsors of evaluation efforts, are constantly sifting and winnowing potential evaluation problems. When the needs for information exceed some threshold, the sponsor can allocate resources to initiate an evaluation project. The evaluator controls Stage III, methodology, in the same way the sponsor controls Stage I, the stimulus. The sponsor is unlikely to have up-to-date know-how of evaluation methods. Sponsors and evaluators share control over the development of causal models and the findings. The dialogue between evaluators and sponsors in Stage II (model formation) and Stage IV (documentation of results) leads to success or failure for the project.

Figure 25 : Behaviorally Based Evaluation Processes

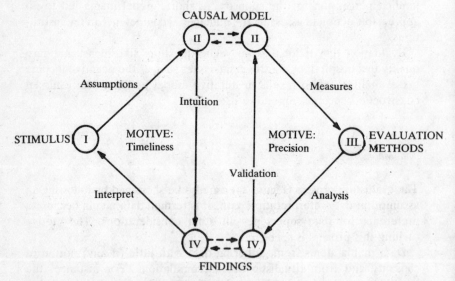

Reprinted with permission from Nutt, P.C., 'On Managed Evaluation Processes,' *Technological Forecasting and Social Change*, Vol. 17, No. 4 (1980)

Preferred Paths

The sponsor's preferred path leads to a 'stimulus-model-results' evaluation process, as shown in Figure 25. The sponsor makes assumptions in order to build the causal model and uses the model to visualize ways to overcome problems implicit in the stimulus. Their motive is timeliness; a detailed investigation is perceived to take too long. Churchman points out that managers often believe they should be able to tease out findings without the expense and frustration of formal data collection. The manager examines his causal model, may get the opinions of staff and peers, and then draws conclusions without the aid of tiresome academic fumbling. Administrators rich in experience believe they can draw on this experience to overcome the need for many evaluation projects . . . .

Improving the Evaluation Dialogue

Sponsors and evaluators adopt distinct paths because they have distinct roles and skills. Sponsors must excel in diagnostic skills (deciding when additional evaluation information can materially aid the organization is particularly important). Methodological skills are the forte of the evaluator, so these skills are stressed. Neither skill can supplant the other.

Evaluators attempt to validate, using a model. The results may lack relevance because they were not exposed to the forces motivating the evaluation. Validation does not occur unless the findings are interpreted in terms of the sponsor's needs. Validation using a model leads to stacks of unread consultant and staff reports. Often, relevant and thought-provoking information fails to influence decisions in organizations because its validation lacked field testing and because the information was not carefully interpreted to the sponsor.

Sponsors can rely too often on their intuition. Churchman contends that a strict reliance on intuition leads to dogmatic managers. They become professional skeptics who contend evaluation has little chance of illuminating complex issues, and relativists who believe that a mosaic of obscure contingencies dictate the success of interventions. These and other manifestations of the practical school dominate many policy-level positions in organizations. Unfortunately, many problems are counter-intuitive.

Remedies to these problems lie in the dialogue that occurs in Stages II and IV. To illustrate, the causal model may be developed jointly by the sponsor and evaluator, as shown in Figure 26. Both can educate. The evaluator learns more about the motivations behind the study and the necessity of key assumptions. The evaluator may be able to relax constraints by pointing out how evaluation methods with greater power can be used when certain assumptions are changed. This dialogue aids the evaluator and sponsor to enrich the causal model, trimming out restrictive assumptions and devising measurable program and performance factors.

Figure 26 : Some Dialogues

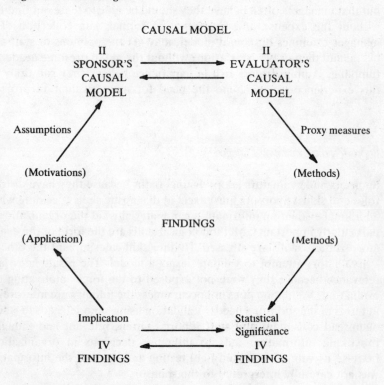

Reprinted with permission from Nutt, P.C., 'On Managed Evaluation Process,' *Technological Forecasting and Social Change*, Vol. 17, No. 4 (1980).

Sponsor-evaluator dialogue is also essential in explaining the meaning of evaluation findings, also illustrated in Figure 26. Evaluators can aid sponsors by fully exploring the implications of the evaluation information. Reports or presentations should be jointly developed to describe policy guides and to provide the sponsor with an interpretation, a story, or an anecdote that can be used to illustrate key points. The evaluators must help the sponsor understand the limitations of the evaluation's conclusion-drawing power. The sponsor aids the evaluator by reemphasizing the motivation for the study and how the information will be used. Again, this dialogue permits the sponsor to make full and complete use of the evaluation information.

Managing the Evaluation Process

Avoiding Evaluation

The threatening nature of evaluation sets it apart from many other collaborative staff-administrator activities. When an evaluation is conducted someone may lose, and lose badly, if the results do not support the predictions, programs, or commitments of an organisation's power figures. Survival, stability, and growth are goals that often dominate the work world of administrators. Evaluation focuses on past accomplishments and may turn them into deficits. For these reasons, administrators attempting to advance or maintain their power position against the intrusion of competitors often resist evaluation. In other instances, programs become highly entrenched and, as Suchman points out, are based upon a large collection of inadequately tested assumptions and defended by staff and field personnel with strong vested interests in the continuation of the program as it is. Testimonials and assurances of success are periodically demanded from program administrators, forcing the administrator into a total program commitment. Such commitments entice the administrators, and others with vested interests in the programs, to avoid evaluation, fearing its findings.

To avoid evaluation, administrators often engage in rationalization, including the following:

1. Alleging long-range effects: A prediction is made that the effects of a program will not show up for some time, making longitudinal studies essential. For instance, a major university conducted a pilot test of a suicide prevention program, using a computer interview. The preliminary evaluation suggested that the interview was more effective than the psychiatrists. The results were put away for five years, to determine its 'long-term effects'.

2. Contending important effects resist measurement: A contention is often made that instruments cannot detect program effects. The program is described as having subtle, general, or small effects that will evade detection by anything but very costly evaluation and that evaluation funds could be better used to deliver program services . . . . Those attempting quality-of-care studies of nursing are confronted with claims that even unobtrusive measures will [somehow] disturb the patient care process and that 'tender, loving care' is not measurable anyway.

3. Refusing to withhold services: Experimental and control groups may be called unreasonable because they withhold services from the needy . . . .

Pseudoevaluation

. . . When evaluation can no longer be resisted, or when these rationalizations have been dismissed, those with vested interests often engage in pseudoevaluation. Pseudoevaluation is carried out to manage the evaluation process so that a thoughtful assessment of a program is impossible. Some evaluation abuses... are listed below:

1. Eyewash: An attempt to justify a weak or bad program by focusing evaluation on these aspects of the program expected to fare well. Referring to Figure 26, the sponsor makes assumptions and suggests causal relations that he suspects (or knows) will provide findings supportive of the program.

2. Whitewash: Covering up the prospect of program failure by soliciting testimonials to distract evaluation efforts. The left-hand loop in Figure 2, embracing the assumption-intuition-interpretation activities by sponsor, can be used to whitewash. Accreditation teams for hospitals and academic programs often act on testimonials in the form of reports and presentations which extoll their virtues, and not on formal performance measures . . . . The testimonial is hoped to dose the link between assumptions and interpretation. Whitewash is often successful because requests to evaluate, like the continuing education example, are proforma: a serious attempt at assessment is not expected. In other cases, program failures are covered up by eloborate reasoning stemming from intuitive assessments, and by favorable comments in or out of context.

3. Submarine: Attempt to eliminate or destroy a good program. Submarining often stems from administrative in-fighting over rights to succession or turf. Again, the left-hand side of Figure 24 is used, but in this case negative information is posited or solicited. Objective evaluation is avoided as it may reveal positive program features . . . . For example, the programs, missions, and guideliners of Regional Medical Programs were altered by administrative edicts so frequently and pervasively that . . . the Regional Medical Programs were phased out because 'they failed to settle on a mission'.

4. Posture: Using evaluation as a gesture to create the aura of scientific objectivity. The sponsor looks good when his/her organization or unit sponsors self-assessment or appears forward-looking when new opportunities are being carefully examined. The sponsor encourages the evaluator to move through all stages (Figure 26) but withholds resources

and personal sanction. No results are expected or even desired . . . . Activities labelled 'fact finding' in public agencies often signal this type of evaluation.

5. Substitution: Shifting attention to less relevant, or defensible, aspects of a program to disguise failure. All stages in Figure 26 are covered but the interpretation activity is selective, reporting only positive program features. These tactics are often attempted with varying success.

6. Delay: Postponement tactics can be used to thwart evaluation. The scope of the project can be studied at length and then restudied to point out to those pushing for evaluation that a proper study takes time. After repeated failure to build a model, a case can be made that evaluation just isn't worth the effort . . . . Delay is probably the most common form of pseudoevaluation, and is often signalled by task forces, elaborate agendas, and the sudden emergence of a preference for group decision-making in otherwise autocratic administrators.

7. Reconstruction: Attempts can be made to piece together programs in the light of beneficial changes in performance indicators. The causal model is built to reflect the performance data. For instance, a Blue Cross organization mounted a variety of cost containment programs in response to a state's legislative mandates. First, one intervention is attempted and then another, with the last intervention often based on a spin-off of the previous program. If costs begin to show a measurable decline, a frantic search for a causal agent is mounted to reconstruct the program.

8. Inadvertent programs: Data found to verify the beneficial effects of inadvertent interventions can be relabelled as planned interventions to enhance the prestige of administrators. A causal relationship is discovered, following a routine performance audit. Screndipitous outcomes often stimulate data collection, to refine the effectiveness measures and to isolate a defensible causal agent, under the administrator's control. The sponsor verifies the veracity of the data, and then frames an evaluation question which the data can confirm. The process has but one step: intuition . . . .

9. Hand-picked panels: Site visit teams are often used to evaluate programs. Outsiders often set up expectations based on experiences that are not transferable. By selecting a site visit team whose experiences, and thus biases and expectations, are similar to those operating in the program, the program can be sanctified. Or to eliminate an unwanted program, a site team may be selected, whose members are likely to be hostile to the practices of the program . . . .

10. Fixed Indices: Evaluation sponsors dictate criteria and criteria weights. Measures of the criteria are fixed to steer the evaluator toward issues the sponsor wants considered. The sponsor restricts the evaluator's

scope of inquiry by dictating the measures and by restricting the evaluator's role in interpreting the results (see Figure 26). Interpretation is reserved for the sponsor and no dialogue is permitted (see Figure 24) . . . . Well-endowed hospitals, for instance, publicize those indices that measure institutional solvency. Fixed indices are also used to make a point. When pupil-teacher ratios are falling, school systems compare them to other schools to justify budget increases.

Fuzzy Interpretations

As a last resort, sponsors may develop tactics to aid them in explaining away negative findings, should they occur. The results are made fuzzy to raise questions which may discredit the findings. Suchman contends that even well-conducted evaluation projects can be rendered suspect when someone in a position of power makes one of several claims. These include the following:

1. Alleging a poorly selected target group: The effects of the program were claimed to be understated because those who could benefit most from the services, or respond best to the intervention, did not participate in the study. In short, a biased source of the target group is alleged. Randomization makes this claim implausible but the benefits of randomization are seldom understood, so it can be alleged anyway. A variant on this theme is to claim that those needing the services were in the control group. Again, randomization will make this claim implausible.

2. Claims of concentrated effects: Some service recipients improved immensely, but the claim is made that these benefits were washed out by those who did not need the services. The selective effect argument is difficult to combat unless individual cases can be traced to isolate high benefiting participants.

3. Claims of faulty program machanisms: A more intensive program is advanced as necessary to produce positive results. Ths claim was advanced by Head Start advocates, who were able to initiate 'follow through', a program designed to work with low-income children after they began grade school.

4. Claim of bias: All sorts of claims can be made which imply bias. Contending that control groups were improperly selected, measures were taken without reliability checks, and the wrong measurements were used, can discredit evaluation findings. The 'Hawthorne Effect' (people responding to the evaluation situation, not the program) can always be alleged because the Hawthorne had taken on the status of an empirical law.

8. ACTION RESEARCH

INTRODUCTION

For trainers and consultants, it is particularly important to take action research into fields beyond (and cutting deeper than) evaluation and other 'problem solving' activities, at least as these terms are commonly used. Evaluation examines already established programs and problem solving is limited by accepted assumptions and problem formulations based on them. Beyond these, lies action research which probes into the assumptions and general directions themselves, to throw light on program and organizational goals and on improving the processes for reaching these goals. Again, underlying these at various levels, are issues of the consultant trainers' own development, *their* perceptions, assumptions and ways of giving professional and personal meaning to their world of work. While action research for 'solving' problems and for operational purposes, such as evaluation, easily carry an energetic, no-nonsense, definitive overtone, these wider areas have a quieter exploratory, developmental image. But across these differences it is the range of concern and tone which is the essence they share: the research is for action. It is *not* of the essence that the concern be triggered by features of the immediate situation, that action be immediate or final, or that the actor feel out of breath or propelled by his brilliance and decisiveness into feeling on top of the world.

Practitioners—trainers, managers, community workers—interested in searching for answers to questions about how to improve their action and involve themselves in research, whether or not they are aware of it, can become what Schon calls 'reflective practitioners' if they reflect on their action choices and deliberately search for alternative paths. We include three readings from Schon in this section: on the nature of 'reflection-in-action' and on reflective research and experimenting by practitioners. In his first reading, Schon enumerates four types of research 'outside the immediate context of practice (yet) in order to enhance the practitioner's capacity for reflection-in-action': frame analysis—how the practitioner forms problems and roles; 'repertoire-building' research; research on 'fundamental methods of inquiry and overarching theories'; and research on the process of reflection-in-action.

For Pareek and Khanna (8.2) action research denotes any research that focusses on 'a particular problem' in which the processes are 'consciously used and perfected' for decision and action for improving practice. They then walk the reader through an eight-step sequence centered on hypothesis formulation and testing. Schon (8.3) concentrates instead on experimentation. Experimentation may or may not have a hypothesis. It may be exploratory or 'move-testing'—to see not only 'whether you get what you intend but whether you then in fact like what you get'. He sees the practitioner in continuous 'transaction with the situation, he shapes it and makes himself part of it'. In the course of this, he develops a stance towards inquiry. This involves 'a kind of double vision. He must act in accordance with the view he has adopted [and] his choices become more committing, . . . more nearly irreversible'. But he must *also* be ready 'to break it open later in order to make new sense of his transactions with the situation'.

We have included two more readings to delineate the proper field of action research and its main processes. One suggests the boundary between action research and organization development. Since O.D. has become a specialist function for which executives often draw on outside expertise, this reading also touches on the broader issue of the role and function of the specialist outsider in action research and on the nature of the relationship between practitioner and research (with which a later reading, by Schon, will deal in more detail). We close this first, orienting set of readings with an overview by Chin, of the uses to which action research (as we use the term here) can be put and the differences it makes to design and outcomes. Chin limits action research of affecting 'conduct', but we prefer its wider reference, to include research that practitioners can do themselves and also guide researchers to do together with themselves.

The 'Revolutionary Demands' of Reflective Practice

The next set of readings, deals with the relationships between practitioners and researchers and the 'revolutionary demand' that reflective practice makes on the operating as well as on the helping institutions: 'flexible procedures, differentiated responses, qualitative appreciation of complex processes, and decentralized responsibility for judgement and action [and] . . . attention to conflicting values and purposes'. These are all 'in contrast to the normal bureaucratic emphasis on technical rationality'. Programs for the centralized organization of research, gracefully suggests Lewis Thomas (8.8) need 'thinking about . . . .

If it is centrally organized, the system must be designed primarily for the elicitation of disbelief and the celebration of surprise . . . [and] so that the separate imaginations in different human minds can be pooled. [This is] more a kind of game than a systematic business . . . . What it needs is for the air to be made right'.

The final paper pulls together the various strands of readings in this section in order to focus on how practitioners may through some systematic training be helped to develop their competences in action research.

8.1 *Reflective Research by Practitioners*[1]

DONALD A. SCHON

. . . there are kinds of research which can be undertaken outside the immediate context of practice in order to enhance the practitioner's capacity for reflection-in-action. 'Reflective research', as I shall call it, may be of four types, each of which already exists at least in embroyo . . . .

Frame analysis: At any given time in the life of a profession, certain ways of framing problems and roles come into good currency. When Quist frames the problem of the design of the school as one of 'imposing a discipline on the screwy site', and when Dean Wilson frames the problem of malnourishment as one of 'gaps in a process of nutrient flow', they bound the phenomena to which they will pay attention. Their frames determine their strategies of attention and thereby set the directions in which they will try to change the situation, the values which will shape their practice.

Repertoire-building research: . . . when practice situations do not fit available theories of action, models of phenomena, or techniques of control, they may nevertheless be seen as familiar situations, cases, or precedents. Repertoire-building research serves the function of accumulating and describing such exemplars in ways useful to reflection-in-action, and it varies from profession to profession . . . a sequence of astutely chosen questions leads . . . through a process of inquiry which serves both to structure the 'solution space' of the situation at hand and to demonstrate a mode of thinking about business problems

[1] From Donald A. Schon, *The Reflective Practitioner: How Professionals Think in Action*, Basic Books, New York, 1983, pp. 306–11.

Repertoire-building research is widely practiced, but tends to focus on the starting situation, the actions taken, and the results achieved. Such cases may usefully display linkages between features of action, outcome, and context, but they do not reveal the path of inquiry which leads from an initial framing of the situation to the eventual outcome . . . . When a case study more nearly presents the evolution of inquiry, it may provide the reader with exemplars in the double sense I have described.

Research on fundamental methods of inquiry and overarching theories . . . . By methods and theories fundamental to a practice, I mean those that some practitioners have learned to use as springboards for making sense of new situations which seem, at first glance, not to fit them . . . . Research on such fundamental theories and methods may be of two kinds. Researchers may try to discover how this process of recognition and restructuring works by examining episodes of practice . . . . This sort of research may help other practitioners to enter into a way of seeing, restructuring, and intervening which they may wish to make their own.

In the second sense, research on fundamental theories and methods would take the form of an 'action science'. An action science would concern itself with situations of uniqueness, uncertainty, and instability which do not lend themselves to the application of theories and techniques derived from science in the mode of technical rationality. It would aim at the development of themes from which, in these sorts of situations, practitioners may construct theories and methods of their own.

The idea of an action science has a precursor in the work of Kurt Lewin, much of which has the thematic character which enables practitioners to use it in their own reflection-in-action. Such notions as 'gate-keeper roles', 'democratic and authoritarian group climates', and 'unfreezing' are metaphors from which managers, for example, can build and test their own on-the-spot theories of action.

The development of action science cannot be achieved by researchers who keep themselves removed from contexts of action, nor by practitioners who have limited time, inclination, or competence for systematic reflection. Its development will require new ways of integrating reflective research and practice.

Research on the process of reflection-in-action: . . . by asking a question like, 'How are you thinking about it now?', we produce an intended or unintended intervention which changes the subject's understanding and shifts the direction of action.

In all such cases, the subject's feelings about the task, about his own performance, and about his relation to the researcher are essential parts of the process under study. 'Hawthorne effects' are unavoidable. The researcher cannot exempt himself and ignores at his peril his own contribution to the social context of the experiment. He is, in Geoffrey Vicker's phrase, an agent-experient who must try to become aware of his own influences on the phenomena he is trying to understand . . . . When the researcher adopts a strategy of combined observation and intervention (and in the last analysis he may be capable of no other strategy), he may find that he can help his subject to reflect-in-action by allowing himself to experience and reveal his own confusion . . . .

As we try to understand the nature of reflection-in-action and the conditions that encourage or inhibit it, we study a cognitive process greatly influenced by 'cognitive emotions' and by the social context of inquiry. In order to study reflection-in-action, we must observe someone engaged in action. We may set a task for performance, . . . or may try to learn how someone is thinking and acting as he carries out a task he has set for himself. In some cases, we may interview a subject or ask him to think out loud as he works on the task. In other cases, we may combine research and intervention . . . .

8.2 *The Process of Action Research*[2]

UDAI PAREEK AND ADARSH KHANNA

Action research is an attempt to help the practitioners develop scientific ways of thinking and acting and to seek actions that will result in the improvement of practices . . . the question where research begins, and on what basis a particular study can be distinguished as a research study from a common-sense approach to problem solving. The practical answer . . . can be given in terms of awareness of the processes involved . . . . If the various processes are consciously used and perfected for the solution of a particular problem, we can say that research is being undertaken; . . . This . . . does not in any sense minimize the value of attempts made at problem-solving by persons without being aware of the processes involved. Such attempts may be highly valuable and useful. But to avoid confusion, the term research should be used only for the efforts which are made consciously by the individuals concerned.

Need for Change: It is necessary that the practitioner be dissatisfied with the existing practices . . . complacency comes in the way of research.

[2] From Udai Pareek and Adarsh Khanna, 'Action Research in Education', *Shiksha*, Vol. XIV, July 1961, pp. 131–55.

Problem Selection: . . . diagnosis has to be made of the various difficulties. It is always useful to identify a problem area in terms of difficulties rather than in terms of goals, because awareness of difficulties is often sharper than awareness of goals.

After the broad problem area has been identified, there is need to sharpen and focus the problem. Global problems cannot be attacked easily. It is necessary to break the broad problem into specific problems that can be taken up for research . . . for example, the problem should be real and not imaginary, be important to the practitioner, be simple and well defined, be concerned with the practitioner, and require simple tools for its solution . . . . The problem should be discussed in causative terms. A number of causes for a particular difficulty may be thought about and taken down. The problem when focused upon should be precise; . . . if it is too broad, a good research design cannot be prepared; if it is too narrow, research becomes spurious. The pinpointing or bringing the problem into focus is not easy, as accepted patterns of thinking get in the way of correct analysis of the problem. The only way of analysis is continuous questioning and fact gathering.

Search for Hypothesis: When a problem is pinpointed and brought into focus, a number of possible solutions emerge in the mind. It is useful to think of various hypotheses in this way . . . weigh them, to see their pros and cons. A preliminary investigation and collection of evidence may sometimes be needed for the imaginary testing of the hypotheses. The various resources available should be fully utilized for this purpose. If research consultants or advisors are easily available, they may be consulted at this stage.

Choice of Hypothesis: After the imaginary testing of the hypotheses, . . . a number of criteria may be considered . . . for example, . . . that the hypothesis chosen is important enough, is easy to implement, is simple, takes into account the resources available, does not conflict with the established patterns of organizational norms, does not involve much expenditure, does not interfere with the routine activities of the practitioners much, and is concrete and precise.

Design of Action: . . . It is necessary to work out details of the design of action, in defined steps with time targets, if possible . . . important elements have to be controlled. The importance of human relations cannot be overstressed in this connection. From time to time expert consultation may be needed for making simple research methods and statistical techniques comprehensible to the practitioners.

Evaluation: . . . It is necessary to use simple methods to measure change . . . .

Generalizations: . . . It has been suggested that generalizations are made at two major levels—generalization as to the event and the possibility of its occurrence, and generalization as to the degree of relationship that exists between any two or more factors and variables. The first is roughly the concept of reliability and the second roughly the concept of causation. Generalizations in a simple way may be taken to mean generalizations applicable to the future groups with whom the practitioner works.

8.3 Experimenting in Practice[3]

DONALD A. SCHON

Seeing as, is not enough . . . . When a practitioner sees a new situation as some element of his repertoire, he gets a new way of seeing it and a new possibility for action in it, but the adequacy and utility of his new view must still be discovered in action. Reflection-in-action necessarily involves experiment . . . .

In the most generic sense, to experiment is to act in order to see what the action leads to. The most fundamental experimental question is 'What if?'.

When action is undertaken only to see what follows, without accompanying predictions or expectations. I shall call it *exploratory experiment*. This is much what an infant does when he explores the world around him, what an artist does when he juxtaposes colors to see what effect they make, and what a newcomer does when he wanders around a strange neighborhood. It is also what a scientist often does when he first encounters and probes a strange substance to see how it will respond. Exploratory experiment is essential to the sort of science that does not appear in the scientific journals, because it has been screened out of the scientists' accounts of experimental results (perhaps because it does not conform to the norms of controlled experiment). Exploratory experiment is the probing, playful activity by which we get a feel for things. It succeeds when it leads to the discovery of something there.

There is another way in which we sometimes do things in order to see what happens: we take action in order to produce an intended change. A carpenter who wants to make a structure stable tries fastening a board across the angle of a corner. A chess player advances his pawn in order

---

[3] From Donald A. Schon, *The Reflective Practitioner: How Professionals Think in Action*, Basic Books, New York, 1983, pp. 14–64.

to protect his queen. A parent gives his child a quarter to keep the child from crying. I shall call these *move-testing experiments*. Any deliberate action undertaken with an end in mind is, in this sense, an experiment. In the simplest case, where there are no unintended outcomes and one either gets the intended consequences or does not, I shall say that the move is *affirmed* when it produces what is intended for it and is *negated* when it does not. In more complicated cases, however, moves produce effects beyond those intended. One can get very good things without intending them, and very bad things may accompany the achievement of intended results. Here the test of the affirmation of a move is not only 'Do you get what you intended?' but 'Do you like what you get?'. In chess, when you accidentally checkmate your opponent, the move is good and you do not take it back because its results are unexpected. On the other hand, giving a child a quarter may not only get him to stop crying, but also teach him to make money by crying—and the unintended effect is not so good. In these cases, a better description of the logic of move-testing experiments is this: Do you like what you get from the action, taking its consequences as a whole? If you do, then the move is affirmed. If you do not, it is negated.

[In] a third kind of experimenting, *hypothesis testing* . . . the experiment succeeds when it effects an intended discrimination among competing hypotheses. If, for a given hypothesis, its predicted consequences fit what is observed, and the predictions derived from alternative hypotheses conflict with observation, then we can say that the first hypothesis has been *confirmed* and the others, *disconfirmed* . . . . In the on-the-spot experimenting characteristic of reflection-in-action, the logic of hypothesis testing is essentially the same as it is in the research context. If a carpenter asks himself, What makes this structure stable? and begins to experiment to find out—trying now one device, now another—he is basically in the same business as the research scientist. He puts forward hypotheses and, within the limits of the constraining feature of the practice context, tries to discriminate among them—taking as disconfirmation of a hypothesis, the failure to get the consequences predicted from it. The logic of his experimental inference is the same as the researcher's.

What is it, then, that is distinctive about the experimenting that goes on in practice?

The practice context is different from the research context in several important ways, all of which have to do with the relationship between changing things and understanding them. The practitioner has an interest in transforming the situation from what it is to something he likes better. He also has an interest in understanding the situation, but it is in the service of his interest in change.

When the practitioner reflects-in-action in a case he perceives as unique, paying attention to phenomena and surfacing his intuitive understanding of them, his experimenting is at once exploratory, move testing, and hypothesis testing. The three functions are fulfilled by the very same actions. And from this fact follows the distinctive character of experimenting in practice . . . .

The practitioners' moves also function as exploratory probes of their situations. Their moves stimulate the situation's back-talk, which causes them to appreciate things in the situation that go beyond their initial perceptions of the problem . . . the exploratory experiment consists in the practitioner's conversation with the situation, in the back-talk which he elicits and appreciates . . . further, the practitioner's reframing of the problem of the situation carries with it a hypothesis about the situation. He surfaces the model of the phenomena associated with his student's framing of the problem, which he rejects. He proposes a new problem and with it, a new model of the phenomena, which he proceeds to treat as a hypothesis to be tested.

When we compare the practitioner's hypothesis-testing experiment to the method of controlled experiment, however, there are several notable differences.

The practitioner makes his hypothesis come true. He acts as though his hypothesis were in the imperative mood. He says, in effect, 'Let it be the case that X . . .', and shapes the situation so that X becomes true . . . . The practitioner's hypothesis testing consists of moves that change the phenomena to make the hypothesis fit.

The practitioner violates the canon of controlled experiment which calls for objectivity and distance. In controlled experiment, the inquirer is supposed to refrain from imposing his biases and interests on the situation under study. He is supposed to avoid what, in the context of human beings, is popularly called the 'Hawthorne Effect'. It is true that in laboratory experiments, experimenters are also expected to manipulate the experimental phenomena . . . . But *their* experiment has to do with a *type* of naturally occurring phenomenon which they study through the artificial situation of the laboratory. The manipulate the artificial situation, but leave the naturally occurring phenomena alone. Moreover, the canon of experimental method prohibits them from influencing the experimental situation to make it conform to their hypotheses; on the contrary, they are expected to strive for disconfirmation.

In the inquiries of (practitioners), the unique situation at hand is the domain of inquiry. As the inquirers influence it, they influence the totality of their object of study. And they seek to exert influence in such a way as to confirm, not refute, their hypotheses.

Nevertheless, their situations are not wholly manipulable. They may resist the inquirers' attempts to shape them and in so doing, may yield unintended effects . . . . Thus, the practitioners' hypothesis-testing experiments are not wholly self-fulfilling.

Their hypothesis-testing experiment is a game with the situation. They seek to make the situation conform to their hypothesis but remain open to the possibility that it will not. Thus, their hypothesis-testing activity is neither self-fulfilling prophecy, which insures against the apprehension of disconfirming data, nor is it the neutral hypothesis testing of the method of controlled experiment, which calls for the experimenter to avoid influencing the object of study and to embrace disconfirming data. The practice situation is neither clay to be molded at will, nor an independent, self-sufficient object of study from which the inquirer keeps his distance.

The inquirer's relation to this situation is *transactional*. He shapes the situation, but in conversation with it, so that his own models and appreciations are also shaped by the situation. The phenomena that he seeks to understand are partly of his own making; he is *in* the situation that he seeks to understand.

This is another way of saying that the action by which he tests his hypothesis is also a move by which he tries to effect a desired change in the situation, and a probe by which he explores it. He understands the situation by trying to change it, and considers the resulting changes not as a defect of experimental method but as the essence of its success.

This fact has an important bearing on the practitioner's answer to the question: When should I stop experimenting?

In the context of controlled experiment, . . . the experimenter might keep on experimenting indefinitely—as long as he is able to invent new, plausible hypotheses which might resist refutation more effectively than those he has already tried. But in the practice situations . . . where experimental actions is also a move and a probe, where the inquirer's interest in changing the situation takes precedence over his interest in understanding it—hypothesis testing is bounded by appreciations. It is initiated by the perception of something troubling in promising, and it is terminated by the production of changes one finds on the whole satisfactory, or by the discovery of new features which give the situation new meaning and change the nature of the questions explored. Such events bring hypothesis testing to a close even when the inquirer has not exhausted his store of plausible alternative hypotheses . . . .

It is true that the larger inquiry continues beyond these findings, its further directions set by them. But the experimenter need discriminate among contending hypotheses only to the point where his moves are affirmed or yield new appreciations of the situation. Thus, hypothesis-testing experiment has a more limited function in practice than in research. And because of this, constraints on controlled experiment in the practice situation are less disruptive of inquiry than they would otherwise be.

On the other hand, the practice context places demands on hypothesis testing which are not present in the context of research. The hypothesis must lend itself to embodiment in a move . . . .

These distinctive features of experimenting in practice carry with them distinctive norms for rigor. The inquirer who reflects-in-action plays a game with the situation in which he is bound by considerations relevant to the three levels of experiment—exploration, move testing, and hypothesis testing. His primary interest is in changing the situations. But if he ignores its resistances to change, he falls into mere self-fulfilling prophecy. He experiments rigorously when he strives to make the situation conform to his view of it, while at the same time he remains open to the evidence of his failure to do so. He must learn by reflection on the situation's resistance that his hypothesis is inadequate, and in what way, or that his framing of the problem is inadequate, and in what way. Moreover, he plays his game in relation to a moving target, changing the phenomena as he experiments. Whether he ought to reflect-in-action, and how he ought to experiment, will depend on the changes produced by his earlier moves . . . .

Stance Toward Inquiry

A practitioner's stance toward inquiry is his attitude toward the reality with which he deals.

According to the model of Technical Rationality, there is an objectively knowable world, independent of the practitioner's values and views. In order to gain technical knowledge of it, the practitioner must maintain a clear boundary between himself and his object of inquiry. In order to exert technical control over it, he must observe it and keep his distance from it—as Bacon said, commanding Nature by obeying her. His stance toward inquiry is that of spectator/manipulator.

In a practitioner's reflective conversation with a situation that he treats as unique and uncertain, he functions as an agent/experient. Through his transaction with the situation, he shapes it and makes himself a part of it. Hence, the sense he makes of the situation must include his own contribution to it. Yet he recognizes that the situation, having a life of its own distinct from his intentions, may foil his projects and reveal new meanings.

From this paradoxical source derive the several features of a stance toward inquiry which are as necessary to reflection-in-action as the norms of on-the-spot experiment and the uses of virtual worlds.

The inquirer must impose an order of his own, jumping rather than falling into his transactions with the situation. Thus, the Supervisor tries to get the Resident to recognize his contribution to the patient's stalemate and to see in the transference a medium for inquiry and intervention. Thus, Quist tries to get Petra to see that coherence does not exist in the site but must be imposed upon it by the designer. But the inquirer must also take responsibility for the order he impresses. As Quist draws to scale and the Supervisor probes the Resident's stories, they engage in a disciplined pursuit of the implications of their chosen frames.

At the same time that the inquirer tries to shape the situation to his frame, he must hold himself open to the situation's back-talk. He must be willing to enter into new confusions and uncertainties. Hence, he must adopt a kind of double vision. He must act in accordance with the view he has adopted, but he must recognize that he can always break it open later, indeed, must break it open later in order to make new sense of his transaction with the situation. This becomes more difficult to do as the process continues. His choices become more committing, his moves, more nearly irreversible. As the risk of uncertainty increases, so does the temptation to treat the view as the reality. Nevertheless, if the inquirer maintains his double vision, even while deepening his commitment to a chosen frame, he increases his chances of arriving at a deeper and broader coherence of artifact and idea.

His ability to do this depends on certain relatively constant elements that he may bring to a situation otherwise in flux: an overarching theory, an appreciative system, and a stance of reflection-in-action which can become, in some practitioners, an ethic for inquiry.

8.4 *Action Research and Organizational Development*[4]

UDAI PAREEK

Although the concept of action research (AR) is close to that of organization development (OD), there are some differences between the two. These are summarised in Figure 27. The concept of OD may be defined

[4] From S. Chattopadhyay and Udai Pareek (eds.), *Managing Organizational Change*, Oxford & IBH, New Delhi, 1982, pp. 25–26.

as 'a planned effort, initiated by process specialist(s) to help an organization to develop its diagnostic skills, coping capabilities, linkage strategies in the form of temporary and semi-permanent systems and a culture of mutuality'. It emphasizes the use of applied behavioural science. In action research, this is not an essential condition, and action research can be conducted in any area on any problem in the organization. OD is mostly regarded as a program of change which starts from the top in the organization. AR on the other hand, can be initiated at any level, depending on where the problem is felt, and who is involved in it. In OD, change is attempted throughout the organization, and the total organization is used for the diagnosis and designing of interventions. AR is always problem-oriented, and some problems can be taken up without getting into other areas of the organization. While OD emphasizes the development of persons, the main emphasis of AR is on building research competence in the organization, and helping people to develop skills of diagnosis, action planning (designing intervention) and evaluation. The main concern of AR is praxis—the integration of theory and research, and also of process. The main concern of OD, on the other hand, is that of process.

Probably the main difference between the two approaches is with regard to the integration of outside expertise and internal resources. In OD the duality is still maintained—the outside consultant is an expert in process work (applied behavioural science), and continues to play the role as an outsider. In AR, the outside expert and the inside people work in partnership for managing change. This may be a subtle difference, but it has implications for the joint responsibility for change.

Figure 27: Organization Development and Action Research

OD	AR
Emphasizes the use of applied behavioural science.	No such emphasis; work can be done in any area.
Emphasizes work from the top.	Emphasizes work at the level at which the problem is felt.
Emphasizes work throughout the whole organization.	Emphasizes solving a specific problem at the concerned level.
Emphasizes building organizational health.	Emphasizes building research competence.
More concern for process.	More concern for praxis.
Maintains duality between the outside consultant and the organization.	Works towards partnership.

8.5 *Design and Utility Factors according to Research Use*[5]

ROBERT CHIN

Loosening up of the positions of researcher and practitioner in areas which do not affect the core goals of each role will make for better working relations . . . attempts to explore the flexibility of research activities [and] justify some of these research choices in terms of the educational practitioners' requirement . . . move the researcher closer to the practitioner. We assume that the canons of scientific method are not violated. We are concerned with the various forms which scientific inquiry may take. We suggest that there are distinguishably different purposes in conducting research on programs of action and that the purposes affect our design, the factors studied, the kinds of conclusions we may draw, and the contribution we make. Our efforts will be more feasible and, in turn, more useful, when we are cognizant of our primary goals, or combination of goals, in conducting research on programs of action designed to improve training . . . an orientation to the development of systematic knowledge underlies many of the positions to be stated.

Our approach uses the language of independent, dependent, and criterion variables, since we are concerned with the determining conditions of events. Independent variables are those variables that are altered from their usual state in order to see what happens to the event. A program of action, education, or training is created or altered to see what improvements occur. The term criterion variable is used here to refer to the selected dependent variables which are considered to be at the 'criterion', the 'pay-off', or success-failure level. That is, criterion variables are deliberately selected from the gamut of dependent variables, on the basis of some practical interest other than scientific requirements.

The six uses of research we distinguish below are not always separable in a project. More frequently than not, however, we can determine the primary aim, or usable result, of a study. A chart is presented as a concise statement of our judgements about the variables, design and control, and the kinds of utility they may have to practitioners.

[5] From Franklin Patterson *et al.* (eds.), *The Adolescent Citizen*, The Free Press, New York, 1960, pp. 247–66.

8.6 *Practitioners and Researchers in Partnership*[6]

DONALD A. SCHON

. . . there is a disturbing tendency for research and practice to follow divergent paths. Practitioners and researchers tend increasingly to live in different worlds, pursue different enterprises, and have little to say to one another. Teachers have gained relatively little from cognitive psychology; political and administrative practice has gained little from the policy sciences; and management science has contributed relatively little to the practice of management. The divergence of research and practice exacerbates the practitioner's dilemma which I have called 'rigor or relevance' and tempts the practitioner to force practice situations into molds derived from research.

Clearly, then, when we reject the traditional view of professional knowledge, recognizing that practitioners may become reflective researchers in situations of uncertainty, instability, uniqueness, and conflict, we have recast the relationship between research and practice. For on this perspective, research is an activity of practitioners. It is triggered by features of the practice situation, undertaken on the spot, and immediately linked to action. There is no question of an 'exchange' between research and practice of the 'implementation' of research results, when the frame or theory-testing experiments of the practitioners at the same time transform the practice situation. Here the exchange between research and practice is immediate, and reflection-in-action is its own implementation.

Researchers and practitioners: In the kinds of reflective research I have outlined, researchers and practitioners enter into modes of collaboration very different from the forms of exchange envisaged under the model of applied science. The practitioner does not function here as a mere user of the researcher's product. He reveals to the reflective researcher the ways of thinking that he brings to his practice, and draws on reflective research as an aid to his own reflection-in-action. Moreover, the reflective researcher cannot maintain distance from, much less superiority to, the experience of practice. Whether he is engaged in frame analysis, repertoire building, action science, or the study of reflection-in-action, he must somehow gain an inside view of the experience of practice. Reflective research requires a partnership of practitioner-researchers and research-practitioners.

[6] From Donald A. Schon, *The Reflective Practitioner: How Professionals Think in Action*, Basic Books, New York, 1983, pp. 323–25, 338.

This partnership may take a variety of forms. Groups of practitioners may support one another in reflective research . . . . The reflective researcher may take on the role of consultant to the practitioner. Reflective research may become a part of continuing education for practitioners . . . . The researcher may stand to the practitioner in a relationship of participant observation. The practitioner may take time out to become a reflective researcher, moving in and out of research and practice careers.

To the extent that such partnerships grow in importance and begin to occupy an important place in the research enterprises of the professionals schools, universities and practice institutions will enter into new relationships. University faculty will become interested in professional practice, not only as a source of problems for study or internships for students, but as a source of access to reflective practice. As a consequence, a new meaning will be given to activities usually considered peripheral to the conduct of the research university. Field work, consultation, and continuing education, often considered as second-class activities or as necessary evils, will rise to first-class status as vehicles for research, the main business of the university.

Conversely, practice institutions may come to see themselves incresingly as centers of research and education. As the teaching hospital has long functioned under a model of applied science as a research and educational institution, so business firms, law offices, may recognize the reflection-in-action of their members and make a place for the reflective research which will support it.

The agenda of reflection research will be generated out of dialogue between reflective researchers and practitioner-researchers, and will be constrained by the requirement that the research be of the kind that practitioners can also undertake. In consequence, there will be a new approach to the sometimes vexing question of the implementation of research. Implementation will be built into the process of reflective research, for practitioners will gain and use insights derived from it as they participate in it.

The roles of practitioner and researcher will have permeable boundaries, and research and practice careers will intertwine as a matter of course. While the relative weight given to reflective research or to practice might vary considerably in the course of a career, one would normally expect practitioners to function on occasion as reflective researchers, and vice versa.

Nevertheless, it is unlikely that the new roles and relationships of practice and research will wholly displace the old. In such fields as medicine, dentistry, agronomy, and engineering, where relatively stable zones of practice lend themselves to the model of applied science, it is more likely that the two systems of relationship will coexist. But how? If the universities allow them to compartmentalize, there will be a major loss of opportunity which could contribute to the university's decline. If the universities seek new integrations of research and practice, of reflective research and applied science,then they will have to make the epistemology of practice a focus not only for intellectual attention but for institutional redesign.

Institutions for Reflective Practice: . . . To the extent that an institution seeks to accommodate to the reflection-in-action of its professional members, it must meet several extraordinary conditions. In contrast to the normal bureaucratic emphasis on uniform procedures, objective measures of performance, and centre/periphery systems of control, a reflective institution must place a high priority on flexible procedures, differentiated responses, qualitative appreciation of complex processes, and decentralized responsibility for judgement and action. In contrast to the normal bureaucratic emphasis on technical rationality, a reflective institution must make a place for attention to conflicting values and purposes. But these extraordinary conditions are also necessary for significant organizational learning.

The predicament of the reflective practitioner in a bureaucracy is another face of the predicament of organizational learning. Reflection-in-action is essential to the process by which individuals function as agents of significant organizational learning, and it is at the same time a threat to organizational stability. An organization capable of examining and restructuring its central principles and values demands a learning system capable of sustaining this tension and converting it to productive public inquiry. An organization conducive to reflective practice makes the same revolutionary demand . . . .

Within the universities, the professional schools, in so far as they become centers of reflective research, may become increasingly independent of the disciplinary departments and increasingly autonomous in their evolution of their own standards of rigor and relevance in research. One might then expect a reduction of the status differential between the research disciplines and the professional schools and with this, a reduction in the dilemmas of the schools of the minor professions.

8.7 *The Role of Institutions in Promoting Action Research*[7]

UDAI PAREEK

The model of action research . . . has implications for both research and consulting work. This distinction between the two ceases when these are

[7] From S. Chattopadhyay and Udai Pareek (eds.), *Managing Organizational Change*, Oxford University Press & IBH, New Delhi, 1982, pp. 35–36.

used for solving problems of an organization, involving those who are facing the problem. The joint search for problem solving, the use of the experience generated according to a well prepared scientific design, and raising the pertinent questions about goals and values are the main characteristic of this approach. It is as much valid for effective consulting as for applied research work.

This model has implications for the design of research institutions. Research and teaching institutions according to this design cannot take a stand of merely generating knowledge and not get involved in action in an organization or in a community. The present structure of the teaching and research institutes would not allow them to play an effective role in using action research approach. This distinction will certainly continue to be maintained, but the involvement of the academic institutes in action would grow much more, resulting in higher mutual learning. The design of the academic institution should become much more flexible and creative in order to move into such a direction. Clark has suggested that 'boundary organization' may have to be developed to effectively undertake action research of this kind. Boundary organization is defined as 'one which receives inputs from, and provides inputs for, the institution on whose boundary it exists'.

The flexibility of such an organization in leading its members to the community or other organizations in which action research is being conducted, and borrowing people from such settings may be required for the effectiveness of action research. It is encouraging to learn that recently the agricultural university in Trichur has decided to appoint progressive and successful farmers as visiting professors. The boundary institute may break the traditional limitations, on the one hand, of academic institutions which want to keep themselves clean and not soil their hands in direct action, and, on the other hand, of the traditional attitude of the community and work organization towards academic institutions, who consider the latter as primarily contributing to knowledge and not to the improvement of practice. This is a challenging task. The institutions of management which have made innovative interventions in various fields may be best suited to think about the organizational design innovations for academic institutions to play a crucial role in linking theory, practice and process.

8.8 *Organizing for Disbelief and Surprise*[8]

LEWIS THOMAS

The essential wildness of science as a manifestation of human behavior

[8] From Lewis Thomas, *The Lives of a Cell*, Viking Press, New York, 1974, pp. 100–102.

is not generally perceived. As we extract new things of value from it, we also keep discovering parts of the activity that seem in need of better control, more efficiency, less unpredictability. We'd like to pay less for it and get our money's worth on some more orderly, business-like schedule. The Washington planners are trying to be helpful in this, and there are new programs for the centralized organization of science all over the place, especially in the biomedical field.

It needs thinking about. There is an almost ungovernable, biologic mechanism at work in scientific behavior at its best, and this should not be overlooked.

The difficulties are more conspicuous when the problems are very hard and complicated and the facts not yet in. Solutions cannot be arrived at for problems of this sort, until the science has been lifted through a preliminary, turbulent zone of outright astonishment. Therefore, what must be planned for, in the laboratories engaged in the work, is the totally unforeseeable. If it is centrally organized, the system must be designed primarily for the elicitation of disbelief and the celebration of surprise.

Scientists at work have the look of creatures following genetic instructions; they seem to be under the influence of a deeply placed human instinct. They are, despite their efforts at dignity, rather like young animals engaged in save play. When they are near to an answer, their hair stands on end, they sweat, they are awash in their own adrenalin. To grab the answer, and grab it first, is for them a more powerful drive than feeding or breeding or protecting themselves against the elements.

It sometimes looks like a lonely activity, but it is as much the opposite of lonely as human behavior can be. There is nothing so social, so communal, so interdependent. An active field of science is like an immense intellectual anthill; the individual almost vanishes into the mass of minds tumbling over each other, carrying information from place to place, passing it around at the speed of light.

There are special kinds of information that seem to be chemotactic. As soon as a trace is released, receptors at the back of the neck are caused to tremble, there is a massive convergence of motile minds flying upwind on a gradient of surprise, crowding around the source. It is an infiltration of intellects, an inflammation.

There is nothing to touch the spectacle. In the midst of what seems a collective derangement of minds in total disorder, with bits of information being scattered about, torn to shreds, disintegrated, reconstituted, engulfed, in a kind of activity that seems a random and agitated as that of bees in a disturbed part of the hive, there suddenly emerges, with the purity of a slow phrase of music, a single new piece of truth about nature.

In short, it works. It is the most powerful and productive of the things human beings have learned to do together in many centuries, more effective than farming, or hunting and fishing, or building cathedrals, or making money.

It is instinctive behavior, in my view, and I do not understand how it works. It cannot be prearranged in any precise way; the minds cannot be lined up in tidy rows and given directions from printed sheets. You cannot get it done by instructing each mind to make this or that piece, for central committees to fit with the pieces made by other instructed minds. It does not work this way.

What it needs is for the air to be made right. If you want a bee to make honey, you do not issue protocols on solar navigation or carbohydrate chemistry, you put him together with other bees (and you'd better do this quickly, for solitary bees do not stay alive) and you do what you can to arrange the general environment around the hive. If the air is right, the science will come in its own season, like pure honey.

There is something like aggression in the activity, but it differs from other forms of aggressive behavior in having no sort of destruction as the objective. While it is going on, it looks and feels like aggression: get at it, uncover it, bring it out, grab it, it's mine! It is like a primitive running hunt, but there is nothing at the end of it to be injured. More probably, the end is a sigh. But then, if the air is right and the science is going well, the sigh is immediately interrupted, there is a yawping new question and the wild, tumbling activity begins once more, out of control all over again.

8.9 *Workshop for Action Research Trainers*[9]

STEPHEN M. COREY AND UDAI PAREEK

We have the population of educational practitioners in our mind— teachers, administrators, supervisors—who volunteer to participate. Before doing so, they must have the workshop's purposes and methods explained to them carefully. The workshop will be appreciably less effective if its members are deputed. We are assuming furthermore that each person volunteering to be a participant in the workshop will already have developed sufficient dissatisfaction with his own professional practices to want to work to improve them. In other words, he is aware

[9] From Stephen M. Corey and Udai Pareek, 'The In-Service Training Action Research Workshop', *Journal of Education and Psychology*, New Delhi, 1967, pp. 25–33.

of some teaching or administrative or supervisory difficulty that is interfering with his effectiveness and he is motivated to do something about it.

What are the Major Purposes of the Action Research Workshop?

The workshop we have in mind and are describing has two central purposes. The first is to help the participants get experimentation under way in their own institutions—experimentation intended to make them more effective professional workers. For this experimentation to be more than trial and error, it must be subjected to some discipline. Learning how to be disciplined and objective and pay continuous attention to facts and evidence is the first task worked on in the workshop. The second function is to begin to teach the sensitivities, concepts, and skills that are required for successful small-group work. Most of the difficulties in an institution cannot be coped with successfully unless several of the persons involved in the difficulty work together cooperatively. If these cooperative efforts are to be maximally successful, the people engaged in them must be able to work productively in small, face-to-face, task-oriented groups.

What Preparations Should Precede the Workshop?

Such a workshop assumes that a great deal of planning and work have been done before the participants arrive. On the basis of their expressed interest, resulting from studying a carefully prepared memorandum describing the intended workshop, no more than twenty participants have been invited to attend. It is well to ask them to submit in advance the particular difficulty they plan to work on. This assures some preliminary thinking. Plans for convening the workshop in the campus of a well-known training institution or a college or a university, under the general direction and chairmanship of someone who deals with problems of institutional change, must be completed. Facilities for the workshop, including a rather large classroom for general sessions and several places where small groups can work, as well as mimeographing and typing facilities, must be arranged for. It is well to have available a small library of references. There should be at least one consultant available full time—a person who is thoroughly familiar with action research procedures and problems. Members of the college or university teacher training faculty should be available on a part-time and 'when needed' basis. The best possible living arrangements should be provided.

What Is the Role of an Action Research Consultant?

Every action research training workshop should have, as we have already stated, one full-time resource person who has had experience working with educational practitioners who want to undertake experimentation to improve their own practices. Generally, it is this consultant who will prepare the materials needed for the workshops, deliver the lecturettes, and arrange for the demonstrations and other training activities. This consultant will also be available for conferences with the participants regarding the problems they are facing as they plan their own action research projects. Members of the college or university faculty who are available for consultation should probably be expected to spend one or two hours each day conferring with the participants. They might benefit, too, from attendance at the general sessions of the workshop where action research procedures and small group work are talked about and demonstrated.

What Will Be the Variety of Workshop Activities?

One central intention of the workshop must be to demonstrate the benefits of action research in the operations of the workshop itself. The workshop small-group procedures must also demonstrate the best of such procedures. The very complexity of what it is the workshop is trying to accomplish should lead to a wide variety of activities. Some of the more important of these activities are named and briefly explained below:

General Sessions. General sessions are meetings of the entire workshop personnel, including the consultants. The main activity in most general sessions will be a lecturette-cum-discussion or a lecturette-cum-demonstration. During any single general session an attempt is made (a) to provide theory or conceptualization; (b) to demonstrate the application of the theory to practice; (c) to involve the participants in a discussion of what they have heard or seen; and (d) to provide an opportunity to raise questions with the consultants.

Small-Group Work. The total workshop group will frequently be divided into small groups for discussion or other purposes. It is almost always advantageous to keep these working groups small. One of the best arrangements to get serious work done is in groups of three (the triad). Part of the workshop will involve training the triads in order to improve the quality of the help each can give to, and receive from, the other two members.

Commitment Reports. It is usually desirable to conclude the workshop by having each participant describe to the others the experimentation he will engage in when he returns to his job. These reports not only enable all workshop participants to know what the others are planning to do, they also constitute something of a public pledge to do it which greatly increases the likelihood that the things learned at the workshop each day are evaluated

Evaluation. In an effective workshop, each day's activities are evaluated and an attempt is made to modify the next day's activities in the light of these evaluation data. This is best done by using, at the end of each day,some kind of simple 'postmeeting evaluation' form or questionnaire which makes it easy for each participant to report the way he feels about the things that have been done during the day.

Follow-up. Specific and definite arrangements to follow up on the effects of the workshop as they extend into the future are always desirable. In other words, whoever is responsible for planning and staging the workshop makes a strenuous effort to be sure that what the participants plan to do is done. In this connection, he attempts to provide continuing help to the participants as they try to get their experimentation under way. It is much easier to plan under the stimulus of the workshop environment than it is to carry the plans out when the workshop is over and the participants have returned to their 'back-home' working situations.

Practice Laboratory. The most effective in-service workshops provide participants with numerous opportunities to practice the skills they will need, to make their experimentation successful. Arrangements are made actually to construct instruments for procuring evidence. Complicated human relation situations are 'role-played' so as to get the feel of dealing with them. Instructional materials that are integral to the experimentation are prepared. The workshop, in other words, is much more than 'talking about' experimentation.

On the basis of their experience in several in-service training action research workshops, the authors are suggesting below one pattern of activities for five consecutive daily sessions. Numerous modifications would, of course, be made in these suggestions in the case of any specific workshop. Many of these modifications would result from involving the participants in the planning of the session by session activities.

PART III

Institutions and Large Systems

9. TRAINING CENTRES AND OTHER INSTITUTIONS

INTRODUCTION

An early paper from the then new Tavistock Institute of Human Relations in England has the intriguing title, 'The hospital as a defence against anxiety'.[1] It showed how directors, managers and staff groups at all levels used organizational structures and processes to protect themselves as barricades against inner turmoils, against unfinished struggles between departments and professions, and against having to face challenging tasks and situations. The readings in this part are chosen with an eye to helping consultant trainers avoid colluding with analogous tendencies, to make their programs into a defence against anxieties of their own or of their clients', for instance, through encouraging excessive expectations from training or simplistic diagnoses of developmental problems and solutions. They focus on the proper functions of training and consulting in the wider organizational and cultural contexts and on the systemic development of their professions, qualitatively as well as on a sufficient scale.

Particular institutions, such as training centers, staff colleges and consulting groups can be powerhouses of innovation, standard setting and normative developments. But even when they are, and do not degenerate instead into places for quite routine operations, they constitute only components in large and varied systems for staff and organizational development. We focus on them here, because they provide the immediate settings for training, consulting, and professional development, offer important points of reference and represent a logical step towards broadening a practitioner's perspective.

The first two readings present useful ways of thinking about an institution. The first is a brief orderly account of 'open socio-technical systems thinking'. Attempts to improve only the people in this interdependent dyad—the 'socio' part—disappoint just as surely as concentrating on technological dimension does. These two are to be treated

[1] From Menzies, I, E.P., *Human Relations*, 1951 reprinted as 'A Case Study in the Functioning of Social Systems as a Defence against Anxiety, *Tavistock Pamphlet no. 3*, Tavistock Publication, London, U.K., 1961.

together. Essential additional elements to include in system thinking are time and environment.

An institution building schema is presented next. The reading presents the model as a whole, examines two of its 'internal variables'—institutional doctrine and leadership—in the light of a study of twenty institutions engaged in the same task at one time and then draws some implications for institutional consultation.

Criteria and Processes for Interventions

The next set of three readings is about interventions. Mat Miles (9.4), identifies criteria for organizational health. It translates ten dimensions of organization development work in diverse settings to the particular needs of educational institutions. Work on six dimensions seems important: self-study, 'what might be called organizational introspection'; relational emphasis; increased data flow; norms as change targets; a temporary system approach to problem-solving, to developing new norms of working and to designing improved structures and processes to try out; and effective expert facilitation. Expert help is temporary: 'the organization itself continues the self-corrective processes which have been begun by the intervention'. Next, Marvin Weisbord distills four useful practices from his consulting in recent years. Together, they constitute so significant a shift from classical lines that he senses himself in 'third wave consulting' rather like Juanita Brown. Third wave consulting focussed on action potential (rather than problems), system as a whole rather than a part, the future (rather than the present) and on 'structuring tasks that people can do for themselves'. Gant, South and Hansen (9.6) write about interventions as 'temporary systems'.

The last two readings are about developing institutions. Ravi Matthai describes his experiences as a director working on the norms, processes and structures of the Indian Institute of Management, Ahmedabad. 'The first and most important task was to build a tradition of attitudes [with] structure . . . subservient . . . just enough for the accomplishment of primary tasks'. Among the issues to be worked out through practice and reflections were, 'how, operationally, to reconcile individual creativity with effective group functioning', e.g., in decision-making; how to shield the new Institute from outside pressures for conformity; how to involve faculty in administrative tasks; and how to combine the complex and fluid processes chosen for developing the Institute with sufficient institute-wide planning, including planning for resources and for participation in long-term national-building tasks. It took over ten years to work out these issues. Only then were 'more formal and systematic planning and the organization for it' worked out by a Reorganization Committee and accepted by 'a mature and confident faculty'. The processes Matthai describes have little in them of formal authority and decision-making from the higher levels of an organizational hierarchy. Instead, much work was done towards 'the creation of settings', the title of Sarason's book about building institutions (1.8).

The final reading presents a schema for the crises and dilemmas that seem to occur at various stages of institution development, together with some directions for resolving them.

9.1 *Socio-Technical Systems Thinking*[2]

ERIC L. TRIST

Considering enterprises as 'open socio-technical systems', helps to provide a more realistic picture of how they are both influenced by, and able to, act back on their environment. It points in particular to the various ways in which enterprises are enabled by their structural and functional characteristics ('system constants') to cope with the 'lacks' and 'gluts' in their available environment. Unlike mechanical and other inanimate systems they possess the property of 'equi-finality'; they may achieve a steady state from differing initial conditions and in differing ways. Thus in coping by internal changes they are not limited to simple quantitative change and increased uniformity but may, and usually do, elaborate new structures and take on new functions . . . .

Inherent in the socio-technical approach is the notion that the attainment of optimum conditions in any one dimension does not necessarily result in a set of conditions optimum for the system as a whole. If the structures of the various dimensions are not consistent, interference will occur, leading to a state of disequilibrium, so that achievement of the overall goal will to some degree be endangered and in the limit, made impossible. The optimization of the whole tends to require a less than optimum state for each separate dimension . . . . This approach does not imply that in all circumstances a detailed study of all three dimensions must be carried out. It does, however, underline the importance, when

---

[2] From Eric L. Trist, Murray Higgin, and Pollock, *Organizational Choice*, Tavistock Publications, London, 1963, pp. 6–7.

any aspect of a production system is examined, of taking into account the manner and extent of its interdependence with the other dimensions.

9.2 And in Practice[3]

WILLIAM A. PASMORE AND JOHN J. SHERWOOD

. . . In practice, working toward the joint optimization of the social and technological systems of an organization is a complex process that requires a thorough understanding of: (1) the social processes that occur in organizations and the variety of theories and methods that exist to make more efficient use of human resources; (2) the technological process used by the organization and the constraints that it places on the design and operation of the social system; (3) the theory of open systems, because no two organizations are exactly alike or are faced with the same environmental demands; and (4) the mechanics of change, both in the execution of the initial sociotechnical system design and in provision for the continual adaptation of the organization to new environmental demands.

. . . Sociotechnical theory has evolved into a set of fairly stable and recognizable propositions. These specify, (1) that the design of the organization must fit its goals; (2) that employees must be actively involved in designing the structure of the organization; (3) that variances in production or service must be controlled as close to their source as possible; (4) that subsystems must be designed around relatively whole and recognizable tasks; (5) that support systems must be congruent with the design of the organization; (6) that a high quality of work life should be provided; and (7) that changes should continue to be made as necessary to meet environmental demands.

9.3 Institution-building Theory[4]

ROLF P. LYNTON AND JOHN M. THOMAS

I-B theory deals with three kinds of components: internal organizational

[3] From William A. Pasmore and John J. Sherwood, *Sociotechnical Systems: A Sourcebook*, University Associates Inc., San Diego, CA, 1978, pp. 3–5.

[4] From Rolf P. Lynton and John M. Thomas, 'Institution-building Theory and an Analysis', *Southern Review of Public Administration*, USA, December 1980, pp. 305–20.

variables, linkage variables which define specific environmental relationships, and the interactions among them . . . . Figure 28 sets out the simplest version. Figure 29 shows a dynamic model . . . .

In the early 1960s, institution-building studies were touched off by the urge to find better means and methods for international assitance and for evaluating [their] effectiveness . . . . The formulations developed so far have been used mostly in projects involving U.S. technical assistance in Africa, Asia, and Latin America—projects that required new institutions or the major expansion and pervasive renewal of existing institutions. The concepts which the I-B model incorporates have proved useful both in designing new organizations and in developing innovative subsystems within existing organizations as well as in understanding failures.

University Population Programs (UPP)

. . . Prominent in the doctrines of effective programs in the UPP project were formal statements which explicitly addressed: (a) the disciplinary composition of the program; (b) its goals and priorities within and outside the university; and (c) the design of joint decision mechanisms to be used for the allocation of funds and for frequent and full reporting of activities to established university bodies. The academic bases for population studies were defined. Doctrines also specified procedures for negotiating differences and for securing university-wide approval for changes in program direction and priorities. The 'relationship to [emerging] societal preference and priorities' was characterized by an effort directly to involve policy and implementation agencies in decisions concerning the development of program activities. It was assumed that program activities should be treated as 'doctrine translated into action' . . . .

Common issues in program leadership. The I-B perspective also highlights certain issues associated with the leadership of organization change. Three leadership issues were particularly prominent in the programs observed in this analysis.

First, in a majority of cases, significant conflict emerged between the need for leadership specifically oriented to *internal* policy formation and structure and the need to manage external linkages . . . .

A second leadership issue arose from difficulties of integrating program 'doctrine' with specific *program activities* and with the design of *organizational structure*. Most programs had great difficulty in developing leadership with competence in all three areas.

Figure 28 : The Institution Building Model

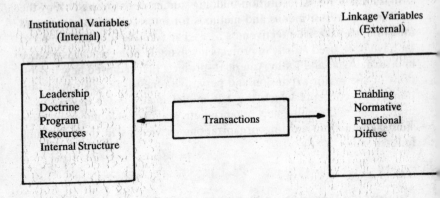

Figure 29 : The Institution Building Process

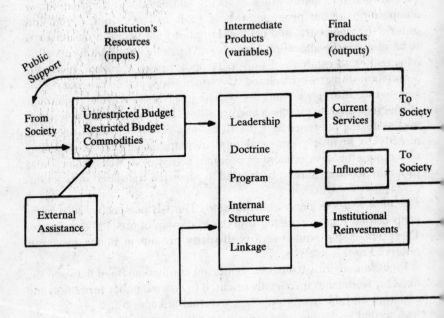

Finally, in UPP programs with effective leadership, the structure of governance reflected the pattern of enabling and normative linkages required by the organization . . . who was to be included in governance was, in fact, the first key decision taken by the initiators of effective programs . . . . This decision was a strong influence on the substance of program doctrine. In turn, a clear, well-communicated doctrine, which reflected the commitment of those included in the governance of the program, then legitimated and protected the autonomy of the program.

Implications of the I-B Model for Consultation

. . . the value of diagnostic models for planning organizational change efforts cannot be overestimated . . . one of the key problems facing consultants during the diagnostic phase of a project is that they are usually more concerned with understanding and improving their relationship with the client organization than they are in understanding specific organizational problems . . . . Ideally, however, a diagnostic framework should enable both activities to occur simultaneously and to be mutually reinforcing: the consultant-client relationship, particularly when considered in terms of strategic leverage-points for consultant interventions, should emerge from, and be defined by, an explicit mapping of the organization's critical developmental problems.

Without a diagnostic framework which can guide the allocation of the consultant's work as well as contribute to a viable consultant-client relationship, the consultant will all too often become a significant problem and sometimes will fail altogether. One reason for the extra risks involved in such situations is that, in consulting for institution-building, several key components in the process, e.g., program leadership, and enabling and normative linkages, are highly sensitive and not readily accessible to an outsider. Yet, accurate data about these variables are also essential for the consultant to work effectively and are needed very early. With the I-B model, the consultant and the client can jointly identify variables on which the consultant's help is welcome and on which data are required. Collaboration in the use of this type of diagnostic framework can also facilitate questions about the client's allocation of resources to key components.

The alternatives to a collaborative relationship between consultant and client have grave consequences. Two are common. If the consultant muscles his way into these sensitive components of institution-building, the least (serious) consequence will be lowered commitment to innovation in the client organization. This has been common in I-B projects funded by an outside agency, as in federal or state-assisted projects or in international assistance through governments or foundations. The other alternative, which has also been common, is for the consultant to stay clear of the sensitive components of institution-building and to concentrate on developing others which are accessible and yield what may appear to be benefits; e.g., program activities and additional resources. . . . consultation on this basis is inadequate. In several cases (in the UPP study) this myopia resulted in costly distortion of institutional goals and loss of innovation which became difficult to reverse; in at least one program, rectification proved impossible and the program folded after eight years.

Still another important implication of the I-B diagnostic framework for consultation stems from its emphasis upon a proactive stance towards the environment . . . . Most scenarios of planned organizational change still leave managers and consultants collecting and using information about the environment in order for the organization to *adapt* itself to the environment.

Increasingly common conditions make a more proactive stance *vis-à-vis* the environment particularly desirable. One is the high turbulence . . . in the environments of an increasing number of organizations . . . . Even where power and influence are limited, a proactive stance can still increase the flow of information and the organization's ability to 'forecast' environmental conditions. The I-B diagnostic framework is useful for differentiating between the types of information to secure from various linkages and for locating responsibilities in the organization for using information and maintaining the viability of each type of environmental linkage.

A second significant condition which makes the proactive stance important for an organization is relatively high autonomy of units in the environment on which the organization depends for the use of its outputs or for its resources, or for both. This is most obviously the case for service organizations, e.g., health systems and political organizations. The autonomy of these units is especially high where the organization receives its funds from one source, e.g., the government, in order to deliver services to a third party, e.g., people in the slums; where the culture of the organization is sharply different from the culture of the people for whom the services are meant; and where intended recipients of outputs are unorganized. High autonomy also characterizes coordination and interagency mechanisms and, less obviously but importantly, even innovative sub-systems within many kinds of organizations, including industrial ones . . . . (For UPPs) the environment is full of other organizations which (they) must seek to influence but for whom interaction with the program is optional and subject to little or no organizational control.

9.4 *Organizational Health in Training Institutions*[5]

MATTHEW B. MILES

Organizational health can be seen as a set of fairly durable second-order system properties, which tend to transcend short-run effectiveness . . . . A steadily ineffective organization would presumably not be healthy; . . . . But notice that an organization may cope effectively in the short run (as for example by a speed-up or a harsh cost-cutting drive), but at the cost of longer run variables, such as those noted below. The classic example, of course, is an efficiency drive which cuts short-run costs and results in long-run labor dissatisfaction and high turnover.

To illustrate in more detail what is meant by 'second-order property', here is a list of ten dimensions of organizational health that seem plausible to me . . . . The first three dimensions are relatively 'tasky', in that they deal with organizational goals, the transmission of messages, and the way in which decisions are made.

1. Goal focus. In a healthy organization, the goal (or more usually goals) of the system would be reasonably clear to the system members, and reasonably well accepted by them. This clarity and acceptance, however, should be seen as a necessary but insufficient condition for organizational health. The goals must also be achievable with existing or available resources and be appropriate—more or less congruent with the demands of the environment. The last feature may be most critical.

2. Communication adequacy. Since organizations are not simultaneous face-to-face systems like small groups, the movement of information within them becomes crucial. This dimension of organizational health implies that there is relatively distortion-free communication 'vertically', 'horizontally', and across the boundary of the system to and from the surrounding environment. That is, information travels reasonably well—just as the healthy person 'knows himself' with a minimum level of repression, distortion, etc. In the healthy organization, there is good and prompt sensing of internal strains; there are enough data about problems of the system to ensure that a good diagnosis of system difficulties can be made. People have the information they need, and have gotten it without exerting undue efforts, such as moseying up to the superintendent's secretary, reading the local newspaper, or calling excessive numbers of special meetings.

[5] From Matthew B. Miles, 'Planned Change and Organizational Health: Figure and Ground', in R.O. Carlson *et al.*, *Change Processes in the Public School*, Columbia University Press, New York, 1965 pp. 369–81.

3. Optimal power equalization. In a healthy organization, the distribution of influence is relatively equitable. Subordinates (if there is a formal authority chart) can influence upward, and even more important, they perceive that their boss can do likewise with his boss. In such an organization, intergroup struggles for power would not be bitter, though intergroup conflict (as in all human systems known to man) would undoubtedly be present. The basic stance of persons in such an organization, as they look up, sideways and down, is that of collaboration rather than explicit or implicit coercion. The units of the organization (persons in roles, work groups, etc.) would stand in an interdependent relationship to each other, with rather less emphasis on the ability of a 'master' part to control the entire operation. The exertion of influence in a healthy organization would presumably rest on the competence of the influencer *vis-à-vis* the issue at hand, his stake in the outcome, and the amount of knowledge or data he has—rather than on his organizational position, personal charisma, or other factors with little direct relevance to the problem at hand.

.... A second group of three dimensions deals essentially with the internal state of the system, and its inhabitants' 'maintenance' needs. These are resource utilization, cohesiveness, and morale.

4. Resource utilization. We say of a healthy person, that he is 'working up to his potential'. At the organization level, 'health' would imply that the system's inputs, particularly the personnel, are used effectively. The overall coordination is such that people are neither overloaded nor idling. There is a minimal sense of strain, generally speaking (in the sense that trying to do something with a weak or inappropriate structure puts strain on that structure). In the healthy organization, people may be working very hard indeed, but they feel that they are not working against themselves or against the organization. The fit between people's own dispositions and the role demands of the system is good. Beyond this, people feel reasonably 'self actualized': they not only 'feel good' in their jobs, but they have a genuine sense of learning, growing, and developing as persons in the process of making their organizational contribution.

5. Cohesiveness. . . . the organization knows 'who it is'. Its members feel attracted to membership in the organization. They want to stay with it, be influenced by it, and exert their own influence in the collaborative style suggested above.

6. Morale. The history of this concept in the social-psychological literature is so appalling that I hesitate to introduce it at all . . . . Yet it still seems useful to evoke, at the organization level, . . . a summated set of individual sentiments, centering around feelings of well-being,

satisfaction, and pleasure, as opposed to feelings of discomfort, unwished-for strain and dissatisfaction . . . in a healthy organization it is hard to entertain the idea that the dominant personal response of organization members would be anything else than one of well-being.

Finally, there are four more dimensions of organizational health, which deal with growth and changefulness: the notions of innovativeness, autonomy, adaptation *vis-à-vis* the environment, and problem-solving adequacy.

7. Innovativeness. A healthy system would tend to invent new procedures, move toward new goals, produce new kinds of products, diversify itself, and become more rather than less differentiated over time. In a sense, such a system could be set to grow, develop, and change, rather than remaining routinized and standard.

8. Autonomy . . . . A healthy organization . . . does not respond passively to demands from the outside, feeling itself the tool of the environment, and it would not respond destructively or rebelliously to perceived demands either. It would tend to have a kind of independence from the environment, in the same sense that the healthy person, while he has transactions with others, does not treat their responses as determinative of his own behavior.

9. Adaptation. The notions of autonomy and innovativeness are both connected with the idea that a healthy . . . organization is in realistic, effective contact with the surroundings. When environmental demands and organization resources do not match, a problem-solving, restructuring approach evolves in which both the environment and the organization become different in some respect. More adequate, continued coping of the organization, as a result of changes in the local system, the relevant portions of the environment, or more usually both, occurs. And such a system has sufficient stability and stress tolerance to manage the difficulties which occur during the adaptation process . . . .

10. Problem-solving adequacy. Finally, any healthy organism—even one as theoretically impervious to fallibility as a computer—always has problems, strains, difficulties, and instances of ineffective coping. The issue is not the presence or absence of problems, therefore, but the manner in which the . . . organization copes with problems. Argyris has suggested that in an effective system, problems are solved with minimal energy; they stay solved; and the problem solving mechanisms used are not weakened, but maintained or strengthened. An adequate organization, then, has well-developed structures and procedures for sensing the existence of problems, for inventing possible solutions, for deciding on the solutions, for implementing them, and for evaluating their effectiveness. Such an organization would conceive of its own operations

(whether directed outward to goal achievement, inward to maintenance, or inward-outward to problems of adaptation) as being controllable. We would see active coping with problems rather than passive withdrawing, compulsive responses, scapegoating, or denial.

The Special Case of Educational Organizations

. . . educational systems have special properties which condition the propositions of organizational theory in reasonably predictable ways . . . .

1. Goal ambiguity. For many different reasons, it has seemed difficult to specify the output of educational organizations very precisely. Some of this is realistic: change in human beings is going on, with presumably cumulative effects over a long period of time. But part of this output measurement difficulty also seems to be a form of organizational defense or protection against criticism from the surrounding environment . . . .

This ambiguity and pseudo consensus around output measurement encourages the institutionalization and ossification of teaching procedures. If it cannot really be determined whether one course of action leads to more output than another, then why stop lecturing?. . . .

2. Input variability. Another, possibly unique, property of educational organizations is a very wide variation in input from the environment, particularly in relation to participants and personnel. The range of intellectual ability, interpersonal skill, and knowledge of subject matter among teachers is probably at least as great as that among pupils. This variability causes considerable stress in educational organizations and develops the need to provide teaching personnel with methods and procedures which are (in effect) teacherproof.

3. Role performance invisibility. Classrooms are in effect the production departments of the educational enterprise; in them trainers work. Yet, this role performance is relatively invisible to status equals or superiors. Learners can observe, usually very acutely, the quality of a teacher's execution of his role, but they are not allowed to comment on this, and have few, if any, sanctions to bring to bear. Thus, rewards in the teaching profession seem relatively detached from others' estimates of one's performance; the average teacher gains most satisfaction from intrinsic properties of the role behavior involved. Teaching thus becomes a craft-like occupation, rather than a profession, and substitute criteria for teaching effectiveness, such as 'interest of the kids', begin to appear and are used vigorously. Perhaps this is what teachers mean when they say it is not difficult to know when they are doing a good job.

4. Low interdependence. A further characteristic of educational organizations, when compared with thing-producing systems, seems to be a relatively low interdependence of parts. Teacher A's failure to teach anything to the participants affects the job-relevant behavior of Teacher B very little—except in a rather diffuse, blaming sense.

This low interdependence has several consequences. First, it tends to reinforce the pyramidal 'man-to-man' style of supervision which Likert and others have shown to be inimical to organizational effectiveness.

The reported stresses and strains in most accounts of team teaching—an attempt to increase interdependence in educational organizations—are mute testimony to the strength with which 'separatist' norms have become institutionalized . . . .

5. Vulnerability. Educational institutions are subject to control, criticism, and a wide variety of 'legitimate' demands from the surrounding environment: everyone is a stockholder. To the system inhabitants, the organizational skill seems extremely thin. Many kinds of ingenious defenses are adopted to solve this problem. This state of affairs represents a serious failure of adaptation skills of organizations and tends to reduce autonomy sharply.

6. Lay-professional control problems. Many educational institutions are governed by laymen. Even where the board is 'well-trained' and leaves the execution of policy to the administration, notice that the question of educational policy determination still remains a moot one.

And there are internal lay-professional problems as well. In many respects, the administrator may find himself far behind the capabilities of particular trainers (in terms of expert knowledge), and he is in this sense a layman as well. The problems of organizations with high proportions of professionals have been studied vigorously (for example, hospitals and research organizations); I only wish to indicate here that the fruits of such study so far have found little application in educational institutions.

7. Low technological investment. Lastly, it seems very clear that the amount of technology per worker in institutions is relatively low. From 60 to 90 per cent of an educational institution's budget ordinarily goes to salary, with a fraction for equipment and materials . . . . This has consequences: social transactions, rather than sociotechnical transactions, come to be the major mode of organizational production. Because of this, it is possible that education has never made it out of the folk culture stage. And we are back once again to goal ambiguity and its problems.

. . . in terms of the (ten) dimensions above, the major difficulties to be expected . . . center around goal focus (as a consequence of goal ambiguity); difficulties in communication adequacy and power equalization stemming from low interdependence; and perhaps most centrally, failures in innovativeness autonomy adaptation, and problem-solving adequacy, because of vulnerability and lay-professional conflict.

The Induction of Organizational Health

. . . the usual aim of an intervention is to start internal change processes going in the system . . . rather than only causing an immediate change. Below are described six interventions aimed at improving organization health.

1. Team training. In this approach, the members of an intact work group meet for a period of several days away from their offices, with consultant help. They examine their own effectiveness as a problem-solving team, the role of each member in the group and how it affects the group and the person himself, and the operations of the group in relation to its organizational environment. This problem solving may be based on fairly careful prior data collection from individuals as to their views on the current problems of the system; these data are summarized and form the beginning of the group's agenda. Occasionally, exercises and theoretical material on group and organization functioning may be supplied by the outside consultant.

Under these circumstances, the members of the group usually improve in their abilities to express feelings directly, and to listen to—and understand—each other. Communication adequacy is thus considerably increased. The members also deal with internal conflicts in the team and learn to solve problems more effectively as a unit, thus presumably increasing their ability to meet the demands placed upon them by other parts of the system. Over a period of time, beginning with the top decision-making group of the system, this intervention may be repeated with other groups as well. Industrial programs of this sort have been described by Argyris and Blake and Mouton[6].

2. Survey feedback. In this approach, data bearing on attitudes, opinions, and beliefs of members of a system are collected via a questionnaire. An external researcher summarizes the data for the organization as a whole and for each of a number of relevant work groups. Each work group, under the guidance of its own superior, and perhaps with consultant help, examines its own summarized data, in comparison with those for the organization as a whole. The group makes plans for change

---

[6] Chris, Argyris, *Interpersonal Competence and Organizational Effectiveness*, Dorsey Press, Homewood, Ill., 1962.

Robert Blake and Jane S. Mouton, *The Managerial Grid*, Gulf Publishing Co., Houston, Texas, 1966.

stemming from these discussions and carries them out. The focus of this intervention is on many or all of the work groups within a total setting. The aim is to free up communication, leading to goal clarification and problem solving work. The relative objectification involved in looking at data helps to reduce feelings of being misunderstood and isolated, and makes problems more susceptible to solution, rather than retaining them as a focus for blaming, scapegoating, griping, and so on. For an account of survey feedback procedure, see Mann[7].

3. Role workshop. Sometimes called the 'horizontal slice' meeting, this intervention involves all the people in a particular role (for example, elementary principal). They fill out research instruments dealing with role expectations which various others hold for them, the fit between their own wishes and these expectations, their actual role performance, etc. These data are summarized and form the vehicle for a series of activities (discussion, role practice, decision-making exercises, problem solving, and so on) at a workshop attended by all the people in the role. The main focus here is on role clarity, effectiveness, and improved fit between the person and the role. By sharing common role problems, people occupying the role may develop alternative solutions which result in better performance of that role and more 'self-actualized' operation in general.

4. 'Target setting' and supporting activities. In this approach, periodic meetings are held between a superior and each of his subordinates, separately. In an institution this might involve a principal and his trainers. The work of each subordinate is reviewed in relation to organizational and personal goals, and the supervisor and subordinate agree collaboratively on new targets for the subordinate's work and personal development. These 'targets' are in turn reviewed after some work time (usually six months or so) has elapsed. During that period, other activities such as role meetings, consultation, self-operated data collection, academic courses, and workshops, may be engaged in by the subordinate to develop needed skills and understandings as he works toward the collaboratively set goals. The focus of attention here is the working relationship between superior and subordinate, and the degree to which they are together able to help the subordinate grow and develop on the job. Improved trust, feelings of support, better and more satisfying role performance, and more open communication usually result . . . .

5. Organizational diagnosis and problem-solving. This intervention involves a residential meeting of members of an intact work group,

[7] F.C. Mann, 'Studying and Creating Change', in W.G. Bennis, K.D. Benne, and R. Chin, *The Planning of Change: Readings in the Applied Behavioral Sciences*, Holt, Rinehart & Winston, Inc., New York, 1961, pp. 605–15.

usually at the top of the organization (or in small organizations, up to size 40–50, the entire workforce). They meet for several days to identify problems facing the system, and the reasons for the existence of these; to invest possible solutions; to decide on needed system changes; and to plan implementation of these through regular channels and newly constructed ones. The procedure differs from team training as described above, in that relatively less attention is given to team relationships and interpersonal effectiveness as such and more to system problems in the large. The main focus of attention is on the organization and its current functioning. The improvement of problem solving activity and communication adequacy are typical results[8] . . . .

6. Organizational experiments. In this approach, a major organizational variable of interest is changed directly, by agreement of the responsible administrators and needed implementation efforts . . . . Such an approach requires the careful collection of pre-post data, and the use of control groups in order to test the consequences of the change. The halo of 'experiment' is an aid to acceptance, since the arrangement is seen as not only temporary but scientific and responsibly managed. Such an approach ordinarily includes a feedback stage, in which the results are examined carefully and implications for the continuing functioning of the organization drawn.

These, then, are six possible approaches to the induction of organizational health. Certain common threads appear to flow through all of them.

1. Self-study. These approaches reject the 'technocratic' change model involving the recommendations of a detached expert, and actively involve the system itself in what might be called organizational introspection. The same holds true for approaches involving group self-study for various teams in the organization, and personal introspection and reexamination by role occupants.

In common with the action research movement in education, these approaches also carry the assumption that an operant stance on the part of the organization is both theoretically and practically preferable to the problems involved in dependence on outsiders for system change.

2. Relational emphasis. These approaches do not conceive of the organization as a collection of jobs with isolated persons in them, but as a network of groups and role relationships; it is the functioning of these groups and relationships, as such, which requires examination and self-operated, experimental alteration. The aim is not to ferret out and change

[8] See current Indian studies in, for example, *Proceedings of First National Conference of Human Resources Development Network*, Madras, September 1987.

the 'attitude' of old-fogey Principal A, but to focus on the relationships and group settings in which Principal A's attitudes are evoked.

3. Increased data flow. These approaches all involve the heightening or intensification of communication, especially vertically, but also diagonally and horizontally. New feedback loops are often built into the existing system. The use of status-equalizing devices such as intensive residential meetings also encourages fuller and freer flow of information through channels which may have been blocked or have always carried distorted messages.

4. Norms as a change target. By focusing on groups and relationships, and increasing data flow, these approaches have the effect of altering existing norms which regulate interpersonal transactions in the organization. If, for example, a work group where the norms are 'play it close to the vest, and don't disagree with the boss' engages in a team training session, it is quite likely—since all group members have participated in the experience—that norms such as 'be open about your feelings whether or not they tally with the boss' wishes' will develop. These approaches thus have a strong culture-change component, based on intensive, data-based interaction with others.

5. Temporary system approach. But norm changing is by definition very difficult under the usual pressures of day-to-day operation in the organization. 'Business as usual' has to prevail. Most of the interventions described involve the use of residential meetings, which constitute a detached, 'cultural island' approach to organizational introspection and self-correction. They are in effect temporary systems, where new norms can develop, and where, given the suspension of the usual pressures, meaningful changes can be made in the structure and functioning of the permanent system.

6. Expert facilitation. All of these interventions also include the presence of a semidetached consultant figure, whose main functions are to facilitate, provoke, and support the effects of the system to understand itself, free up communication, and engage in more adequate problem solving behaviour. The outsider role, however, is seen as impermanent; it is only associated with the system during the actual period of the intervention itself. If the intervention is successful, the organization itself continues the self-corrective processes which have been begun by the intervention.

Whether or not these interventions, . . . can be used plausibly with people-processing organizations such as schools, is an interesting question . . . it is quite likely that the very act of carrying out small-scale projects in planned change can undoubtedly strengthen the health of an educational organization—but only if direct attention is paid concurrently to the state of the organization. The basic innovative project, we believe, must be one of organization development itself.

9.5 *Third-Wave Consulting: Four Useful Practices*[9]

MARVIN R. WEISBORD

. . . In reviewing my projects over 25 years, I find recurring patterns—related to leadership, energizing situations, and energizing people—under which I do better work. The leaders I have learned most from seem to me to have certain knacks. They focus attention on worthy aspirations; they mobilize energy by involving others; they seem willing to face the unknown without 'answers' . . . .

Useful Practice 1: Assess the Potential for Action

Instead of diagnosing 'gaps', I find myself asking under what conditions I could make a contribution. That leads me away from problem lists toward an assessment of leadership, business opportunities, and sources of energy.

Condition 1: committed leadership . . . . Consultants make better contributions when a person in authority says, 'I think this is so important that I'm willing to take a risk too'. I'm wary of requests to fix somebody else or to supply unilateral 'expert' answers.

Condition 2: good business opportunities . . . . I listen sympathetically to the 'people problem' list, but I don't focus on it. Rather, I focus on the opportunities for cooperative action—chances to innovate products/services and/or ways of making/delivering them . . . .

Condition 3: energized people. The third dimension is a little trickier. We all drag our feet some days and burst with energy on others. What can a consultant do about this? Claes Janssen, a Swedish social psychologist, has devised a simple tool for visualizing potential energy. Each person, group, department, company, says Janssen, lives in a 'four-room apartment' . . . .

[9] From Marvin R. Weisbord, 'Toward Third-Wave Managing and Consulting', *Organizational Dynamics*, Spring 1985, pp. 4–20. This article is adapted from his book, *Productive Workplaces: Organizing and Managing for Community*, Jossey-Bass Publishers, San Francisco, USA, 1987.

We move from room to room, depending on perceptions, feelings, and aspirations, triggered by external events. The rooms represent cyclical phases . . . . It's a circle game. Our feelings and behavior go up and down as outside pressures impinge on our own 'life space'. How much energy we have for support and commitment depends upon which room we're in . . . .

Figure 30: Action-Taking in the Four-Room Apartment

Contentment Room	*Renewal Room*
What clients say: 'I like it just the way it is'.	What clients say: 'We 've got more possibilities than we can ever use. I don't know that to do first.'
What a consultant should do: Leave people alone, unless you think the building's on fire	What a consultant should do: Offer assistance through simple, mutually arranged tasks.
Denial Room	*Confusion Room*
What clients say: 'What, me worry?! Everthing's fine—I think . . .' What a consultant should do: Ask questions. Give support. Heighten awareness. Do not offer advice.	What clients say: 'This is the damnedest mess I ever saw. Helllpp!' What a consultant should do: Structure tasks. Focus on the future. Get people together Ask for/offer help.

. . . The activities I like best—because they involve whole systems—are joint planning of business strategy (external focus), work redesign (internal focus), and reorganizations that embody both strategy and structure. In each mode, the people most affected help devise and test various structural models, using consulting help. I don't mean to make this sound easy as pie. I usually find myself in long 'should we/shouln't we' dialogs—hours or days of hashing out the pros and cons of opening the action to many others, whether there's time to do it all, whether short term results will suffer, what good alternatives exist. Above all, each of us uses the dialogs to decide whether to become personally involved.

So I look for a leader, a business opportunity, and a 'should we/shouldn't we' discussion. If we decide to team up, I help people plan how to raise a crowd, structure a task, and provide some (left brain) methods for getting started. As right brains are activated, they take care of what can't be planned in advance.

Useful Practice 2: Get the 'Whole System' in the Room

There are many ways to get a 'whole system' together. A system can be there. for example, in your head—a conceptual rather than logistical feat that most people can master . . . .

However, knowing what's going on is not the same as enacting productive community. People need shared perceptions to make their contributions. That means getting together to live the open system. How many functions, levels, managers, operators, staff, line can be mustered to work on their own organization all at once? Could customers and suppliers be involved? My inclination is to push for 'more' and let others say what's 'realistic'. When people from top and bottom meet across lines of status, function, sex, race, and hierarchy, and when 'problems' can be seen as systemic rather than discrete, wonderful new (and unpredictable) things happen. These can't be 'planned' except in the sense of making them more probable. Such happenings lead to more creative and committed actions, more secure and engaging work . . . .

There is a further benefit to having a whole system present. New patterns of action that are achieved in the room are often carried outside of it because all the relevant parties enacted them together. There is less 'sell' needed when three or four levels are able to come to the same conclusion at the same time.

Useful Practice 3: Focus on the Future

This practice derives from work by the late Ronald Lippitt, the coiner, with Kurt Lewin, of the term group dynamics 40 years ago . . . . He has people visualize preferred futures in rich detail—as they wish things to be two, three, and even five years into the future. This simple concept has enormous power. While untangling present problems leads to depression, imagining scenarios energizes common values. Taking a stand for a desired future provides purposeful guidance for goal setting, planning, and skill building . . . .

Useful Practice 4: Structure Tasks that People Can Do For Themselves

What structures make it possible for people to learn, focus on the future, and action plan for themselves (when leadership, opportunity and energy exist)? A conference series designed by clients and consultants together is one way to bring the productive community alive. These are task-focused, working conferences to reorganize work or refocus effort; they shouldn't serve as add-ons or data dumps . . . .

. . . Merrelyn Emery, a leading advocate of this perspective, points out that the purpose of consulting techniques is to create a learning climate, not solutions. This is a subtle and important distinction . . . . Creating a learning climate, points out Emery, results in 'an almost immediate increase in energy, common sense, and goodwill'.

Summary Observation: . . . Anybody who offers to sell you an exemption from the clarifying experience of muddling through to renewal is a charlatan . . . . When the 'whole system' gets into one room, when people have valued tasks to accomplish, I believe the right diagnoses and action steps occur in 'real time' . . . .

9.6 *Developing a Temporary Educational System* [10]

JACK GANT, ORON SOUTH, AND JOHN H. HANSEN

. . . a temporary educational system is, by definition, a product of, and an influence on, the permanent systems that comprise its constituencies. Those constituencies include the funding or sponsoring agency, the permanent systems to which staff and participants belong, and the site organization where the temporary system will operate. The members of the permanent systems (constituencies) have needs, goals, expectations, skills, and resources which will be combined in the temporary system to produce a program that is unique. The temporary system, then, starts and ends with its focus on the permanent systems.

Each of the constituencies of the system contributes to its development in various ways at various times. They may reinforce mutual interests and, at times, may conflict when priorities or expectations differ. Collaboration is critical to the development process if all the parties are to benefit.

The development of a temporary system may be described as a set of five interrelated, progressive stages or phases including planning, building, operating, closing, and following up . . . . During the planning phase the dimensions of the temporary system are defined; during the

[10] From Jack Gant, Oron South and John H. Hansen; with the assistance of Hart, Binky and Mills, Johnie, *Temporary Systems*, 1977, pp. 65–74.

building phase the system's dimensions are adjusted to accommodate the needs, objectives, and resources of new members. The primary focus of the operating stage is teaching and learning in order to achieve the program's objectives. During the closing phase, participants will be involved in activities designed to transfer what they have learned to the permanent systems to which they will return. The follow-up phase occurs in the permanent systems where learnings are now being applied and disseminated. See Figure 31.

Figure 31: Temporary System Components

Planning	*Building*	*Operating*	*Closing*	*Following-up*
Goal Setting	Acquaintanceship	Microdesign	Forward Action Planning	Providing Support
Recruiting and Selecting Participants and Staff	Stating and Redefining Goals	Forming and Using Work Groups	Forward Support Planning	Evaluating
Specifying Norms	Redefining Roles	Conflict Management	Forward Network Planning	
Data Planning	Building the Governance System	Decision Making	Planning for Evaluation	
Choosing Time and Territory	Identifying and Using Resources	Recreation		
Locating and Allocating Resources	Monitoring			
Macrodesign				
Analyzing Constraints				

Throughout the five phases, the system becomes stronger. New members are involved; objectives increase and learning resources are added. Figure 32 on the following page suggests that the temporary system evolves upward in a spiral fashion.

The environment of the system is designed to maximize the chances that each member feels safe enough to risk active involvement as the system grows. Each stage relies on previous stages; each stage contributes to subsequent stages.

While each of the phases in the development of the temporary system differs in some ways from the others, some common elements can be identified. Each phase has a purpose and a membership which is engaged in fulfilling that purpose. During each phase, a specific set of tasks must be accomplished so that required outcomes are produced. The following is a description of each phase accompanied by suggestions for performing key tasks.

Figure 32 : The Spiral Nature

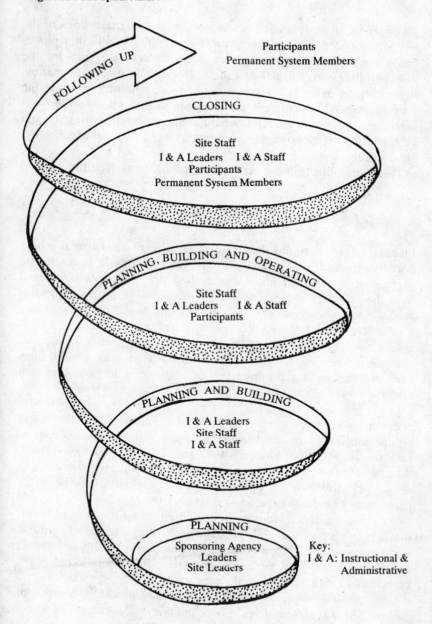

Planning

The purpose of the planning phase is to define the dimensions of the temporary system. The planning process is critical to all other phases and is conducted by representatives of the sponsoring agency and the administrative and instruction leaders. During this stage they address the questions: What is the system going to accomplish? Who are the participants? What resources are available to the system? When and where will the system operate? What are the primary activities that will be conducted? What information is needed by planners and participants? How will the system function?

These questions lead the planners to specific tasks. The tasks are:

1. Goal Setting

Planners engage in stating the changes that are expected to occur among participants and, ultimately, the changes that should occur in the permanent systems. Planners can assume that participants, relieved from the pressures of the permanent systems, will be prepared to work hard. On the other hand, time and resources are limited in the temporary system. Therefore, goals must be clearly stated, measurable, and achievable within the time allotted. Goals are likely to specify anticipated changes in knowledge, skills, attitudes, or interpersonal relationships and may also involve commitments of participants to tasks they will undertake once they have returned to the permanent systems.

In the process of goal setting, planners of temporary systems should consider both their own expectations and the expectations of constituent groups. Objectives are always set with a focus on the permanent system, i.e., the organization which receives participants upon their return. Agency sponsors, participant representatives, planners and instructors should all be involved in the goal setting process. Goals should be set for participants to indicate expected outcomes of the program. Goals should also be set for the temporary system itself to spell out how it will function to support the goals of participants. Planners should continue to be aware of long-range goals of the permanent system and should ensure that these goals are known to participants and reflected in the objectives specified for the temporary system.

Goals should be set by interfacing with key people in constituent groups. These representatives may be interviewed, surveyed, or where the constituent group is large and diverse, a Delphi technique may be useful. Planners should be careful to limit objectives to a manageable and achievable number. Though they must take care not to overload the system, they must be certain to provide time, space and opportunities for staff and participants to modify or add to the objectives.

2. Recruiting and Selecting Participants and Staff

In some temporary systems, participant selection, which is accomplished prior to the planning team, is a task of the sponsoring agency. Planners may have the task of selecting the instructional staff, administrative staff and participants. For each group, planners establish the selection criteria that are compatible with the system's goals. In order to minimize socialization problems and internal conflicts, participants are likely to be highly specific groups of personnel who can devote themselves to the system's learning tasks.

3. Specifying Norms

Determining the social behaviors that should characterize the temporary system, is a task of the planners. Any social system develops norms which define and govern group behavior. In temporary systems, planners have the unique opportunity to establish norms that are specifically intended to encourage learning and creativity. The norms of the temporary system may be different from the norms of the permanent systems and may include:

1. Egalitarianism. The hierarchy is minimized and all members may initiate ideas or participate in decisions that affect them.

2. Authenticity. Members are expected to be open, frank, and honest and to be free to express feelings.

3. Innovativeness. Members are encouraged to be curious, to seek solutions to problems, to raise questions and try new answers.

4. Effortfulness. Limited time in the temporary system is likely to encourage people to work hard to achieve the goals. Energies are channeled into the learning tasks.

5. Risk Taking. When removed from their permanent systems, participants are likely to be willing to try new behaviors or take on unfamiliar roles and tasks.

6. Experimentalism. In solving problems, experimentalism is encouraged by the fact that a temporary system protects members from the usual consequences of failure.

7. Interdependence. The standard supports available in the permanent system are not available. Members, therefore, come to rely on each other to achieve the goals set forth by the temporary system.

8. Open Conflict Management. Participants of a temporary system are expected to deal with conflicts among themselves openly, rather than to conceal disagreements . . . .

The planners or designers should apply the specified norms to the planning process. In this way, the planners can be assured that they are capable of modeling the norms which they are specifying for the temporary system because they will have applied them and established them in their own planning process. One way in which members can determine whether or not the norms are being observed is to review planning meetings. Such questions as: 'How are we working', as opposed to 'What are we achieving?', is a good question to use as the planning team evaluates its way of work.

4. Data Planning

Planners need a variety of types of information to steer the development of the temporary system. The information is to be used for planning, for monitoring the system during its operation, and for planning follow-up activities once the system is closed.

Evaluators of the temporary system participate in the data planning process. Evaluation is based upon system goals and is likely to require the collection of data before, during, and after the program.

If an outside evaluation team is to be used for evaluating the success of the temporary system, it is essential that the planners negotiate early with the evaluation team. Agreement should be reached on what data are required, the method of collecting the data, and questions to be answered by the data. It is extremely important that the data collection process NOT interfere with the operation of the temporary system . . . .

Another decision on evaluation and data collection concerns feedback to staff and participants. Unless otherwise established by the funding agency, even data collected by outside evaluators should be fed back to staff and participants . . . . Staff should have veto power over any research data to be collected. Participants should also be informed and their agreement sought.

5. Choosing Time and Territory

The site of the temporary system must provide work space, recreational facilities, housing, and meals. Representatives from the site organization should participate in planning and should be aware of any unusual demands that the temporary system might place on that permanent system.

The site should be far enough away from the permanent system to protect it from permanent system interruptions and distractions, yet, close enough for week-end excitement if the temporary system is to cover more than one week.

The learning facilities should be flexible (and have) a retreat atmosphere . . . .

6. Locating and Allocating Resources

. . . Goals and resources are closely related. Time, money and energy are applied to the achievement of each goal and should be distributed to maximize the success of the various program activities. The planners should keep in mind that the time of the personnel (planners, participants and staff) is the most expensive resource . . . .

7. Macrodesigning

Planners design an overall flow of activities that will occur during the operation of the system . . . . The macrodesign attends to such living and learning needs of the participants and staff as:

a The physical environment;

b The human resources inside and outside the system;

c Involvement of the participants in a two-way influence in goal setting, contract defining, and problem solving;

d A reduction of dependency needs on staff and increased participant responsibility and skills; and

e Openness to redesign on the basis of data from the ongoing process . . . .

The living and learning needs require attention in both macro and microdesigning.

In putting the macrodesign together, decisions are made on time boundaries, major themes, unit or weekly objectives, the unit of planning and delivery, and outside resources. In considering time boundaries, plan the starting and ending time so that all participants and staff can begin and end the temporary system together. Early departures erode the temporary system and diminish the impact of the closing phase of the system.

8. Analyzing Constraints

During the planning process, planners need to be aware of any constraints in the system which might interfere with attainment of the goals. Constraints may be logistic or material; they may relate to people or resources.

Careful analysis may remove some of the constraints. Others may be unavoidable and should be shared with participants.

9. Pre-System Communication

Prior to their arrival at the program site, participants should receive information about the temporary system . . . a statement of the goals of the system and . . . the commitment they are making when they become members of the temporary system . . . . Pre-system communication affects the norms of the temporary system and should be carried out in a manner consistent with the desired norms.

9.7 Building a New Institution—Practical Issues[11]

RAVI J. MATTHAI

A fly sat on the axle wheel of a chariot, and said, 'What a dust do I raise'.

Francis Bacon

This note emphasises problems that arose from the beliefs, attitudes and behavior patterns which influence the Institute's growth.

Beliefs

For many years the Institute was, perhaps, underorganized. It was believed that the first and most important task was to build a tradition of attitudes. The structure of the Institute was subservient and secondary to this. Whatever organizational system was introduced, it was thought that the community's attitudes would determine whether or not it functioned successfully. The Institute's structure, as a facilitating mechanism, was, in the early years, just enough for the accomplishment of primary tasks. There was a conscious avoidance of seemingly neat but rigid forms. As a result, many aspects of the Institute's operations were

[11] From Ravi Matthai, Udai Pareek and T.V. Rao (eds.), *Institution Building in Education and Research*, All India Management Association, New Delhi, 1977, pp. 69–87.

relatively unstructured, sometimes to a point of discomfort. But it was hoped that the structures would be created from the development of attitudes, which structures could, as they emerged, be engineered appropriately to form a coherent whole. Such structures that emerged from the community would, it was believed, tend to be self-regulating. With this belief in mind, even detailed integrated planning was sacrificed until, it was felt, attitudes would sustain the creative use of this process.

It was assumed that the Institute's growth depended on the competence, creativity, and initiative of the faculty. Competence would be largely determined through faculty selection and development. If people with a creative potential were selected, it was assumed that they would best express themselves in conditions of free expression, minimum restrictions and adequate facilities. Initiative, it was thought, would be shown if there was a strong enough motivation, if what came to be called 'academic entrepreneurship' was encouraged and recognized, and if the faculty, as individuals and as a group, developed sufficient confidence in themselves to expose their creations to the world. The faculty's confidence would develop if they were trusted and confidence was shown in their integrity and work. It would also be affected by the market's acceptance of, demand and respect for, faculty and their output. While on the one hand it was thought that the faculty would build the institution, on the other it was also felt that if, even at the earliest stages, the Institute could gain a fair measure of market acceptance, this would reinforce the confidence of faculty in themselves. The circumstances should be created in which faculty, even if they had not 'made their names', could gain access to the market by virtue of their being members of the IIMA faculty. A community that lacked confidence might build for 'defence' rather than 'attack'. This emphasised the urgency with which it was thought necessary to develop strong boundary relations and the role of Director as the 'gate-keeper' was to transmit to the market his own sense of confidence in faculty capabilities, confidence in the group and in individuals. The messages so transmitted must be in terms of 'us' not 'me' and in terms of the Institute's faculty, not 'my' faculty. This was considered important since the Director's role was to build the Institute and not himself and since it was assumed that the development of faculty confidence would, in the long term, be weakened by an over-personalised institution and by the existence or appearance of faculty dependence on an individual. In some senses, this might be considered presumptuous on the part of the Director, but there were examples in India to serve as warnings of the long-term damage that resulted from such over-personalisation. This, therefore, was one of the dominant considerations in the evolution of the Institute's working environment.

Individuality and the Group

'Creativity' posed a problem. The Institute was concerned with the application of knowledge in the resolution of problems. This implied a considerable emphasis on multi-disciplinary work and hence an emphasis on working in groups. However, it was thought that creativity was primarily an individual characteristic and that group work would only evolve after individuals had progressed towards finding their work identity and had gained sufficient confidence in themselves to trust their peers. In the early years of the Institute, therefore, there was a strong emphasis on faculty individuality. For the faculty, this meant a considerable degree of independence from formal authority in making choices.

If, however, at the same time, the faculty were to develop confidence in building the Institute, in taking initiative to develop new activities and in managing the activities of the Institute, these individuals had to work in operational groups which would be capable of making decisions regarding the activities for which they were responsible. Each activity had a faculty committee with a faculty member as chairman. But in order to create the circumstances in which individuality and free expression would not be circumscribed, the chairmen were given the responsibility for the acitivity without *de jure* hierarchical authority. The chairman could not dictate decisions to his committee. He had to win over his committee. He could not in any sense give orders to faculty members involved in the activity for which he was responsible. Again, he had to win them over. His responsibility was given by the Director but authority stemmed from his acceptance by his peers.

The problem, therefore, was how, operationally, to reconcile individual creativity with effective group functioning.

The Freedoms

In these circumstances, the vague and much abused notion of 'academic freedom' was introduced. It was viewed as freedom of the faculty to express their opinions without fear of reprisal, freedom to initiate academic activities within the broad objectives of the Institute, freedom of the individual to plan his work to his satisfaction, freedom to innovate according to his creative thinking, freedom of movement to achieve his academic goals, freedom from external pressures, freedom from the pressure of excessive authority. These are vague phrases but the attempt was made to translate them into reality.

Freedom of expression in academic work was not a problem. The integrity of the faculty expressed itself in relation to problems discussed in the classroom or analysed through research. Occasionally an embarrassing situation would arise as a result of faculty severely criticising some part of the Institute's client system. But it was taken for granted that this sort of situation was bound to arise if this freedom were to mean anything. The Director's role was then to reconcile the client system to such free expression on the grounds that the Institute's strength and usefulness would be in the competence and integrity of its faculty. This was vital since a great part of the Institute's strength would come from its equal acceptance by different parts of the client system, e.g., industry, government and trade unions, whose goals frequently diverged. Freedom of academic expression was therefore consciously linked with building the Institute's image of impartiality. Within the Institute this emphasised faculty integrity, but the faculty's own concern with the client system and their sense of fair play often tempered these expressions with tact and understanding. In the early years, until an adequate level of self-confidence was built, the Director saw his role in terms of partly insulating the internal community from what he believed to be external pressures which were inimical to the Institute's goals and the culture he wished to see develop, whether these pressures were parochial, political, financial or of various vested interests.

However, the more difficult problems arose in relation to meaningful and constructive freedom of expression within the Institute community. This was particularly so in the early years when norms of behavior had not yet evolved into any recognisable form. There were four directions, amongst others, which this expression took—freedom of expression in relation to the constituted authorities (Society, Board of Governors, and the Director), in relation to the organization for academic administration, the non-faculty groups in the community, and in the personal relationships amongst the faculty themselves.

Background

It should be borne in mind that it was in the early years that these problems occurred. The faculty was composed of people with industrial experience, experience in government, with a purely academic experience up to and beyond the Ph.D. level and a very few that combined such backgrounds. An important element that gave cohesiveness to the early faculty was that the first fifteen or so faculty were sent, in small groups, to the International Teachers Programme at the Harvard Business School. The idea was to give them a common learning experience, a common living experience, and a common cultural experience away from the pressures of their place of work . . . .

This strategy in terms of its objective was most successful but the 'follow through' required that this cohesiveness be used to develop an indigenous culture which would typify IIMA. The full-time Director who joined IIMA in August 1965, wondered whether this would create too strong and specific a focus of foreign acculturation and thought that, given the base that had been created, a greater degree of diversity was then desirable. From 1967 the use of the IIP on this basis was discontinued.

In deciding the policy on faculty recruitment from 1966, it was felt that recruitment from academic institutions in India should be minimised. Such local recruitment would merely redistribute existing talent within the country and would not add to the pool of talent available in India. The drive was, therefore, to bring back to India people who were working abroad, either completing their Ph.Ds. or, having done so, were teaching and researching in foreign universities. Many of the faculty so recruited were educated in the basic disciplines . . . and had had no opportunity to test their interest in 'application'. The motivation and reference groups of these various sections of the faculty varied, as did their desire and need to come to grips with the realities of organizational problems . . . .

The faculty development policy aimed at sending existing faculty or potential faculty chosen from the non-faculty research staff of IIMA, the graduating student body of the Institute, or from the open market, to Ph.D. programmes in universities in the USA. In some cases, faculty with work experience were sent to the HBS MBA programme and this was the only MBA programme used.

When the effect of these recruitment and development policies began to be felt, a greater diversity in approach, in disciplines, pedagogical preferences, research capabilities and temperament was injected into the campus community and at the same time faculty saw further avenues for self-development opening.

The faculty was young. The average age would have been in the early thirties. Though, by 1965, all academic activities were being administered by IIMA's own faculty, they were, at the time, as new to these roles as the Director was to his.

Faculty housing was being built on the Institute's 65-acre campus and from 1966 an increasing proportion of faculty moved on to the campus.

Faculty and Institution Building

In the context of such circumstances as existed at the time, it was hoped that the motivation to be creative and to take initiative would be influenced by the faculty feeling that they were in fact playing a part in building the Institute and were simultaneously building themselves, rather than merely carrying out a job which was given to them as paid employees of the Institute.

However, a faculty member's professional satisfaction is derived from his academic output and the recognition of his competence by his students, peers, reference groups, and the Institute. It is understandable, therefore, that he would resist accepting an administrative burden . . . . Nevertheless, the intention was to get as many faculty as possible involved in academic administration. At the same time, with the encouragement of individuality and free expression, it was thought necessary to convey to the faculty that accepting such administrative positions should be of their own volition and that it was clearly possible for them to reject the Director's request, which they sometimes did, without any fear of recrimination or repercussions. Even those who agreed to undertake these tasks frequently suggested that full-time administrators should be used to take over these positions or, at any rate, the administrative aspects. These suggestions were invariably rejected by the Director in the belief that this involvement of the faculty was vital to the development of faculty attitudes towards institutional tasks. At the most, some administrative assistance was provided. The problem therefore was how to achieve this essential faculty participation in institution building without using the direct force of authority.

The problem of involving faculty in academic administration was made more difficult by faculty concern about the importance given to administrative work in faculty evaluation. Once again, the Director's assurance in faculty meetings that institution building at that stage of the Institute's development was as important as the other academic activities raised three questions asked by the faculty—as to whether this should be so, whether in fact administration was being over-emphasised. Individually also, some faculty members asked the Director for reassurance that their administrative work if well done would be recognized at the time of their evaluation. 'What guarantee is there that I will benefit from those administrative chores?'. In the reward and punishment system, the attempt was made to ensure that good academic administration was recognized on a par with academic work. However, this in turn caused some resentment on the part of those who disagreed with the policy of equating administrative and academic work . . . .

Administration, Rules and the Use of Judgement

. . . Authority derived from rules might tend to treat them as ends and not means. It was also believed that a creative faculty would be most productive if the emphasis was on their motivation to work rather than on controlling them with rules and regulations. The outcome was that in the early years, except for the rules laid down by the Government of India common to all national educational institutions . . . few rules were set down in writing. The attitude towards rules, particularly terms of service, was that they were constraints imposed to ensure a basic commonality amongst the national institutes which was considered necessary by the government. The pressure however to adopt more Government rules than this unavoidable minimum was resisted. However, the Institute was slow to set down alternative rules of its own. Co-ordination was sought through group discussions in, for example, activity committees and areas. Policy guidelines for faculty activity were laid down by committees but restrictive rules were kept to a minimum. It was hoped that norms of behavior would evolve from such discussions and co-operative management of activities by which faculty would impose upon themselves the behavioral restraint necessary for the accomplishment of institutional tasks.

In this sense, it was also thought that decision-making, particularly in the earliest stages of institutional growth, should not be governed by precedents. The attitude was one of being apprehensive about perpetuating errors of decision-making at a stage when they were bound to occur. This attitude could be expressed in the statement: 'Learn from your errors; don't institutionalise them'. Where the rules, such as they were, hampered the accomplishment of academic tasks, they were broken with little compunction. Such deviations from the rules could only be sanctioned by the Director and this meant that a considerable degree of detail ended up on the Director's table. It also meant that judgement was to be used frequently and that the use of judgement was not to be overwhelmed by the comforting protection of the bureaucratic application of rules.

The three criteria used in the exercise of judgement by the Director were simple. In question form they were:

How important is the related task? Is the deviation necessary for the accomplishment of the task and is it justified? (Sometimes, given the situation at that point of time, the deviation was necessary but might not have been justified due to, for example, a lack of planning. The deviation might have been sanctioned but the reservation would be conveyed to the faculty member).

Given this attitude, the occasional misuse of such a permissive system did not result in the multiplication of rules, but in the stricter use of judgement in relation to the individual concerned. The aim was to establish relationships of trust and the assumed prerequisite was faculty self-discipline rather than the imposed discipline of authority and regulation. Control was kept as light as possible and exercised primarily through the overall evaluation of an individual and an activity rather than through the minute regulation of each part.

The fact that such a nebulous system functioned is itself a tribute to the integrity, maturity and motivation of the faculty.

Such a system, however, again focused aggression on the Director since, in the final analysis, it was his judgement that was questioned by those dissatisfied with a decision. These circumstances gave rise to many problems but fortunately none of them were of such a magnitude as to endanger the system. It was not uncommon that such use of judgement was regarded as not being 'objective', and this was perhaps reinforced by the fact that the Director did not explain publicly the apparent discrepancies between individual cases.

The freedom to express aggression against authority was primarily used in three contexts—the corridors, faculty and committee meetings, and in the Director's office. 'Corridor' expressions were heard but not acted upon directly. However, the Director took very seriously expressions at committee meetings or at personal meetings in his office. In an attempt to be 'open-minded', decisions already made by the Director was occasionally reversed by him. However, it was not uncommon for the assertion to be made in the corridors, after an aggressive meeting on personal issues in the Director's office, that if you were aggressive enough with the Director he would 'back down'. Whether or not this was the case, whether aggression paid off or whether there was a genuine desire to be fair-minded, the norm of privacy in relation to such personal issues ensured that the Director could never make a counter-assertion. Perhaps, therefore, encouragement of aggression against authority could be said to have been built into the system. The lack of rules, however, was also found to be uncomfortable. Faculty members wanted to know 'where they stood'. They wanted to know more specifically how to allocate their time between academic activities and how to plan their work such that their plans would be acceptable to the Institute. They wished to know more explicitly their 'rights and obligations', what was permissible and what was not. The suggestion that faculty discuss their doubts with the Director, which they did frequently, was not adequate and not as comfortable as having a written document on which to rely. At a faculty meeting specifically convened to discuss the Institute's academic climate, the view was commonly expressed that there was 'too much freedom', and that there was need to document institutional guidelines and rules. Eventually, in 1971, a note on faculty evaluation was circulated to the faculty.

Individuality and Behavioral Styles in Academic Administration

In these circumstances that led to a somewhat aggressive individuality, the working of academic administrative committees often posed problems. Appointments to all academic administrative positions were made by the Director. The alternative of elections, which was occasionally suggested by faculty, was turned down by the faculty themselves. The Director also opposed the use of 'political democratic' mechanisms in an educational institution.

The norm was suggested, but . . . did not always work, that committee decisions should be the outcome of discussing the substantive merits of points of view and resolving them in terms of what was best from the Institute's point of view, rather than forcing an issue by a vote. In the early stages, it was common that rigid points of view were held. An impasse was frequently created and the issue was then referred to the Director. Sometimes this was the result of the attitude of a committee member and sometimes of the committee chairman's style of operation. Styles varied widely, from the wholly passive to the overwhelmingly aggressive. Neither extreme worked successfully. The quality of decisions in the former case was often doubtful and the latter extreme, more often that not, resulted in interpersonal crises that necessitated the Director's intervention. Some thought that management required efficiency, and efficiency required speed of decision-making—the frequent analogy of an industrial myth. The chairman was as capable as any member of asserting his point of view, perhaps more so because of his responsibility. Sometimes a different view was regarded as a personal attack and at other times impatience was expressed with the inefficient meanderings of a group of individualistic prima donnas. The emphasis is on 'sometimes'. These situations were a minority and most often committee behavior was remarkably constructive and patient. Initially when such situations occurred, the Director intervened, but later, at the risk of appearing to 'duck' the decision, he forced the issues back to the committee. This had two diverse effects. With smaller committees consensus decisions became the rule and references to the Director for intervention became extremely rare. With large committees consisting of a majority of the faculty, the committees more frequently resorted to voting. But over the years, as the community became more used to the system, the chairmen and members of groups became increasingly sophisticated in dealing with situations that arose from statements which began with phrases such as 'As a matter of principle. . .' or 'If I may be frank...' or 'With due respect to my colleagues . . .' which phrases were often a prelude to the introduction of that faculty member's hidden agenda . . . .

Behavioral Styles and Faculty Initiative

The importance of faculty taking the initiative to start new activities and to innovate with regard to existing ones was frequently discussed at meetings and individually with the Director. Generally the ideas put forward were taken seriously and efforts were made to implement them. Whether the idea started with the Director or a faculty member, if a faculty member was interested in it and accepted the responsibility for its implementation, the initiative was left squarely with him. He had the freedom to design the activity, choose his colleagues, establish the necessary boundary relations and raise resources. It was the deliberate intention of the Director that he should take a back seat and that the faculty member should get the credit and the 'visibility'. Whenever the Director was asked to help in persuading other faculty to participate, or in establishing contacts outside, or in raising resources, he endeavoured to play this supportive role but tried to ensure that the faculty member maintained the lead. This, again, placed a heavier burden on the faculty member than if the Director had assumed a greater part of the initiative. It was felt that the concentration of action with the Director would on the one hand inevitably slow down the rate of growth of activities and diminish their effectiveness and, on the other hand, would dampen the initiative of the faculty.

Numerous problems arose. In some cases there was resentment against this burden being placed on faculty shoulders . . . more serious problems arose when attempts were made to start long-term on-going activities at the Institute in which the faculty members who took the initiative and responsibility showed even the slightest hesitation in regarding their colleagues as peers. Faculty support and participation, vital for long-term institution building activities, were soon lost if the self-assertive leadership style was combined with a possessiveness expressed in references to 'my activity', 'my project', 'my faculty', 'my clients', 'faculty assisting me'.

Planning

A conspicuous gap in the operations of the Institute was the overall planning function. This might be evident from the circumstances described so far. The two-year post-graduate programme and executive development programmes were planned in advance of the year to which the plan was relevant. Medium or long-term plans were not made. Research was planned by individuals or by specific project groups . . . . Consulting. by the nature of the activity, was not planned. Planning across activities was therefore done at two levels. The individual faculty member planned for an academic year in relation to all the activities in which he wished to work or had agreed to get involved. The Director planned the whole Institute for the following year and for five years. These plans, however, were intended, firstly, as a basis for obtaining grants from the government, and, secondly, to serve as his targets for the range and size of academic activities and so far faculty, staff and facility requirements. Such integration of individual plans as was done was done by the Director, but this was inadequate. There was no mechanism for integrated planning between the individual faculty and the Director. The reasons for not acting upon the various suggestions made to appoint a Joint Director or Dean of Planning were: first, that it was felt that in the early stages of the Institute's development there should be no intervening mechanisms between the individual faculty member in terms of his total work and the Director, which mechanism or position could be viewed as a buffer; secondly, that a detailed integrative planning process might inhibit faculty initiative at a time when it was thought to be essential. For this reason, the target-setting five-year plan drawn up by the Director was not communicated to the faculty. Thirdly, it was felt that such planning mechanisms, if they were to be used imaginatively as stimulants and not curbs, should be expressly needed by those whose work was to be planned at a stage of growth when the institution was viable enough in its size and range of activities and in the maturity of attitudes to consider 'consolidation' as an alternative to continued rapid growth.

This need was expressed by the 1971–72 Re-organization Committee and accepted by the faculty. More formal and systematic planning and the organization for it were introduced in late 1972. Unsuccessful attempts were made in the early years to plan research, but today the planning of research is becoming a reality. The Institute continues to grow but in a planned and integrated manner. This process itself, with a mature and confident faculty, will give to academic administrators a surer authority to accomplish their tasks through the clearer acceptance of the process and their roles by their peers.

9.8 *Crises, Dilemmas, and Resolutions in Institutional Development[12]*

ROLF P. LYNTON AND UDAI PAREEK

From our work in new institutions and from watching sister institutions start and grow we have become conscious of important similarities in the 'life cycles' of all institutions—to transpose the term Erik Erikson uses for an individual. Rough though the analogy may be, even a brief systematic description of the uniformities may interest those charged with setting up new institutions, as well as innovating principals who are attempting to move existing institutions toward greater maturity. The uniformities are systematically set out in Figure 33. They are ordered into three concepts. One is the crisis; not in the sense of an emergency, but of a constellation of forces internal and external that insistently pose a dilemma—the second concept. The dilemma is not a problem to be solved, once and for all; the constellation of forces does not dissolve. The alternatives it offers are tempting but a false choice. What the dilemma demands is resolution—the third concept: resolution sufficiently deep to embrace both. Working out such a resolution calls, in the first place, for quiet pause from day-to-day activities, a disengagement for reflection, a turning inward. For this disengagement, Erikson uses the word 'moratorium'. The moratorium is not itself the resolution but sets up a condition for discovering it.

The crises occur in a certain predictable order: We have called them birth, identity, growth, maturity, development. Each has characteristic patterns and issues. They overlap, and occasionally there may be a regression, but the sequence broadly stands. Only after the current dilemma is resolved and the crisis passed, is the institution ready for the next phase of its development. This phase in turn will shape towards a crisis. Characteristically unresolved, any crisis persists and prevents further development. So every phase holds the seeds of institutional death. 'Doom' would be a better word: growth stifled, an atmosphere of death. The institution may continue to exist; institutions usually do. But it is at a halt.

[12] From Rolf P. Lynton and Udai Pareek, *Training for Development*, Kumarian Press, Connecticut, 1978, pp. 357–58.

Figure 33: Crises in the Life of an Institution

Crises	Characteristic Features	Dilemma	Resolution
1. *Birth*	A few individuals full of ideas and zest. Frenzied activity. Attention oriented outward—power points, sister institutions, customers.	When should the institution be born and how large? Planning for every contingency or have a crash program?	Strong continuing leadership.
2. *Identity* a) Seeking identity	Search for main focus or foci. Conflict and uncertainty. Internal competition for attention.	Perfection of one thing or value on all comers?	Clearly explicit long-range objectives as a priority system for decision-making.
b) Seeking acceptance	Search for relationships with existing systems. Inter-organizational jealousies. Attention outward.	Stress likeness and conformity or stress novelty and differences?	Moratorium to establish standards, largely in isolation.
c) Seeking balance	One or two activities have made a quick start, threaten to dwarf or belittle others. Jealousies within.	Curb fast starters of let them run loose?	Focus on lagging functions to encourage their momentum.
3. *Growth*	Great demands for services, mostly short-term. Temptation to take on too much load. Meeting demands increases demands.	Consolidate and develop slowly or expand in all promising directions?	Moratorium to re-examine objectives and priorities. Publicize long-range plans.
4. *Maturity*	Success revives inter-organizational jealousies, even threatens sponsors. Attacks on autonomy and independence.	Forego identity and submit or revolt and break away?	Develop interdependent relationships focused on tasks.
5. *Development*	Self-satisfaction. Temptation to rest on laurels. Reluctance to work out new ideas.	Fossilize or break up into progressive and conservative, young and old?	Check objectives against changing situation, rejuvenate institution, build in indices of relevance.

10. LARGE SYSTEMS DEVELOPMENT

INTRODUCTION

Insight has consequences. Effective professional practice—even responsible citizenship—now requires trainer consultants to include broad cultural, socio-technical and political dimensions in their active work with participants and organizational clients. In many programs, eg., poverty alleviation in rural and urban areas, empowerment of oppressed populations, environmental protection, public services, and development planning administration, large systems are in fact the direct clients. Half the readings in Section 5 laid out concepts with which to reduce the complexities and 'turbulence' involved in planning large system interventions: the set displayed ways to offset inherent tendencies of individual units, i.e., subsystems, to wall themselves off, impossibly seeking salvation on their own (5.1), and to avoid innovation (5.2); to distinguish in the general environment the 'relevant' parts, to concentrate efforts on working out particular developments (5.3) and the set of five kinds of linkages to organize and manage for this purpose (5.4); and to divide up and sequence the work—content and constituencies-so that all things need not be attempted, with everybody involved, all at the same time (5.5 and 5.6). This conceptual work has undercut notions that large system work is impossible, impractical or too costly; or that it is unnecessary, on the grounds that private (a subsystem) good promotes the good of the polity at large, that small-scale development will multiply and affect practices throughout the system on its own, by virtue of its success; or that work on multiplication strategies can be postponed till after pilot projects have been established and proved efficacious.

The readings in this final section concentrate on the implementation of large scale interventions: learnings from actual experiences. These learnings provide feedback for planning future interventions—there is growing evidence in fact that the prevailing separation of planning from implementation is itself dysfunctional, and very damaging in social development programs (e.g. education, health and social welfare, social upliftment, rural extension). From the conceptual readings in Section 5—from mapmaking in heads and on charts on walls—we now proceed to reports and analyses of work on the ground, in the municipalities, rural districts and country-wide settings to which the maps refer.

'Learning theatres' for Inter-Organizational domains

The first reading is from Eric Trist's recent work on intermediary mechanisms, i.e., those that (could) bridge current gaps between policy makers, strategists, funders and implementing agencies, and 'people's participation'. How such structure, bound and related intermediary mechanisms such that they include the requisite set of (sufficiently homogeneous/heterogeneous) units to be effective 'learning threatres for building domains'. Some of these domains centre on, and take cues for, their development and working from a 'referent organization', others are networks without such a center.

Effective learning theatres for large scale development have structural and managerial characteristics which fit some national cultures better than others. From a longitudinal study in many countries, Hofstede (10.2) has distilled four 'value dimensions' as especially important: interdependence among people; how a society handles inequalities; how far it 'tries to control the future or to let it happen'; and how it relates achievement motivation to caring relationships and concerns with the quality of life.

In the next two readings, two Indians—a professor of management as well as a consultant and a scientist administrator of international renown—comment on the development culture in India. Chattopadhyay (10.3) finds widespread preoccupation with power and dependence on people in power, and with using collective efforts for self-protection and the exploitation of others. Unbounded power attributed to senior members in traditional joint families tends to perpetuate such impasses to development. For Vikram Sarabhai (10.4), they constitute 'a crisis of obsolescence'; but he goes on to describe a major national organization of scientists—which, in that same general environment, has been structured and operates in favor of development. That its chief executive combined 'policy making, executive and scientific roles and himself headed four key agencies, and wielded great power and authority in the top echelons of government' may be essential for breaking through major cultural impasses. Essential too, may be his confirmed active participation in the research and colleagueship in the laboratory. 'The creation of administrative practices (and institutional structures) appropriate to a given technology or a set of tasks comes with knowledge of the technology of tasks concerned . . . (and) cannot be done on the basis of borrowed knowledge'. Lewis Thomas' appreciation (10.5) of Woodshole in Maine,

USA as 'a human institution possessed of a life of its own, self-regenerating, touched all round by human muddle but constantly improved, embellished by it' underscores key characteristics of creative, developmental systems. In North American culture 'neither the spectacularly eminent . . . directors down through the century nor . . . numberless committees, nor the six hundred-man [sic!] corporation, nor even the trustees, have ever been able to do more than hold the lightest reins over this institution [which] seems to have a mind of its own, which it makes up in its own way'.

For uncovering the cultural assumptions in a system, Edgar Scheins' piece (10.6) offers a ten-step procedure. It is a collaborative procedure; both inside and outside perspectives are essential. Essential too, for planned development, is to articulate the findings, for decision makers to take into account in their planning.

From Small- to Large-Scale

A set of four readings follow. These explore national strategies for promoting development, including the multiplication of successful local projects and approaching development through maximising learnings. Arturo Israel (10.7) extracts practical distinctions from 'the patterns of success and failure' in World Bank-supported programs. Contrary to expectations, the patterns distinguish between sectors and activities rather than between countries. Developments in low-specificity and non-competitive sectors take longer and have to be measured differently but, again contrary to expectations, they may be more crucial and urgent than developments in other sectors (which tend to take care of themselves and are culturally less involving). 'Developing societies are dazzled with technology, but their real breakthrough will come at the other end of the spectrum'. The reading lays out a set of mechanisms to 'compensate for lack of specificity'.

Charismatic leadership, long, devoted work, independent funding and lean administration characterize most small discrete development projects in many countries which have achieved impressive results . . . . Pyle's study shows that their independence of bureaucratic and political conditions in the larger society has a price: it limits their scale, permanently. Such projects do not become large and widespread programs. He subjects nine successful health services projects in one of India's largest states, to analyse from three perspectives: a 'rational actor's' which deals primarily with the program's form; a 'management' analysis which deals with problems and constraints preventing successful transition from small projects to large-scale programs; and a political analysis. The reading includes a tabulation of the main features of each perspective. Pyle concludes that projects considered for expansion into programs need to be tested 'structurally . . . within the existing bureaucratic and political settings' and that attempts to expand to a programmatic scale need to be incremental so as to allow modifications indicated by practical experience to be made, including modifications in program strategy. Cousins (10.9) incorporates Pyle's findings in an integrated list of key issues in scaling up from studies by seven authors and his own long experiences (in urban and rural development).

Korten, one of these authors, conceptualizes the 'learning process approach', using several successful rural development programs in India, Thailand and the Philippines as a base. This approach to planning is very different from the usual 'blueprint approach', with its separations of pre-planning from strategy, resource decision and program 'execution', on the lines of manufacturing enterprises. In these successful programs, in contrast, 'villagers and program personnel shared their knowledge and resources to create a fit between needs, actions and capacities . . . and built a larger organization around the requirements of what [they] learned'. Learning to be effective, to be efficient and to expand are three stages in the overall process.

'Rules of Thumb'

Last, in this section and also closing the volume, is a recently reprinted piece by Herbert Shephard which pulls together the many strands of the trainer consultant's work which we have tried to encompass in this volume: personal, colleagial, technical, immediate/concrete and also longer term and systemic. He pioneered much and these 'rules of thumb' from his long experience are wisdom presented lightly. The piece was reprinted soon after his death in 1985 and may, here, stand in tribute.

10.1 *Inter-Organizational Domains and Referent Organizations*[1]

ERIC L. TRIST

Complex societies in fast-changing environments give rise to sets or

[1] From Eric Trist, 'Referent Organizations and the Development of Inter-Organizational Domains', *Human Relations*, Vol. 36, No. 3, 1983, pp. 269 and 273–76.

systems of problems (meta-problems) rather than discrete problems. These are beyond the capacity of single organizations to meet. Interorganizational collaboration is required by groups of organizations at what is called the 'domain' level. The required capability at this level is mediated by 'referent organizations' . . . .

. . . It is important to realize that domains are cognitive as well as organizational structures, else one can only too easily fall into the trap of thinking of them as objectively given, quasipermanent fixtures in the social fabric, rather than as ways we have chosen to construe various facets of it. Domains are based on what Vickers called 'acts of appreciation'. Appreciation is a complex perceptual and conceptual process which melds together judgements of reality and judgements of value. A new appreciation is made as a new meta-problem is recognized. As the appreciation becomes more widely shared, a domain begins to be identified. It is most important that the identity of the domain is not mistaken through errors in the appreciative process, otherwise all subsequent social shaping becomes mismatched with what is required to deal with the meta-problem. As an identity is acquired, the domain begins to take a direction which makes a path into the future as to what may be attempted in the way of courses of action. All this entails some overall social shaping as regards boundaries and size: what organizations are to be included, heterogeneity, homogeneity, etc. Along with this, an internal structure evolves as the various stakeholders learn to accommodate their partially conflicting interests while securing their common ground. Locales begin to be established.

. . . Can we improve the work of appreciation? Can we learn to speed it up? When the locale is a region or a community, the smaller scale and greater immediacy seem to enable more to be accomplished. Such locales may constitute our most accessible learning theatres for building domains.

Functions of Referent Organizations

There are two broad classes of domains which are complementary: those which display some kind of centering in terms of a referent organization (of which there are several variations) and those which remain uncentered and retain a purely network character. These latter comprise social movements concerned with the articulation of latent value alternatives . . . environmental probes into possible futures. But they are not in themselves purposeful . . . a referent organization must not usurp the functions of the constituent organizations, yet to be effective it must provide appropriate leadership.

. . . The first [function of a referent organization] is a regulation as distinct from operation—operations are the business of the constituent organizations. Regulation entails setting the ground rules, determining the criteria for membership, maintaining the values from which goals and objectives are derived, undertaking conflict resolution, and sanctioning activities. But a referent organization also has a time perspective which tends to be longer term than that of the constituent organizations. It is consequence, rather than result-oriented . . . so that it begins to assume considerable responsibility for the future of the domain. This entails the appreciation of emergent trends and issues and the working out with the constituent organizations of desirable futures and modifying practice accordingly. Mobilization of resources may be an especially important item, as is developing a network of external relations. This is an interactive planning role (Ackoff, 1974) which is an extension of the regulative function.

The life of referent organizations is by its very nature discontinuous, entailing the bringing together in various contexts of representatives of the constituent organizations. A staff is therefore necessary to provide infrastructure support, but the staff must be prevented from taking over the appreciative work of the leadership which is generalist rather than specialist.

10.2 *Cultural Dimensions in Management and Planning*[2]

GEERT HOFSTEDE

People build organizations according to their values, and societies are composed of institutions and organizations that reflect the dominant values within their culture. Organization theorists are slowly realising that their theories are much less universal than they once assumed: theories also reflect the culture of the society in which they were developed . . . . The technical side of management is less culture-dependent than the human side but because the two interact, no management activity can be culture-free . . . . Management within a society is very much constrained by its cultural context, because it is impossible to coordinate the actions of people without a deep understanding of their values, beliefs and expressions.

. . [This] also applies to planning in particular. Planning is also symbolic activity, which may or may not have an impact on what

[2] From Geert Hofstede, 'Cultural Dimensions in Management and Planning', *Organization Forum*, Vol. I, No. 1, 1985, pp. 12–15.

happens afterwards. Even if it has not, it will, in some cultures, still be functional because it allows management to feel secure . . . .

The Scope of Cultural Differences Around the World

. . . differences among countries reflect the existence of four underlying value dimensions along which the countries could be positioned. The four dimensions represent elements of common structure in the cultural systems of the countries. They are based on four very fundamental issues in human societies to which every society has to find its particular answers . . .

1. Individualism versus Collectivism (i.e.)—the degree of interdependence a society maintains among individuals . . . .
2. Large versus Small Power Distance (i.e.)—how a society handles inequalities among people when they occur. This has obvious consequences for the way people build their institutions and organizations.
3. Strong versus Weak Uncertainty Avoidance (i.e.)—how a society reacts to the fact that . . . the future is unknown: whether it tries to control the future or to let it happen . . . .
4. Masculinity versus Femininity. Masculinity stands for a preference in a society for achievement, heroism, assertiveness, and material success. Its opposite, Femininity, stands for a preference for relationships, modesty, caring for the weak, and the quality of life. The fundamental issue addressed by this dimension is the way in which a society allocates social (as opposed to biological) roles to the sexes . . . there is solid evidence that the four dimensions are, indeed, universal. Together they account only for a small part of the differences in cultural systems around the world, but this small part is important if it comes to understanding the functioning of work organizations and the people within them.

10.3 *Indian Images and Management*[3]

GORANGA P. CHATTOPADHYAY

One of the recurring assumptions that members make is that task belongs to the management, . . . people behave as if the onus of

[3] From Goranga P. Chattopadhyay *et al.*, *When the Twain Meet: Western Theory and Eastern Insights in Exploring Indian Organizations*, A.H. Wheeler & Co., Calcutta, 1986, pp. 136–38 and 145–46.

determining what is inside a person and what is outside of his inner world lies with others, i.e., leadership is always someone else's job . . . members further experience institutional organizations as tools for exploitation of, among other things, their faith to which they are committed . . . . [They] do not struggle or question their faith. They take a strategy of exploiting what may still be available in line with their faith—a sort of making the best of a bad situation rather than going for excellence—by mobilising people who are experienced as similar to oneself.

. . . the term 'management' in any enterprise usually means either the next higher level or the chief executive and at best a few of his colleagues. It is as if the task of the enterprise belongs to them and, therefore, most managers are actually non-managers who get managed by others. A response to this assumption is the second process—more and more enterprises are spawning managers' and officers' associations which are organizations of perceived like-minded people, to exploit what may still be available for themselves.

This does seem to point towards an unconscious process of channeling activities to get power. The seniormost managers are perceived as the most powerful, almost omnipotent figures, who own the task and have all the power to manage others. In that situation others then try to mobilise power through collective effort and grab what residues they can get for themselves . . . as if entropy and doom are inevitable, regeneration of resources and fathering the future is impossible. The senior managers blame the juniors, right down to the workers, for not being committed to work. Everyone above the level of workers blame the seniors of getting the best out of the situation while the workers are seen as not committed. The workers see all the seniors as grabbing all the available goodies. Consequently, the motive is to grab more power to either get the juniors to work or the seniors to make a better division of the spoils . . . .

Power as a Means of Invading Others' Boundaries

. . . to survive one has to either invade other people's boundaries or allow others to invade one's boundary . . . . Those who have . . . chosen other interpretations have been branded as traitors, anarchists and so on, though in their own experience they have been freedom fighters or seekers of truth. [This] culture is experienced as one where the individual has to understand the interpretation of those who are in positions of authority, in order to survive. This results in turning all authority into power. This is, I believe, a very typical Indian social construct . . . the probable result of an unconscious transfer of infantile and childhood images of authority in the joint family to the work situation. In the joint family, more often than not, the head behaves as though his role has no boundary and as a result others too feel that their role boundaries are being transgressed and demolished. In such situations, it is very difficult to firmly hold on to ideas of rights and obligations of role-holders. Consequently people seem to think more in terms of privileges to be granted by the head of the family.

Hope of survival in such situations, as also in workplaces, leads to identification with power figures, and growth is equated to getting more power, i.e., growth is measured in terms of one's capacity to become like those who are in power. Management thus becomes synonymous with control through power . . . . A very negative consequence of imbibing this culture is a belief that, given the choice, people will be anarchic . . . .

Today . . . the cultural memory is strongly held in the unconscious, strengthened by our child rearing practices, in our notion of being a developing country which is given 'aid' by the developed ones, our education system and our enterprises.

10.4 *Organizing for Developmental Tasks: A Case in Applied Science*[4]

VIKRAM S. SARABHAI

Inherent in a programme of accelerated development . . . there is a suppression of some of the natural constraints which prevent divergence. And as the rate of innovation, discovery, and everything else in the world gets faster, so does the obsolescence of people and things become ever more acute.

. . . The contradiction between desired longevity and a world of increasing change is obvious. An inevitable result of all this is the disillusionment of the young concerning the understanding and behaviour of the middle aged and the old. Equally serious is the inability of those who wield power and influence over world affairs to adopt values and behaviour inherent in an order where accelerating change, rather than stability, is dominant.

[4] From Vikram S. Sarabhai, *Management for Development*, Vikas Publishing House Pvt. Ltd., New Delhi, India, 1974, pp. 6–7, 24–25, 88–89, 104–5.

I suggest that today we witness a crisis of obsolescence . . .

Organization for Inter-faces and Overlaps

. . . an impressive demonstration is possible if we are prepared to create organizations with operating cultures and traditions which are appropriate to specific tasks. Most meaningful tasks of national development rarely lie within the four corners of responsibilities of any one Ministry, as enshrined in the 'Allocation of Business Rules'. On the contrary . . . an organization which has built into it the ideas of overlap, ambiguity, and multiplicity of aspects is not less orderly than a simplistic structure within a single national agency. They represent a thicker, tougher, more subtle, and more complex view of structure.

Homi Bhabha's Approach

(i) . . . Bhabha's approach to building institutions was to build the organization around men. No organization chart stood in the way of recognizing and rewarding talent.

He conveyed confidence in the ability of men, and the men usually rose to the occasion. Bhabha 'protected' his scientists from bureaucratic procedures and organized administration largely as a service rather than a control function.

(ii) The combination of policy making, executive, and scientific roles, providing the chief executive power, freedom, and authority were important; Bhabha was the Chairman of the Commission, the Secretary of the Department and the Director of the A.E.E.T. and the T.I.F.R. The combination of these four roles provided the chief executive with sufficient freedom and flexibility in decision-making and commitment of resources. It meant that the chief executive had powers and responsibilities which permitted full accountability. It also meant that Bhabha was able to keep his 'grassroots' in scientific research. It was this facility of working as a policy maker, organizer, and administrator, on the one hand, and participating in the scientific work at the 'coalface' level, on the other, that provided him the on-going understanding to motivate and manage his research workers. In research laboratories and in other developmental tasks, it seems important that the chief executive, besides policy making and administration, maintains direct contact with his professional role. The creation of administrative practices appropriate to a given technology or a set of tasks, comes with a knowledge of the technology of tasks concerned.

(iii) The early beginnings of any institution are crucial, and the 'culture' (or lack of it) brought by the first entrants play a significant role in establishing norms, procedures, and practices. Therefore, their number should be large enough to achieve a critical size to permit positive interactions . . . the greatest possible freedom was given to the staff to develop new ideas and fruitful lines of work. Institutions grew on the ability of various groups to expand fruitfully.

. . . Bhabha was aware that different tasks and institutions required different types of administrative practices, and that the transfer of government administrative practices, either to industrial enterprises or research and development, produced inefficiencies and lack of morale. Thus he said:

The type of administration required for the growth of science and technology is quite different from the type of administration required for the operation of industrial enterprises, and both of these are again quite different from the type of administration required for such matters as the preservation of law and order, administration of justice, finance, and so on . . . . The administration of scientific research and development . . . cannot be done on the basis of borrowed knowledge.

Bhabha introduced administrative practices in the T.I.F.R. and later in the D.A.E. which were alien to established university and government procedures. Scientists and engineers were paid according to their merit and maturity rather than in terms of organizational position and status. Promotion did not imply handing over charge of one task and going over to another. Positions were created whenever competent people were available for identified tasks. As with personnel functions, Bhabha established for procurement as well as for civil construction, procedures in which major decisions were taken by the scientists concerned.

Another factor that was important in Bhabha's approach, was to provide to scientists and technologists, opportunities of building their own know-how, and of gaining experience even at the risk of failures. Thus, he said, 'the emphasis has been throughout on developing know-how indigenously and on growing people able to tackle the tasks which lie ahead. The generation of self-confidence and the ability to engineer and execute industrial projects without foreign technical assistance have been major objectives'.

10.5 *A Self-Renewing Paradigm*[5]

LEWIS THOMAS

The Marine Biological Laboratory in Woods Hole is a paradigm, a human institution possessed of a life of its own, self-regenerating, touched all around by human muddle but constantly improved, embellished by it. The place was put together, given life, sustained into today's version of its maturity and prepared for further elaboration and changes in its complexity, by what can only be described as a bunch of people. Neither the spectacularly eminent men who have served as directors down through the century nor the numberless committees by which it is seasonally raddled, nor the six hundred-man corporation that nominally owns and operates it, nor even the trustees, have ever been able to do more than hold the lightest reins over this institution; it seems to have a mind of its own, which it makes up in its own way.

Successive generations of people in bunches, never seeming very well organized, have been building the MBL since it was chartered in 1888. It actually started earlier, in 1871, when Woods Hole, Massachusetts, was selected for a Bureau of Fisheries Station and the news got round that all sorts of marine and estuarine life could be found here in the collisions between the Gulf Stream and northern currents offshore, plus birds to watch. Academic types drifted down from Boston, looked around, began explaining things to each other, and the place was off and running.

The MBL has grown slowly but steadily from the outset, sprouting new buildings from time to time, taking on new functions, expanding, drawing to itself by a sort of tropism greater numbers of biological scientists each summer, attracting students from all parts of the world. Today, it stands as the uniquely national center for biology in this country; it is the National Biological Laboratory without being officially designated (or yet funded) as such. Its influence on the growth and development of biologic science has been equivalent to that of many of the country's universities combined, for it has had its pick of the world's scientific talent for each summer's research and teaching. If you ask around, you will find that any number of today's leading figures in biology and medicine were informally ushered into their careers by the summer course in physiology; a still greater number picked up this or that idea for their key experiments while spending time as summer visitors in the laboratories, and others simply came for a holiday and got

[5] From Lewis Thomas, *The Lives of a Cell*, The Viking Press, New York, 1974, pp. 58–63.

enough good notions to keep their laboratories back home busy for a full year. Someone has counted thirty Nobel Laureates who have worked at the MBL at one time or another.

It is amazing that such an institution, exerting so much influence on academic science, has been able to remain so absolutely autonomous. It has, to be sure, linkages of various kinds, arrangements with outside universities for certain graduate programs, and it adheres delicately, somewhat ambiguously, to the Woods Hole Oceanographic Institute just up the street. But it has never come under the domination of any outside institution or governmental agency, nor has it ever been told what to do by any outside group. Internally, the important institutional decisions seem to have been made by a process of accommodation and adaptation, with resistible forces always meeting movable objects . . . .

There is no way of predicting what the future will be like for an institution such as the MBL. One way or another, it will evolve. It may shift soon into a new phase, with a year-round program for teaching and research and a year-round staff, but it will have to accomplish this without jeopardizing the immense power of its summer programs, or all institutional hell will break loose. It will have to find new ways for relating to the universities, if its graduate programs are to expand as they should. It will have to develop new symbiotic relations with the Oceanographic Institute, since both places have so much at stake. And it will have to find more money, much more—the kind of money that only federal governments possess—without losing any of its own initiative.

It will be an interesting place to watch, in the years ahead. In a rational world, things ought to go as well for the MBL as they have in the past, and it should become an even larger and more agile collective intelligence. If you can think of good questions to ask about the life of the earth, it should be as good a place as any to go for answers.

It is now, in fact. You might begin at the local beach, which functions as a sort of ganglion. It is called Stony Beach, because it used to be covered, painfully, by small stones. Long ago, somehow, some committee of scientists, prodded by footsore wives, found enough money to cover it with a layer of sand. It is the most minor of beaches, hardly big enough for a committee, but close enough to the laboratories so that the investigators can walk down for a sandwich lunch with their children on sunny weekdays. From time to time, pure physicists turn up, with only a few minutes to spare from a meeting at the National Academy summer headquarters, tired from making forecasts on classifiedly obscure matters, wearing the look of doom. The physicists are another species, whiter-skinned, towel-draped against the sun, unearthly, the soles of their feet so sensitive that they limp on sand.

A small boy, five-ish, with myopia and glasses, emerges from the water, characteristically, although his hair is dripping his glasses are bone dry; he has already begun to master technique. As he picks his way between the conversations, heading for his mother, who is explaining homology between DNA in chloroplasts and bacteria, he is shaking his head slowly in wonderment, looking at something brown and gelatinous held in his hand, saying, 'That is very interesting water'. At Stony Beach, the water is regarded as primarily interesting, even by small boys.

On weekends, in hot midsummer, you can see how the governing mechanisms work. It is so crowded that one must pick one's way on tiptoe to find a seat, but there is always a lot of standing up anyway; biologists seem to prefer standing on beaches, talking at each other, gesturing to indicate the way things are assembled, bending down to draw diagrams in the sand. By the end of the day, the sand is crisscrossed with a mesh of ordinates, abscissas, curves to account for everything in nature.

You can hear the sound from the beach at a distance, before you see the people. It is that most extraordinary noise, half-shout, half-song, made by confluent, simultaneously raised human voices, explaining things to each other.

You hear a similar sound at the close of the Friday Evening Lecture, the MBL's weekly grand occasion, when the guest lecturers from around the world turn up to present their most stunning pieces of science. As the audience flows out of the auditorium, there is the same jubilant descant, the great sound of crowded people explaining things to each other as fast as their minds will work. You cannot make out individual words in the mass, except that the recurrent phrase, 'But look-'keeps bobbing above the surf of language.

Not many institutions can produce this spontaneous music at will, summer after summer, year after year. It takes a special gift, and the MBL appears to have been born with it. Perhaps this is an aspect of the way we build language after all. The scale is very small, and it is not at all clear how . . . .

10.6 *Revealing a Cultural Paradigm*[6]

EDGAR H. SCHEIN

It is one thing to define basic cultural essence as the pattern of assumptions that underlie what people value and do; it is quite another thing to

[6] From Edgar H. Schein, *Organizational Culture and Leadership*, Jossey-Bass Publishers, San Francisco, 1985, pp. 112–19.

determine what that underlying pattern of assumptions actually is . . . only a *joint* effort between an insider and an outsider can decipher the essential assumptions and their patterns of interrelationships . . . for two basic reasons:

1. *To avoid the subjectivity bias.* The outsider cannot experience the categories of meaning that the insider uses because he has not lived long enough in the culture to learn the semantic nuances, how one set of categories connects to other sets of categories, how meanings are translated into behavior, and how such behavioral rules apply situationally. What the newcomer learns at entry reveals surface layers of the culture; only when inner boundaries are crossed is the member told what really goes on and how to think about it . . . .

2. *To overcome internal invisibility.* The insider cannot tell the outsider what the basic assumptions are and how they are patterned, because they have dropped out of awareness and are taken for granted. The insider can become aware of them only by trying to explain to the outsider why certain things that puzzle the outsider happen the way they do, or by correcting interpretations that the outsider is making. This process requires work on the part of both the insider and outsider over a period of time. The nature of this work can be likened to trying to bring to the surface something that is hidden but not concealed deliberately. It is so taken for granted that it escapes notice, but it is perfectly visible once it has surfaced into consciousness.

Ten Steps

1. *Entry and Focus on Surprises.* The interested outsider enters the organization . . . and begins to experience the culture, both actively through systematic observation and passively through encountering 'surprises'—things that are different from what the outsider expects. In Action, I was most surprised by the high level of interpersonal conflict which seemed to be immune to my interventions. In Multi, I was most surprised by the fact that my communications did not circulate freely. Both of these proved to be important symptoms or artifacts of deep cultural assumptions.

2. *Systematic Observation and Checking.* The outsider engages in systematic observation to calibrate the surprising experiences as best he can and to verify that the 'surprising' events are indeed repeatable experiences and thus likely to be a reflection of the culture, not merely random or idiosyncratic events.

3. *Locating a Motivated Insider.* The outsider must now find someone

in the culture who is analytically capable of deciphering what is going on and who is motivated to do so. It is the insider's motivation to obtain some kind of help or clarity that makes this a 'clinical' rather than an ethnographic approach. Often the insider initiates the project by seeking help of some kind and then becomes involved as a participant in unraveling aspects of the culture . . . .

4. *Revealing the Surprises, Puzzlements, and Hunches.* Once a relationship has been established with the insider, the outsider can reveal his observations, surprises, reactions, and even his own projections, theories, and hunches about what is going on in the culture . . . . I generally avoid abstractions and generalizations; instead, I stick very closely to my own personal reactions to events, thereby allowing the insider to consider the possibility that my idiosyncrasy rather than a cultural force is operating . . . .

5. *Joint Exploration to Find Explanation.* The insider attempts to explain to the outsider what the surprising even means, or, if the outsider has a hunch, the insider elaborates on or corrects the outsider's interpretation. Both parties now have to probe systematically for the underlying assumptions and the patterns among them . . . both people must relate the observations to the various theoretical categories to see where there is most clearly a connection and where the data clearly reveal an underlying assumption. In this process, the outsider must assume the role of a clinical interviewer who is helping the insider search in his own mind for the deeper levels of explanation that can help both persons decipher the basic assumptions of the culture . . . . In practice this activity usually takes place when both parties are relaxed, may be at the end of a consulting day or over a meal, or at a session deliberately designed to be diagnostic . . . .

6. *Formalizing Hypotheses.* The output of step 5 is explanations that make sense, stated in the form of underlying assumptions, but these assumptions can be taken only as hunches about the culture at this point and must be formalized into hypotheses. Both the insider and the outsider must determine what further data would constitute a valid test of whether such an assumption is operating. Such data might be in the form of operational values that should be derivable from the assumptions, or actual behavior that one should be able to observe if the assumption holds . . . .

7. *Systematic Checking and Consolidation.* Through new interviews or observations, the interested insider and the outsider now search for new evidence . . . . At this point in the process, the outsider knows enough to know where to look, what to look for, and whom to ask. Questionnaires, content analysis of documents, stories and other artifact, formal interviews, systematic observations, and all the other techniques of gathering social data now become highly relevant.

8. *Pushing to the Level of Assumptions.* One of the most difficult steps in the deciphering process comes when one must go beyond the articulated values and attempt to understand the deeper layer of assumptions behind them . . . and how that assumption affects behaviour . . . .

9. *Perpetual Recalibration.* As new data surface, and as the outsider becomes better acquainted with the culture, he can refine and modify the model of the culture that he has begun to construct, and he can test that model on other interested insiders. But they must be interested and analytical, because otherwise they may not recognize the assumptions by which they operate. Worse, they may get defensive if they feel that a judgement is being made or embarrassed that their behavior has been 'exposed' . . . .

I have had counterproductive experiences both in Action and in Multi when I attempted to lecture to insiders about their culture, even if they requested the lecture . . . in cultural analysis the reaction of people to cultural descriptions provides important further data on what the culture is all about.

10. *Formal Written Description.* As a final test of our understanding of the assumptions of a given organizational culture, it is necessary to write down the assumptions and to show how they relate to each other in a meaningful pattern to articulate the paradigm . . . some description is an essential step in the method of deciphering.

The interested insider can go over the written description as a further test of accuracy, but it is not at all clear that making such a written description generally available is helpful . . . . How the cultural data are used, then, is a function of what problems the client system wishes to address . . . . For example, I once asked, 'If your culture really assumes that every individual must think for himself, how is that consistent with your wish to have senior management make decisions and push them down the system?'.

10.7 National Strategies[7]

ARTURO ISRAEL

Usually, strategies for improving institutional performance focus on individual agencies or groups of them. This study, however, suggests

[7] From Arturo Israel, *Institutional Development: Incentives to Performance*, Johns Hopkins University Press, Baltimore, 1987, pp. 111–17 and 150–61.

that performance can be improved through countrywide policies and measures that affect most or all agencies. In fact, experience indicates that major improvements in performance often materialize in a country only after national policies and measures are established or modified.

When competition and specificity are taken as central explanations of institutional performance, the first and probably most important corollary is that low-specificity and noncompetitive activities cannot, by definition, achieve the same level or kind of performance as high-specificity and competitive ones. The effectiveness of low-specificity and noncompetitive activities has to be measured by different standards.

A second corollary of using the concepts of specificity and competition is that institutional improvement in low-specificity and noncompetitive activities will take longer than in high-specificity and competitive ones. If velocity of change is taken as a measure of performance, low-specificity and noncompetitive activities will be ranked as doing poorly. Evaluations of their performance will therefore have to use different measures.

A third corollary has to do with the possibility of substitution between specificity and competition as factors inducing better institutional performance . . . .

A fourth corollary is that improved institutional performance is part and parcel of the process of modernization . . . . The challenge (for developing countries) is to modernize as fast as possible, but without unduly changing the character of their people-oriented activities . . . . Great progress could be made if key decision makers would change their attitude toward these issues and face insufficient institutional capacity as just one more of the resources lacking in a developing economy.

Emphasis on Low-Specificity and Noncompetitive Activities

If increased awareness is the first order of business, the second is to give priority in institutional development strategies to the low-specificity (low-technology and people-oriented) activities. This priority is vital for countries at lower levels of development, particularly if their high-technology activities operate as enclaves. The real intellectual challenge will be to design solutions for these activities without simply copying those that have worked in the high-specificity ones. Several biases will have to be overcome, such as the tendency to assume that progress will be made merely by introducing partial organizational improvements and a few management techniques or by concentrating on the quantifiable aspects of an operation and on planning and design instead of on implementation . . . .

A question that arises now is whether this proposed emphasis on the institutional aspects of low-specificity and noncompetitive activities makes sense as a development strategy, since it neglects the modern sectors. To this, there are several answers. First, the low-specificity and noncompetitive activities in a developing economy will represent the largest proportion of the total activities, and the less developed the country, the larger that proportion; the strategy thus attempts to tackle the largest and weakest segments. Second, the modern and competitive activities will, . . . take care of themselves pretty well (relatively speaking, of course), and their effectiveness can be improved much more than those of the low-specificity and noncompetitive activities with relatively minor efforts. Third, . . . since many of the activities deal with the rural areas and the poorest segments of the population, emphasizing them is tantamount to reiterating the priority attached by the development community to the eradication of poverty; it coincides with the emphasis given to agriculture in the most recent development strategies; and it strengthens the argument that development programs oriented to agriculture and poverty eradication are among the most productive.

Perhaps the most difficult obstacle to this strategy is the long-standing belief in all societies, including the developed ones, that hard technology deserves the highest priority. To conclude that low-specificity activities are the most important and in many ways the most difficult requires an intellectual jump which will be hard to achieve in practically all developing societies. At present, attitudes and incentives are oriented in the other direction . . . . Developing societies are dazzled with technology, but their real breakthrough will come at the other end of the spectrum.

Mechanisms to Compensate for Lack of Specificity

. . . the characteristics of low-specificity activities (e.g. human services) make it extremely difficult to arrive at clear operational guidelines for them, which is presumably why management science has neglected them . . . people-oriented activities need strong incentives, but their low specificity makes the design and implementation of strong incentives almost impossible. Similarly, low-specificity activities need flexibility to operate effectively, which means that their objectives and incentives should not be specified in too much detail.

The techniques and approaches for simulating specificity can be divided' into several categories: general strategies, recruitment, staff incentives, training, management, managerial techniques, and organizational structures. Undoubtedly, other classifications are possible, but the main interest here is the general thrust of the analysis.

Recruitment

One real dilemma is that many of the characteristics that make individuals especially effective in people-oriented activities are innate and cannot be taught . . . the difficulty comes in actually attempting to hire hundreds or thousands of poorly educated individuals to expand rural primary education or health services . . . .

The problem may be less severe than it first appears. There is evidence that effectiveness in low-specificity activities is also heavily linked to motivation, particularly at low levels . . . that the abilities required are possessed by many people and [that these] are brought out by the greater professionalization and motivation which manifests itself in better work behavior.

Training

. . . Innate talent and successful practical experience should be valued more than educational background. This applies to the highest levels of management as well as to agents dealing with farmers and villagers. Experience in building primary health care systems strongly confirms this point . . . training has to be much more continuous in low-specificity activities because it is a matter of repeated adaptation to new situations. How continuous depends on the circumstances. The knowledge imparted is only partially cumulative and, especially in the case of staff with relatively little education, it is not realistic to expect low-level personnel to adapt their skills and solutions to the changing realities. Second, training for low-specificity activities should concentrate less on teaching specific techniques and more on offering a mixture of traditional formal training in techniques, on-the-job training, and professional support to help the agents deal with operational problems. This structure of training is adapted to low-specificity activities and applies to all levels of staff . . . .

Management

Management of low-specificity and especially people-oriented activities is distinguished, first, by a relatively greater need to deal with the political, economic, and cultural environment because it can affect a people-oriented activity in many ways. High and middle-level managers need constantly to assess which external pressures are under their control and which are not and adapt their operations to changes in the external environment. In some instances, these external influences are such that the chief executive should be someone particularly capable of managing the political dimension, which should be his main concern, and someone else should be delegated to be in charge of operations . . . .

The second characteristic of the management role in people-oriented activities is the more extreme need to adapt managerial techniques and approaches to the local culture . . . thorough knowledge of the locality and a sensitivity to local needs means that in most cases the managers should be local people.

. . . managers—especially at the middle level—need to cultivate a management style that is open to pressures, or 'incentives', from lower-level staff and from clients and beneficiaries. This will require important changes in the way most people-oriented activities are now managed, and changes in the managerial culture in many countries. Managers will need to improve communications with workers in the field and become much more oriented toward field operations: they will have to get used to leaving their offices in the capital or provincial city more often for direct contact with their subordinates in the small towns and villages.

. . . This point is at the heart of the differences between technology-oriented and people-oriented activities. Each decision made by an agent will have an element of uniqueness—whether advising a farmer on methods of production, persuading a villager to boil water, or solving a problem for a client of a ministry. The agent decides alone, on the spot. It is therefore essential that he gets professional support, in addition to continuous training and opportunities to compare his experience with other agents. Most agents have little education or experience and should not be left to make difficult decisions in isolation. . . .

Managers in these cases should have as much feedback from their agents as possible, so as to monitor progress and change approaches; they should take part in a continuous dialogue with each agent . . . . Managers in low-specificity activities should also put special emphasis on tracing and measuring the effects of the actions performed by their staff, either individually or in groups.

The best management styles . . . for people-oriented activities might have to be somewhat looser or more democratic than is desirable for technology-oriented ones—that is, it should not rely excessively on quantitative objectives and specific controls. A loose style does not preclude great precision and tightness in certain aspects of the operation, however. In rural extension work, for example, management can ensure that visits to farmers are made on a strict schedule, but it cannot define too rigidly what the extensionist should do on each visit.

10.8 Using Projects for Large Program Development: Rational, Organizational and Political Constraints[8]

DAVID F. PYLE

. . . the existing *organizational* structure (of government) does not 'fit' the new strategy. Consequently, the chances for effective implementation of the innovative, community-level approach were dramatically reduced . . . some officials recognized the need for structural modifications (e.g., effective decentralization, community interaction) . . . but adaptations or modifications were resisted by the existing organizational infrastructure.

. . . [Too] the projects could not be used as a comparative model since they operated in a virtual *political* vacuum, i.e., they circumvented or were not deeply involved in either macro- or micro-level political issues . . . the existing political structure did not obstruct project activities . . . [but] once the project-developed model was adopted on a larger scale, political factors became intimately involved in the implementation of the program and had a dramatic effect on the scheme's chances for success.

. . . four propositions . . . were substantiated by . . . experience:

- Governmental commitment at the macro-level (i.e., policy rhetoric and budgetary support) was a necessary but not sufficient condition for impact without micro-level commitment (i.e., willingness to make the structural changes required for program impact);
- Elite/interest groups did not actively support programs which primarily serve the poorer socioeconomic groups;
- Political factors reduced accountability, both from below and from above;
- Political actors encouraged dependency and discouraged self-reliance.

The three perspectives are summarized in Figure 34.

[8] From David F. Pyle, *From Project to Program*, Doctoral Dissertation, MIT, 1981, pp. 245–50, 258–62.

Figure 34: Summary of Three-Dimensional Analysis of Projects and Programs

		Projects	*Program*
I.	***Rational Actor***		
	1. *Selection*		
	sex	female	male
	education	low-level	higher-level
	coverage	1000–2000/VHW	1000/CHW
	2. *Training*	two weeks or less; on-the-job	three months; little retraining
	3. *Materials*	few essential medicines; regular supply	not all drugs listed were supplied
	4. *Remuneration (CHN)*	not a problem	considered too low
II.	***Management***		
	1. *Orientation*	*results*	*procedure*
	objectives	specific	vague/general
	target group	MCH services to vulnerables made priority	entire population receives broad spectrum of services
	indicators of success	output or intermediate	input
	organization	team (CHW important member)	specialists dominate (CHW appendage)
	training	problem-solving based on feedback	routine; didactic
	2. *Morale*		
	motivation	service oriented value system; reorientation	urban oriented
	incentives		
	– pay	modest	modest
	– promotion	based on merit; advancement possible	based on seniority; advancement limited
	– participatory management	involved	follow orders
	– job satisfaction	support provided	support lacking
	3. *Control*		
	supervision	supportive	no direct control over CHWs
	information systems	simple, effective feedback	huge number; not utilized as feedback
	4. *Flexibility*	trial and error; adjust as necessary; time; sequential programming	hierarchical; centralized; rigid bureaucracy
	5. *Community Interaction*		
	understanding		
	– program of community	community diagnosis	limited
	– community of program	ensured	limited
	participation	limited	none

Figure 34 (Continued)

		Projects	Program
	involvement	financial demand made on community	discouraged
	organization	encourage formation of community groups	no effort to stimulate
III.	*Political*		
	1. *Commitment*		
	macro	leadership committed	rhetorical and financial support
	micro	limited effect on projects	inhibit program impact
	2. *Elite/Interest Groups*		
	urban	not a factor or reoriented	urban bias and elite recruitment
	rural	circumvented	no support; use to their advantage
	3. *Accountability*		
	from above	strictly maintained	political connections prevent control
	from below	involvement/ownership	patron-client relationships preclude
	4. *Self-sufficiency*	self-reliance encouraged	dependency encouraged; reluctance to make demands on constituents

Policy Implications

1. To improve the chances for program implementation, . . . having a clear idea of what the obstacles to impact are before the scheme is launched [is important];

2. Once the program is in operation, the evaluation of social development programs must be broadened and deepened to include . . . the underlying managerial and political factors to explain why the programs are or are not functioning as planned. This is particularly important in regard to the new basic needs, social service programs which attempt to deliver services at the village level to the most disadvantaged groups . . . .

3. If expansion is desired it must be carried out incrementally, both in terms of scale and time. The expansion, from projects covering no more than 100,000 to 200,000 populations to a program with between 7 to 8 million beneficiaries is far more ambitious than it is sensible . . . . The

greater the distance between the existing structure and the required structure, the less the chance of successful transition and the more carefully and slowly the expansion must be carried out . . . .

. . . the intervention must be tested 'structurally'. That is, the model being considered for expansion must be observed within the existing bureaucratic and political settings. However, this cannot or should not be done on a full operational basis. An intermediate step is called for. A reasonable approach would be to take a single administrative unit (such as a district in India) which would explore the approach to both the administrative/managerial constraints as well as micro-level (and even some macro-level) political factors. For the incremental expansion in scale to be worthwhile, the program managers must have the proper feedback mechanism to identify problems as well as the flexibility to modify the structure as required. Expanding in such a controlled, carefully observed manner would enable the government to identify and appreciate what structural impediments exist and what changes are required before full-scale implementation is attempted . . . . [This] will take time. We are faced with some of the most fundamental and difficult tasks in development . . . . The greatest danger . . . is that we attempt to accomplish too much too soon and in the process discredit a valid and valuable intervention.

10.9 *Key Issues in Scaling UP*[9]

WILLIAM J. COUSINS

The following is an attempt to make a combined and integrated list of the key issues in scaling up, based upon the ideas of Bosnjak Nyi Nyi, Myers, Korten, Pyle, Paul and the writer:

1. *Continuous learning from community level experience* . . . effective community level projects must begin, not with blueprints for action handed down from above, but with *profound understanding of the survival patterns of poor people* and the generation of activities, goods and services in partnership with them which can be understood and maintained by the people themselves.

A process of dialogue which allows continuous learning and exchange of ideas between those who are living in poor communities and outside

[9] From William J. Cousins, *Scaling Up and Scaling Down*, Unpublished MS, 1987, pp. 11–24.

change agents will be more likely to produce change in the conditions of life than a process which includes only community groups, or only change agents with pre-package plans. *The process of interaction between community members and change agents should be a process of mutual learning and dialogue.* The change agent should promote dialogue and facilitate the articulation of the interests of the people. They should be knowledgeable about power relations and social stratification in the community and actively search for strategies which respond to the greatest needs. They should also share their technical knowledge and explain their points of view; especially when they feel that the people are uninformed as to the alternatives and consequences of their chosen course of action.

2. *Learning while doing. Information-sharing, monitoring and evaluation:* . . . . It is both a vertical and a horizontal process, . . . vertical in the sense that planners and policy makers learn from local experience and *vice versa* . . . horizontal in the sense that there is information-sharing among projects with similar objectives . . . qualitative information from local projects can enrich decision-makers' understanding of quantitative data from secondary sources . . . .

3. *Community involvement* . . . involvement compensates, in part, for their lack of negotiating power in the existing economic, social and political situation . . . . [Too], they are already 'involved' in the health care of their families, no matter what form it takes . . . . A good primary health care programme must start where they are and become involved with them in an effort to improve the level of health care systematically and systemically . . . local level experiences can contribute to a better formulation of regional and national policies . . . .

4. *Replicability of local projects* . . . During the initial period of community diagnosis and project formulation, criteria for project replicability . . . can improve a community's chances of generating successful local improvements and/or long-term development [and] also help in designing national programmes for the benefit of the poor and the poorest.

5. *The need for flexibility* . . . national programmes seek uniformity, standardization of procedures and simplification of action designs rather than diversity and flexibility to suit a variety of local conditions . . . . This leads to the 'blueprint fallacy' i.e., the tendency to apply a model which has been successful in one or a few places to all places . . . .

6. *Political will and popular demand (will).* Encouraging political will requires understanding of the political circumstances of a country and of the styles and priorities of the political leadership . . . . The enhancing of popular demand can be achieved through the horizontal communication of project experiences as well as through the mass media . . . .

7. *Bureaucratic and professional will* . . . working methods, rules and traditional ways of allocating resources have to be modified and made more flexible. Above all, many of their attitudes must be changed . . . . The important roles of para-professionals, community health workers and NGOs must be recognised . . . rather than planning in terms of 'the delivery of a package of services' (pre-packaged by definition), it is necessary to develop flexible plans which can be adjusted appropriately to local conditions . . . .

8. *Management and organizational planning* . . . . There is a need for up-to-date job descriptions and training, detailed individual programmes of work, and staff participation in the programme evaluation and supervision to change training to the form actually needed . . . . It will also be necessary for the government health system to analyze its normative standards and procedures, recognizing that a number of decisions will have to be made at the regional and local level by organizations composed of community as well as government representatives. Thus, one required change will be increased decentralization with the purpose of supporting local initiatives rather than controlling them . . . . It also means a gearing up of the organizational and management capacity at the local level [and] . . . . As expansion occurs, management needs change in significant ways . . . .

9. *Recruitment and training,* . . . there must be much more flexibility in staff recruitment at the local level—with perhaps less emphasis upon formal education and more emphasis upon motivation and commitment, demonstrated ability to work with people effectively and leadership skills . . . .

10. *Costs: Reallocation of financial and human resources.* . . . Converging health, health-related and other social welfare programmes not only have a synergistic effect but also generate resources from all the different sectors which can be combined for the benefit of the people. This is the reason that Bosnjak advocates 'an active search for new partners' at the local level. At the highest levels of government, such convergence requires policy decisions and co-ordinated action (Tabibzadeh, 1985).

11. *Marrying planning and implementation.* . . . the roles of researchers, as well as planners and administrators, have been combined in the most successful projects which expanded significantly . . . [also] individuals who were successful and effective in the original project were assigned to guide the learning experiences of others until they too gained the knowledge, commitment, and the skills to make the programme work.

10.10 *Rural Development Programming: The Learning Process Approach* [10]

DAVID KORTEN

In examining a number of successful rural development programs in Asia it became evident that each found a particular solution to the requirement for fit appropriate to its time and circumstance. If we look to these experiences for a program or an organizational blueprint for replication elsewhere, we are only likely to be disappointed. It is to the process of their development that we must look for the most useful lessons. The nature and significance of this process is best understood by contrasting it with a more conventional approach to development programming, understood as the 'blueprint' approach . . . .

The 'Blueprint' Approach

This approach, with its emphasis on careful pre-planning, reflects the text-book version of how development programming is supposed to work . . . . Its clear-cut order, allocation of funds for precisely-stated outcomes, reliance on 'hard' data and expert judgement, and the clearly-stated implementation schedules make project justification easy in budget presentations. It is a programming approach quite appropriate to certain types of development projects—most notably physical infrastructure projects—where the task and outcomes are defined, environment stable, and cost predictable. Unfortunately, however, in rural development, the objectives are more often multiple, ill-defined, and subject to negotiated change; task requirements are unclear; environments are constantly changing; and costs are unpredictable. Although knowledge is severely limited, the blue-print approach calls for behaving as if it were nearly perfect. Where there is need to build institutional capacity for sustained action on unfamiliar development problems, it assumes that development actions are terminal and that hastily assembled temporary organizations will suffice. Where the need is for a close integration of knowledge-building, decision-making, and action-taking roles, it sharply differentiates the functions and even the institutional locations of the researcher, the planner and the administrator.

Awareness is becoming widespread that the blueprint approach is

[10] From David Korten, *Rural Development Participation Review*, Vol. II, No. 2, Development Committee, Cornel Univ., Ithaca, NY, 1981, pp. 1, 4–8.

inadequate . . . but its assumptions and procedures continue to dominate most rural development programming and to provide the core content of most training courses in development management. This is unlikely to change until viable options are understood and supported.

The Learning Process Approach

Examination of (three) Asian success cases suggests that the blueprint approach never played more than an incidental role in their development. None was designed and implemented. Each emerged out of a long-term learning process in which villagers and program personnel shared their knowledge and resources to create a fit between needs, actions, and the capacities of the assisting organization. Each had a leader who spent time in the villages with an idea, tried it, accepted and corrected his errors, and built a larger organization around the requirements of what he learned.

In each instance, the overall process can be broken down into three stages, each with its own unique learning requirement (see Figure 35). The elements of each stage can be described roughly as follows:

Figure 35: Program Learning Curves

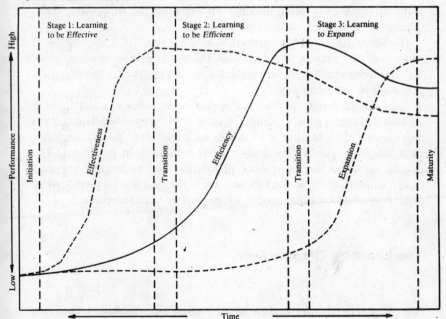

Note: There are likely to be trade-offs between effectiveness, efficiency and expansion which will lead to some loss of effectiveness as efficiency increases and to losses in both effectiveness and efficiency during expansion.

Stage 1: Learning to be Effective. One or more teams of highly qualified personnel are sent to one or more villages which constitute their learning laboratory or pilot site. Here they develop a familiarity with the problem in question, from the beneficiary's perspective and try out some promising approaches to addressing jointly identified needs. They may be supported by a variety of external resource persons with expertise in the social, managerial, and related technical sciences. Errors will be common and the resource inputs required will be high, relative to results. It is assumed that rapid adaptive action will be taken as errors in initial assumptions are identified.

Stage 2: Learning to be Efficient. As insights are gained into what to do, attention is redirected to learning how to do it more efficiently, eliminating activities which are relatively non-productive and working out simplified problem-solving routines for handling critical activities within the grasp of less skilled persons. New learning laboratory sites may be selectively established to test and further refine such methods—simultaneously giving additional personnel experience in their application
. . . .

Stage 3: Learning to Expand. Then attention is again redirected, this time to the phased development of a supporting organization geared to the requirements of carrying out the prescribed activities on a larger scale. It requires building into the organization the supporting skills, management systems, structures and values.

The three stages as represented here are a simplified abstraction of what in reality may be a very disorderly and largely intuitive process. Yet the abstraction helps to explicate an alternative to the blueprint approach to programming.

A key point worth special note is that in the cases examined, there was no thought given to simply testing a program model in a pilot context and then leaving it to others to implement. To the contrary, each was distinguished by a substantial continuity of personnel. The people who had the experience of figuring out an original program design capable of doing the job were the same people who then built an organization around that model adapted to its requirements.

The Learning Organization

Any pre-planned intervention into a varied and constantly changing socio-technical system inevitably will be in error by some margin; the outcome will nearly always deviate from the outcome intended. It is the response to this error that tells the true character of the organization and its leadership.

In the self-deceiving organization, those in authority treat error as synonymous with failure and seek to place blame on some guilty party. In response, the organization's members become skilled in hiding such errors . . . .

In the defeated organization, the source or error is assumed to stem from forces beyond the control of the organization's members. Thus, while adverse factors may be discussed in rich detail, no action is taken. When individual members feel impotent and therefore refer all problems to their superiors for action, they render their superiors equally impotent, ultimately immobilizing the entire organization.

In the learning organization, error is treated as an essential source of information. Since some margin of error is treated as inevitable, particularly in the early stages of the learning process, it is viewed neither as a sign of failure, nor of environment perversity. Error is discussed candidly in such organizations, but in the context of lessons learned and corrective actions being attempted. There may be no surer indicator that an organization has effective leadership . . . .

What is all too rare is for the social scientists to help an organization build its capacity to actually use social science knowledge and data as a normal part of its operating routine. What the case studies suggest as needed is a willingness to experiment with new research methods by researchers committed to providing action agency personnel with simple tools to facilitate their rapid collection and interpretation of social data directly relevant to action for which they are responsible. The task is to make a demystified social science available as every person's tool, turning agency personnel, and in some instances the villagers themselves, into more effective action researchers.

This most often seems to involve disciplined observation, guided interviews and informant panels rather than formal surveys; emphasizing timeliness over rigor; employing oral more than written communication; offering informed interpretation rather than extensive statistical analysis; making narrative rather than numerical presentations; and giving attention to the processes unfolding and to intermediate outcome data required for rapid adaptation, rather than dwelling on detailed assessment of 'final' outcomes. Rather than provide the static profiles found in the typical socio-economic survey, it involves a quest to understand the dynamics of the socio-technical systems that govern village life, to provide a basis for operational-level predictions of the consequences of given development interventions. It means identifying target group members and behaviors in terms relevant to program action rather than simply producing aggregated statistics.

Application to an Established Bureaucracy

The framework of the learning process approach can be applied in either of two ways. One is by building an entirely new program and organization—from the bottom up . . . . The other is by introducing an analogue of this same process within an established organization which seeks to build a new capacity for effective . . . action. The methodologies for the latter application are presently being worked out by the Philippine's National Irrigation Administration (NIA) in an effort directed toward strengthening its capacity to work in effective support of small farmer owned and operated [communal] gravity-fed irrigation systems.

Concerned that the communal irrigation system it was assisting often fell into disrepair and disuse soon after rehabilitation construction was completed, NIA officials concluded that attention was needed to strengthen the water user associations concurrently at work on physical construction. They first selected for special attention two systems scheduled for assistance. Since the NIA had no community organizers of its own, a number of experienced organizers were hired on a temporary basis to work with NIA engineers on these systems. The idea was to integrate the social and technical aspects of the work—developing the social and technical capacity of the water user association through active involvement of its members in such activities as planning system layout, obtaining water rights and rights of way, organizing volunteer labor inputs to system construction, and exerting control over project expenditures . . . the experience established that such integration was at once important and difficult to achieve.

In one community, local power struggles emerged which led to a two-year postponement of construction plans. In the second community, a high level of cohesion greatly facilitated farmer involvement, but seldom in ways which made life easier for project staff. Delays resulted from farmer demands for scheduling and design changes. The use of volunteer labor posed unfamiliar problems of supervision worked out only through lengthy meetings. The engineers did not always welcome farmer interest in monitoring purchases and limiting the staff's personal use of vehicles operated on gasoline charged to the farmers' loan account. Particularly tense, was a conflict in judgment between farmers and engineers as to whether the materials chosen for dam construction would withstand the force of local floods. Farmers said no. Engineers said yes. (The farmers won a Pyrrhic victory when the dam, finally constructed to the engineers' specifications, washed out a few months after completion.)

At this stage, the pilot projects were a failure from the standpoint of any normal evaluation criteria. But it was quite evident to those involved that the weakness was not in the basic concept—it was in the as-yet-limited capacity of the NIA to make it work. And the experience provided extensive insights as to what was required to develop that capacity on both the technical and institutional sides. A major commitment to further learning was implied, involving major changes in the NIA's structure and operating procedures.

A series of new pilot projects was initiated, the designs of which were carefully worked out to incorporate the lessons of the earlier Laur experience. New personnel were brought in and thoroughly trained in these lessons. A top-level national communal irrigation committee was established to coordinate the learning process under the leadership of NIA Assistant Administrator Benjamin Bagadion, a man with total dedication to the idea of independent farmer owned and operated irrigation systems. The committee included central level NIA officials, representatives of related action agencies, and senior members of collaborating academic and research institutions—each of whom had a major day-to-day commitment to the effort. A new social science research program supported by the Ford Foundation was introduced to build within the NIA the new skills, methods, and systems it would require for its new participative approach. Social scientists from the Institute of Philippine Culture developed guidelines for rapid collection and assessment by NIA field staff of 'institutional profiles' which contained social-institutional data critical to project selection and planning. They also observed field activities and produced monthly 'process documentation' reports which provided non-evaluative narrative feedback on key process events.

Concurrently, management experts from the Asian Institute of Management assessed the fit between requirements of the new methods for assisting communals and the existing NIA management systems, advised on new management roles and procedures, assisted in planning the organizational change process, and coordinated workshops for NIA managers and engineers on the new methods. On the technical side, an agricultural engineering team from the International Rice Research Institute and the University of the Philippines at Los Banos was developing simplified methods for diagnosis and correction of common water management problems by farmers and NIA engineers, and designing water management systems suited to the needs of small water user associations.

Once the new methods for assisting the communal projects seemed to be proving more successful in the second round of pilot projects or learning laboratories, a second set of twelve sites was chosen, one in each region of the country, to test their broader application and to begin building the basis for the expansion stage. As of mid-1980, the NIA was perhaps half-way through the learning process on which it had embarked three and a half years earlier. It was likely to be a total of seven or eight years before the new capacity would be in place throughout the agency. Such a lengthy undertaking does not fit well with normal donor programming cycles and requires uncommon commitment, patience, and continuity of leadership. But it may be exactly the type of undertaking in which any major agency concerned with being effective in assisting the rural poor must become engaged . . . . The challenge is to integrate action-taking, knowledge-creation, and institution-building into a coherent learning process . . . .

10.11 *Rules of Thumb for Change Agents*[11]

HERBERT A. SHEPHARD

The following aphorisms are not so much bits of advice (although they are stated that way) as things to think about when you are being a change agent, a consultant, an organization or community development practitioner—or, when you are just being yourself trying to bring about something that involves other people.

Rule 1: Stay Alive. This rule counsels against self-sacrifice on behalf of a cause that you do not wish to be your last . . . .

This is not to say that one should never take a stand, or a survival risk. But such risks should be taken as part of a purposeful strategy of change and appropriately timed and targeted. When they are taken under such circumstances, one is very much alive.

But Rule 1 is much more than a survival rule. The rule means that you should let your whole being be involved in the undertaking. Since most of us have never been in touch with our whole beings, it means a lot of putting together of parts that have been divided, of using internal communications channels that have been closed or were never opened.

Staying alive means loving yourself. Self-disparagement leads to the suppression of potentials, to a win-lose formulation of the world, and to wasting life in defensive maneuvering.

Staying alive means staying in touch with your purpose. It means using your skills, your emotions, your labels and positions, rather than being used by them. It means not being trapped in other people's games. It means turning yourself on and off, rather than being dependent

[11] Herbert A. Shephard, *OD Practitioner*, Vol. 17, No. 4, December 1985.

on the situation. It means choosing with a view to the consequences as well as the impulse. It means going with the flow even while swimming against it. It means living in several worlds without being swallowed up in any. It means seeing dilemmas as opportunities for creativity. It means greeting absurdity with laughter while trying to unscramble it. It means capturing the moment in the light of the future. It means seeing the environment through the eyes of your purpose.

Rule II: Start Where the System is. This is such ancient wisdom that one might expect its meaning had been fully explored and apprehended. Yet in practice the rule—and the system—are often violated . . . . Starting where the system is, can be called the Empathy Rule. To communicate effectively, to obtain a basis for building sound strategy, the change agent needs to understand how the client sees himself and his situation, and needs to understand the culture of the system . . . sometimes where the client is, is wondering where the change agent is.

Rarely is the client in any one place at any one time. That is she/he may be ready to pursue any of several paths. The task is to walk together on the most promising path.

Even unwitting or accidental violations of the empathy rule can destroy the situation . . . . Sometimes starting where the client is, which sounds both ethically and technically virtuous, can lead to some ethically puzzling situations.

Empathy permits the development of a mutual attachment between client and consultant. The resulting relationship may be one in which their creativities are joined, a mutual growth relationship. But it can also become one in which the client becomes dependent and is manipulated by the consultant. The ethical issues are not associated with starting where the system is, but with how one moves with it.

Rule III: Never Work Uphill. This is a comprehensive rule, and a number of other rules are corollaries or examples of it. It is an appeal for an organic rather than a mechanistic approach to change, for a collaborative approach to change, for building strength and building on strength. It has a number of implications that bear on the choices the change agent makes about how to use him/herself, and it says something about life.

Corollary 1: Don't Build Hills as You Go. This corollary cautions against working in a way that builds resistance to movement in the direction you have chosen as desirable. For example, a program which has a favorable effect on one portion of a population may have the opposite effect on other portions of the population. Perhaps the commonest error of this kind has been in the employment of T-group training in organizations: turning on the participants and turning off the people who didn't attend, in one easy lesson.

Corollary 2: Work in the Most Promising Arena. The physician-patient relationship is often regarded as analogous to the consultant-client relationship. The results for system change of this analogy can be unfortunate. For example, the organization development consultant is likely to be greeted with delight by executives who see in his speciality the solution to a hopeless situation in an outlying plant. Some organization development consultants have disappeared for years because of the irresistibility of such challenges . . . .

Corollary 3: Build Resources. Don't do anything alone that could be accomplished more easily or more certainly by a team . . . .

The change agent's task is an heroic one, but the need to be a hero does not facilitate team building. As a result, many change agents lose effectiveness by becoming spread too thin. Effectiveness can be enhanced by investing in the development of partners.

Corollary 4: Don't Over-organize. The democratic ideology and theories of participative management that many change agents possess can sometimes interfere with commonsense.

Corollary 5: Don't Argue If You Can't Win. Win-Lose strategies are to be avoided because they deepen conflict instead of resolving it. But the change agent should build her/his support constituency as large and deep and strong as possible so that she/he can continue to risk.

Corollary 6: Play God a Little. If the change agent doesn't make the critical value decisions, someone else will be happy to do so. Will a given situation contribute to your fulfillment? Are you creating a better world for yourself and others, or are you keeping a system in operation that should be allowed to die? . . . the change agent does need a value perspective for making choices like that.

Rule IV: Innovation Requires a Good Idea, Initiative and a Few Friends. Little can be accomplished alone, and the effects of social and cultural forces on individual perception are so distorting that the change agent needs a partner, if only to maintain perspective and purpose.

The quality of the partner is as important as the quality of the idea. Like the change agent, partners must be relatively autonomous people. Persons who are authority-oriented—who need to rebel or need to submit—are not reliable partners: the rebels take the wrong risks and the good soldiers don't take any. And rarely do they command the respect and trust from others that is needed if an innovation is to be supported.

The partners need not be numerous.

A change agent . . . reports that he knows of only one case of successful interdepartmental collaboration in mutually designing, funding and managing a joint project. It was accomplished through the collaboration of himself and three similarly-minded young men, one from each of four agencies. They were friends and met weekly for lunch. They conceived the project, and planned strategies for implementing it. Each person undertook to interest and influence the relevant key people in his own agency. The four served one another as consultants and helpers in influencing opinion and bringing the decision-makers together.

An alternative statement of Rule IV is as follows: Find the people . . . in the system whose values are congruent with those of the change agent, who possess vitality and imagination, who are willing to work overtime, and who are eager to learn. Such people are usually glad to have someone like the change agent join in getting something important accomplished, and a careful search is likely to turn up quite a few. In fact, there may be enough of them to accomplish general system change, if they can team up in appropriate ways.

In building such teamwork, the change agent's abilities will be fully challenged as he joins them in establishing conditions for trust and creativity; dealing with their anxieties about being seen as subversive; enhancing their leadership, consulting, problem-solving, diagnosing and innovating skills; and developing appropriate group norms and policies.

Rule V: Load Experiments for Success. This sounds like counsel to avoid risk taking. But the decision to experiment always entails risk. After that decision has been made, take all precautions.

The rule also sounds scientifically immoral. But whether an experiment produces the expected results depends upon the experimenter's depth of insight into the conditions and processes involved. Of course, what is experimental is what is new to the system; it may or may not be new to the change agent.

Build an umbrella over the experiment . . . . Use the Hawthorne effect. Even poorly conceived experiments are often made to succeed when the participants feel ownership . . . the first persons to be invited should be those who consistently turn all their experiences into constructive learning. Similarly, in introducing team development processes into a system, begin with the best functioning team.

Maintain voluntarism. This is not easy to do in systems where invitations are understood to be commands, but nothing vital can be built on such motives as duty, obedience, security-seeking or responsiveness to social pressure.

Rule VI: Light Many Fires. Not only does a large, monolithic development or change program have high visibility and other qualities of a good target, it also tends to prevent subsystems from feeling ownership of, and consequent commitment to, the program.

The meaning of this rule is more orderly than the random prescription— light many fires—suggests. Any part of a system is the way it is, partly because of the way the rest of the system is. To work towards change in one subsystem is to become one more determinant of its performance. Not only is the change agent working uphill, but as soon as he turns his back, other forces in the system will press the subsystem back towards its previous performance mode.

If many interdependent subsystems are catalyzed, and the change agent brings them together to facilitate one another's efforts, the entire system can begin to move.

Understanding patterns of interdependency among subsystems can lead to a strategy of fire-setting.

Rule VII: Keep an Optimistic Bias . . . . This rule does not advise ignoring destructive forces. But its positive prescription is that the change agent be especially alert to the constructive forces which are often masked and suppressed in a problem-oriented, envious culture.

People have as great an innate capacity for joy as for resentment, but resentment causes them to overlook opportunities for joy . . . .

Individuals and groups locked in destructive kinds of conflict focus on their differences. The change agent's job is to help them discover and build on their commonalities, so that they will have a foundation of respect and trust which will permit them to use their differences as a source of creativity . . . .

Rule VIII: Capture the Moment. A good sense of relevance and timing is often treated as though it were a 'gift' or 'intuition' rather than something that can be learned, something spontaneous rather than something planned. The opposite is nearer the truth. One is more likely to 'capture the moment' when everything one has learned is readily available.

Perhaps it's our training in linear cause-and-effect thinking and the neglect of our capacities for imagery that makes us so often unable to see the multiple potential of the moment. Entering the situation 'blank' is not the answer. One needs to have as many frameworks for seeing and strategies for acting available as possible. But it's not enough to involve only one's head in the situation; one's heart has to get involved too. Cornelia Otis Skinner once said that the first law of the stage is to love your audience. You can love your audience only if you love yourself. If you have relatively full access to your organized experience, to yourself and to the situation, you will capture the moment more often.

ACKNOWLEDGEMENTS

1.1 Erik H. Erikson, Adult Crises and Growth: Identity, Intimacy, Generativity. Reprinted from Erik H. Erikson, *Identity, Youth and Crises*. New York: W.W. Norton & Company, Inc., 1968.

1.2 Daniel J. Levinson, Four Adult Transitions. Reprinted from Daniel J. Levinson with Charlotte N. Darrow, Edward B. Klein, Maria H. Levinson, Braxton McKee, *The Seasons of a Man's Life*. New York: Ballantine Books, 1978.

1.3 Sudhir Kakar, Giant Strides and Personal Costs in Developing Societies. Reprinted from Sudhir Kakar, *Identity and Adulthood*. Bombay: Oxford University Press, 1979. Used by permission of the author.

1.4 Arthur N. Turner and George F.F. Lombard, Knowledge, Practice and Values. Reprinted from Arthur N. Turner and George F.F. Lombard, *Interpersonal Behaviour and Administration*. New York: The Free Press, 1969. Used by permission of George F.F. Lombard.

1.5 David A. Kolb *et al.*, Experiential Learning. Reprinted from David A. Kolb, Irwin M. Rubin and James M. McIntyre, *Organizational Psychology: An Experiential Approach to Organizational Behavior*, 4e, © 1984, pp. 45–46. Reprinted by permission of Prentice Hall, Inc., Englewood Cliffs, New Jersey.

1.6 Donald A. Schon, Reframing the Problem: Practitioner Dialogue with the Situation. Reprinted from Donald A. Schon, *The Reflective Practitioner: How Professionals Think in Action*. Copyright © 1983 by Basic Books. Reprinted by permission of Basic Books, a division of HarperCollins Publishers.

1.7 A.K. Rice, Training for Leadership. Reprinted from *Training for Leadership*. London: Tavistock Publications Ltd., 1965.

1.8 Seymour B. Sarason, The Creation of Settings. Reprinted from Seymour B. Sarason, *The Creation of Settings and Future Societies*. San Francisco: Jossey-Bass, 1972, pp. 2–3 and 283–84.

1.9 Paulo Friere, Liberation Education. Reproduced from a lecture by Paulo Friere at Harvard University in Spring 1961.

1.10 Natasha Josefowitz, Double Binds. Reprinted from Good Management Potential, in *Paths to Power: A Woman's Guide from First Job to Top Executive*. Reading, Mass.: Addison-Wesley, 1980.

1.11 Carl R. Rogers, Personal Thoughts on Teaching and Learning. Reprinted from Carl R. Rogers, *On Becoming a Person*. Copyright © 1961 by Houghton Mifflin Company, Boston. Used with permission.

2.1 Irwin R. Weschler *et al.*, from Personal Dynamics to Interventions. Reprinted from I.R. Weschler and E.S. Schein (eds.), *Issues in Human Relations Training*, Washington, D.C.: NTL Selected Readings Series, Number 5, 1962. With the permission of Bob Tannenbaum.

2.2 Rolf P. Lynton, Close/Personal or Distant/Impersonal Faculty in Residential Settings. Reprinted from Rolf P. Lynton, *The Tide of Learning: The Aloka Experience*. London: Routledge and Kegan Paul, 1961. With the permission of the author.

2.3 Sudhir Kakar, Healer and Client. Reprinted from Sudhir Kakar, *Shamans, Mystics and Doctors*. New Delhi: Oxford University Press, 1982. With the permission of the author.

2.4 Carl Jung, The Development of Personality. Reprinted from Jung, C.J., *Collected Works, Vol. 17*. Copyright © 1954 and © 1982 Princeton University Press. Reprinted by permission of Princeton University Press.

2.5 Martin Buber, On Becoming Aware. Reprinted from Martin Buber, *Between Man and Man*. New York: MacMillan, 1985. Permission granted by the Estate of Martin Buber.

2.6 Certified Consultants International, Values and Ethics for Organizational Development Professionals. Reprinted from Certified Consultants International, Draft Statement. Nashville, Tenn., 1986. Permission assumed as no reply.

2.7 Erik H. Erikson, Conviction and Competence. Reprinted from Erik H. Erikson, *Dimensions of a New Identity*. New York: W.W. Norton, 1974.

2.8 Fritz J. Roethlisberger, Skillful Behavior. Reprinted from George F.F. Lombard (ed), *The Elusive Phenomena* by Fritz J. Roethlisberger, Boston, MA: Division of Research, Harvard Business School, 1977, pp. 350–53, 392–93.

3.1 Rolf P. Lynton, Building Trainers into a Team. Reprinted from Rolf P. Lynton, *The Tide of Learning: The Aloka Experience*. London: Routledge and Kegan Paul, 1960. Used with the permission of the author.

3.2 Suzanna Finn Eichhorn, Individual Differences and Team Development. Reprinted from Suzanna Finn Eichhorn, *Becoming: The Actualization of Individual Differences in Five Student Health Teams*. New York: Institute for Health Team Development, Montefiore Hospital and Medical Centre. Used with the permission of the author.

3.3 Lewis Thomas, On Meetings as Collective Monologues and Listening without Meeting. Reprinted from Lewis Thomas, *The Medusa and the Snail: More Notes of a Biology Watcher*. New York: The Viking Press, 1974. Permission assumed as no reply.

3.4 Charles Seashore, Building Support Systems. Reprinted from Gerald Caplan and Maria Willilea (eds.), *Support Systems and Mutual Help*. Florida: Grune & Stratton, Inc., 1976.

3.5 Howard Kirshenbaum and Barbara Glaser, The Professional Support Group. Reprinted from H. Kirshenbaum and B. Glaser, *Developing Support Groups: A Manual for Facilitators and Participants*. San Diego, CA: University Associates Inc., 1978. Used with permission.

3.6 David H. Jenkins, Differentiating the Observation-for-Feedback Function. Reprinted from Warren Bennis *et al.*, *The Planning of Change*. New York: Richard & Winston Inc., 1961.

3.7 Charles Seashore and Elmer Van Egmond, Consulting Help with Problem Solving. Reprinted from Warren Bennis *et al.*, *The Planning of Change*. New York: Richard & Winston, Inc., 1961.

3.8 Peter L. Berger and Thomas Luckmann, Constraints on Significant Learning. Reprinted from Peter L. Berger and Thomas Luckmann, *Social Construction of Reality: A Treatise in the Sociology of Knowledge*. New York: Doubleday, 1966.

3.9 Bruce D. Reed, Attachment and Autonomous Activity: 'Oscillation'. Reprinted from Bruce D. Reed, *The Dynamics of Religion*. London: Darton, Longman and Todd Ltd. Copyright © 1978 Darton, Longman and Todd Ltd. Used with permission of the publishers.

3.10 Laurens Van der Post, Alone Time for Reflection. Reprinted from Laurens Van der Post, *Yet Being Someone Other*. London: The Hogarth Press, 1982.

3.11 Laurens Van der Post, With a Teacher, Guru, Mentor. Reprinted from Laurens Van der Post, *Yet Being Someone Other*. London: The Hogarth Press, 1982.

3.12 Lewis Thomas, Conjoint Intelligence. Reprinted from Lewis Thomas, *The Lives of a Cell: Notes of a Biology Watcher*. New York: Viking, 1974.

4.1 Benjamin Franklin, Two Different Worlds. Reprinted from Benjamin Franklin, *Remarks Concerning the Savages of North America*. Passey: Private Press of Franklin, 1784. Used with the permission of the New York Public Library.

4.2 Cyril Sofer, In Multiple Roles and Settings. Reprinted from Cyril Sofer, *The Organization from Within*. London: Tavistock, 1961.

4.3 Cyril Sofer, Fact-finding or New Perspectives. Reprinted from Cyril Sofer, *The Organization from Within*. London: Tavistock, 1961.

4.4 Matthew B. Miles, In the Trainer Role. Reprinted from Matthew B. Miles, *Learning to Work in Groups*. New York: Teachers College Press. Copyright © 1980 by Teachers College Columbia University. Reprinted by permission of the publisher. All rights reserved.

4.5 D.P. Champion, David H. Kiel and Jean A. McLendon, Choosing a Consulting Role. Reprinted from *Training & Development Journal*, Vol. 44, No. 2 (February 1990). Used with permission of the journal.

4.6 Juanita Brown, A Shifting Paradigm. Reprinted from A Shifting Paradigm for Organizational Consultation, In *Vision/Action*, The Journal of the Bay Area OD Network (June 1987). Used by permission of the author.

4.7 Donald A. Schon, The Reflective Contract. Reprinted from Donald A. Schon, *The Reflective Practitioner: How Professionals Think in Action*. New York: Basic Books. Copyright © 1983 by Basic Books. Reprinted by permission of Basic Books, a division of HarperCollins Publishers.

4.8 Rolf P. Lynton, As Monitor/Researcher of his own Praxis. Reprinted from Rolf P. Lynton, *Boomerangs and Alligators: Professional Education in the Public Interest*. Unpublished manuscript. Used by permission of the author.

5.1 Rolf P. Lynton, Innovative Subsystems. Reprinted from Linking an Innovative Subsystem into the System, in *Administrative Science Quarterly*, Vol. 14 (1969). Used by permission of the author.

5.2 Fred E. Emery and Eric L. Trist, Organizational Environments. Reprinted from Fred E. Emery and Eric L. Trist, The Causal Texture of Organizational Environments, in *Human Relations*, Vol. 18 (1965). Used by permission of Plenum Publishing Corporation.

5.3 Rolf P. Lynton and John M. Thomas, Institution Building Theory for Use in Consultation. Reprinted from Dharni P. Sinha (ed.), *Consultants and Consulting Styles*. New Delhi: Vision Books, 1982. Used by permission of the author (Rolf P. Lynton).

5.4 William Foote Whyte, Limiting Factors Strategy. Reprinted from William Foote Whyte, Potatoe Peasants and Professors: A Development Strategy for Peru, in *Sociological Practice*, Vol. 2, No. 1 (1977).

5.5 Joe Thomas, Needs Assessment. Reprinted from J. William Pfeiffer and Leonard D. Goodstein (eds.), *The 1984 Annual for Facilitators, Trainers and Consultants*. San Diego, CA: University Associates, Inc., 1984. Used with permission.

5.6 Betty Mathews and K. Pisharoti, Job Specifications as a Basis for Training Design.

Reprinted from Betty Mathews and K. Pisharoti, *Job Description as a Basis for Training Design* (Action Research Monograph No. 2) Gandhigram, India: Institute of Rural Health and Family Planning, 1966.

5.7 Leland P. Bradford, A Laboratory Strategy. Reprinted from Leland P. Bradford, Human Relations Training, a paper partially based on *Explorations in Human Relations Training*. Washington, D.C.: National Training Laboratories, 1954.

5.8 H. Oliver Holt, Programmed Instruction. Reprinted from H. Oliver Holt, Programmed Self-instruction, *Bell Telephone Magazine*. 1973 (Spring).

5.9 Walter C. McGaghie, G.E. Miller, A.W. Sakod, T.V. Telder, Competency-based Curricula. Reprinted from W.C. McGaghie, G.E. Miller, A.W. Sakod, and T.V. Telder, *Competency-based Curriculum Development in Medical Education*. Geneva: WHO, 1978.

5.10 Stephen M. Corey, The Instructional Process. Reprinted from Stephen M. Corey, *Programmed Instruction*, the 1967 Yearbook of the National Society for the Study of Education.

6.1 Udai Pareek, A Classification of Training Methods. Reprinted from the Pedagogy of Behavior Simulation, in *Indian Educational Review*, Vol. 16 (1981). Used by permission of the author.

6.2 Donald T. Simpson, Selecting Appropriate Methods. Reprinted from J. William Pfeiffer and Leonard D. Goodstein (eds.), *The 1983 Annual for Facilitators, Trainers and Consultants*. San Diego, CA: University Associates, Inc., 1983. Used with permission.

6.3 Ronne Toker Jacobs and Barbara Schneider Fulfrman, Learner and Training Styles. Reprinted from J. William Pfeiffer and Leonard D. Goodstein (eds.), *The 1984 Annual for Facilitators, Trainers and Consultants*. San Diego, CA: University Associates, Inc., 1984. Used with permission.

6.4 Harriet Ronken Lynton and Rolf P. Lynton, The Case Method. Reprinted from *Asican Cases*. Mysore, India: Aloka Centre for Advanced Study and Training, 1960.

6.5 Udai Pareek, Simulating Reality: Role Playing. Reprinted from Udai Pareek, Role Playing as a Human Relations Training Technique, in *Indian Journal of Social Work*, Vol. XI (1960). Used by permission of the author.

6.6 Jerry L. Fryrear and Stephen A. Schneider, Self-Modeling and Behavior Rehearsal. Reprinted from J. William Pfeiffer and Leonard D. Goodstein (eds.), *The 1983 Annual for Facilitators, Trainers and Consultants*. San Diego, CA: University Associates, Inc. 1983. Used with permission.

6.7 Art Freedman, Re-entry from Training: A Concept. Reprinted from J. William Pfeiffer and John E. Jones (eds.), *The 1980 Annual Handbook for Group Facilitators*. San Diego, CA: University Associates, Inc., 1980. Used with permission.

7.1 Paul C. Nutt, The Evaluation Process: Components and a Model. Reprinted from Paul C. Nutt, *Evaluation Concepts and Methods: Shaping Policy for the Health Administrator*, Bridgeport, CT: Robert B. Luce.

7.2 Arturo Israel, Distractions and Distortions. Reprinted from Arturo Israel, *Institutional Development: Incentives to Performance*. Published for The World Bank by The Johns Hopkins University Press, Baltimore/London, 1987, pp. 162–63, 111–17, 150–61.

7.3 Lawrence F. Salmen, Participant–Observer Evaluation. Reprinted from Lawrence F. Salmen, *Listen to the People: Participant–Observer Evaluation of Development Projects*. Copyright © 1987 by the International Bank for Reconstruction and Development/The World Bank. Reprinted by permission of Oxford University Press, Inc.

7.4 Udai Pareek, A Comprehensive Framework for Evaluating Training. Reprinted from R.K. Misra and S. Ravishankar (eds.), *Management Development and Training in Public Enterprises*. New Delhi: Ajanta, 1983. Used by the author's permission.

7.5 Udai Pareek and T.V. Rao, Evaluating Training Programmes. Reprinted from Udai Pareek and T.V. Rao, *Handbook for Trainers in Educational Management*. Bangkok: UNESCO, 1981. Used by permission of the author.

7.6 D. Schwartz and G. Lippitt, Evaluating the Consulting Process. Reprinted from D. Schwartz and G. Lippitt, Evaluating the Consulting Process, in *Journal of European Training*, Vol. 4, No. 5 (1975). Used by permission of MCB University Press Limited.

7.7 M.Q. Patton, Utilization-focused Evaluation. Reprinted from M.Q. Patton, *Utilization-focused Evaluation*. Newbury Park, CA: Sage Publications, Inc. Copyright © 1978. Reprinted by permission of Sage Publications. Inc.

7.8 Paul C. Nutt, Characteristic Impasses and Ways to Manage. Reprinted from Paul C. Nutt, *Evaluation Concepts and Methods: Shaping Policy for the Health Administrator*. Bridgeport, CT: Robert B. Luce.

8.1 Donald A. Schon, Reflective Research by Practitioners. Reprinted from Donald A. Schon, *The Reflective Practitioner: How Professionals Think in Action*. New York: Basic Books. Copyright © 1983 by Basic Books. Reprinted by permission of Basic Books, a division of HarperCollins Publishers.

8.2 Udai Pareek and Adarsh Khanna, The Process of Action Research. Reprinted from Udai Pareek and Adarsh Khanna, Action Research in Education, in *Shiksha*, Vol. XIV (July 1961).

8.3 Donald A. Schon, Experimenting in Practice. Reprinted from Donald A. Schon, *The Reflective Practitioner: How Professionals Think in Action*. New York: Basic Books. Copyright © 1983 by Basic Books. Reprinted by permission of Basic Books, a division of HarperCollins Publishers.

8.4 Udai Pareek, Action Research and Organizational Development. Reprinted from S. Chattopadhyay and U. Pareek (eds.), *Managing Organizational Change*. New Delhi: Oxford and IBH, 1982. Used by permission of the author.

8.5 Robert Chin, Design and Utility Factors according to Research Use. Reprinted from Franklin Patterson *et al.* (eds.), *The Adolescent Citizen*. New York: The Free Press of Glencoe, Inc., 1960.

8.6 Donald A. Schon, Practitioners and Researchers in Partnership. Reprinted from Donald A. Schon, *The Reflective Practitioner: How Professionals Think in Action*. New York: Basic Books. Copyright © 1983 by Basic Books. Reprinted by permission of Basic Books, a division of HarperCollins Publishers.

8.7 Udai Pareek, The Role of Institutions in Promoting Action Research. Reprinted from S. Chattopadhyay and U. Pareek (eds.), *Managing Organizational Change*. New Delhi: Oxford and IBH, 1982. Used with permission of the author.

8.8 Lewis Thomas, Organizing for Disbelief and Surprise. Reprinted from Lewis Thomas, *The Lives of a Cell*. New York: Viking, 1974.

8.9 Stephen M. Corey and Udai Pareek, Workshop for Action Research Trainers. Reprinted from Stephen M. Corey and Udai Pareek, The In-Service Training Action Research Workshop, in *Journal of Education and Psychology* (1967).

9.1 Eric L. Trist, Conceptual Framework 1: Socio-Technical Systems Thinking. Reprinted from E.L. Trist *et al.*, *Organizational Choice*, London: Tavistock, 1963.

9.2 William A. Pasmore and John J. Sherwood, And in Practice. Reprinted from W.A. Pasmore and J.J. Sherwood, *Sociotechnical Systems: A Sourcebook*. San Diego, CA: University Associates, Inc., 1978. Used with permission.

9.3 Rolf P. Lynton and John M. Thomas. Conceptual Framework B: Institution-building Theory. Reprinted from Institution-building Theory and an Analysis, in *Southern Review of Public Administration* (December 1980).

9.4 Matthew B. Miles, Organizational Health in Training Institutions. Reprinted from Matthew B. Miles, Planned Change and Organizational Health: Figure and Ground, in R.O. Carlson, *et al.*, *Change Processes in the Public School*. New York: Columbia University Press, 1965. Used by permission.

9.5 Marvin R. Weisbord, Third-Wave Consulting: Four Useful Practices. Reprinted from Marvin R. Weisbord, Toward Third-Wave Managing and Consulting, in *Organizational Dynamics* (Spring 1985). Used by permission of the author.

9.6 Jack Gant *et al.*, Developing a Temporary Educational System. Reprinted from Jack Gant *et al.*, *Temporary Systems*. 1977.

9.7 Ravi J. Matthai, Building a New Institution—Practical Issues. Reprinted from Ravi Matthai, Udai Pareek and T.V. Rao (eds.), *Institution Building in Education and Research*. New Delhi: All India Management Association, 1977. Used with the permission of Udai Pareek.

9.8 Rolf P. Lynton and Udai Pareek, Crises, Dilemmas, and Resolutions in Institutional Development. Reprinted from Rolf P. Lynton and Udai Pareek, *Training for Development*. Connecticut: Kumarian Press, 1978. Used with permission of the authors.

10.1 Eric Trist, Inter-Organizational Domains and Referent Organizations. Reprinted from Eric Trist, Referent Organizations and the Development of Inter-Organizational Domains, in *Human Relations*, Vol. 36, No. 3 (1983), pp. 269, 273–76. Used by permission of Plenum Publishing Corporation.

10.2 Geert Hofstede, Cultural Dimensions in Management and Planning. Reprinted from Geert Hofstede, Cultural Dimensions in Management and Planning, in *Organization Forum*, Vol. 1, No. 1 (1985). Used by permission of the author.

10.3 Goranga P. Chattopadhyay, Indian Images and Management. Reprinted from Goranga P. Chattopadhyay *et al.*, *When the Twain Meet: Western Theory and Eastern Insights in Exploring Indian Organizations*. Calcutta: A.H. Wheeler & Co., 1986. Used by permission of the author.

10.4 Vikram S. Sarabhai, Organizing for Developmental Tasks: A Case in Applied Science. Reprinted from Vikram S. Sarabhai, *Management for Development*, New Delhi: Vikas, 1974.

10.5 Lewis Thomas, A Self-Renewing Paradigm. Reprinted from Lewis Thomas, *The Lives of a Cell*. New York: Viking, 1974.

10.6 Edgar H. Schein, Revealing a Cultural Paradigm. Reprinted from Edgar H. Schein, *Organizational Culture and Leadership*. San Francisco: Jossey-Bass, 1985, pp. 112–19.

10.7 Arturo Israel, National Strategies. Reprinted from Arturo Israel, *Institutional Development: Incentives to Performance*. Published for The World Bank by The Johns Hopkins University Press, Baltimore/London, 1987, pp. 162–63, 111–17, 150–61.

10.8 David F. Pyle, Using Projects for Large Program Development: Rational, Organizational and Political Constraints. Reprinted from David F. Pyle, *From Project to Program*. Doctoral Dissertation, MIT, 1981. Used by permission of the author.

10.9 William J. Cousins, Key Issues in Scaling Up. Reprinted from William J. Cousins, *Scaling Up and Scaling Down*. Unpublished manuscript, 1987. Used by permission of the author.

10.10 David Korten, Rural Development Programming: The Learning Process Approach. Reprinted from David Korten in *Rural Development Participation Review*, Vol. II, No. 2 (1981). Used by permission of the author.

10.11 Herbert A. Shephard, Rules of Thumb for Change Agents. Reprinted from *OD Practitioner*, Vol. 17, No. 4 (December 1985).

INDEX